World Politics 01/02

Twenty-Second Edition

EDITOR

Helen E. Purkitt
United States Naval Academy

Dr. Helen Purkitt obtained her Ph.D. in international relations from the University of Southern California. She is professor of political science at the U.S. Naval Academy. Her research and teaching interests include political psychology, African politics, international relations theory, and environmental security. She is currently researching South Africa's former biological weapons program and completing an experimental study of framing effects in budget decision-making. Recent publications include "A Problem Centered Approach for Understanding Foreign Policy: Some Examples from U.S. Foreign Policy Toward Southern Africa" in S. Nagel (Ed.) *Global International Policy: Among and Within Nations.* Marcel-Dekker, 2000; "Predicting Environmental Security Trends and Events in Africa: A Proto-Type Monitoring System of Environmental and Political Problems in Southern Africa," International Symposium of Forecasting, Washington, D.C., U.S. Government, 1999; and "Problem Representations and Political Expertise: Evidence From 'Think Aloud Protocols of South African Elites," in D. Sylvan and J. F. Voss (eds.), *Problem Representation in International Relations* (Cambridge University Press, 1998).

McGraw-Hill/Dushkin
530 Old Whitfield Street, Guilford, Connecticut 06437

Visit us on the Internet
http://www.dushkin.com

Credits

1. New World Order
Unit photo—United Nations photo.
2. World Economy
Unit photo—© by Cindy Brown/Sweet By & By.
3. Weapons of Mass Destruction
Unit photo—© 2001 by PhotoDisc, Inc.
4. North America
Unit photo—Courtesy of The Capitol Building.
5. Latin America
Unit photo—United Nations photo by T. Sennett.
6. Europe
Unit photo—Associated Press photo by Michael Euler.
7. Former Soviet Union
Unit photo—United Nations photo by P. Teuscher.
8. The Pacific Basin
Unit photo—United Nations photo by John Isaac.
9. Middle East and Africa
Unit photo—Associated Press photo by Jassim Mohammed.
10. International Organizations and Global Issues
Unit photo—United Nations photo.

Copyright

Cataloging in Publication Data
Main entry under title: Annual Editions: World Politics. 2001/2002.
1. International relations. 2. United States—Foreign relations. I. Purkitt, Helen, *comp.*
II. Title: World politics.
ISBN 0-07-243301-9 327'.05 80-643193 ISSN 0198-0300

Twenty-Second Edition

Cover image © 2001 by PhotoDisc, Inc.

Printed in the United States of America 1234567890BAHBAH54321 Printed on Recycled Paper

Editors/Advisory Board Staff

Members of the Advisory Board are instrumental in the final selection of articles for each edition of ANNUAL EDITIONS. Their review of articles for content, level, currentness, and appropriateness provides critical direction to the editor and staff. We think that you will find their careful consideration well reflected in this volume.

EDITOR

Helen Purkitt
United States Naval Academy

ADVISORY BOARD

EDITORIAL STAFF

TECHNOLOGY STAFF

PRODUCTION STAFF

To the Reader

In publishing ANNUAL EDITIONS we recognize the enormous role played by the magazines, newspapers, and journals of the public press in providing current, first-rate educational information in a broad spectrum of interest areas. Many of these articles are appropriate for students, researchers, and professionals seeking accurate, current material to help bridge the gap between principles and theories and the real world. These articles, however, become more useful for study when those of lasting value are carefully collected, organized, indexed, and reproduced in a low-cost format, which provides easy and permanent access when the material is needed. That is the role played by ANNUAL EDITIONS.

Annual Editions: World Politics 01/02 is aimed at filling a void in materials for learning about world politics and foreign policy. The articles are chosen for those who are new to the study of world politics. The objective of this compilation is to stimulate interest in learning more about international issues that often seem remote and irrelevant, but that can have profound consequences for economic well-being, security, and survival.

International relations can be viewed as a complex and dynamic system of actions and reactions by a diverse set of actors that produce new situations that require further actions. The readings in this volume have been chosen to convey the complexities and dynamic interdependence of actors in contemporary international relations.

This interdependence means that events in places as far away as Latin America, Asia, the Middle East, and Africa affect the United States, just as America's actions, and inaction, have significant repercussions for other states. Interdependence also refers to the increased role of nonstate actors such as international corporations, the United Nations, nongovernmental organizations and actors, and the Cable News Network (CNN). These nonstate actors increasingly influence the scope, nature, and pace of change in the international system. International events proceed at such a rapid pace, however, that often what is said about international affairs today may be outdated by tomorrow. It is important, therefore, that readers develop a mental framework or theory of the international system as a complex system of loosely connected and diverse sets of actors who interact around an ever-changing agenda of international issues. This collection of articles about international events provides up-to-date information, commentaries about the current set of issues on the world agenda, and analyses of the significance of these issues and emerging trends for the structure and functioning of the post–cold war international system.

A variety of political perspectives are offered in each unit to make readers more aware of the complex and differing aspects of international relations stressed by different analysts. Usually the underlying ideological assumptions are implicit aspects of the analysis. By becoming more aware of the assumptions underlying contemporary analyses of international relations, one can become a more discriminating consumer of alternative perspectives about the world.

This twenty-second edition of *Annual Editions: World Politics* is divided into 10 units. The end of the cold war means that we can no longer view international relations through the prism of a bipolar system. Instead, national, regional, and subregional issues are increasingly important aspects of international relations in the emerging multipolar and multidimensional world system.

The first three units summarize themes and broad areas of international concerns in a period of high uncertainty about future security threats. Each article in unit 1 offers an alternative view of the important trends emerging in world politics at the beginning of the twenty-first century.

It is important to understand the linkages between economic and political trends in an era of increasing globalism. The articles in unit 2 discuss the key actors, issues, and trends relevant to understanding contemporary problems in the international political economic system.

Articles in unit 3 discuss specific issues and emerging trends related to the spread of weapons of mass destruction. As the technology and materials necessary to produce nuclear, chemical, and biological weapons proliferate, the world is faced with new and unprecedented security threats. A number of questions related to how to deter, defend against, and cope with the effects of weapons of mass destruction, which are used against civilians by either hostile nation-states or terrorist groups, must be answered. Authorities must now prepare to defend against these new threats at the local, national, and international levels of world society.

Articles in units 4 through 9 focus on the impact of international and regional trends in six geographical areas or subsystems: North America, Latin America, Europe, Russia and the other independent nation-states of the former Soviet Union, the Pacific Basin, and the Middle East and Sub-Saharan Africa. A common theme running through these articles is the increased challenges facing local, national, and regional political authorities who must simultaneously cope with the problems generated by economic globalism and subnational political changes.

The final unit of this reader, unit 10, examines unresolved issues and new trends in the post–cold war era related to the role of the United Nations, the IMF and World Bank, and other nonstate actors in coping with international economic and political conflicts. This final section begins with an article that questions the ability of the United Nations Security Council to be the guardian of international peace and security without more support from the United States and other major powers. Subsequent articles focus on the role of new types of international actors and trends, including the role played by modern mercenaries, and the increased use of "child soldiers." A recent UN publication warns that water shortages, global warming and nitrogen pollution constitute new threats to future world security unless politicians act now to curb conspicuous overconsumption in the world's richest countries.

I would like to thank Ian Nielsen and his associates at McGraw-Hill/Dushkin for their help in putting this volume together and previous users of *Annual Editions: World Politics,* who took the time to contribute articles or comments on this collection of readings. Please continue to provide feedback to guide the annual revision of this anthology by filling out the postage-paid *article rating form* on the last page of this book.

Helen Purkitt

Helen E. Purkitt
Editor

Contents

UNIT 1

New World Order

Three articles consider some of the challenges facing the world: the impact of local conflicts on foreign policy, major influences on domestic and international security, and the consequences of globalization.

World Economy

Five articles examine the global marketplace as politics redefine the rules of the economic game.

The concepts in bold italics are developed in the article. For further expansion please refer to the Topic Guide and the Index.

Weapons of Mass Destruction

Three selections discuss nuclear proliferation and the use of toxic weapons.

The concepts in bold italics are developed in the article. For further expansion please refer to the Topic Guide and the Index.

North America

These six articles discuss current and future United States and Canadian roles in world policy and international trade.

The concepts in bold italics are developed in the article. For further expansion please refer to the Topic Guide and the Index.

Latin America

Three selections consider Latin American relations in the Western Hemisphere with regard to politics, economic reform, and trade.

Europe

Four selections review some of the historic events that will alter Western and Central Europe. Topics include the European Union's search for a foreign policy and Central/Eastern Europe's strivings toward democracy.

The concepts in bold italics are developed in the article. For further expansion please refer to the Topic Guide and the Index.

UNIT 7

Former Soviet Union

Three articles examine the current state of Russia's economy, politics, military, and foreign policy.

UNIT 8

The Pacific Basin

Three articles examine some of the countries instrumental in the economic evolution of the Pacific Basin.

Middle East and Africa

Six articles review the current state of the Middle East and Africa with regard to conflict, extremism, and democratic trends.

The concepts in bold italics are developed in the article. For further expansion please refer to the Topic Guide and the Index.

International Organizations and Global Issues

Four articles discuss international organizations and world peace, UN reform, and the use of mercenaries and children in the conduct of modern war.

The concepts in bold italics are developed in the article. For further expansion please refer to the Topic Guide and the Index.

Topic Guide

This topic guide suggests how the selections in this book relate to the subjects covered in your course.

The Web icon ( ) under the topic articles easily identifies the relevant Web sites, which are numbered and annotated on the next two pages. By linking the articles and the Web sites by topic, this ANNUAL EDITIONS reader becomes a powerful learning and research tool.

TOPIC AREA	TREATED IN
Africa	34. Africa's Security Issues Through 2010 35. Nigeria: The Politics of Marginalization 36. Turning-Point for AIDS? 38. Outsourcing War 56. Children Under Arms ***3, 6, 8, 10, 11, 12, 28, 34, 35***
Alternative Visions of World Politics	1. Globalization: What's New? What's Not? 2. Ethnic Warfare on the Wane 3. Humanitarian Intervention 7. Helping the World's Poorest 40. Dillema That Confronts the World ***1, 2, 5, 8, 31, 33, 34, 36***
Arms Control and Arms Trade	9. Folly of Arms Control 10. Asian Nuclear Reaction Chain 11. Missile Defences 15. No-First-Use for NATO? 33. Trap That Suits Saddam—and the U.S. ***3, 9, 14, 15***
Asia	10. Asian Nuclear Reaction Chain 28. Does China Matter? 29. Kimaraderie, at Last 30. Towards a Tripartite World ***3, 5, 6, 11, 12, 25, 26***
Balkans	24. Free at Last ***3, 6, 15, 21***
Canada	15. No-First-Use for NATO? 16. Canada Battles With Its Vision of Peace 17. Canada's Water: Hands Off ***3, 6, 16, 17, 18***
Democracy	18. International Relations of Latin America and the Caribbean 20. Is Latin America Doomed to Failure? 23. Europe After Communism 24. Free at Last 25. Putin in Power 35. Nigeria: The Politics of Marginalization ***1, 18, 28***
Environmental Conflicts	17. Canada's Water: Hands Off 40. Dilemma That Confronts the World ***7, 17***
Ethnic Conflict	2. Ethnic Warfare on the Wane 19. Coca Leaf War 26. Chaos in the Caucasus 31. Frightening Fall-Out 34. Africa's Security Issues Through 2010 35. Nigeria: The Politics of Marginalization ***3, 14, 15, 17, 21, 23, 24, 28***
Europe (Central)	23. Europe After Communism 24. Free at Last ***3, 6, 14, 20, 21, 22***
Europe (Western)	21. Their Own Army? 22. Search for a Common Foreign Policy ***3, 6, 10, 12, 19, 20, 21, 22***
Foreign Investment	5. Color of Hot Money 6. Trade Agenda 7. Helping the World's Poorest 8. Can Debt Relief Make a Difference? ***6, 9, 10, 12***
Globalism	1. Globalization: What's New? What's Not? 5. Color of Hot Money 6. Trade Agenda 7. Helping the World's Poorest 8. Can Debt Relief Make a Difference? 14. Home Alone 30. Towards a Tripartite World
Human Rights and Human Security	3. Humanitarian Intervention 16. Canada Battles With Its Vision of Peace 36. Turning-Point for AIDS? ***8, 32, 33, 34, 35***
International Organizations and Treaties	9. Folly of Arms Control 33. Trap That Suits Saddam—and the U.S. 37. Peacekeeping: The UN's Missions Impossible 38. Outsourcing War 39. Children Under Arms ***8, 10, 12, 14, 17, 31, 33, 35***
Low-Intensity Conflict	2. Ethnic Warfare on the Wane 19. Coca Leaf War 26. Chaos in the Caucasus 29. Kimaraderie, at Last 31. Frightening Fall-Out 32. License to Kill: Usama bin Ladin's Declaration of Jihad 33. Trap That Suits Saddam—and the U.S. 34. Africa's Security Issues Through 2010 35. Nigeria: The Politics of Marginalization 38. Outsourcing War ***1, 2, 3, 5, 6, 31, 34***
Middle East	31. Frightening Fall-Out

World Wide Web Sites

DUSHKIN ONLINE

AE: World Politics

The following World Wide Web sites have been carefully researched and selected to support the articles found in this reader. The sites are cross-referenced by number and the Web icon ( ) in the topic guide. In addition, it is possible to link directly to these Web sites through our DUSHKIN ONLINE support site at *http://www.dushkin.com/online/*.

The following sites were available at the time of publication. Visit our Web site—we update DUSHKIN ONLINE regularly to reflect any changes.

General Sources

1. Belfer Center for Science and International Affairs (BCSIA)

http://www.ksg.harvard.edu/bcsia/

BCSIA is a center for research, teaching, and training in international affairs.

2. Carnegie Endowment for International Peace

http://www.ceip.org

One of the goals of this organization is to stimulate discussion and learning among experts and the public on a wide range of international issues. The site provides links to the journal *Foreign Policy* and to the Moscow Center.

3. Central Intelligence Agency

http://www.odci.gov

Use this official home page to learn about many facets of the CIA and to get connections to other sites and resources, such as *The CIA Factbook,* which provides extensive statistical information about every country in the world.

4. Crisisweb: The International Crisis Group (ICG)

http://www.crisisweb.org

ICG is an organization "committed to strengthening the capacity of the international community to anticipate, understand, and act to prevent and contain conflict." Go to this site to view the latest reports and research concerning conflicts around the world.

5. The Heritage Foundation

http://www.heritage.org

This page offers discussion about and links to many sites of the Heritage Foundation and other organizations having to do with foreign policy and foreign affairs.

6. World Wide Web Virtual Library: International Affairs Resources

http://www.etown.edu/vl/

Surf this site and its links to learn about specific countries and regions, to research think tanks and organizations, and to study such vital topics as international law, development, the international economy, human rights, and peacekeeping.

New World Order

7. Global Trends 2005 Project

http://www.csis.org/gt2005/

The Center for Strategic and International Studies explores the coming global trends and challenges of the new millenium. Read their summary report at this Web site. Also access Enterprises for the Environment, Global Information Infrastructure Commission, and Americas at this site.

8. Human Rights Web

http://www.hrweb.org

This useful site offers ideas on how individuals can get involved in helping to protect human rights around the world.

World Economy

9. International Political Economy Network

http://csf.colorado.edu/ipe/

This premier site for research and scholarship includes electronic archives.

10. Organization for Economic Cooperation and Development/FDI Statistics

http://www.oecd.org/daf/investment/

Explore world trade and investment trends and statistics on this site. It provides links to many related topics and addresses global economic issues on a country-by-country basis.

11. Virtual Seminar in Global Political Economy/Global Cities & Social Movements

http://csf.colorado.edu/gpe/gpe95b/resources.html

This site of Internet resources is rich in links to subjects of interest in regional environmental studies, covering topics such as sustainable cities, megacities, and urban planning.

12. World Bank

http://www.worldbank.org

News (press releases, summaries of new projects, speeches) and coverage of numerous topics regarding development, countries, and regions are provided at this site. Go to the research and growth section of this site to access specific research and data regarding the world economy.

Weapons of Mass Destruction

13. The Bulletin of the Atomic Scientists

http://www.bullatomsci.org

This site allows you to read more about the Doomsday Clock and other issues as well as topics related to nuclear weaponry, arms control, and disarmament.

14. ISN International Relations and Security Network

http://www.isn.ethz.ch

This site, maintained by the Center for Security Studies and Conflict Research, is a clearinghouse for extensive information on international relations and security policy.

15. Terrorism Research Center

http://www.terrorism.com

The Terrorism Research Center features definitions and research on terrorism, counterterrorism documents, a comprehensive list of Web links, and profiles of terrorist and counterterrorist groups.

North America

16. The Henry L. Stimson Center

http://www.stimson.org

Stimson, a nonpartisan organization, focuses on issues where policy, technology, and politics intersect. Use this site to find varying assessments of U.S. foreign policy in the post–cold war world and to research many other topics.

17. The North American Institute

http://www.santafe.edu/~naminet/index.html

NAMI, a trinational public-affairs organization, is concerned with the emerging "regional space" of Canada, the United

States, and Mexico and the development of a North American community. It provides links for study of trade, the environment, and institutional developments.

Latin America

18. Inter-American Dialogue

http://www.iadialog.org

This is the Web site for IAD, a premier U.S. center for policy analysis, communication, and exchange in Western Hemisphere affairs. The 100-member organization has helped to shape the agenda of issues and choices in hemispheric relations.

Europe

19. Central Europe Online

http://www.centraleurope.com

This site contains daily updated information under headings such as news on the Web today, economics, trade, and currency.

20. Europa: European Union

http://europa.eu.int

This server site of the European Union will lead you to the history of the EU (and its predecessors), descriptions of EU policies, institutions, and goals, and documentation of treaties and other materials.

21. NATO Integrated Data Service

http://www.nato.int/structur/nids/nids.htm

NIDS was created to bring information on security-related matters to the widest possible audience. Check out this Web site to review North Atlantic Treaty Organization documentation, to read *NATO Review,* and to explore key issues in the field of European security and transatlantic cooperation.

22. Social Science Information Gateway

http://sosig.esrc.bris.ac.uk

A project of the Economic and Social Research Council (ESRC), this is an online catalogue of thousands of Internet resources relevant to political education and research.

Former Soviet Union

23. Russia Today

http://www.russiatoday.com

This site includes headline news, resources, government, politics, election results, and pressing issues.

24. Russian and East European Network Information Center, University of Texas at Austin

http://reenic.utexas.edu/reenic.html

This is *the* Web site for information on the former Soviet Union.

The Pacific Basin

25. ASEAN Web

http://www.asean.or.id

This site of the Association of South East Asian Nations provides an overview of Asia: Web resources, summits, economic affairs, political foundations, and regional cooperation.

26. Inside China Today

http://www.insidechina.com

Part of the European Internet Network, this site leads you to information on all of China, including recent news, government, and related sites.

27. Japan Ministry of Foreign Affairs

http://www.mofa.go.jp

Visit this official site for Japanese foreign policy statements and press releases, archives, and discussions of regional and global relations.

The Middle East and Africa

28. Africa News Online

http://www.africanews.org

Open this site for up-to-date information on all of Africa, with reports from Africa's leading newspapers, magazines, and news agencies. Coverage is country-by-country and regional. Internet links are among the resource pages.

29. ArabNet

http://www.arab.net

This page of ArabNet, the online resource for the Arab world in the Middle East and North Africa, presents links to 22 Arab countries. Each country page classifies information using a standardized system.

30. Israel Information Service

http://www.accessv.com/~yehuda/

Search the directories in this site for such information as policy speeches, interviews, and briefings; discussion of Israel and the UN; and Web sites of Israel's government.

International Organizations and Global Issues

31. Commission on Global Governance

http://www.cgg.ch

This site provides access to *The Report of the Commission on Global Governance,* produced by an international group of leaders who want to find ways in which the global community can better manage its affairs.

32. InterAction

http://www.interaction.org

InterAction encourages grassroots action, engages policy makers on advocacy issues, and uses this site to inform people on its initiatives to expand international humanitarian relief and development/assistance programs.

33. Nonprofit Organizations on the Internet

http://www.ai.mit.edu/people/ellens/Non/non-old.html

This site includes some NGO links and contains a meta-index of nonprofit organizations.

34. The North-South Institute

http://www.nsi-ins.ca/ensi/index.html

Searching this site of the North-South Institute—which works to strengthen international development cooperation and enhance gender and social equity—will help you find information and debates on a variety of global issues.

35. United Nations Home Page

http://www.un.org

Here is the gateway to information about the United Nations. Also see *http://www.undp.org/missions/usa/usna.htm* for the U.S. Mission at the UN.

We highly recommend that you review our Web site for expanded information and our other product lines. We are continually updating and adding links to our Web site in order to offer you the most usable and useful information that will support and expand the value of your Annual Editions. You can reach us at: *http://www.dushkin.com/annualeditions/*.

Unit 1

Unit Selections

1. **Globalization: What's New? What's Not? (And So What?)** Robert O. Keohane and Joseph S. Nye Jr.
2. **Ethnic Warfare on the Wane,** Ted Robert Gurr
3. **Humanitarian Intervention: The Lessons Learned,** Chantal de Jonge Oudraat

Key Points to Consider

- What type of conflict do you predict will cause the most serious threats to world peace in the twenty-first century? Explain your reasoning.
- What are the most important types of globalization identified by Robert Keohane and Joseph Nye? What types of events might reverse the current trend of globalization in the world?
- Can you describe a recent ethnic conflict that is following the pattern described by Ted Gurr? Describe how minority/majority relations are being managed.
- Explain why you agree or disagree with the adequacy of the questions proposed by Chantal Oudraat as a guide for determining the best way to intervene in internal conflicts.

Links

www.dushkin.com/online/

7. **Global Trends 2005 Project**
   http://www.csis.org/gt2005/
8. **Human Rights Web**
   http://www.hrweb.org

These sites are annotated on pages 4 and 5.

At the beginning of the twenty-first century, there was a noticeable increase in efforts to predict important changes and to understand new patterns of relationships that may shape international relations. Anyone can engage in this sport as there is little agreement among "futurists" about what to expect regarding causes of tension, types of conflict, or patterns of interaction that may characterize international relations during the twenty-first century.

With the demise of the cold war, analysts focus more on the political and economic ramifications of the emerging international system. Many cite "globalization" as the dominant characteristic of the emerging new system. Globalization refers to the increased global interdependence of economic, communication, and transport systems. Globalization also refers to innovations in computer and other high-tech capabilities and the increased use of these innovations by people in all parts of world society.

A number of disintegrative tendencies are also associated with "globalization," including the rise of cultural extremism in Islamic, Judaic, and Christian cultures; increased economic inequality between the developed and developing sectors of world society; ethnic strife; and the diffusion of high-technology weaponry. Robert Keohane and Joseph Nye re-examine recent trends. They conclude that the modern world system now has several different forms of globalism.

Another distinguishing characteristic of the post–cold war era has been an increase in ethnic and communal conflicts. This trend dominated international relations throughout the past decade. Ted Gurr's data on ethnic conflicts over time indicates that ethnic warfare peaked in the early 1990s and is on the decline in most regions. His analysis suggests that governments now increasingly seek to accommodate ethnic demands using a common set of principles and repertoire of strategies for handling ethnic crises.

This trend may be significant since the 1990s was an era during which several nation-states intervened in domestic conflicts with and without the UN's blessing. Today, some of the most violent local conflicts in remote areas of the developing world are ignored by governments and the media in developed countries while other communal conflicts receive more world attention and involvement by developed countries. Geographic proximity or strategic value for major powers, or because they raise concerns about the possibility of escalation in a world characterized by the proliferation of weapons of mass destruction, are most commonly used as rationales for interventions. Some complex emergencies in the developing world receive attention because of humanitarian concerns or because more self-interested motives relate to the possibility that conditions in collapsed societies may fuel mass migrations, the spread of infectious diseases, and other problems. The disintegration of Yugoslavia and the resulting Balkans war, which were largely ignored by most nation-states for nearly 5 years, is frequently cited as the most likely archetypal conflict that may trigger outside involvement in the future.

Complex political factors that are important root causes of most contemporary civil conflicts include invented nationalism, the legacy of colonialism, state fragmentation, failed leadership, expatriate extremism, and the financial incentives that warlords and other actors have in perpetuating violence. Conventional international diplomacy or outside peacekeeping forces are often the least suited to manage these types of conflict. International peacekeeping and humanitarian interventions are often hampered by the lack of support by major nation-states. Such interventions must also operate within a legal framework, which still emphasizes the right of self-determination and respect for territorial sovereignty of national states, even though no effective governing authority may exist on the ground. In these situations, international conflict resolution approaches are often unable to promote lasting peace or stability. Instead, peace and stability usually depend more on how well local, national, and regional actors are able to manage conflict among communal groups. In "Humanitarian Interventions: The Lessons Learned," Chantal Oudraat describes the legal, political, and logistical questions that should be addressed as nation-states consider the best ways to intervene in internal conflicts.

Long-term peace and security will also depend on how well these actors manage shared resources such as water, while also coping with transnational problems such as the spread of infectious diseases. At the same time, local and national authorities must meet the basic needs of a growing population and promote economic growth. How well political regimes cope with environmental and related challenges is receiving more attention today because it is now recognized that such factors are root causes or triggers that fuel local conflicts. Conflicts in Somalia and Rwanda were not spontaneous outbreaks of clan warfare or ethnic violence. Rather, the underlying strains of hunger, drought, the longer-term lack of cultivable land, the breakdown of traditional clan structures, and, finally, population increases fueled these recent conflicts as did the residue of past political and economic relationships.

Occasionally, problems caused by environmental factors facilitate peace. A devastating drought in Mozambique, in addition to damage caused by prolonged civil war, led warring factions to agree to a negotiated peace settlement in the early 1990s. In a similar fashion, the worsening problems created by drought throughout the Middle East, along with the desires of President Assad of Syria and Prime Minister Barak of Israel, prompted the leaders of the two countries to resume peace talks at the end of 1999. However, the breakdown of the peace process in the Middle East and the resumption of the intifada in 2000 underscore how delicate the peace process is and how difficult it will be to construct lasting peace agreements among parties engaged in protracted conflicts.

While analysts continue to argue about whether water or oil will be the most important strategic resource in the future, there is an emerging consensus that resource scarcity and environmental degradation will complicate existing relationships among nation-states and other actors in future international relations. While other analysts focus on the implications of globalization for future conflicts, some Western analysts are more optimistic about future world trends. Many now attribute the spread of democracy in part to the communication revolution and the ability of marginal groups to interact and communicate using new technological tools such as the Internet. What remains to be seen is whether globalization will promote democracy, establish new international norms of peace and stability, or lead to older forms of international conflicts. Optimists and pessimists, holding rival visions of future world politics, will continue to disagree about globalization.

These disagreements will continue because emerging trends call into question long-standing concepts of security based on competition over armaments and national wealth. Instead, future security may be a function of the strength and durability of subnational and transnational as well as interstate relationships. This proposition, if accurate, requires a new vision and model of international relations.

Globalization: What's New? What's Not? (And So What?)

by Robert O. Keohane and Joseph S. Nye Jr.

"Globalization" emerged as a buzzword in the 1990s, just as "interdependence" did in the 1970s, but the phenomena it refers to are not entirely new. Our characterization of interdependence more than 20 years ago now applies to globalization at the turn of the millennium: "This vague phrase expresses a poorly understood but widespread feeling that the very nature of world politics is changing." Some skeptics believe such terms are beyond redemption for analytic use. Yet the public understands the image of the globe, and the new word conveys an increased sense of vulnerability to distant causes. For example, as helicopters fumigated New York City in 1999 to eradicate a lethal new virus, the press announced that the pathogen might have arrived in the bloodstream of a traveler, in a bird smuggled through customs, or in a mosquito that had flown into a jet. Fears of "bioinvasion" led some environmental groups to call for a reduction in global trade and travel.

Like all popular concepts meant to cover a variety of phenomena, both "interdependence" and "globalization" have many meanings. To understand what people are talking about when they use the terms and to make them useful for analysis, we must begin by asking whether interdependence and globalization are simply two words for the same thing, or whether there is something new going on.

The Dimensions of Globalism

The two words are not exactly parallel. Interdependence refers to a condition, a state of affairs. It can increase, as it has been doing on most dimensions since the end of World War II; or it can decline, as it did, at least in economic terms, during the Great Depression of the 1930s. Globalization implies that something is increasing: There is more of it. Hence, our definitions start not with globalization but with "globalism," a condition that can increase or decrease.

Globalism is a state of the world involving networks of interdependence at multicontinental distances. The linkages occur through flow and influences of capital and goods, information and ideas, and people and forces, as well as environmentally and biologically relevant substances (such as acid rain or pathogens). Globalization and deglobalization refer to the increase or decline of globalism.

Interdependence refers to situations characterized by reciprocal effects among countries or among actors in different countries. Hence, globalism is a type of interdependence, but with two special characteristics. First, globalism refers to networks of connections (multiple relationships), not to single linkages. We would refer to economic or military interdependence between the United States and Japan, but not to globalism between the United States and Japan. U.S.-Japanese interdependence is part of contemporary globalism, but is not by itself globalism.

Second, for a network of relationships to be considered "global," it must include multicontinental distances, not simply regional networks. Distance is a continuous variable, ranging from adjacency (between, say, the United States and Canada) to opposite sides of the globe (for instance, Great Britain and

Australia). Any sharp distinction between long-distance and regional interdependence is therefore arbitrary, and there is no point in deciding whether intermediate relationships—say, between Japan and India or between Egypt and South Africa—would qualify. Yet globalism would be an odd word for proximate regional relationships. Globalization refers to the shrinkage of distance on a large scale [see box "Distance: It's Not Quite Dead"]. It can be contrasted with localization, nationalization, or regionalization.

Some examples may help. Islam's rapid diffusion from Arabia across Asia to what is now Indonesia was a clear instance of globalization, but the initial movement of Hinduism across the Indian subcontinent was not. Ties among the countries of the Asia Pacific Economic Cooperation forum qualify as multicontinental interdependence, because these countries include the Americas as well as Asia and Australia; but ties among members of the Association of Southeast Asian Nations are regional.

Globalism does not imply universality. At the turn of the millennium, more than a quarter of the American population used the World Wide Web compared with one hundredth of 1 percent of the population of South Asia. Most people in the world today do not have telephones; hundreds of millions live as peasants in remote villages with only slight connections to world markets or the global flow of ideas. Indeed, globalization is accompanied by increasing gaps, in many respects, between the rich and the poor. It implies neither homogenization nor equity.

Interdependence and globalism are both multidimensional phenomena. All too often, they are defined in strictly economic terms, as if the world economy defined globalism. But there are several, equally important forms of globalism:

- *Economic globalism* involves long-distance flows of goods, services, and capital, as well as the information and perceptions that accompany market exchange. It also involves the organization of the processes that are linked to these flows, such as the organization of low-wage production in Asia for the U.S. and European markets.
- *Military globalism* refers to long-distance networks of interdependence in which force, and the threat or promise of force, are employed. A good example of military globalism is the "balance of terror" between the United Sates and the Soviet Union during the cold war. The two countries' strategic interdependence was acute and well recognized. Not only did it produce world-straddling alliances, but either side could have used intercontinental missiles to destroy the other within 30 minutes. Their interdependence was distinctive not because it was totally new, but because the scale and speed of the potential conflict arising from it were so enormous.
- *Environmental globalism* refers to the long-distance transport of materials in the atmosphere or oceans, or of biological substances such as pathogens or genetic materials, that affect human health and well-being. The depletion of the stratospheric ozone layer as a result of ozone-depleting chemicals is an example of environmental globalism, as is the spread of the AIDS virus from west equatorial Africa around the world since the end of the 1970s. Some environmental globalism may be entirely natural, but much of the recent change has been induced by human activity.
- *Social and cultural globalism* involves the movement of ideas, information, images, and people (who, of course, carry ideas and information with them). Examples include the movement of religions or the diffusion of scientific knowledge. An important facet of social globalism involves the imitation of one society's practices and institutions by others: what some sociologists refer to as "isomorphism." Often, however, social globalism has followed military and economic globalism. Ideas, information, and people follow armies and economic flows, and in doing so, transform societies and markets. At its most profound level, social globalism affects the consciousness of individuals and their attitudes toward culture, politics, and personal identity. Indeed, social and cultural globalism interacts with other types of globalism, because military, environmental, and economic activity convey information and generate ideas, which may then flow across geographical and political boundaries. In the current era, as the growth of the Internet reduces costs and globalizes communications, the flow of ideas is increasingly independent of other forms of globalization.

This division of globalism into separate dimensions is inevitably somewhat arbitrary. Nonetheless, it is useful for analysis, because changes in the various dimensions of globalization do not necessarily occur simultaneously. One can sensibly say, for instance, that economic globalization took place between approximately 1850 and 1914, manifested in imperialism and increased trade and capital flows between politically independent countries; and that such globalization was largely reversed between 1914 and 1945. That is, economic globalism rose between 1850 and 1914 and fell between 1914 and 1945. However, military globalism rose to new heights during the two world wars, as did many aspects of social globalism. The worldwide influenza epidemic of 1918–19, which took 30 million lives, was propagated in part by the flows of soldiers around the world. So did globalism decline or rise between 1914 and 1945? It depends on what dimension of globalism one is examining.

Contemporary Globalism

When people speak colloquially about globalization, they typically refer to recent increases in globalism. In this context, comments such as "globalization is fundamentally new" make sense but are nevertheless misleading. We prefer to speak of globalism as a phenomenon with ancient roots and of globalization as the process of increasing globalism, now or in the past.

The issue is not how old globalism is, but rather how "thin" or "thick" it is at any given time. As an example of "thin globalization," the Silk Road provided an economic and cultural link between ancient Europe and Asia, but the route was plied by a small group of hardy traders, and the goods that were traded back and forth had a direct impact primarily on a small (and relatively elite) stratum of consumers along the road. In contrast, "thick" relations of globalization, as described by political scientist David Held and others, involve many relationships that are intensive as well as extensive: long-distance flows that are large and continuous, affecting the lives of many people. The operations of global financial markets today, for instance, affect people from Peoria to Penang. Globalization is the process by which globalism becomes increasingly thick.

Globalism today is different from globalism of the 19th century, when European imperialism provided much of its political structure, and higher transport and communications costs meant fewer people were directly involved. But is there anything about globalism today that is fundamentally different from just 20 years ago? To say that something is "fundamentally" different is always problematic, since absolute discontinuities do not exist in human history. Every era builds on others, and historians can always find precursors for phenomena of the present. Journalist Thomas Friedman argues that contemporary globalization goes "farther, faster, deeper, and cheaper . . ." The degree of thickening of globalism may be giving to three changes not just in degree but in kind: increased density of networks, increased "institutional velocity," and increased transnational participation.

Density of Networks

Economists use the term "network effects" to refer to situations where a product becomes more valuable once many people use it—take, for example, the Internet. Joseph Stiglitz, former chief economist of the World Bank, has argued that a knowledge-based economy generates "powerful spillover effects, often spreading like fire and triggering further innovation and setting off chain reactions of new inventions." Moreover, as interdependence and globalism have become thicker, systemic relationships among different networks have become more important. There are more interconnections. Intensive economic interdependence affects social and environmental interdependence; awareness of these connections in turn affects economic relationships. For instance, the expansion of trade can generate industrial activity in countries with low environmental standards, mobilizing environmental activists to carry their message to these newly industrializing but environmentally lax countries. The resulting activities may affect environmental interdependence (for instance, by reducing cross-boundary pollution) but may generate resentment in the newly industrializing countries, affecting social and economic relations.

The worldwide impact of the financial crisis that began in Thailand in July 1997 illustrates the extent of these network interconnections. Unexpectedly, what first appeared as an isolated banking and currency crisis in a small "emerging market" country had severe global effects. It generated financial panic

Distance: It's Not Quite Dead

The "Death of Distance" is the battle cry of the information age. In some domains, this refrain is true; as a generalization, however, it is a half-truth. First, participation in global interdependence has increased, but many people of the world are only tenuously connected to any communications networks that transcend their states, or even their localities. Many peasant villages in Asia, Africa, and Latin America are only connected to the world as a whole through slow and often thin economic, social, and political links. Even for those people linked extensively to global communications networks, it is more accurate to say that the significance of distance varies greatly by issue area.

For instance, **economic globalism** has been most marked in financial markets. Distance is indeed irrelevant—except for time zones—if a stock can be sold instantaneously in New York or Hong Kong by an investor in Abidjan to one in Moscow. Indeed, if the stock is sold online, it may be only a fiction that it was "sold on the New York Stock Exchange." But physical goods move more slowly than capital, because automobiles and cut flowers cannot be transformed into digits on a computer. Orders for such items can be sent without regard to distance, but the cars or flowers have to move physically from Tokyo or Bogotá to Jakarta or Calgary. Such movement is taking place faster than ever—flowers are now sent thousands of miles by jet aircraft—but it is by no means instantaneous or cheap.

Variability by distance applies to **cultural globalism** as well. The actual movement of ideas and information is virtually instantaneous, but how well new concepts are understood and accepted depends on how much the assumptions, attitudes, and expectations of different groups of people vary. We can refer to these differences as "cultural distance," which has been shaped by past migrations of people and ideas and is, in turn, constrained by geography. The U.S. president can talk simultaneously to people in Berlin, Belgrade, Buenos Aires, Beijing, Beirut, Mumbai, and Bujumbura—but the same words will be interpreted very differently in these seven cities. Likewise, U.S. popular culture may be interpreted by youth in some cultures as validating fundamentally new values and lifestyles, but viewed in other settings as nothing more than trivial symbols, expressed only in baseball caps, T-shirts, and music. And for some youth in the same city, such as Tehran, such symbols are representative of the Great Satan, or of liberation. Cultural distance resists homogenization. Finally, elements of **social globalism** that rely on the migration of people are highly constrained by distance and by legal jurisdictions, because travel remains costly for most people in the world, and governments everywhere seek to control and limit migration.

Similar variability by distance occurs with **environmental globalism.** We may live on "only one earth," but pollution of rivers directly affects only those downstream, and the poisonous air of many cities in the former Soviet empire and developing countries is lethal mostly to people within local and regional basins. The most lethal pollution is local. Even global phenomena such as the depletion of the ozone layer and global warming vary by latitude and climatic factors.

There is also great variability by distance in **military globalism.** Only a few countries have intercontinental missiles, and only the United States has the logistical and command and control capabilities for global reach with conventional forces. Most countries are local or at best regional powers. At the same time, weak local actors can use other networks of globalism to cause damage. Even nonstate actors can do so, as witnessed when a transnational terrorist group bombed the World Trade Center in New York.

—R.O.K. & J.S.N.

elsewhere in Asia, particularly in South Korea and Indonesia; prompted emergency meetings at the highest level of world finance and huge "bail-out" packages orchestrated by the International Monetary Fund (IMF); and led eventually to a widespread loss of confidence in emerging markets and the efficacy of international financial institutions. Before that contagious loss of confidence was stemmed, Russia had defaulted on its debt, and a U.S.-based hedge fund had to be rescued suddenly through a plan brokered by the Federal Reserve Bank of New York. Even after recovery had begun, Brazil required an IMF loan, coupled with a devaluation, to avoid financial collapse in 1999.

Economic globalism is nothing new. Indeed, the relative magnitude of cross-border investment in 1997 was not unprecedented. Capital markets were by some measures more integrated at the beginning than at the end of the 20th century. The net outflow of capital from Great Britain in the four decades before 1914 averaged 5 percent of gross domestic product, compared with 2 to 3 percent for Japan over the last decade. The financial crisis of 1997–99 was not the first to be global in scale: "Black Tuesday" on Wall Street in 1929 and the collapse of Austria's Creditanstalt bank in 1931 triggered a worldwide financial crisis and depression. In the 1970s, skyrocketing oil prices prompted the Organization of Petroleum Exporting Countries to lend surplus funds to developed nations, and banks in those countries made a profit by relending that money to developing countries in Latin

America and Africa (which needed the money to fund expansionary fiscal policies). But the money dried up with the global recession of 1981–83: By late 1986, more than 40 countries worldwide were mired in severe external debt.

But some features of the 1997–99 crisis distinguish it from previous ones. Most economists, governments, and international financial institutions failed to anticipate the crisis, and complex new financial instruments made it difficult to understand. Even countries that had previously been praised for their sound economic policies and performance were no less susceptible to the financial contagion triggered by speculative attacks and unpredictable changes in market sentiment. The World Bank had recently published a report entitled "The East Asian Miracle" (1993), and investment flows to Asia had risen rapidly to a new peak in 1997, remaining high until the crisis hit. In December 1998, Federal Reserve Board Chairman Alan Greenspan said: "I have learned more about how this new international financial system works in the last 12 months than in the previous 20 years." Sheer magnitude, complexity, and speed distinguish contemporary globalization from earlier periods: Whereas the debt crisis of the 1980s was a slow-motion train wreck that took place over a period of years, the Asian meltdown struck immediately and spread over a period of months.

The point is that the increasing thickness of globalism—the density of networks of interdependence—is not just a difference in degree. Thickness means that different relationships of interdependence intersect more deeply at more points. Hence, the effects of events in one geographical area, on one dimension, can have profound effects in other geographical areas, on other dimensions. As in scientific theories of "chaos," and in weather systems, small events in one place can have catalytic effects, so that their consequences later, and elsewhere, are vast. Such systems are difficult to understand, and their effects are therefore often unpredictable. Furthermore, when these are human systems, people are often hard at work trying to outwit others, to gain an economic, social, or military advantage precisely by acting in unpredictable ways. As a result, globalism will likely be accompanied by pervasive uncertainty. There will be continual competition between increased complexity and uncertainty, and efforts by governments, market participants, and others to comprehend and manage these increasingly complex interconnected systems.

May I interconnect you?

Globalization, therefore, does not merely affect governance; it is affected by governance. Frequent financial crises of the magnitude of the crisis of 1997–99 could lead to popular movements to limit interdependence and to a reversal of economic globalization. Chaotic uncertainty is too high a price for most people to pay for somewhat higher average levels of prosperity. Unless some of its aspects can be effectively governed, globalization may be unsustainable in its current form.

Institutional Velocity

The information revolution is at the heart of economic and social globalization. It has made possible the transnational organization of work and the expansion of markets, thereby facilitating a new international division of labor. As Adam Smith famously declared in *The Wealth of Nations,* "the division of labor is limited by the extent of the market." Military globalism predated the information revolution, reaching its height during World War II and the cold war; but the nature of military interdependence has been transformed by information technology. The pollution that has contributed to environmental globalism has its sources in the coal-oil-steel-auto-chemical economy that was largely created between the middle of the 19th and 20th centuries and has become globalized only recently; but the information revolution may have a major impact on attempts to counter

The increasing thickness of globalism—the density of networks of interdependence—is not just a difference in degree.

and reverse the negative effects of this form of globalism.

Sometimes these changes are incorrectly viewed in terms of the velocity of information flows. The biggest change in velocity came with the steamship and especially the telegraph: The transatlantic cable of 1866 reduced the time of transmission of information between London and New York by over a week—hence, by a factor of about a thousand. The telephone, by contrast, increased the velocity of such messages by a few minutes (since telephone messages do not require decoding), and the Internet, as compared with the telephone, by not much at all. The real difference lies in the reduced cost of communicating, not in the velocity of any individual communication. And the effects are therefore felt in the increased intensity rather than the extensity of globalism. In 1877 it was expensive to send telegrams across the Atlantic, and in 1927 or even 1977 it was expensive to telephone transcontinentally. Corporations and the rich used transcontinental telephones, but ordinary people wrote letters unless there was an emergency. But in 2000, if you have access to a computer, the Internet is virtually free and transpacific telephone calls may cost only a few cents per minute. The volume of communications has increased by many orders of magnitude, and the intensity of globalism has been able to expand exponentially.

Markets react more quickly than before, because information diffuses so much more rapidly and huge sums of capital can be moved at a moment's notice. Multinational enterprises have changed their organizational structures, integrating production more closely on a transnational basis and entering into more networks and alliances, as global capitalism has become more competitive and more subject to rapid change. Nongovernmental organizations (NGOs) have vastly expanded their levels of activity.

With respect to globalism and velocity, therefore, one can distinguish between the velocity of a given communication—"message velocity"—and "institutional velocity." Message velocity has changed little for the population centers of relatively rich countries since the telegraph became more or less universal toward the end of the 19th century. But institutional velocity—how rapidly a system and the units within it change—is a function not so much of message velocity than of the intensity of contact—the "thickness" of globalism. In the late 1970s, the news cycle was the same as it had been for decades: People found out the day's headlines by watching the evening news and got the more complete story and analysis from the morning paper. But the introduction of 24-hour cable news in 1980 and the subsequent emergence of the Internet have made news cycles shorter and have put a larger premium on small advantages in speed. Until recently, one newspaper did not normally "scoop" another by receiving and processing information an hour earlier than another: As long as the information could be processed before the daily paper "went to bed," it was timely. But in 2000, an hour—or even a few minutes—makes a critical difference for a cable television network in terms of being "on top of a story" or "behind the curve." Institutional velocity has accelerated more than message velocity. Institutional velocity reflects not only individual linkages but networks and interconnections among networks. This phenomenon is where the real change lies.

Transnational Participation and Complex Interdependence

Reduced costs of communications have increased the number of participating actors and increased the relevance of "complex interdependence." This concept describes a hypothetical world with three characteristics: multiple channels between societies, with multiple actors, not just states; multiple issues, not arranged in any clear hierarchy; and the irrelevance of the threat or use of force among states linked by complex interdependence.

We used the concept of complex interdependence in the 1970s principally to describe emerging relationships among pluralist democracies. Manifestly it did not characterize relations between the United States and the Soviet Union, nor did it typify the politics of the Middle East, East Asia, Africa, or even parts of Latin America. However, we did ar-

Interstate use and threat of military force have virtually disappeared in certain areas of the world.

gue that international monetary relations approximated some aspects of complex interdependence in the 1970s and that some bilateral relationships—French-German and U.S.-Canadian, for example—approximated all three conditions of complex interdependence. In a world of complex interdependence, we argued, politics would be different. The goals and instruments of state policy—and the processes of agenda setting and issue linkage—would all be different, as would the significance of international organizations.

Translated into the language of globalism, the politics of complex interdependence would be one in which levels of economic, environmental, and social globalism are high and military globalism is low. Regional instances of security communities—where states have reliable expectations that force will not be used—include Scandinavia since the early 20th century. Arguably, intercontinental complex interdependence was limited during the cold war to areas protected by the United States, such as the Atlantic security community. Indeed, U.S. power and policy were crucial to the construction of postwar international institutions, ranging from NATO to the IMF, which protected and supported complex interdependence. Since 1989, the decline of military globalism and the extension of social and economic globalism to the former Soviet empire have implied the expansion of areas of complex interdependence, at least to the new and aspiring members of NATO in Eastern Europe. Moreover, economic and social globalism seem to have created incentives for leaders in South America to settle territorial quarrels, out of fear both of being distracted from tasks of economic and social development and of scaring away needed investment capital.

Even today complex interdependence is far from universal. Military force was used by or threatened against states throughout the 1990s, from the Taiwan Strait to Iraq, from Kuwait to the former Yugoslavia; from Kashmir to Congo. Civil wars are endemic in much of sub-Saharan Africa and sometimes have escalated into international warfare, as when the Democratic Republic of Congo's civil war engulfed five neighboring countries. The information revolution and the voracious appetite of television viewers for dramatic visual images have heightened global awareness of some of these civil conflicts and made them more immediate, contributing to pressure for humanitarian intervention, as in Bosnia and Kosovo. The various dimensions of globalization—in this case, the social and military dimensions—intersect, but the results are not necessarily conducive to greater harmony. Nevertheless, interstate use and threat of military force have virtually disappeared in certain areas of the world—notably among the advanced, information-era democracies bordering the Atlantic and the Pacific, as well as among a number of their less wealthy neighbors in Latin America and increasingly in Eastern-Central Europe.

The dimension of complex interdependence that has changed the most since the 1970s is participation in channels of contact among societies. There has been a vast expansion of such channels as a result of the dramatic fall in the costs of communication over large distances. It is no longer necessary to be a rich organization to be able to communicate on a real-time basis with people around the globe. Friedman calls this change the "democratization" of technology, finance, and information, because diminished costs have made what were once luxuries available to a much broader range of society.

"Democratization" is probably the wrong word, however, since in markets money votes, and people start out with unequal stakes. There is no equality, for example, in capital markets, despite the new financial instruments that permit more people to participate. "Pluralization" might be a better word, suggesting the vast increase in the number and variety of participants in global networks. The number of international NGOs more than quadrupled from about 6,000 to over 26,000 in the 1990s alone. Whether they are large organizations such as Greenpeace or Amnesty International, or the proverbial "three kooks with modems and a fax machine," NGOs can now raise their voices as never before. In 1999, NGOs worldwide used the Internet to coordinate a massive protest against the World Trade Organization meeting in Seattle. Whether these organizations can forge a coherent and credible coalition has become the key political question.

This vast expansion of transnational channels of contact, at multicontinental distances, generated by the media and a profusion of NGOs, has helped expand the third dimension of complex interdependence: the multiple issues connecting societies. More and more issues are up for grabs internationally, including regulations and practices—ranging from pharmaceutical testing to accounting and product standards to banking regulation—that were formerly regarded as the prerogatives of national governments. The Uruguay Round of multilateral trade negotiations of the late 1980s and early 1990s focused on services, once virtually untouched by international regimes; and the financial crisis of 1997–99 led to both public and private efforts to globalize the transparent financial reporting that has become prevalent in advanced industrialized countries.

Increased participation at a distance and greater approximation of complex interdependence do not imply the end of politics. On the contrary, power remains important. Even in domains characterized by complex interdependence, politics reflects asymmetrical economic, social, and environmental interdependence, not just among states but also among nonstate actors, and through transgovernmental relations. Complex interdependence is not a description of the world, but rather an ideal concept abstracting from reality. It is, however, an ideal concept that increasingly corresponds to reality in many parts of the world, even at transcontinental distances—and that corresponds more closely than obsolete images of world politics as simply interstate relations that focus solely on force and security.

So what really is new in contemporary globalism? Intensive, or thick, network interconnections that have systemic effects, often unanticipated. But such thick globalism is not uniform: It varies by region, locality, and issue area. It is less a matter of communications message velocity than of declining cost, which does speed up what we call systemic and institutional velocity. Globalization shrinks distance, but it does not make distance irrelevant. And the filters provided by domestic politics and political institutions play a major role in determining what effects globalization really has and how well various countries adapt to it. Finally, reduced costs have enabled more actors to participate in world politics at greater distances, leading larger areas of world politics to approximate the ideal type of complex interdependence.

Although the system of sovereign states is likely to continue as the dominant structure in the world, the content of world politics is changing. More dimensions than ever—but not all—are beginning to approach our idealized concept of complex interdependence. Such trends can be set back, perhaps even reversed, by cataclysmic events, as happened in earlier phases of globalization. History always has surprises. But history's surprises always occur against the background of what has gone before. The surprises of the early 21st century will, no doubt, be profoundly affected by the processes of contemporary globalization that we have tried to analyze here.

Want to Know More?

Interdependence became a buzzword in the 1970s, thanks in part to the landmark works of two economists: Richard N. Cooper's ***The Economics of Interdependence: Economic Policy in the Atlantic Community*** (New York: McGraw Hill, 1968) and Raymond Vernon's ***Sovereignty at Bay: The Multinational Spread of U.S. Enterprises*** (New York: Basic Books, 1971). Political scientists Robert O. Keohane and Joseph S. Nye Jr. have published a number of works on the topic, including ***Transnational Relations and World Politics*** (Cambridge: Harvard University Press, 1972) and ***Power and Interdependence: World Politics in Transition*** (Boston: Little, Brown, and Company, 1977; forthcoming third edition, New York: Longman, 2000).

Technological and economic change did not stop in the 1980s, even as the "little cold war" was refocusing public attention, foundation resources, and academic fashions on the more traditional security agenda. With the cold war's end, the resulting growth in interdependence became so clear that journalist Thomas Friedman's well-written book on globalization, ***The Lexus and the Olive Tree*** (New York: Farrar Straus and Giroux, 1999) became a bestseller. (Friedman engaged *Le Monde diplomatique's* Ignacio Ramonet in a lively debate over globalization in the Fall 1999 issue of FOREIGN POLICY.) William Greider presents a skeptical post-cold-war view in his ***One World, Ready or Not: The Manic Logic of Global Capitalism*** (New York: Simon & Schuster, 1997).

The most complete academic survey of globalization to date is the magisterial ***Global Transformations: Politics, Economics, and Culture*** (Stanford: Stanford University Press, 1999), by David Held, Anthony McGrew, David Goldblatt, and Jonathan Perraton. Saskia Sassen presents an interesting sociological perspective in ***Globalization and Its Discontents: Essays on the New Mobility of People and Money*** (New York: New Press, 1997). Frances Cairncross takes a somewhat breathless view of the information revolution in ***The Death of Distance: How the Communications Revolution Will Change Our Lives*** (Boston: Harvard Business School Press, 1997). Margaret E. Keck and Kathryn Sikkink's book ***Activists Beyond Borders: Advocacy Networks in International Politics*** (Ithaca: Cornell University Press, 1998) offers a historical perspective on the evolution of global norms, and Jared M. Diamond's ***Guns, Germs, and Steel: The Fates of Human Societies*** (New York: W.W. Norton & Company, 1997) examines the various dimensions of globalism over a span of centuries.

Karl Polanyi's ***The Great Transformation*** (New York: Farrar & Rinehart, 1944; Beacon Press, 1985) remains a classic account of the rise and fall of 19th-century economic globalism. Dani Rodrik's ***Has Globalization Gone Too Far?*** (Washington: Institute for International Economics, 1997) updates these concerns for the current era. Jeffrey G. Williamson's chapter, **"Globalization and the Labor Market,"** in Philippe Aghion and Jeffrey G. Williamson, eds., ***Growth, Inequality and Globalization: Theory, History, and Policy*** (Cambridge: Cambridge University Press, 1998) is an excellent source for important historical data.

For links to relevant Web sites, as well as a comprehensive index of related FOREIGN POLICY articles, access **www.foreignpolicy.com.**

ROBERT O. KEOHANE *is James B. Duke professor of political science at Duke University.* JOSEPH S. NYE JR. *is dean of the John F. Kennedy School of Government at Harvard University. This article is drawn from the third edition of their book* Power and Interdependence: World Politics in Transition (*New York: Longman, 2000*).

Ethnic Warfare on the Wane

Ted Robert Gurr

A NEW WAY TO MANAGE NATIONALIST PASSIONS

IN NOVEMBER 1999, Indonesia's new president, Abdurrahman Wahid, promised in both Jakarta and Washington to hold a referendum on autonomy in the secessionist province of Aceh. His government reportedly started negotiating with representatives of the Free Aceh movement—something flatly unthinkable under Wahid's autocratic predecessor, Suharto.

Wahid's actions are hardly isolated. Indeed, they bespeak a new global strategy to contain ethnic conflict. Its essential principles are that threats to divide a country should be managed by the devolution of state power and that communal fighting about access to the state's power and resources should be restrained by recognizing group rights and sharing power. The conventional wisdom, of course, is that tribal and nationalist fighting is still rising frighteningly. But in fact, the rash of ethnic warfare peaked in the early 1990s—countered, in most regions, by the application of these principles.

The brutality of the conflicts in Kosovo, East Timor, and Rwanda—and the messiness of the international responses to them—obscures the larger shift from confrontation toward accommodation. But the trends are there: a sharp decline in new ethnic wars, the settlement of many old ones, and proactive efforts by states and international organizations to recognize group rights and channel ethnic disputes into conventional politics. In Kosovo and East Timor, intervention was chosen only after other means failed. The fact that the United States, NATO, the United Nations, and Australia intervened was itself a testament to the underlying premise that managing ethnic conflict has become an international responsibility.

Evidence about the shift toward accommodation comes from tracking some 300 politically active ethnic and religious groups over half a century.[1] The eruption of ethnic warfare in the early 1990s was the culmination of a long-term general trend that began in the 1950s and peaked shortly after the end of the Cold War. The breakup of the Soviet Union and Yugoslavia opened the door to new ethnic and national claims, and about a dozen new ethnic wars erupted in the erstwhile Soviet empire between 1988 and 1992. In the southern hemisphere, more than two dozen ethnic wars began or resumed in roughly the same period, most of them not directly related to the end of the Cold War.

By mid-decade, a strategic shift was under way. Over the course of the 1990s, the number of ethnic groups using violent tactics fell modestly (from 115 to 95). But a more important indicator was the balance between escalation and de-escalation: of the 59 armed ethnic conflicts under way in early 1999, 23 were de-escalating, 29 had no short-term trend, and only 7 were escalating—including Kosovo. By the late 1990s, the most common strategy among ethnic groups was not armed conflict but prosaic politics.

Another way of tracking the trends is by timing when new episodes of ethnic and political conflict start. Two-thirds of all new campaigns of protest and rebellion since 1985 began between 1989 and 1993; few have started since. The decline in new protest movements foreshadows a continued decline in armed conflict. Recent history shows that ten years of nonviolent political action generally precede the start of a new ethnic rebellion. Since the number of new ethnically based protest campaigns has declined—from a global average of ten per year in the late 1980s to four per year since 1995—the pool of potential future rebellions is shrinking.

A third perspective on the overall trends comes from examining wars of self-determination, such as those in Aceh, Sri Lanka, southern Sudan, and

Trends in Ethnic Conflicts in 1999

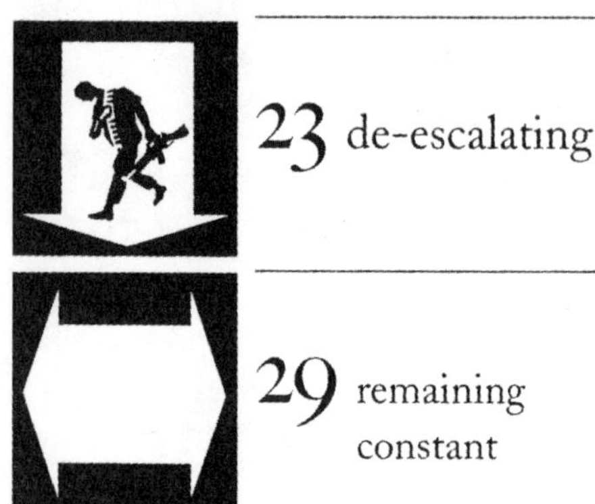

7 escalating (includes Kosovo)

Nagorno-Karabakh. Their protagonists claim the right to their own communally based zones or demand unification with their ethnic kindred across state borders. These wars are among the most deadly and protracted of all ethnic conflicts, and their spillovers have posed the greatest regional security threats of the post–Cold War decade. But they also are being contained. Between 1993 and the beginning of 2000, the number of wars of self-determination has been halved. During the 1990s, 16 separatist wars were settled by negotiated peace agreements, and 10 others were checked by cease-fires and ongoing negotiations. Fewer separatist wars are being fought today—18 by my count—than at any time since the early 1970s. This steep decline puts the Kosovo rebellion in perspective. The bombings and ambushes by the Kosovo Liberation Army in late 1997 started the only new ethnic war in Europe since 1994.

Less visible than the shift toward settling separatist wars is a parallel trend toward accommodating ethnic demands that have not yet escalated into armed conflict. Leaders of ethnic movements appeal to minorities' resentment about rights denied—political participation, autonomy, and cultural recognition. In the 1990s, separatists almost always justified such claims by invoking international norms. But minority groups are doing better these days, so such appeals now sometimes fall on deaf ears. Discrimination eased for more than a third of the groups monitored by the Minorities at Risk Project between 1990 and 1998, mainly because governments formally recognized and guaranteed their political and cultural rights. The new democracies of Europe, Asia, and Latin America were especially likely to protect and promote minority rights. Even authoritarian governments were not immune to this trend, especially in Asia. Vietnam and Indonesia both lifted some restrictions on their Chinese minorities, although for reasons that had more to do with improving relations with mainland China and maintaining access to Chinese capital than any newfound fealty to group rights. Still, the overall trend is unmistakable: ethnic conflict is on the wane.

THE NEW NEW THING

NO "INVISIBLE HAND" guided the global decline in serious ethnic conflict during the 1990s. Rather, it was the result of concerted efforts by a great many people and organizations, including domestic and international peacemakers and some of the antagonists themselves. Relations between ethnic groups and governments changed in the 1990s in ways that suggest that a new regime governing minority-majority relations is being built—a widely held set of principles about how to handle intergroup relations in heterogeneous states, a common repertoire of strategies for handling crises, and an emerging domestic and international consensus on how to respond to ethnic repression and violence.

The first and most basic principle of this emerging regime is recognizing and actively protecting minority peoples' rights. This means freedom from discrimination based on race, national origin, language, or religion; it also entails institutional remedies that organized ethnic groups can use to protect and promote their collective cultural and political interests. A corollary is the right of national peoples to exercise some autonomy within existing states. After all, it follows that if minorities who make up a majority of one region of a multiethnic democracy have the right to protect and promote their collective interests, they should have the right to local or regional self-governance.

Western democracies have taken the lead here. After World War II, the Atlantic democracies emphasized the protection of individuals, but during the early 1990s, Western advocates shifted their emphasis from individual rights to the collective rights of national minorities. The Organization for Security and Cooperation in Europe (OSCE) and the Council of Europe adopted standards in 1990–95 that prohibit forced assimilation and population transfers, endorse autonomy for minorities within existing states, and acknowledge that minority claims are legitimate subjects of international discussion at both U.N. and European regional organizations.

Virtually all European democracies have implemented these principles. In the first stage of democratization in postcommunist Europe, some ethnic leaders manipulated democracy to stoke nationalist passions at the expense of minorities like the Russians in the

Baltics, the Hungarians in Slovakia and Romania, and the Serbs in Croatia. In most of these countries, a combination of diplomatic engagement by European institutions and elections checked the new wave of discrimination. The status of Hungarians in Slovakia and Romania improved markedly in the late 1990s, when old-line communists-turned-nationalists were ousted by coalitions that included ethnic parties. European diplomatic initiatives and OSCE missions helped persuade Baltic nationalists to moderate their treatment of Russians. Croatia's new, more moderate government today promises to respect the minorities that suffered from former President Franjo Tudjman's ultranationalism. That leaves Serbia as the last holdout, and once Slobodan Miloševic's successor takes office, the Serbian government, too, will probably give more than lip service to minority rights.

For several reasons, however, creating autonomy within the state for minorities is harder than simply banning discrimination. Most governing elites want to hold on to central authority. Many also fear that autonomy will lead to outright secession. Finally, negotiating arrangements that satisfy all parties and address each situation's unique quirks is not easy.

The second fear—autonomy as a slippery slope—is not supported by the facts on the ground. In very few contemporary instances did negotiated autonomy lead to independence. Sometimes an autonomous regional government pushes hard for greater authority, as the Basques have done in Spain. But the ethnic statelets that won de facto independence in the 1990s—Somaliland, Abkhazia, the Trans-Dniester Republic, and Iraqi Kurdistan—did so in the absence of negotiations, not because of them. Those truly looking to reduce ethnic bloodshed should embrace autonomy, not fear it.

There are now many models of autonomy agreements to draw on. The best-known such pacts were reached through negotiated settlements of wars of self-determination, like the Oslo accords between Israel and the Palestine Liberation Organization and Northern Ireland's Good Friday agreement. Less has been written about the conflict-containing agreements that established a federal state for India's Mizo people in 1986, an autonomous republic for the Gaguaz minority in Moldova in 1994, and regional autonomy for the Chakma tribal group in Bangladesh's Chittagong Hills in 1997.

Some authoritarian leaders have also recognized that negotiations can end protracted conflicts. In the mid-1990s the junta that rules Burma concluded ceasefire agreements and offered concessions that checked protracted separatist rebellions by the Kachin and Mon peoples of northern Burma, although similar efforts failed to end resistance by the more numerous Shans and Karens who live in the south and east of the country.

In most recent wars of self-determination, fighting usually began with demands for complete independence and ended with negotiated or de facto autonomy within the state. There are many reasons why most ethnic nationalist leaders are willing to settle for 50 cents (or less) on the dollar, but it usually comes down to being strategically and politically overmatched. Nationalists willing to continue fighting for total independence, like the rebel leaders in Chechnya and East Timor, are rare. Central governments, on the other hand, tend increasingly to conclude that it is cheaper to negotiate regional and cultural autonomy and redistribute some funds than it is to fight endless insurgencies—especially when other states and international organizations are encouraging them to negotiate. The Turkish government's obdurate resistance to organized Kurdish political participation has become an anachronism; even Saddam Hussein is more open to cooperation with (some) Kurdish groups than Turkish nationalists are.

> Most recent ethnic wars began with demands for complete independence and ended with autonomy.

If the parties in separatist wars recognize that the costs of accommodation are probably less than the costs of prolonged conflict, it is only a short step to mutual decisions to settle after an initial show of forceful resolve rather than after prolonged warfare. Gagauz and Moldovan nationalists came to such a conclusion in 1992, as did Tuareg rebels and the governments of Mali and Niger in the mid-1990s. Nationalist Serbia became the pariah state and the bombing range of Europe in 1999 precisely because it refused to negotiate with the Kosovars throughout the 1990s and (most immediately) blatantly violated principles about group rights accepted elsewhere in the region.

Protecting collective rights is one of the three elements of the new preferred strategy for managing ethnic heterogeneity. Democracy is another; it provides the institutional means whereby minorities in most societies secure their rights and pursue their collective interests. Of course, other institutional mechanisms can protect groups' interests—take, for example, the communal power-sharing arrangements found in many nondemocratic African states. Nonetheless, European-style democracy is widely held to be the most reliable guarantee of minority rights. It is, after all, inherent in the logic of democratic politics that all peoples in heterogeneous societies should have equal civil and political rights, and democracy also implies resolving civil conflicts by peaceful means.

ACCOMMODATING BEHAVIOR

A THIRD ELEMENT of this new regime is the principle that disputes over self-determination are best settled by negotiation and mutual accommodation. One of democratic Russia's most important but least-noticed achievements has been its negotiation of power-sharing agreements with Tatarstan, Bashkiria, and some 40 other regions in the Russian Federation, only some of which have non-Russian nationalities. The agreement between Russia proper and Tatarstan went the greatest symbolic distance: strikingly, it actually treated the parties as equals. (This pact could and should have been a model for settling the dispute between Moscow and Chechnya, but Chechen leaders were interested only in total independence.)

The principle that serious ethnic disputes should be settled by negotiation is backed up actively by most major powers, the U.N., and some regional organizations, especially in Europe and Africa. These entities mix diplomacy, mediation, sweeteners, and threats to encourage accommodation. Preventive diplomacy is widely popular—not only because early engagement can be cheaper than belated crisis management but because it is the preferred instrument of the new regime. Coercive intervention, as in Kosovo, is the international system's response of last resort to gross violations of human rights and to ethnic wars that threaten regional security.

Four regional and global forces reinforce the trend toward accommodation in mixed societies. First is the active promotion of democratic institutions and practices by the Atlantic democracies. Modern democracies fight one another rarely and temper their repression against internal opponents. Before-and-after comparisons of national and minority peoples in new democracies show that their status usually improves substantially during democratic transitions.

A second buttressing factor is engagement by the U.N., regional bodies, and interested nongovernmental organizations on behalf of minority rights. International entities such as the OSCE, the Council of Europe, the Organization for African Unity, and the Organization of the Islamic Conference have often used diplomacy and mediation to soften their members' policies toward minorities and move ongoing conflicts toward agreement. The Organization of the Islamic Conference, not usually considered a peacemaker, was for two decades the key international player supporting a negotiated settlement to the Muslim Moros' separatist war in the Philippines.

Third is the virtually universal consensus among the international political class—the global foreign policy elite—in favor of reestablishing and maintaining global and regional order. Empire-building is out of fashion. Interstate rivalries in the 1990s focused mainly on economic productivity and competition for markets, and wars of any stripe threaten regional order and prosperity. Hence the U.N., the United States, regional powers, and the regional organizations of Europe, Latin America, and Africa have sought to contain local conflicts by preventive measures where possible and by mediation and peace-keeping where necessary.

Finally, the costs of ethnic conflict have become evident to both governing elites and rebel leaders. The material and social costs of civil war have been bitterly acknowledged in countries where postwar settlements are taking hold—in Bosnia, the Philippines, Mozambique, and elsewhere. The lesson drawn by outside observers of the mid-1990s war in Chechnya was that the Russian military could not defeat highly motivated guerrillas—remember Afghanistan. But the lesson the protagonists in Chechnya should have learned was that the war was not worth fighting; neither side gained much that could not have been won through negotiations before the Russian tanks rolled. Caution about the likely costs of war and the unlikely chances of victory on either side probably helped check ethnic rebellions elsewhere on Russia's periphery and in most Soviet successor states. NATO'S spring 1999 campaign against Serbia conveyed a similar message to other states whose leaders have refused to compromise with ethnic nationalists. The lesson has reached as far as Beijing, where the Kosovo crisis reportedly prompted Communist Party officials to begin drafting alternative policies for dealing with restless Tibetans and Uigurs.

NOT SO EASY

OF COURSE, conventional wisdom sees things somewhat differently. Most Western policymakers and foreign affairs analysts view ethnic conflict as getting worse, not becoming more manageable. What about communal warfare and genocide in central Africa, ethnic cleansing in Kosovo, Muslim and Hindu fundamentalism, or regional rebellions in Indonesia? The answer is a paradox. Objectively, there are substantially fewer such conflicts now than in the early 1990s. But they now get more public attention—precisely because they challenge the emerging norms that favor group rights and the peaceful accommodation of ethnic conflicts. Bloody crises also rivet Western publics because they threaten the comforting assumption that the "international community" can guarantee local and regional security.

Why, then, was Kosovo wracked by massacres and ethnic cleansing despite international doctrines of minority rights, past examples of ethnic conflicts that were successfully settled, and a world willing to get engaged? For starters, in no sense was ethnic war in Kosovo unprecedented. Indeed, Kosovo was the most dreaded flash point in post-Bosnia Europe. Empirically, a decade of political activism and protest typically precedes ethnic wars. Kosovo fit the pattern neatly: its ethnic Albanians resisted the dissolution of the province's regional government in 1989 by forming a parallel government, but the first Kosovar terrorist attacks did not begin until 1997. Large-scale armed conflict began a year later. Miloševic's ultranationalist policies and intransigence fundamentally contradicted European and international principles about minority rights, but international attempts to prevent calamity faltered. True, the Bush administration warned the Yugoslav government in December 1992 not to repress the Kosovars, but the issue was not addressed in the 1995 Dayton Accord that the Clinton administration negotiated to end the war in Bosnia, and the Serbs' October 1998 preparations for another round of ethnic cleansing elicited little international response. The failure, then, was not so much due to international spinelessness as to sheer disbelief that the Serbs would try it again.

The world system emerging from the settlement of ethnic and regional conflicts is more complex than its Cold War predecessor. So containing ethnic conflict requires more foresight and better-coordinated international responses, as demonstrated in Kosovo and East Timor. The new liberal wisdom holds that sovereignty can be trumped by humanitarianism and that the international cavalry will ride to the rescue of minorities who face genocide. Chechen and Tibetan nationalists remain unconvinced.

The liberal vision is still too neat. Better to think of the system as multilayered, with three interdependent sets of political actors: states; ethnic movements, some within an existing country and some straddling several of them; and the regional and international organizations that are increasingly responsible for managing relations between the other two. States remain the paramount actors, and the powerful among them can still get away with the sort of thing that the Russians are doing in Chechnya and the Chinese are doing in Tibet. But most states, even major powers, are held back by a growing network of mutual obligations regarding minorities, regional organizations, multinationals, and world bodies. Countries that ignore those obligations risk their future world status, prosperity, and amicable foreign relations.

The new regime is not fully developed, and a depressingly long list of states and ethnic movements that reject its principles will challenge it violently. Few states in the Muslim world, for example, are prepared to grant full political and cultural rights to religious minorities. Some protracted ethnic conflicts are almost immune to regional and international influence. The struggles in places such as Afghanistan and Sudan probably will remain intractable unless and until one side wins decisively. The odds are against durable settlements for the longstanding conflicts between Kurdish nationalists and Iraq and Turkey or the containment of communal strife between Hutu and Tutsi in Rwanda. Some ethnic wars are being held in check by cease-fires and contested agreements that could easily come apart—consider Georgia, Azerbaijan, Iraqi Kurdistan, Bougainville, or Northern Ireland. South Asia alone is home to a dozen thorny ethnic and political conflicts. Since the 1950s, India has faced a series of separatist challenges, especially in the northeast; no sooner has one movement been accommodated than another emerges. Some conflicts that have been "settled" in the traditional way—by overwhelming force—could flare up again; think of what Burma did in the Karen and Shan states, or of Indonesia's crackdown in the provinces of Aceh and Irian Jaya, or China in Tibet. Repression without accommodation regularly leads to renewed resistance and rebellion, as it did in Indonesia after Jakarta began its democratic transition. So international efforts should focus on helping rulers negotiate with rebellious groups, providing both sides with incentives for choosing autonomy rather than secession.

> The world simply did not believe that the Serbs would try ethnic cleansing again.

The greatest challenges to the new international way of containing ethnic conflicts are in Africa. In a vast conflict zone from Sudan and Ethiopia through the Great Lakes region to Angola's highlands and the Congo, rivalries between states and communities form an extraordinarily complex web. The U.N. hopes to send 500 observers and 5,000 peacekeepers to the region to help implement the Lusaka accords and thereby stop the fighting, but this plan ignores the blunt political reality that many of the armed bands do not want their conflicts managed. If the Lusaka accords and the peacekeeping mission were to fail, the credibility of future international attempts to ease the area's misery would be undercut. Instead, the world should concentrate on trying to negotiate settlements on the conflict zone's periphery, notably in Sudan and Angola.

Other challenges lie in West Africa. Revolutionary and ethnic wars have been doused in Niger, Mali, and Liberia but sporadically flare up in Sierra Leone and Chad. The greatest risk here has been that of civil war in Nigeria, which is divided between Muslims in the north and Christians in the south and has many of the factors that elsewhere predict ethnic warfare—a legacy of repressive rule, the emergence of militant ethnic nationalist groups, and a lack of international engagement. The prospects of ethnic war in Nigeria depend on how well its transition to democracy goes. The highest priority for preventive engagement in West Africa should therefore be supporting Nigeria's democratization, in the course of which the Ijaw, Ogoni, and Yoruba peoples' grievances against the northern-dominated regime should be addressed.

This survey highlights the highest-priority ethnic conflicts, which urgently need remedies and preventive action. But by whom and how? The answers depend on which actors have the will, the political leverage, and the resources to act. Kosovo, East Timor, and Chechnya illustrate that the reach of the new strategy for managing ethnic conflict depends equally on whether that doctrine is accepted by the combatants and on the will and ability of regional and international organizations to implement it. International and regional bodies are most likely to effectively prevent conflict in areas where the Western powers have vital interests, which means Europe, Latin America, and the Middle East. African and Asian conflicts are more remote and therefore more resistant to outside influence. The strategy there should be to encourage and assist regional organizations, especially the Organization of African Unity and the Association of Southeast Asian Nations (which, if quietly encouraged, may expand beyond its usual agenda of regional economics). When prevention fails or is not pursued in the first place, the international challenges are different: providing humanitarian aid and keeping the fighting from spreading throughout the region.

AFTER ETHNICITY

THE EVOLUTION of good international practices for managing ethnic conflict is one of the signal accomplishments of the first post–Cold War decade. It also has had some unintended consequences. The most obvious is that accommodation of ethnic claims encourages new groups and political entrepreneurs to make similar demands in the hope of gaining concessions and power. Some latecomers are the Cornish in Britain, the Reang tribe in India, and the Mongols in China—each of which is now represented by organizations calling for autonomy and more public resources. But the pool of potential ethnic contenders is not infinite, and we have already heard from most of them. Ethnic identity and interest per se do not risk unforeseen ethnic wars; rather, the danger is hegemonic elites who use the state to promote their own people's interests at the expense of others. The "push" of state corruption and minority repression probably will be a more important source of future ethnic wars than the "pull" of opportunity.

A less obvious threat is the potential emergence of alternative forms of popular opposition. During the last several decades, the entrepreneurs behind ethnic political movements tapped into a reservoir of resentment about material inequality, political exclusion, and government predation and channeled it to their purposes. They drew on some of the same grievances that once fueled revolutionary movements. In fact, some conflicts are hybrids: ethnic wars when seen through one set of analytic lenses and revolutionary wars when seen through another. Leftists in Guatemala recruited indigenous Mayans to fill the ranks of a revolutionary movement, Jonas Savimbi built his rebel movement through the support of Angola's Mbundu people, and Laurent Kabila led a revolutionary army to Kinshasa made up of Tutsi, Luba, and other disaffected tribal peoples in the eastern Congo.

The larger point is that popular support for mass movements is to some degree fungible. All but a few of the Cold War's socialist movements failed, discrediting revolutionary rhetoric and action for most of their target audience, the urban and rural poor. Ethnic-national movements have met greater political success, but their appeal is limited to groups with some prior sense of cultural identity. And since ethnic conflicts tend to end in compromise, disillusionment is inevitable. So the field is open for other forms of mass opposition that may supplant ethnic movements, just as ethnic nationalism in its time preempted most revolutionary movements. Faith, in the form of militant Islam, Christianity, or Buddhism, can also motivate mass movements: consider the Falun Gong, a personal and spiritual movement whose persecution by the Chinese government virtually ensures its politicization. Today, class, ethnicity, and faith are the three main alternative sources of mass movements, and class-based and religious movements may well drain away some of the popular support that now energizes ethnic political movements. With a little bit of luck and a great deal of international engagement, ethnic conflict's heyday will belong to the last century.

NOTES

1. All evidence herein comes from the Minorities at Risk Project. The data and interpretations are reported in greater detail in the author's forthcoming book, *Peoples Versus States: Minorities at Risk in the New Century*, forthcoming from the United States Institute of Peace Press. Coded data, chronologies, and assessments for all groups are available from the project's Web site at www.bsos.umd.edu/cidcm/mar.

TED ROBERT GURR is Distinguished University Professor at the University of Maryland. He directs the Minorities at Risk Project at the university's Center for International Development and Conflict Management.

Humanitarian Intervention: The Lessons Learned

In determining how they should react to internal crises in other countries, the nations of the world need to answer three questions: "First, under what conditions should international actors intervene in internal conflicts? . . . When international action is required, which international actors should take the lead and who should participate in these operations? . . . [And third,] What are the best ways of carrying out international interventions in internal conflicts?"

CHANTAL DE JONGE OUDRAAT

The Kosovo crisis in 1999 and the Sierra Leone hostage debacle in 2000 have reignited a recurring debate in international policy circles over humanitarian intervention.[1] This debate focuses on the legal, political, and operational conundrums of coercive actions for humanitarian purposes, and will only intensify in the future. Indeed, internal conflicts are difficult to ignore in a globalizing world.

The legal obstacles to humanitarian intervention were highlighted by North Atlantic Treaty Organization (NATO) threats to intervene without United Nations Security Council authorization in the conflict between the Yugoslav government and the secessionist Kosovar Albanians. Throughout the summer and autumn of 1998, China and Russia strongly opposed a possible NATO intervention and threatened to veto any attempt to secure UN authorization for such action. In March 1999, as violence within Kosovo increased, the United States and its NATO allies nonetheless went ahead and, without consulting the UN Security Council or General Assembly, launched a 78-day air war against Belgrade. Consequently, unlike in the early 1990s, the debate at the end of the decade focused not on the question of whether humanitarian considerations could be characterized as "threats to international peace and security" and thus justify intervention in states' domestic affairs, but rather whether such interventions needed the authorization of the UN Security Council.

The March 1999 intervention in Kosovo and Serbia also highlights today's policy dilemmas. Clearly, communal strife is difficult to ignore in an increasingly interdependent and globalized world; images of gross human rights abuses will frequently create pressures on outside powers to intervene. Yet, allowing for the use of force in humanitarian emergencies without UN Security Council authorization could easily lead to erosion of the general rule on the prohibition of the use of force and efforts to restrict its use in relations between states. It could also contribute to a weakening of the United Nations.

UN Secretary General Kofi Annan is acutely aware of this dilemma and the dangers associated with it. In September 1999 he took this debate to the UN General Assembly and urged states to develop criteria to permit humanitarian interventions in the absence of a consensus in the Security Council. Annan asked Algeria, China, and India—countries that vehemently opposed the United States–NATO intervention in Yugoslavia and spoke against humanitarian intervention in the 1999 General Assembly debate—what they would have done if, in the case of the 1994 Rwanda genocide, a coalition of states had been prepared to act in defense of the Tutsi population, but did not receive prompt Security Council authorization. "Should such a coalition have stood aside," he asked, "and allowed the horror to unfold?" Similarly, those who heralded the Kosovo operation were asked what type of precedent the action had set. To what extent had that intervention undermined the prohibition on the use of force and the system created after World War II to deal with such security threats?

The political and operational conundrums of international interventions in internal conflicts for humanitarian purposes again sprang up in Sierra Leone in May 2000 and were illustrated by the international response—or rather the lack thereof—to the taking hostage of 500 UN soldiers by rebel forces.[2] Members of the Security Council immediately voiced their concern about the situation. United States Ambassador to the United Nations Richard Holbrooke called the situation in Sierra Leone "unacceptable to the United Nations" said that it "should be unacceptable to all [UN] member states." "We can't turn away from crises like these," he stressed. Similarly, United States Secretary of State Madeleine Albright stated that the hostage-taking was "unacceptable" and that it "needed to be reversed." Despite these strong rhetorical reactions, little was done.[3] Britain sent 800 troops to rescue its citizens in Sierra Leone, and the United States, which had been heavily involved in the Sierra Leone peace negotiations in 1999, sent the Reverend Jesse Jackson as an envoy to neighboring Liberia in an attempt to enlist President Charles Taylor's help in liberating the UN hostages. Taylor was both the "godfather" and the "quartermaster" of those who had taken UN peacekeepers hostage. The United States also offered to fly troop reinforcements from Bangladesh to Sierra Leone. However, because the United States rate for the transport of troops greatly exceeded regular commercial rates, the UN Secretariat declined this offer.

Sierra Leone showed that the political and operational lessons from failed UN missions in Rwanda, Bosnia, and earlier in Somalia had not been learned. The same mistakes continued to be made. For example, the UN had learned in Bosnia and Rwanda that lightly armed peacekeepers should not be sent into a violent or potentially violent situation. Yet, the UN Security Council did exactly that in Sierra Leone in 1999, and set out to do the same in the Democratic Republic of Congo (the former Zaire) in 2000. Similarly, the early 1990s had shown the importance of matching mission mandates with sufficient resources. Yet, the Zambian peacekeepers in Sierra Leone were not equipped to carry out a mandate to enforce the peace. This mismatch was reminiscent of the agonizing UN missions of the early 1990s, and it pointed to the domestic and international political constraints inherent in humanitarian interventions. The challenge is mobilizing sufficient domestic and international political support to see these missions through.

Meeting this challenge requires international actors to answer three questions. First, under what conditions should international actors intervene in internal conflicts? (This "whether to intervene" question has both legal and political components.) The second question is: When international action is required, which international actors should take the lead and who should participate in these operations? (This is the "who should intervene" question.) And the third question is: What are the best ways of carrying out international interventions in internal conflicts? (This is the "how to intervene" question.) Answering these questions requires an examination of recent practice. This in turn will help identify policy challenges for the future.

OBSTACLES TO INTERVENTION

At the heart of the humanitarian intervention debate lies the question of whether force can be used lawfully in situations other than those foreseen by the UN charter. This debate features different legal schools of thought and is defined by the practice and the declaratory policies of states, which often are not in line with each other.

Under Chapter VII of the UN charter, the Security Council can impose coercive measures and disregard the general principle of nonintervention in states' domestic affairs if it determines that a particular problem poses a "threat to international peace and security." In the 1990s, the Security Council showed great creativity in defining such threats. It increasingly deemed internal conflicts and gross violations of human rights to be legitimate reasons for international action. By the end of the 1990s, the idea that states should not be allowed to hide behind the shield of sovereignty when gross violations of human rights occur on their territory had firmly taken root. Still, many states remain hesitant to accept a right of humanitarian intervention outside the UN framework. They believe that the current system, under which the Security Council determines whether a situation merits the imposition of economic sanctions or military intervention, is the best guarantee that economic embargoes and military interventions will not be launched for self-serving political reasons.

Most legal scholars and governments argue that the UN charter contains a general prohibition on the use of force. This prohibition is embodied in Article 2(4): "All Members shall refrain in their international relations from the threat or use of force against the territorial integrity or political independence of any state, or in any other manner inconsistent with the Purposes of the United Nations."

Scholars and governments generally maintain that the charter allows for only two exceptions to this rule. One is in response to an armed attack (Article 51). The other is when the use of force is authorized by the Security Council to maintain or restore international peace and security (Article 42).

Every approach that would allow for humanitarian intervention contains possibilities for abuse, and none provides a guarantee to future victims of genocide or gross violations of human rights.

That said, some legal scholars maintain that Article 2(4) does not contain a general and comprehensive prohibition on the use of force. They argue that it merely regulates the conditions under which force is prohibited, but allows exceptions beyond the two mentioned in the charter (Articles 51 and 42). They defend the notion that the charter permits the use of force in other circumstances. State practice, despite declaratory policies to the contrary, seems to concur with this view. Over the years, governments and legal scholars have argued that force can be lawfully used to protect and rescue nationals abroad; free people from colonial domination; fight terrorism; or protect people from gross violations of human rights.

The idea that force can be used to protect a country's nationals abroad (or even nationals of another country) whose lives are in immediate danger or who are in a hostage situation has not formally been accepted as an exception to Article 2(4). Yet a growing number of states have, if not openly condoned, at least not actively opposed such actions.

Interventions to free people from colonial domination received widespread political support in the UN General Assembly in the 1960s and 1970s, but legal scholars disagreed over the legality of the use of force in such cases. While many scholars considered this issue irrelevant with the end of decolonization, the larger questions of self-determination and the liberation of oppressed people remained on the agenda. Indeed, throughout the cold war, socialist states backed military interventions in support of liberation movements and to preserve so-called Marxist gains within the Soviet bloc. The United States defended military interventions to counter communism and to further democracy during this period. Such ideologically based justifications for the use of force were repudiated by the International Court of Justice in its 1986 decision on the Nicaragua case, and they were abandoned with the end of the cold war. The self-determination debate nonetheless resurfaced in the 1990s with the breakups of Yugoslavia and the Soviet Union and with the increased focus on ethnic conflicts. Groups in Bosnia, Chechnya, East Timor, Sri Lanka, and Kosovo all claimed a right to self-determination and justified their use of force and requests for outside help on these grounds. Most legal scholars assert that no right of outside military intervention exists in these types of situations, and the UN Security Council has almost always called on outside powers to show restraint and has imposed arms embargoes. State practice is nonetheless often at odds with legal rules and Security Council injunctions.

Claims regarding the legality of coercive action to combat terrorism, other than in hostage situations, are similarly shaky but have gained some ground. The cruise missile strikes by the United States in August 1998 that destroyed a pharmaceutical plant in Sudan and training facilities in Afghanistan believed to be associated with Osama bin Laden—accused of directing terrorist attacks in 1998 on United States embassies in Kenya and Tanzania—were criticized throughout the world. Yet, UN Security Council resolutions on terrorism in the 1990s testify to greater international concern with terrorism; they acknowledge that terrorism can endanger "the lives and well-being of individuals world-wide as well as the peace and security of all states." Moreover, in 1992 the Security imposed economic sanctions for the first time on a state—Libya—because of its alleged support of international terrorists (the sanctions were lifted in April 1999 after Libya agreed to allow the trial in the Netherlands under Scottish law of the two Libyans accused of bombing an American airliner, killing 270 people, in 1988). In 1996 it imposed economic sanctions on Sudan, and in 1999 it did the same on Afghanistan.[4] The United States has also increasingly resorted to the unilateral adoption of economic sanctions (in 1999, seven countries believed to be supporting international terrorism—Cuba, Iran, Iraq, Libya, North Korea, Sudan, and Syria—were the subject of unilateral United States sanctions, as were 202 terrorist organizations and 59 individuals).

The most divisive issue—which is also the one that received the most attention in the 1990s—is military intervention to protect people from gross violations of human rights. The 1999 UN General Assembly debate showed that most states clearly reject a unilateral right to intervene for humanitarian purposes. China, Russia, and most developing states claim that such a right would allow meddling in their internal affairs. They fear abuse from the United States, in particular, and they strongly condemned NATO's unauthorized intervention in Kosovo.

Armed intervention for humanitarian purposes developed a bad reputation in the nineteenth century, when military interventions by European powers were frequently justified on humanitarian grounds. Since the adoption of the UN charter, states have generally avoided referring to humanitarian purposes when justifying their military interventions, relying instead on broad interpretations of self-defense and claims of providing "assistance" to "legitimate" governments.

The end of the cold war resuscitated the question of military intervention for humanitarian purposes, a concept that has steadily received more supporters. Indeed, compared to the early 1990s, the idea that the UN Security Council can order interventions for humanitarian purposes was commonly accepted by 1999. The Security Council did so, for example, in Bosnia, Somalia, Haiti, and Rwanda. Similarly, it endorsed peace-implementation missions in Kosovo (after the NATO intervention), Indonesia's East Timor, Sierra Leone, and Congo with a Chapter VII—enforcement—mandate. Unauthorized interventions, however, pose problems for most states. Genocide and gross violations of human rights are universally considered morally unacceptable acts. Many analysts and governments agree that, in such cases, economic sanctions and the threat of criminal prosecution are weak deterrents and even weaker instruments of compellence. Yet few have accepted the idea that, in those cases, military intervention must become a duty. The absence of a legal framework for carrying out interventions contributes to the unease states experience when considering such actions. Still, the current system, whereby the UN Security Council determines whether a situation merits military intervention by certifying such a situation as a "threat to international peace and security," is an insufficient warranty that the council will intervene when the next atrocity occurs.

IS A LEGAL FRAMEWORK POSSIBLE?

Developing a legal framework, which would regulate unilateral interventions for humanitarian purposes, would not ensure action. Such a framework, nonetheless, is a necessary condition to help deter and stop future humanitarian disasters. Those who fear that the formulation of a new legal framework for humanitarian intervention would lead to abuse—particularly Western abuse—should be reassured by Western behavior regarding Chechnya, East Timor, Sierra Leone, and Congo. In Chechnya, Russia was permitted to act with impunity. In East Timor, Australia intervened only after having received the consent of the Indonesian government. In Sierra Leone, the Western reaction to the taking hostage of 500 UN peacekeepers in May 2000 consisted of evacuating their nationals from the country. And in Congo, three months after the UN Security Council had authorized the deployment of more than 5,000 troops in February 2000, only a fraction of these troops had actually been committed. None were from the United States.

Several analysts and scholars have put forward proposals that would regulate state practice and make humanitarian intervention legal under specific circumstances. Two different approaches have been developed. The first builds on the framework established in the UN charter. Proponents of this school advocate new interpretations of certain charter articles. The second builds on law outside the UN charter and draws on the inherent rights of states. Advocates of this school argue that states have a unilateral right to humanitarian intervention.

Among the analysts who advocate a new look at the charter, those who suggest an extended reading of Chapter VIII, which deals with regional arrangements, are the most convincing. They propose to broaden the mandate of regional organizations and give them the right, under certain conditions, to authorize the use of force. Like the 1950 "Uniting for Peace" resolution, which gives the UN General Assembly the right to recommend military action if the council is paralyzed, most of these proposals maintain the central role of the UN Security Council and allow for the activation of other loci of authority only if the council is incapable of acting.

At the heart of the humanitarian intervention debate lies the question of whether force can be used lawfully in situations other than those foreseen by the UN charter.

Winrich Kühne, a German analyst at the Stiftung Wissenschaft und Politik in Ebenhausen, Germany, has proposed investing regional organizations with the authority to use force under three conditions: first, when the UN Security Council is unwilling to act or is incapable of acting; second, when the Security Council has not explicitly denied the existence of a humanitarian crisis; and third, when the regional institution in question can act within the confines of a predetermined institutional structure that could authorize such action. Kühne proposes that the Security Council adopt a declaration that would invite regional organizations to develop such mechanisms and that would interpret Article 53 of the charter as giving regional organizations a right of humanitarian intervention when the council is unable or unwilling to act. Bypassing the question of whether NATO is a regional organization under the terms of Chapter VIII, under Kühne's proposal NATO's action in Kosovo would have been lawful.

Kühne's and similar proposals have three problems, however. First, regional organizations are not always the best intervenors in internal conflicts. Members of regional organizations are neighbors, who are the international actors most likely to have ulterior political motives for intervention. Indeed, neighbors often meddle in unhelpful ways in such conflicts (Liberia's support for the Revolutionary United Front in Sierra Leone is but a more recent example). Second, these proposals merely shift the problem from the global to the regional level. Indeed, the decisions of these regional authorities would be based on political considerations and not on agreed-on principles—that is, law. That such decisions would be made collectively would not make them more lawful: "more" means greater *might,* but not necessarily greater *right.* Finally, the Kühne proposal would give the great powers a key role in deciding on interventions. Great powers could block smaller powers from intervening by adopting declarations in the Security Council that would nullify the existence of a humanitarian crisis. But an attempt to block intervention by, for example, NATO would probably not succeed in the council. Indeed, France, Britain, or the United States most likely would veto it. In practice, this would mean that only interventions by regional and subregional organizations in Africa or Asia would be subjected to international scrutiny, since most of the regional and subregional organizations in those continents do not count permanent members of the UN Security Council as their regular members. Although Kühne's proposal was designed to redress insufficient enthusiasm for intervention, its possible abuse might make it unattractive to many developing countries.

Other analysts have argued that states have an inherent right to use force (the United States and Britain defended this right during the Kosovo crisis). This right, they say, is restricted by the UN charter, but not prohibited by it. Many experts have outlined conditions under which military intervention would be lawful, drawing on just-war theories of the nineteenth century that established criteria by which war could be considered just and legitimate. These criteria include: right authority (which actor has the authority to decide on war?); just cause (is the cause legitimate?); right intention (what are the motives behind the launching of the war?); last resort (have other actions been considered?); open declaration (did war start with a declaration?); proportionality (is the act of war proportionate to the harm inflicted?); and reasonable hope (is there a reasonable chance for a successful outcome?).

Serge Sur, a professor of international law at the University of Paris, suggests that humanitarian intervention should be considered lawful under the following conditions. First, states would publicly declare in which cases they would reserve the right to intervene. For example, they could stipulate in a unilateral or collective declaration that they would intervene in cases covered by the statutes of the international criminal tribunals set up for the former Yugoslavia and Rwanda, or those of the International Criminal Court. This right of intervention would be discretionary. States would not be obliged to intervene; neither could third parties hold them responsible for not intervening. Second, states would outline in advance how they would intervene, specifying the military means they would consider employing. In view of the controversy over the use of air power in Kosovo and a military doctrine that allows for

The development of economic sanctions and military strategies should not be seen as independent undertakings.

no deaths on the side of the intervenor, states would outline when they would deploy ground troops. Moreover, states should ensure that the military intervention would not itself become a violation of humanitarian law (several NGOs have argued that certain aspects of NATO's bombing campaign were in violation of humanitarian law, in particular the choice of certain targets and the use of cluster bombs). States also would outline entry and exit strategies. Third, states would articulate how they would coordinate and harmonize their military interventions with efforts for national and international criminal prosecution of those responsible for the humanitarian crisis in question. Such prosecution is foreseen in the Geneva Conventions and is an integral part of international humanitarian law.

Every approach that would allow for humanitarian intervention contains possibilities for abuse, and none provides a guarantee to future victims of genocide or gross violations of human rights. Yet forcing states to define the parameters under which they would consider military intervention for humanitarian purposes might introduce a measure of predictability into the process and could have a deterrent effect on future violators of basic human rights. It would also constitute a start at undercutting arguments about double standards, as well as serving as a hedge against accusations that interventions are solely self-serving.

By emphasizing that a just doctrine of humanitarian intervention is not about legal authority alone, but also about ensuring that interventions have strong political support and sufficient military resources, Sur provides a framework for addressing two additional problems that have plagued coercive actions in the 1990s: political commitment problems and resource problems.

MANAGING THE POLITICS OF HUMANITARIAN INTERVENTIONS

The 1990s saw the UN Security Council increasingly intervene to stop internal conflicts, imposing economic sanctions or authorizing the use of force to stop gross violations of human rights and civil strife that it considered "threats to international peace and security." Since 1989, the Security Council has imposed economic sanctions 15 times—compared to only twice between 1945 and 1988. In 10 of these 15 cases, sanctions were imposed to contain or stop internal conflicts.[5] The use of force other than for self-defense was authorized in 11 cases since 1989, as opposed to 3 times between 1945 and 1988. Ten of these cases concerned internal conflicts.[6] Despite this increase in coercive action, the results have been limited, and in some cases coercive actions have been outright failures (for example, in Bosnia and Somalia).

While some of these failures can be ascribed to faulty operational procedures and inappropriate coercive strategies, most arose because of insufficient political commitment by the intervening powers. Their commitment was restrained by both domestic and international political factors.

Public opinion in Western-style democracies often is moved by media images of humanitarian atrocities, leading citizens to pressure their governments to intervene. At the same time, politicians are hesitant to commit troops to such missions because of the potential for casualties. Indeed, interventions in internal conflict situations are almost always tricky propositions, even if "formally" invited by the warring parties and after the signing of a peace agreement. The military, particularly the United States military, will only support a military intervention if widespread domestic support for such action exists.

Politicians and military commanders believe that domestic support is dependent on keeping combat casualties to a minimum. The conventional wisdom is that the riskier an operation, the weaker the domestic support for it. This explains why American policymakers were wary of intervening in Bosnia, Somalia, Rwanda, and Haiti. It also explains why policymakers generally propose gradual and incremental policies when dealing with humanitarian atrocities. Because they are subject to conflicting domestic political pressures, they often push for half-measures and think in terms of best-case scenarios: wishful thinking is the order of the day when it comes to humanitarian interventions.

However, the cautious attitude of politicians, particularly American politicians, seems questionable. A series of public opinion polls conducted at the University of Maryland as well as a series of studies by the Triangle Institute for Security Studies in North Carolina show that the American public will support military interventions that are morally and politically compelling. For example, in a 1999 poll, people were asked to identify the highest number of American military deaths that would be acceptable to stabilize a democratic government in Congo; a figure of almost 7,000 casualties was given. Similarly, the public was willing to tolerate almost 30,000 deaths to prevent Iraq from obtaining weapons of mass destruction.[7]

Moreover, a 1999 research project by the Program on International Policy Studies of the University of Maryland shows a huge disconnect between policy elites and the public. For example, policy elites consistently think that the American public wants to disengage from the world and has a negative view of the UN, including UN peacekeeping efforts. Poll data, however, show that Americans have a very positive image of the UN and would like to see the organization strengthened, including its military component. Strong majorities (71 percent to 77 percent) believe that the United States and the UN should intervene militarily when gross violations of human rights occur, and they favor the United States contributing troops to such operations.

Constraints on humanitarian interventions are not only of a domestic political nature; international political obstacles are also important. Intervention decisions should be made by the UN Security Council. Whether the council takes action with respect to a specific problem depends on the extent to which the problem threatens regional peace and security, and the extent to which the interests of the council members are engaged, particularly the five permanent members.

Unfortunately, the international political consensus that seemed to emerge at the beginning of the 1990s is crumbling. The new globalized world order of the late 1990s appeared to many states to be an unequal order, favoring one country—the United States—far more than others. As Algerian President Abdelaziz Bouteflika and many other delegates pointed out at the 1999 UN General Assembly debate, the uneven manner in which states developed economically and the ever-widening gap between rich countries and debt-ridden third world countries have not made the establishment of a universally accepted new world order any easier.

Moreover, many states resented Washington's imperial attitude and its willingness to push multilateral organizations aside when they could not agree on a course of action that the United States favored. As a result, organizing collective responses to peace and security threats was becoming increasingly difficult by the end of the 1990s.

International interventions need strong leaders who can coordinate and give focus to the intervention. The UN Secretariat, because of its chronic lack of resources, is often unable to provide this type of leadership. The difficulties of the mission in Sierra Leone and the two other missions undertaken in the wake of NATO's Kosovo intervention—in East Timor and Congo—exemplify the type of problems the UN runs into when it does not have the support of any of the major powers. Unfortunately, the major powers—the United States especially—are often reluctant to engage in humanitarian interventions.

WHO SHOULD INTERVENE?

According to the UN charter, military interventions are to be carried out by armed forces put at the disposal of the Security Council and commanded by the UN Military Staff Committee. Because of the cold war, such an international army was never established. And although the cold war is now over, it seems unlikely that the UN will be endowed with its own army in the near future.

Proposals in the early 1990s calling for the establishment of a UN volunteer military force or the creation of UN peace enforcement units were extremely controversial. In 1993 the UN introduced a standby program that called on member states to earmark some of their forces for UN operations. The limits of this program soon became apparent. Indeed, during the 1994 genocide in Rwanda, the UN secretary general was unable to deploy 5,000 soldiers—despite the pledge of 19 governments to keep 31,000 troops available on a standby basis. By 1995, the idea of standby forces had deteriorated to a standby system under which states made conditional pledges to contribute troops to future UN peacekeeping operations. As of May 2000, 88 states had pledged a total of some 147,900 troops. Yet, few of these states had volunteered troops for the missions in Sierra Leone and Congo.

In sum, as former high-ranking UN official Brian Urquhart put it in a September 17, 1999 *Boston Globe* column, the idea of a UN force is "further than ever from becoming a reality." Troops are put at the disposal of the UN on an ad hoc basis. Most peacekeeping operations—that is, operations where local parties have agreed to the deployment of international forces—are under UN command. Military interventions, including UN enforcement operations, are generally under national command or that of a regional organization because of the operational risk associated with such interventions; a lead state often drives and controls the operation. In Europe, it is NATO, and within NATO it is the United States; in western Africa, it is the Military Observer Group (ECOMOG) of the Economic Community of West African States (ECOWAS), and within ECOMOG it is Nigeria; in East Timor, it is Australia.

Whether a country will intervene or lead a "coalition of the willing" is a function of the international environment (including the legal environment) and national interests (including national military capabilities and domestic political considerations). For large-scale operations, the United States has to take the lead, if only because it alone possesses the capabilities to carry out such operations. Moreover, the involvement—even the limited involvement—of the United States will signal to troublemakers that the effort is serious.

Unfortunately, the United States has a mixed track record in this area. In many cases, the United States failed to take meaningful action: Rwanda, Congo, and East Timor are notable examples. The United States took the lead in Bosnia in 1995 after agonizing for three years about whether and how to get involved in the conflict. In Somalia it took the lead for four months, but then distanced itself from the operation and eventually pulled out altogether. In Haiti, the United States decided and acted only in 1994, three years after Jean-Bertrand Aristide, the democratically elected president, was deposed in a military coup. Similarly, in 1998 and 1999 the United States hesitated about intervening in Kosovo.

Other countries also have taken leadership roles, but these interventions have succeeded only if they have been supported by a regional or global power. Italy, because of its interests in the region and because it was directly affected by the crisis in Albania in 1997, took the lead for Operation Alba. It managed to secure UN Security Council authorization and together with eight other European countries reestablished security in Albania. In 1999, Australia took the lead in East Timor. Given the great powers' lukewarm support of intervention, the success of the Australian mission depended in its early stages on Indonesian cooperation; indeed, Australia intervened only after it had secured approval from the Indonesian government.

The multinational force authorized by the UN Security Council in November 1996 to prevent the starvation of hundreds of thousands of Hutu refugees in Zaire and to create humanitarian corridors to lead them back into Rwanda failed; Washington and Paris were unwilling to lead or provide support for this operation. Canada, which had been given primary responsibility for the mission, was unable to carry out the operation on its own. Similarly, the UN force in Sierra Leone failed miserably to uphold its authority when attacked in May 2000. Only after Britain introduced some 800 well-trained troops did tension begin to subside.

The international political consensus that seemed to emerge at the beginning of the 1990s is crumbling.

Given the reluctance of many Western powers to engage peacekeepers in distant lands and Western fears of combat casualties, some experts have advocated hiring private military corporations for these missions. In the 1990s, private military forces were increasingly used to give logistical support, dispense military advice, provide security services (protection of property and personnel), and participate in combat. For example, in the former Yugoslavia, the United States hired an NGO run by retired United States military personnel—Military Professional Resources Incorporated—to dispense military advice and train Croat forces. In other cases, private military companies were hired by states to fight rebels on their territory. Executive Outcomes—a company run by former South African military officers—was hired by Sierra Leone and Angola to fight rebels on their territory.

Some have pointed out that, in certain cases, these private military forces have helped stop internal strife. David Shearer, a former research associate at the International Institute for Strategic Studies in London, credits Executive Outcomes with bringing the warring parties in Sierra Leone to the negotiating table in 1996. Some also believe that private forces might solve the UN's chronic lack of military personnel in messy and risky situations. Others, however, believe that the activities of these companies should be more closely monitored and regulated.

Indeed, many private security companies operate in a legal vacuum. They mainly do business in Africa, and often countries or rebel groups pay them not in hard currency but in mining rights. At times, mining companies themselves have agreed to buy the services of the private military companies in return for mining rights. In many instances close links exist between the mining companies and the military companies.

Shearer has suggested that the international community should engage these companies, rather than banning them or pretending they do not exist, and apparently this is happening. Increasingly, private security companies perform tasks that governments cannot or will not carry out. International organizations also increasingly engage private security firms, but thus far their role has been limited to the protection of property and civilian personnel. Some believe that success in this domain may lead to employing these firms for combat purposes or enforcement operations. That, however, would amount to giving the UN its own standing forces. Given the reluctance of member states to do that and the lack of UN financial resources, this seems an unlikely prospect.

A clear distinction must be made between hiring the services of security firms for limited and well-defined tasks and hiring them in a peacekeeping capacity, where they would be responsible for the maintenance of public law and order. The United Nations might wish to do the former; it should not be allowed to do the latter. Questions of war and peace and life and death should not be governed by profit motives; doing so would be contrary to everything the UN stands for.

HOW TO INTERVENE

Much has been written about how to intervene. States generally have two main coercive instruments available when considering intervention: the use of force and economic sanctions. (International criminal prosecution, a third available instrument, is not covered here.) Six conditions must be fulfilled for the effective use of such coercive instruments.

First, outside powers need to have a clear idea of the political objectives they hope to achieve. They should try to pursue one objective at a time; multiple objectives muddy the waters. The imposition of sanctions or the use of military force should also not be aimed at punishing troublemakers. Rather, these instruments should be used to change behavior or to bring those responsible to justice.

Second, outside powers need to correctly assess the economic, political, and military characteristics of the target, which will often be nonstate actors.[8] Our knowledge of how coercive actions affect targets—particularly nonstate targets—is limited, a deficiency that hinders the development of a coherent and effective strategy. The imposition of economic sanctions on some targets is ineffective and can even be counterproductive. For example, imposing economic sanctions on parties in poor states (Burundi) or failed states (Somalia) is at best futile. Similarly, the effectiveness of the use of force depends on the characteristics of the target. Aiming the use of force at the "conflict" instead of at the belligerent parties, as was done in the early 1990s in Bosnia and Somalia, led to dramatic policy failures.

Third, one country or international organization has to take the lead in interventions. Leadership gives direction to interventions and is key to building strong coalitions. Moreover, in the absence of a leader, multilateral sanctions regimes will quickly be crippled because of interpretation problems; multiple as well as conflicting purposes may be proposed for military interventions, which frequently leads to failure. In theory, international leadership should come from the UN Security Council; in practice, it comes from individual states. A leader must chart an effective course of action and articulate its position to others. Whether it can do so is a function of its political strength and its military capabilities. Being a leader does not mean bullying others. True leaders know how to translate national interests into regional and international interests and how to persuade other states to get on board.

Fourth, leaders need to build strong international coalitions for proposed coercive undertakings. Obtaining international support for these interventions is a function of national interests and the threat posed to regional and international security and human life. The more countries see an internal conflict as a threat to their own security and to higher values, the easier it will be to construct a coalition to support international intervention. The participation of many states is necessary for the effectiveness of multilateral sanctions regimes. It may also be attractive when it comes to the use of military force; indeed, it may help ensure that sufficient numbers of troops are available for coercive actions. Moreover, multiple involvement may help bring down costs. The United Nations has an important role to play in building and organizing international support for coercive actions, and it can provide legitimacy for them.

Fifth, outside powers need to ensure that enough resources are available for their interventions. Resources may be needed to implement and enforce sanctions regimes, and they may also be needed to compensate some states for losses associated with the implementation of sanctions. Similarly, military interventions must be endowed with sufficient resources. This is not to say that to be successful, such operations must have overwhelming military capabilities, but they need enough firepower and the right mix of forces—air power and ground troops—to get the job done.

Sixth, outside powers need to adopt appropriate strategies. Intervention strategies are the subject of significant debate within the scholarly and policymaking communities. Two main schools of thought exist on the imposition of sanctions and the use of force. The first believes that coercive instruments are most effective when imposed immediately and comprehensively. The second believes that coercive instruments can—and often should—be imposed gradually. Both schools of thought are right some of the time: some cases warrant swift and comprehensive coercive actions; others call for gradual approaches.

The use of economic sanctions and military force should be proportionate to the desired goal. Limited goals do not warrant the imposition of extreme sanctions or the massive use of force. If goals are more ambitious, stronger coercive actions are generally required. If the threat to international peace and security or human life is significant and immediate, strong sanctions and military operations might be needed. Less urgent situations call for more incremental approaches.

The political, economic, and military characteristics of the target should also guide selection of a strategy. For example, authoritarian regimes are less vulnerable to economic sanctions than are democratic regimes; when dealing with an authoritarian regime, it may be advisable to forgo economic sanctions and threaten the use of force immediately. Similarly, small guerrilla groups are generally immune to economic sanctions. Many sanctions regimes stay in place for a long time and often start producing adverse social and humanitarian effects. Such effects, though, rarely lead to the overthrow of politicians or a change in the behavior of the political elites. On the contrary, empirical evidence in the former Yugoslavia, Haiti, and Iraq tends to confirm that prolonged sanctions strengthen—rather than weaken—the political regimes in place. The existence and level of development of a political opposition in the target country are important in this respect. If the opposition is weak, the imposition of comprehensive sanctions may ruin their chances to develop into a real opposition. This happened in the former Yugoslavia, for example.[9] The economic and military characteristics of the target should also guide coercive strategies. Weak economies, for example, should be targeted with gradual and partial sanctions. Robust economies, as well as centrally planned economies, should be hit swiftly and comprehensively; because of their ability to shift resources, they are better able to withstand sanctions.

Similarly, the limited use of force may be sufficient in traditional wars. Indeed, traditional military organizations may be more vulnerable to the coercive uses of force than are guerrilla or insurgent fighters. Much has been written about the force of air power, particularly after Kosovo. Air power remains an extremely problematic tool in internal conflict situations and in situations where gross violations of human rights are taking place. It is often forgotten that the NATO airstrikes in Bosnia—especially those before the 1995 summer offensive—showed the limited utility of air power in these types of situations; it demonstrated that airstrikes cannot substitute for ground forces. The use of air power in the Balkans in 1999 also raises important questions about NATO's targeting policy and its use of cluster bombs.

Coercive strategies should also be flexible. The economic, military, and political characteristics of a target can change over time. The coercer's objectives and means may also change. A strategy that was sound early in a conflict may not be effective later.

Finally, all good strategies should contain exit strategies. But exit strategies should not be confused with exit schedules. Exits must be based on local political and strategic conditions—not arbitrary and rigid timetables. They should also encompass a postintervention strategy designed to tackle long-term economic and political problems. Outside powers considering intervention should realize that interventions entail more than the imposition of economic sanctions or the use of military force. They should be prepared to make long-term—even open-ended—commitments.

The development of economic sanctions and military strategies should not be seen as independent undertakings. Economic sanctions strategies should include determinations about when to escalate and threaten the use of military force. The imposition of economic sanctions and the use of military force should therefore be seen as two points on a coercive continuum and two complementary policy options.

To sum up, the effective use of economic sanctions and military force depends on having a clear purpose; correctly assessing the target, leadership, coalition support; providing sufficient resources to ensure effective implementation; and having an appropriate strategy, including an exit and postintervention strategy. These conditions may seem commonsensical, but many post–cold war interventions have failed to meet these basic standards. And they consequently failed to have the desired effects.

NOTE

1. "Intervention" is defined as a coercive action intended to change the behavior of one or more parties in the country in question. This action may involve the threat or use of economic sanctions and the threat or use of force. Although it may also involve criminal prosecution, this apex of intervention will not be discussed.

2. Members of the Security Council had authorized the peacekeeping operation in Sierra Leone in October 1999 to help implement the peace agreement signed in July 1999 and to prevent war from breaking out again.
3. The UN had been faced with a similar problem in Bosnia throughout 1994 and 1995. In May 1995, when some 300 UN soldiers were taken hostage by Bosnian Serb forces and paraded in front of Western TV cameras, Western countries sent a 10,000-strong Rapid Reaction Force to Bosnia, which prepared the terrain for a larger offensive against the Bosnian Serbs in the summer of 1995. The introduction of this force permitted a redeployment of UN peacekeepers throughout the spring of 1995. It also set the stage for greater coercive action: the NATO bombing campaign against the Bosnian Serbs in August 1995. In Sierra Leone, there were no TV cameras and the UN hostages were not NATO soldiers but mostly Zambian army recruits.
4. Sanctions on Sudan were imposed because of Sudan's refusal to extradite three individuals accused of an assassination attempt on Egyptian President Hosni Mubarak. The sanctions, which went into effect May 10, 1996, consisted of restrictions on the travel of Sudanese diplomatic personnel. Sanctions on Afghanistan were imposed because of the ruling Taliban's refusal to hand over Osama bin Laden and his associates for trial. The sanctions went into effect November 15, 1999, freezing financial assets and requiring UN member states to boycott Taliban-owned aircraft.
5. Sanctions to quell internal conflict were imposed on the republics of the former Yugoslavia, the rump Yugoslavia, the Bosnian Serbs, Somalia, Haiti, Liberia, the guerrilla group Unita in Angola, Rwanda, and Sierra Leone (twice). Sanctions were imposed on Iraq to force it to end its occupation of Kuwait and subsequently to ensure Iraqi compliance with UN Security Council Resolution 687 of April 3, 1991. In the case of Ethiopia and Eritrea, an arms embargo was imposed to stop war between these two countries. Sanctions were imposed on Afghanistan, Libya, and Sudan to force those countries to extradite individuals suspected of terrorist attacks.
6. Military force was authorized in Bosnia, Somalia, Rwanda, Haiti, Zaire, Albania, the Central African Republic, Kosovo, East Timor, Sierra Leone, and Congo. Troops engaged in all these operations received Chapter VII—enforcement—mandates and were authorized to use force for purposes other than self-defense; not all did. Military force was also authorized in Iraq for a more traditional interstate conflict. The Security Council did not authorize the initial military intervention in Kosovo in March 1999, but subsequently authorized an international presence with an enforcement mandate.
7. The poll showed some remarkable discrepancies among the military elite, the civilian elite, and the mass public. Faced with the same question on Congo, the military elite gave 284 and the civilian elite 484 as the number of acceptable deaths. For Iraq, the figures were: military elite, 6,016; civilian elite, 19,045. Finally, respondents were asked how many American deaths would be acceptable to defend Taiwan against invasion by China. The military responded 17,425; the civilian elite 17,554; and the mass public 20,172. See Peter D. Feaver and Christopher Gelpi, "How Many Deaths Are Acceptable? A Surprising Answer," *Washington Post,* November 7, 1999, p. B3.
8. This is in contrast with what happened in the nineteenth and twentieth centuries. It also underscores the idea that the debate over intervention is perhaps not over the decline of the sovereignty of the state, but instead about how the state is reasserting its sovereignty.
9. Recent claims that sanctions brought Milosevic down are wrong. First, the comprehensive sanction regime imposed on Yugoslavia in 1992 was lifted in 1995 with the Dayton peace agreement. In 1998, in response to mounting violence in Kosovo, the UN Security Council imposed an embargo—but no other international economic sanctions were imposed by the council. Second, the unilateral United States and European Union sanctions imposed in 1998 were of a limited nature.

CHANTAL DE JONGE OUDRAAT *is an associate at the Carnegie Endowment for International Peace and a member of the executive board of Women in International Security. This article is adapted from "Intervention in Internal Conflicts: Legal and Political Conundrums," Carnegie Endowment for International Peace (Washington D.C.: August 2000).*

Unit 2

Unit Selections

Key Points to Consider

- What are the most important aspects of the international economy that cannot be explained by contemporary economic theories? Identify important political factors that played a role in each of these events or trends.
- Explain why the increase in international capital flows may lead to more stability in international financial flows.
- Which countries in the world may be able to greatly expand their market share of service exports in the future? Will this growth translate into increased international political influence or power? How important are the principles of fairness and comprehensiveness for the continued trend toward trade liberalization worldwide?
- Do you agree or disagree with Jeffrey Sachs's analysis that rich countries need to mobilize global science and technology in order to address specific problems in the poorest countries? Defend your answer.

Links

www.dushkin.com/online/

9. **International Political Economy Network**
   http://csf.colorado.edu/ipe/
10. **Organization for Economic Cooperation and Development/FDI Statistics**
    http://www.oecd.org/daf/investment/
11. **Virtual Seminar in Global Political Economy/Global Cities & Social Movements**
    http://csf.colorado.edu/gpe/gpe95b/resources.html
12. **World Bank**
    http://www.worldbank.org

These sites are annotated on pages 4 and 5.

Today, economic problems, like the rapid flow of global capital, increases in the price of oil, and the possibility of world recession, are important features of international relations. Stories about the linkages between expanded free trade zones and national trade deficits or worker dislocations are often featured in the media. Governments increasingly focus on issues related to how to promote market shares for national industries in world markets as competition becomes more intense. In the increasingly integrated global economy, national governments must scramble to ensure that deep-seated political disagreements do not interfere with the pursuit of commercial gain by industry.

Recently the United States repealed several laws requiring the imposition of mandatory sanctions as a tool of persuasion while retaining sanctions against a few longstanding enemies—Cuba, Iraq, and Libya. During 1999, the United States lobbied hard to gain China's admission into the World Trade Organization (WTO) and avoided criticizing other important trading partners for human rights violations. The pattern illustrates how a powerful nation-state increasingly shifts national priorities to promote economic prosperity.

As the effects of the Asian financial crisis illustrate, it is important to understand how political factors contribute to major economic problems. Helen Milner summarizes what is known about important economic and political linkages in "International Political Economy: Beyond Hegemonic Stability." The article explains how and why the distribution of power among countries allows hegemonic powers to play key roles in international economics. Milner also discusses how the activities of key international institutions, widely held ideas and beliefs, and domestic politics affect problems and trends in the international economic system. Different interpretations of the financial crisis in Asia highlight more fundamental disagreements about whether the international financial system needs a tune-up or a major overhaul.

Recognition is growing that the International Monetary Fund's (IMF) prescriptions for coping with financial crisis aggravated economic and political problems in several "bail-out countries." The rapid withdrawal of investment flows from countries that experienced short-term liquidity problems also fueled debate about how and how much to reform international institutions and practices that regulate capital flows. These debates reflect more basic disagreements about whether the recent international economic slowdown is a sign of temporary or fundamental problems associated with the modern world capital system. The authors of "The Color of Hot Money" explain why the conventional wisdom that blamed the rapid movement of hedge funds in sparking Asia's recent financial crisis is wrong. Instead, the "hot money" that rushed in and out of emerging markets was short-term loans from troubled banks, not from hedge funds. These authors predict that as capital markets grow and replace traditional bank lending as the primary source of international financing, capital flows are likely to become less volatile.

The publicity surrounding the collapse of the trade talks in Seattle in 1999 underscored the growing importance of the World Trade Organization (WTO). With 120 member-nations, WTO, established in 1995, acts as a global referee of international trade issues, including national "competition policies," international investment, internationally recognized labor rights, and global trade liberalization. The World Trade Organization is moving toward tackling a host of thorny issues related to domestic antitrust practices, labor standards, and the environment that heretofore were the exclusive province of national governments.

The collapse of trade talks at the WTO meeting in Seattle, Washington, underscored the increased role that trade policies are likely to play in domestic politics. The protests reflect the reality that service sector businesses with leading-edge knowledge, skills, or processes in any country are now exportable across national borders. America benefits from this trend in many sectors. The organized labor and environmental protesters who demanded tighter labor and environmental standards at the meeting reflected a number of organized interests in the developed world. While the United States and Europe are concerned with a string of bilateral trade disputes and by their efforts to shepherd China into the World Trade Organization, delegates from developing countries are interested in negotiating new arrangements to foster trade that benefits developing countries.

For many, recent trade talks are unbalanced since the resulting liberalization policies seem to promote trade among developed states and growing inequalities and conflicts between rich and poor countries. Many in the developing world argue that recent trade agreements do not reflect the concerns of most people in developing countries. In most developing countries, trade issues link to larger problems related to poverty. As the number of poor and unemployed people in developing countries increase, developing nation-states increasingly complain that their citizens, who represent three-fourths of humanity, are not benefiting from recent trade agreements.

Global inequalities in trade are being fueled by the fact that 15 percent of Earth's population provides nearly all the world's technology innovations. Jeffrey Sachs, a well-known economist, argues that most people in poor countries live in different ecological zones, face different health conditions, and must overcome agronomic limitations that are very different from those of rich countries. These differences are often the fundamental cause of persistent and worsening poverty.

Many developing countries also find it difficult to compete and prosper in the emerging global economy, since they have to pay 40 to 80 percent of their GNP to service past international loans. Sachs ties several of the problems evident in poor countries to complex market failures. In "Helping the World's Poorest," Sachs argues that recent efforts to provide partial debt relief to Highly Indebted Poor Countries (HIPCs) is only one step in the direction needed to close the gap between the richest and poorest countries. Since conditions for most people in many HIPCs are worsening dramatically, Sachs emphasizes the need for rich countries to mobilize global science and technology in order to address specific problems that help to keep poor countries poor.

The Highly Indebted Poor Countries initiative is a recent effort coordinated by the World Bank and International Monetary Fund to help the poorest of the most heavily indebted nation-states cope with their debt burden by writing off some of their debt owed to multilateral organizations. Some rich countries are also offering to renegotiate or write off a certain percentage of bilateral debts to HIPC countries as well. In 2000, the U.S. Congress approved $435 million to support the HIPC debt relief initiative. While many non-governmental organizations (NGOs) claim this initiative is too limited, others worry that pressures for a speedy process will result in debt relief to countries with bad economic policies and provide little help for other poor countries in the long term.

International Political Economy: Beyond Hegemonic Stability

by Helen V. Milner

International political economy is a growth industry. Beginning its boom after the oil crises in the 1970s shook both world markets and states, the field now encompasses not only a great deal of political economy but of comparative and international politics as well. The end of the Cold War also helped shift attention to the field's main focus: how markets and states affect one another.

Scholars in the field have tried to explain at least four aspects of the international political economy. First, many of its pioneers thought that economics was too narrow to explain central aspects of the international economy. Consider one of the more visible theoretical gaps: Although economic theory showed that free trade was optimal, in reality, protectionism characterized most states' trade policies for years. Seeking to explain such paradoxes created by economic theory, scholars have proposed explanations that are more political. In particular, they have emphasized how politics determines the stability and openness of the international economy, a focus inspired by the trauma of the Great Depression in the 1930s and the desire to avoid repeating any such experience.

Second, scholars have focused on explaining states' foreign economic policy choices. In part, many believe that these choices are the most important factor shaping the nature of the international economy. For example, explaining why states choose to protect their economies, or how they set their exchange rates, or why they give foreign aid have been central preoccupations for the field. These explanations, however, have sought to interpret such choices by adducing domestic and international factors as well as economic and political ones.

Third, the field has paid attention to why certain states grow rapidly and develop over time, while others fail to do so or decline. This interest in the changing positions of states in the world economy has also been approached eclectically. Economic causes for such changes are usually supplemented by political ones, while domestic causes of the rise and decline of states are paired with international factors.

Finally, scholars have been interested in the impact of the international economy on domestic politics, an issue often explored under the rubric of the globalization of national economies.

Researchers in this field have generally sought answers to these kinds of questions by looking into four categories of explanatory factors: 1) the distribution of world power, especially the role of a hegemonic state; 2) the structure, function, and consequences of international institutions; 3) the impact of nonmaterialist factors such as ideas and beliefs; and 4) the effect of domestic politics.

Does Hegemony Breed Stability?

Robert Gilpin, Stephen Krasner, and other scholars from the realist tradition have identified the distribution of power among states as a central factor in explaining the openness and stability of the international economy. "Hegemonic stability theory," first espoused by Charles Kindleberger in the 1970s, focuses on the role of leading states—for example, Great Britain in the nineteenth and the United States in the twentieth centuries—and on how changes in the distribution of capabilities affect the world economy. This theory argued that the overwhelming dominance of one country was necessary for the existence of an open and stable world economy. Such a hegemon served to coordinate and discipline other countries so that each could feel secure enough to open its markets and avoid beggar-thy-neighbor policies. Conversely, the theory asserted that the decline of a hegemon tends to be associated with economic closure, instability, and the creation of competing regional blocs.

During the nineteenth century, Britain exercised a form of economic hegemony over much of the world. Britain's leadership was associated with the globalization of markets, the openness of international trade and capital movements, the rise of multinational corporations, and the general economic and political stability that characterized at least Europe. World War I brought an abrupt end to both British hegemony and the conditions that it had promoted. Increasing protectionism, the formation of regional blocs, and the decline in capital mobility in the 1920s and early 1930s ate away at the foundations of the global economy, contributing to growing economic instability and the depression.

The cause of this tragic chain of events has often been laid at America's doorstep. The United States was, at the end of World War I, the world's strongest economic power. But it steadfastly refused to take on the leadership role that Britain could no longer play. This "irresponsibility" was most vividly exemplified in the minds of many people by the infamous Smoot-Hawley Tariff (1930), which raised the average tax on imports to the United States by about 40 percent. At the beginning of the depression, the United States shut its markets to foreign goods and thus helped propel the world economy into its worst swoon ever. The unwillingness of the United States to coordinate its monetary and currency policies with other countries merely exacerbated the situation. This isolationist posture on the part of the world's economic hegemon had negative consequences for most other countries and the United States itself.

The perils of isolationism seemed to have been well learned by American policymakers after the end of World War II. Then, the United States quickly assumed a leadership role and steadily moved forward to create an open international trade system based on the General Agreement on Tariffs and Trade (GATT) and a stable monetary system founded on the Bretton Woods system. The Marshall Plan was perhaps the direct antithesis of the Smoot-Hawley tariff. It symbolized recognition of America's special role and responsibility for peace and prosperity beyond its borders—indeed, globally. U.S. leadership, it is asserted, helped create the conditions necessary for the steady economic growth experienced by the industrial countries up to the 1970s and the rapid development of countries such as Japan and South Korea.

Concerns about U.S. power arose again in the late 1960s and early 1970s. America's economic advantages over the rest of the world seemed to be rapidly dissipating, while other countries were catching up. In response, protectionist sentiment within the United States grew, leading to many domestic challenges to the traditional policy of freer trade. The stability of international currency markets was also disrupted by American behavior. The simultaneous pursuit of the Vietnam War and the Great Society program helped fuel inflation in the United States, which was exported abroad because of the dollar's role in international exchange. America's allies, especially France and Germany, became very concerned over the impact of this erosion in the dollar's value as the world's reserve currency. Ultimately, these problems led to the U.S. abandonment of the Bretton Woods fixed exchange rate system and to the emergence of a more volatile era of floating exchange rates. Hence, although American policy may have laid the groundwork for the growing globalization of markets, the decline of American leadership prompted many, especially in the United States, to worry about the future stability and direction of the world economy. Critics of U.S. power, however, especially Susan Strange, have either denied any decline in U.S. capabilities or lauded the effects of the decline of "irresponsible" U.S. power.

Why Power Isn't Everything

Nowadays, such concerns about American power have receded. By the mid-1990s, the decline of U.S. hegemony no longer seemed so assured. Claims about the decrease in U.S. power appeared exaggerated given the demise of the Soviet Union, persistent recession in Japan, high unemployment and slow growth in Europe combined with the challenge of integrating Eastern Europe into the European Union, and American industry's return to competitiveness. Moreover, the relationship between hegemony and an open, stable world economy has been cast into doubt by a number of scholars, such as Robert Keohane and David Lake. As U.S. behavior during the interwar period illustrates, the possession of superior resources by a nation does not translate automatically into great influence or beneficial outcomes for the world.

Institutions to Govern the World Economy

One reason why the distribution of power among countries is not seen as the exclusive factor shaping the workings of the international economy is the important role played by international institutions. Keohane has made the most ambitious claims about the role of these institutions. He argues that although hegemony might be necessary for creating such institutions, once begun, they take on a life of their own, and states come to see them as worth preserving. Multilateral institutions such as the United Nations, International Monetary Fund (IMF), World Bank, World Trade Organization (WTO), and EU provide information to states about each others' behavior, reduce the cost of negotiating agreements, and can expose, and sometimes even punish, violations of agreements by states. The claim is that without these institutions the international economy—and international politics—would be much more unstable, less open, and more conflictual. In the case of the EU, for example, many see peace in Western Europe over the past 40 years as partially a product of this institution; and scholars and politicians often cite the maintenance of peace in Europe as a primary motivation for monetary union.

The impact and role of international institutions are controversial. Realists, with their emphasis on power, denigrate the role of such institutions, often seeing them as having little independent impact, and argue that their influence is derived from the actions of the states within them. In the EU example, they might cite the hegemonic role of Germany as the key to monetary union. Others, especially European scholars, believe that many international institutions are controlled by the United States, and thus reflect its interests. In particular, the United States is seen as using the IMF and World Bank as subtle mechanisms to exert its influence on countries. As realists, these scholars emphasize the impact of state power over the character of the institutions themselves.

The Power of Values

The emphasis on power and international institutions misses a central element necessary to explain political behavior: the purposes or goals that states and their leaders choose to pursue with their resources. Nonmaterialist explanations of the international political economy attach key interest to how states' purposes or goals are defined. Two central approaches have taken on the task of explaining this. The "ideas approach," exemplified by the work of Keohane and Judith Goldstein, proposes that the ideas that policymakers carry in their heads are very important in explaining their policy choices. Ideas, whether about the proper role of the state in the economy or the means-ends relationship between economic policy instruments and outcomes, shape how policymakers act.

Dominant ideas—ones that capture the attention of large segments of the policy-making community—define states' actions and coordinate their behaviors in critical ways. Scholars have identified both the rise of the belief in Keynesian macroeconomics after World War II and the later dominance of monetarist beliefs as central explanations for the creation of various international institutions and the coordination of states' policies within them. Some attribute the movement toward European monetary union to the spread of monetarist ideas among European policymakers. In another area, Anne Krueger has shown how changes in the prevailing ideas on how to induce economic development led, in the 1950s, to the use of import substitution policies and, more recently, to their abandonment.

Like scholars who emphasize ideas, the so-called constructivists focus on how policymakers' and states' purposes are defined. This approach goes beyond the adoption of ideas to the definition of social identity. A core proposition of this approach is that the social construction—hence, the term "constructivism" —of states' identities constrains the choices that states can make and propels them toward certain behaviors. For instance, Peter Katzenstein has argued that the Japanese embrace of pacifism since the end of World War II has affected Japan's behavior and its policy choices in the security area. Others have suggested that the construction of a European social identity has helped promote European integration. And certainly the growing concern with nationalism and national identity as sources of conflict or cooperation in international politics has been part of the constructivists' agenda, as evidenced in the work of Ronald Jepperson and Alexander Wendt. These nonmaterialist explanations of the international political economy emphasize states' purposes and choice of goals, which their proponents see as fundamental to states' behavior.

The Impact of Domestic Politics

Domestic political explanations of the international political economy also focus on the definition of states' purposes, but they tend to emphasize political processes and examine the way that national interests are defined through a struggle among domestic actors. Scholars in this area usually focus on two sets of factors: In the first case, they see social groups such as labor organizations, capitalists, multinational corporations, import-competing firms, and ethnic groups as having identifiable preferences about international economic policy that often translate into national policy. Those domestic groups who benefit from international economic exposure or have strong international ties already will favor greater international openness and stability and press their governments to enact policies that promote such market characteristics. The more such groups exist domestically, the greater will be the pressure on policymakers to orient their policies in this direction. For example, Jeffrey Frieden has argued that European monetary union has become more tenable because of the growing external orientation of European firms and banks and their concomitant interest in European economic openness and currency stability.

In the second case, some scholars point to a greater role for the state and policymakers in both the definition and execution of international economic policy. For them, the character of the state is what matters. The institutional structure of the state and its imperviousness to societal pressures shape the policy preferences of political actors and their capacity to implement these preferences. For example, Katzenstein and others identified France and Japan as states with institutional structures that allow technocratically inclined policymakers to play a leading role in defining foreign economic policy and pursuing interventionist policies.

The impact of a state's institutional structures on its development prospects has also been a topic of interest. Why is it that in some countries (mostly in East Asia) the state has played a central role in fostering economic development, while in others (mostly in Africa and Latin America) state action seems to have impaired economic progress? Some scholars such as Chalmers Johnson and Stephan Haggard have concluded that certain institutional characteristics are more conducive than others to making the state an effective promoter of economic development. These institutional traits often enable the state to mediate between the international and domestic economies. More recently, concerns have grown about the extent of democracy within states. Some scholars such as Donald Wittman and Gerald Scully have argued that economic growth and international openness depend greatly on whether a state's institutions are democratic or not.

In more recent work, scholars such as Judith Goldstein, Beth Simmons, and I have tried to focus on both societal actors and state institutions, realizing that each plays a role in shaping foreign economic policy. Moreover, scholars have tried to connect international and domestic factors. Thus, two-level games, which link both the international and domestic environments and societal and state actors, have become more prominent. Robert Putnam's early version of this approach has been refined by others seeking to derive more specific propositions about how all of these factors interact. For example, a number of scholars have shown how divided government affects trade policy choices. These two-level models promise a better understanding of the interaction of the complex factors that create the international political economy.

The Pressures of Globalization

Globalization refers to the increasing integration of national economies into a global one. As mentioned before, globalization peaked in the late nineteenth century, reached its nadir in the early 1940s, and has since rebounded to levels comparable to the earlier highs. Globalization has thus increased, as most agree, but it is far from being complete. For many economists, globalization is a beneficial process since it produces net gains for most countries. More concern has been raised by political scientists over its political effects, especially domestic ones.

In the 1970s, the buzzword for globalization was interdependence. It was argued that rising interdependence was not only changing international politics but also rendering the nation-state obsolete. The expectation was that it would severely limit the range of action that states could take. The state would gradually become less and less important to its citizens as interdependence rose. This debate aroused much controversy and inspired a strong defense of the continuing relevance of the state in international and domestic politics.

In the 1990s, this debate has revived as globalization reaches new heights. Three issues are central to it: First, globalization has been seen as exerting pressure on all states to change their policies and institutions in certain ways. Globalization, scholars have argued, is forcing convergence in policies among countries most exposed to it. Liberalizing trade policy, removing capital controls, opening financial markets to foreign investors, and downsizing the role of the state in the economy are the generic policy prescriptions for effective participation in a global economy. Pressure for the reduction—or even abandonment—of the welfare state in developed countries, and for the liberalization of the economy in developing ones, has been seen as a byproduct of globalization.

Second, globalization has been seen as giving increased power to the holders of capital—investors, multinational firms, and global financial institutions. These actors now can demand that states make changes in their economic policies and can punish them if they do not comply by exiting the country or, better yet, speculating against the country in world currency markets. In contrast, labor has been weakened. Having less freedom to move from country to country, workers find their power to bargain with firms impaired. Membership in unions worldwide has declined, and unions have faced challenges to their acquired power in many states. Globalization moves jobs around the world and imposes constraints on wage increases as never before.

Finally, globalization, it is sometimes claimed, is irreversible. That is, no actor can resist its advance. This again calls into question the role of the nation-state. Can any state resist, or even reshape, the pressures generated by global markets? Or must a state submit to the ineluctable pressures of globalization and lose the capacity to direct its national economy?

On none of these issues is there much consensus. Although many events seem to support the above views—the rush to free trade and capital market liberalization, the reforms of many welfare states, and the creation of independent central banks globally—some critics have seen the other side of the coin. They note that the percentage of government spending in the economy has declined only slightly or not at all (even in Margaret Thatcher's England), countries have maintained extensive and distinct welfare systems, national ways of doing business have persisted, and unions have actually made a resurgence lately in some nations, including in the United States and France. These events suggest that globalization is neither producing convergence nor undermining labor, and may not be irreversible. States in fact are ever more important, for they are the means for countries to resist and reshape the pressures generated by globalization. In this view, strengthening the institutions of the state may be the most effective way for countries to reap the maximum benefits from a world of global markets. These contradictory perspectives on globalization are likely to persist until we have more evidence about its effects.

The relationship between American power and globalization is also a topic of much interest. It is undeniable that U.S. policies have helped create the current international economy. But some claim that globalization is not only a creation of the United States but also a creature controlled by it. Countries such as France and Malaysia have vehemently expressed the view that globalization is basically the extension of American economic practices and ideals to the world, and a tool for the exertion of American power. They see resistance to global market pressures as defiance of the United States. Or, as some South Koreans have claimed during the recent financial crisis there, the IMF is just doing America's bidding. That may be leadership, but it is not the type of leadership these countries would like to see.

Ironically, many Americans see globalization as beyond their country's control. Indeed, in their eyes, the United States is ever more constrained by global forces, just like everyone else: All states must heed the dictates of international bond traders and investors or face the consequences. The United States let globalization out of the bottle and now cannot contain it. This loss of national control is bemoaned by some and applauded by others, but none doubt its reality. What is striking in this debate is the difference in perception between Americans and the rest of the world about the relationship between globalization and American influence.

The impact of globalization remains an area of intense research. The recent economic travails in Asia have underlined how even well-developed states can be affected by international investors and the vast capital flows they now control. How this crisis is resolved will have important consequences for many countries and for the future of the global economy. Will the pressures exerted by international financial actors fundamentally change the relationship between Asian governments and their economies? Will the crisis lead to greater convergence between the economic practices of Asian institutions and those common in the West? Will the famed "industrial policy" practiced by many Asian governments disappear? This issue is especially important for China and other developing countries seeking models of how best to foster economic development.

Such questions beg a look at the role of the state in economic policy, both foreign and domestic. In the aftermath of the two world wars, government intervention in the economy became accepted practice at both the micro and macro levels for eliminating boom and bust cycles in the economy. Indeed, the twentieth century has witnessed the greatest growth in government intervention in the economy ever seen. Globalization and the spread of more "orthodox" economic ideas, however, have undermined confidence in such intervention in many areas. As states' roles in their economies are reduced, what will happen to both the economy and the states? Or is the withdrawal of the state from the economy a passing trend? Will new ideas arise that sanction a greater role for the state in the economy?

Finally, the impact of power and international policies on the global economy is of great interest. After all, political conflict and war after 1914 destroyed the global economy created in the late nineteenth century. What effects will the post-Cold War international system have on the world economy? Will major international conflicts reappear, thus fracturing it into blocs? Will institutions that have helped to keep the peace such as the EU, NATO, and UN disappear, while new political alliances form, reshaping economic flows? Critically, what impact will such changes in the distribution of power and the organization of international politics have on the global economy? These issues will form some of the general research agendas for scholars in international political economy.

Want to Know More?

While students of international political economy hold contradictory perspectives on the causes and effects of globalization, they admire the work of several scholars who have illuminated the pillars of the world economy. A respected primer is Robert Gilpin's ***The Political Economy of International Relations*** (Princeton, NJ: Princeton University Press, 1987). The father of hegemonic stability theory is Charles Kindleberger; see his seminal work, ***The World in Depression, 1929–39*** (Berkeley, CA: University of California Press, 1973). David Lake presents an updated case for the theory in **"Leadership, Hegemony, and the International Economy"** (*International Studies Quarterly*, Winter 1993–94).

The spirited debate over the role of ideas is presented in ***Ideas and Foreign Policy*** (Ithaca, NY: Cornell University Press, 1993), edited by Judith Goldstein and Robert Keohane. Those wanting to learn how societal actors shape foreign economic policy can turn to Ronald Rogowski's ***Commerce and Coalitions*** (Princeton, NJ: Princeton University Press, 1990). Beth Simmons' ***Who Adjusts? Domestic Sources of Foreign Economic Policy During the Interwar Years*** (Princeton, NJ: Princeton University Press, 1994) provides an in-depth exploration of how domestic politics can affect a state's approach to the world economy. Helen Milner's ***Interests, Institutions and Information*** (Princeton, NJ: Princeton University Press, 1997) develops two-level games. Keohane makes ambitious claims about the role of international institutions in ***International Institutions and State Power*** (Boulder, CO: Westview Press, 1989). The national security aspect of this field is outlined in Joanne Gowa's ***Allies, Adversaries, and International Trade*** (Princeton, NJ: Princeton University Press, 1993). Chalmers Johnson considers the effects of a state's institutional structures in his book ***MITI and the Japanese Miracle*** (Stanford, CA: Stanford University Press, 1982). FOREIGN POLICY has published several articles on globalization, including Dani Rodrik's **"Sense and Nonsense in the Globalization Debate"** (Summer 1997).

For links to relevant Web sites, as well as a comprehensive index of related articles, access **www.foreignpolicy.com.**

HELEN V. MILNER *is professor of political science at Columbia University.*

The Color of Hot Money

Martin N. Baily, Diana Farrell, and Susan Lund

All these countries have spent 40 years trying to build up their economies and a moron like Soros comes along with a lot of money to speculate and ruins things.

—Mahathir Mohamad, prime minister of Malaysia, January 1998

TOO DARN HOT

MAHATHIR'S flamboyant rhetoric may be his alone, but his views have gained respectability in the wake of the recent financial crises in Russia and Asia. Famous for moving large sums of money in and out of countries quickly, hedge funds are frequently blamed for destabilizing economies and impoverishing the innocent. As their detractors see it, these funds routinely gamble vast sums of money in shadowy, overleveraged investments, unimpeded by government supervision. And this high-stakes financial poker, critics argue, sparked the volatile "hot-money" flows that undermined emerging markets in 1997 and 1998.

But skeptics thinking about imposing capital controls or otherwise curtailing the activities of hedge funds and other portfolio investors should pause. Those investments were not the prime cause of the volatility of global capital flows. In fact, the hot money in the recent crises came mostly from bank lending, not from hedge funds or other nonbank investments such as pension and mutual funds. International bank lending to emerging markets has often been more volatile than portfolio investments in equities and bonds—because the vast majority of bank lending has taken the form of short-term loans between banks, not long-term project financing. As capital markets continue to grow, eventually replacing traditional bank lending as the primary source of international financing, capital flows are likely to become *less* volatile. Moreover, despite all the focus on hedge funds, they remain small when compared to other market players.

These facts reshape the entire global financial debate, which should instead center on how to help countries shift from bank financing to capital markets where the transition has just begun—while ensuring that their governments and global financial institutions adequately protect investors.

FOLLOW THE MONEY

THAILAND'S financial crisis is a good example of the impact of irresponsible bank lending. Foreign capital flows to that country grew rapidly throughout the 1990s, reaching a peak of $25.5 billion in 1995. Nearly 75 percent of this took the form of bank loans; the remainder was equity and bond investments (including those made by hedge funds) and direct investment by companies. By early 1997, many of these investments were clearly becoming unprofitable, while the Thai banking system was struggling with a growing number of loans that were in default. Foreign banks got out quickly, turning a $1.9 billion inflow in the first quarter of 1997 into a $6.2 billion outflow in the second quarter—a plunge of more than $8 billion within three months. (This figure may even understate the amount withdrawn, since it does not include unused lines of credit that may have been cut.) These outflows put enormous pressure on the baht, which was devalued the following July. Foreign banks continued to pull money out of Thailand rapidly through the rest of 1997 and 1998, triggering a massive liquidity crisis that ultimately spawned a severe economic recession. In addition, $2.5 billion of Thai capital fled the country.

What role did foreign portfolio investors play in all this? In contrast to many banks, they remained calm throughout the initial crisis, continuing to put money into the country even after the baht's devaluation. Portfolio inflows increased by more than 70 percent between the second and third quarters of 1997 and remained positive, albeit much smaller, through the rest of the year and the first half of 1998. Not until late 1998, when it became clear that the economic recession caused by the banking crisis would dampen growth prospects for several years to come, did foreign investors begin to withdraw money from Thailand.

Foreign bank lending proved fickle in the rest of Asia and Russia as well. The five Asian crisis countries (Thailand, Malaysia, South Korea, Indonesia, and the Philippines) received $47.8 billion in foreign bank loans in 1996. This capital inflow turned into a $29.9 billion outflow in 1997—a turnaround of almost $80 billion. Portfolio inflows, in contrast, fell by half but remained positive. The same pattern held for most individual countries, such as South Korea and Malaysia; Indonesia experienced a large outflow of portfolio investments in the fourth quarter of 1997 that became positive again by mid-1998. In most cases, it was money from foreign banks that dried up and fled the country, not money from portfolio investors. (Only in the Philippines, the country least affected by the crisis, did portfolio investors bail out more quickly than foreign banks.) A year later in Russia, foreign bank lenders again were the first to flee.

This pattern is not limited to recent crises. Across the world, foreign bank lending is generally more volatile than portfolio investments. During the 1990s, quarterly swings in the total amount of foreign bank lending were far larger than the ebbs and flows of either portfolio bonds or equities. The volatility of bank-loan flows over this period—the standard deviation of flows divided by the average size of capital flows for the entire world—was 82 percent, as against 50 percent for portfolio flows. The same pattern holds for many individual countries. Between 1992 and 1997, for example, the average volatility in annual foreign bank lending to an individual country was 239 percent. During the same period, average annual volatility in bond flows was only 176 percent and in equity flows 150 percent—still turbulent, but much less so than foreign bank loans.

This instability reflects the nature of international banking today. Many people assume the loans that global banks make are a form of long-term project financing that cannot be withdrawn abruptly. But today's international bank lending often takes the form of short-term interbank loans. At the end of 1997, after the Asian crisis had begun, more than 55 percent of foreign bank loans worldwide were short term, with maturities of less than one year. More than one-third of these were interbank loans that were then applied to many purposes, including the financing of long-term domestic lending. These proportions are even higher in many emerging markets. In Thailand, two-thirds of foreign loans had maturities of less than one year. The vast majority of these went to Thai banks and finance companies, which then used them to support loans of longer duration.

In better days, foreign banks would roll over (that is, extend) most short-term loans as soon as they officially expired, often indefinitely. This became so routine that many emerging-market banks and finance companies imprudently began to rely on this money to fund new, longer-term loans—i.e., borrowing short to lend long. But when trouble appeared on the horizon, foreign banks stopped rolling over these loans as they expired and demanded repayment, thereby precipitating the crisis and forcing capital to flee.

A COMMITMENT PROBLEM

WHAT MAKES international bank lending so volatile? It is not that banks are irrational or foolhardy about the risks involved. The problem lies in the incentives at work in today's fiercely competitive environment. During the 1990s, profit margins on traditional bank lending shrank. As a result, many banks came under pressure from shareholders to bolster their returns by lending to emerging markets, which offered higher interest rates and robust economic growth. The capital requirements of the Bank for International Settlements inadvertently encouraged this trend by making it cheaper for foreign banks to lend to many emerging-market banks than to the largest, most stable corporations. But once they entered these markets, banks tended to pull loans quickly in times of trouble. The unique combination of pressures and incentives thus caused banking institutions to drive the hot money in global financial markets. The fact that all banks share the same incentives and tend to act in unison amplifies market volatility.

The root of volatile bank lending also lies in the nature of the loan contract. Bank loans are mostly illiquid, fixed-price assets—they cannot be quickly converted into cash, and once priced, their interest rate does not go up and down to reflect new information about a borrower (except in the case of a breach of contract or a default). Because the "price" of a loan—the interest rate—does not automatically adjust to changing market conditions, banks adjust the quantity of lending instead. A bank can avoid a default by simply declining to roll over its loans if it sees a borrower in trouble. The short maturities that are common today give banks this flexibility. Bonds and equities, in contrast, adjust to changing market conditions through price rather than quantity. These securities continually reprice to reflect new information as it becomes available. Because prices fall immediately, an investor has no time to sell without incurring a loss. Rather, equity and bond investors have an incentive to hold on to their investment and wait for prices to rise once the market's downward correction has ended.

Paradoxically, advances in bank risk-management techniques exacerbate the volatility of foreign bank lending. With bank loans, the bank itself and its shareholders bear the full risk of a loss. As the 1980s debt crisis illustrated, the loss from foreign lending incurred by a single bank can be tremendous. Citibank, for example, wrote off $3.5 billion in loan losses on Latin American debt in the 1980s. To avoid such debacles, banks have developed sophisticated risk-management models, such as the value-at-risk model. When market risk or credit risk in a particular country increases more than expected, these models indicate that banks must either put up extra capital to cover the risk or reduce their exposure to that market. If banks choose the latter, they can either shed that country's securities or cut lending. But because a selloff of assets typically entails losses, banks are more likely to cut lending.

Many banks had already adopted similar risk-management models before the 1997 financial crisis struck. Not surprisingly, when the credit risk of Asian banks began to rise and banks had to either shed Asian securities or cut lending, they did the latter. The widespread adoption of such risk-management practices in the years leading up to the crisis ultimately magnified the impact of the banks' actions when they raced to cut their exposure in emerging markets in 1997.

The largest portfolio investors generally use different risk-management techniques, in part because the capital of a numerous and diverse group of shareholders is at risk, not that of the funds. Most fund managers would not rapidly pull out of a market unless withdrawals by lots of investors forced them to do so. But the investment strategies of individual investors have been remarkably stable—largely because emerging markets typically make up only a very small percentage of their overall portfolios. (Indeed, customer withdrawals from emerging-market mutual funds did not increase notably during the Asian crisis.) Hence, portfolio investment managers enjoy more flexibility in reacting to risk and have less incentive than banks to withdraw funds when market conditions change.

In the years leading up to the crisis, the sluggish profitability of domestic lending in developed markets made emerging

Hedge funds are marginal players in foreign markets.

markets an attractive alternative. Emerging markets everywhere offered high returns on investment, especially after the lower capital requirements of some of this lending are factored in. Banks carefully minimized the risk to themselves by concentrating on loans with short maturities, which gave them the flexibility to pull out if economic conditions changed. Moreover, they denominated the vast majority of loans to emerging markets in U.S. dollars, thereby eliminating currency risk. In Thailand, for example, 75 percent of foreign loans were in U.S. dollars, even though most of these came from Japanese and European banks. These precautions paid off for banks but increased the risk for borrowers. Hence, most losses in Asia—at least for U.S. banks—came from losses in bond and equity trading and a decline in other Asian business (like securities underwriting), not from loan defaults.

Ironically, the most troubled banks had the greatest incentive to lend to emerging markets. Faced with a mountain of bad debt at home and paltry returns on investment overall, Japanese banks had become the largest lenders to Thailand and Southeast Asia before the crisis. By June 1997, they had extended $97.2 billion in loans to the region, whereas U.S. banks had extended only $23.8 billion. Large French and German banks, prompted by stagnant domestic markets and pressure from competitors, also became prominent lenders to the region. For a time, this lending was highly profitable. Japanese banks could pay one percent interest on deposits and then lend to Thai or South Korean banks at four or five percent interest. But their difficulties at home made them highly sensitive to potential losses, prompting the massive withdrawal of credit to the region at the start of the crisis. Of the $17.5 billion decline in lending to Southeast Asia between June and December 1997, $10.5 billion came from Japanese banks. They simply did not have the financial strength to renew credit to Southeast Asian borrowers in difficult times.

In short, it should not be surprising that foreign bank lending can be highly volatile. Changes in the types of lending activities, the nature of the loan contract, risk-management techniques, and competitive pressures all prompted banks to engage in high-risk lending to emerging markets in a way that minimized the risk to themselves. But how do hedge funds fit in to all this?

THE USUAL SUSPECTS

AT FIRST GLANCE, hedge funds would seem to be the prime suspects behind global market volatility. They are largely unregulated investment funds with few disclosure requirements and a penchant for secrecy. Rather than clustering in global financial centers with large banks and brokers, hedge funds often locate themselves offshore or in outlying areas. They generally use highly dynamic, aggressive trading strategies, darting in and out of markets to arbitrage price differences. They have few investment restrictions and can build highly concentrated portfolios or invest in exotic financial instruments like futures and forward contracts.[1] As the near bankruptcy of Long-Term Capital Management (LTCM) revealed in 1998, hedge funds also can use disproportionately large amounts of borrowed money. Critics allege that this enables them to manipulate markets and even cause financial crashes.

But the impact of hedge funds on international markets is greatly exaggerated. First, hedge funds do not fundamentally differ from other market players, like proprietary traders at commercial and investment banks, who have been using the same types of trading strategies for years. In fact, many hedge funds were started by traders from the major banks. The major difference is that the proprietary trading operations of banks as a group control about twice the amount of assets as do hedge funds.

Compared to other portfolio investors, hedge funds are even smaller. Whereas pension funds, mutual funds, and insurance companies together hold nearly $25 trillion in assets worldwide, hedge funds control only around four percent of that—an estimated $800 billion to $1 trillion. Furthermore, the overleveraged risk-taking of LTCM—which infamously invested sums that were 20 times or more the size of its capital base—is not typical. Van Hedge Fund Advisors reports that roughly a third of hedge funds use no leverage at all, while the average leverage ratio for all hedge funds lies between 4:1 and 7:1. So even counting leveraged assets, hedge funds pale when compared with institutional investors. And although risk-hungry hedge funds put more of their investments into foreign markets than do institutional asset managers, they are marginal players there as well. The relatively small size of hedge funds thus suggests that they alone are unlikely to have caused excessive volatility in most markets.

Instead, it was the herdlike behavior of other market players that rocked the markets in recent years. Again, consider Thailand. In July 1997, the Thai government abandoned its exchange-rate peg and allowed the baht to float, spurring a depreciation that wiped out 56 percent of the currency's value by January 1998. At the time that the peg was dropped, the Bank of Thailand estimated that hedge funds held at most 25 percent of the $28 billion in forward contract sales of the baht. Most of the pressure on the baht actually came from short sales by other market players, the massive outflow of foreign bank loans, the liquidation by domestic companies and banks of their securities positions, and last-minute attempts by corporations and banks to hedge previously unhedged foreign loans. Hedge funds took their positions on the baht after significant pressure had already built up, and they exited the market early. In fact, many hedge funds started taking long positions on the baht and other Asian currencies again in August and September 1997 and lost money doing so. Certainly, a few of the large hedge funds profited handsomely from the initial devaluation of the baht, but they did not precipitate the collapse. Instead, it was caused by the overwhelming pressure exerted by the collective actions of all market participants. As one trader in Thailand noted, "Who wasn't betting against the baht?"

Indeed, hedge funds often play a critical role in curbing market volatility by providing liquidity. Within the hedge fund universe, a great diversity of investment strategies abounds. Relative-value funds, for example, arbitrage price differences between securities; macro funds bet on the direction of the market; and global funds assess the prospects of individual companies. Different hedge funds often end up taking opposite positions in the same market. They are also likely to bet against the market, helping correct an imbalance between buyers and sellers. Hedge funds behave this way because their managers are rewarded for finding overlooked opportunities that produce extraordinary returns rather than for matching an industry benchmark. In short, their enormous flexibility in choosing investment strategies and their restrictions on customer deposits and withdrawals give them the freedom to be contrarian.

In addition, hedge funds can play an important role in promoting price efficiency. Relative-value hedge funds, which profit by correcting anomalies in the relative prices of assets, help to ensure that risk is priced more uniformly and accurately throughout the world. Macro hedge funds help correct the price level within a market when it is out of equilibrium. In developed capital markets, the activities of hedge funds (and the nearly identical activities of proprietary traders at banks) have greatly increased the efficiency of pricing, as seen by the decline in arbitrage opportunities. Thus hedge funds and proprietary traders generally play a positive role in well-functioning capital markets by ensuring that prices accurately reflect market fundamentals and that risks are priced uniformly.

A CAPITAL IDEA

RATHER THAN trying to limit hedge-fund activities, policymakers should focus on the quality of the information that investors use to make decisions. They can accomplish this by improving disclosure, financial transparency, and investor protection. But this goes only so far. They must also recognize that capital markets are replacing banks around the world as the primary source of financing. Today, countries with deep capital markets—such as the United States, the United Kingdom, and Switzerland—are furthest along in this transition. Other countries lag behind due to their lack of economic development (the emerging markets) or the necessary financial and regulatory infrastructure (Japan and much of Europe). Nevertheless, many markets are making the transition, no matter how slowly.

This shift to capital markets will help both individual countries and the world. As explained above, markets will stabilize as more financial instruments begin to adjust through price rather than quantity. Risk will be increasingly diluted as it is spread across a larger investor base, ultimately resulting in lower interest rates for issuers. Competition among intermediaries will increase and improve market efficiency.

To facilitate the transition, developing countries should focus on strengthening the "intangible" structure of modern markets. This would involve adopting global standards for accounting and reporting by both private firms and government institutions, such as national treasuries. (In the case of the latter, this would include reporting on the real level of usable reserves.) Adoption of such standards would also entail more rigorous market supervision and regulation as well as protection of creditors—and all shareholders—even in the event of a borrower's insolvency. For its part, international banking has a role to play during the transition in enforcing rigorous credit-assessment and loan-monitoring practices to emerging markets, where poor skills and low standards are still the norm. Long-term foreign direct investment in emerging-market companies would further improve supervision of management. All these reforms would ultimately lessen volatility.

Although the G-7 group of highly industrialized nations has promoted more open and transparent markets and stronger national financial systems, some governments and economists now talk of slowing down, rather than speeding up, the transition. Discussion of capital controls and the curtailment of hedge-fund activities abounds. Meanwhile, crisis countries are busy bailing out (and in some cases restructuring) weak domestic banking institutions. Such actions—although needed and appropriate—do not constitute a comprehensive solution to the problem.

To counter a retreat by traumatized emerging economies, policymakers must promote domestic capital market development and encourage the transition from banks to capital markets. Although many countries opened their fledgling markets to foreign investors in the 1990s, the crises underscored how woefully underdeveloped the infrastructure of these economies really was. Rather than hiding behind the false security of financial isolation and capital controls, such countries need to equip themselves to become full-fledged participants in the global market. But for that to happen, they and the policymakers who assist them must realize who is actually driving the hot money in international finance.

NOTE

1. In a forward contract, a party agrees to sell a given currency at some point in the future at a given price. Parties enter into such contracts for the purpose of shortselling a currency–that is, borrowing in that currency with the expectation it will depreciate. If it does fall, they pocket the difference between the value of the amount borrowed and the amount repaid.

MARTIN N. BAILY is Chair of the President's Council of Economic Advisers and a former principal of McKinsey & Co. DIANA FARRELL is a principal of McKinsey. SUSAN LUND is a consultant there.

THE TRADE AGENDA
A different, new world order

Trade should be high on the list of priorities for the new American president. But America and Europe must learn to share leadership with other countries

MORE than at any other time in history, a growing economy today needs to be an open economy. And trade policy is essential to an open economy: when doing business with foreign countries, you need agreed ground-rules. But who makes the rules, and what should they be? For half a century, America and Europe have led the way in answering these questions. Now that hegemony is under challenge.

World trade policy has been in a state of flux since last year's debacle in Seattle, when members of the World Trade Organisation (WTO) tried unsuccessfully to launch a new round of trade talks. Contrary to popular wisdom, the reason for the collapse in Seattle was not the presence of several thousand disgruntled demonstrators. Instead, it was a failure of the self-appointed vanguard of America and Europe to respond to the concerns of developing countries. Since Seattle, the big two have been further distracted by a string of ugly bilateral trade disputes and by their efforts to shepherd China into the WTO. It comes as no surprise, therefore, that developing countries are looking to new champions and new arrangements to foster trade.

To understand why many countries are no longer inclined to give America and Europe the benefit of the doubt, consider worldwide trade growth since the Uruguay round of trade talks was completed in 1994. Trade has risen significantly faster than GDP (see chart 1, Trading up). But despite the round's mission to improve market access for developing countries' exports, the share of global exports originating from America and Europe has also grown (see chart 2, Rich beneficiaries). This partly reflects faster growth in rich economies, particularly America. But protectionist subsidies and price-supports have also shown a nasty habit of growing along with GDP. In any event, many developing countries now feel that they were short-changed in the Uruguay round, and they are determined not to let that happen again.

Rising stars

This has come as something of a surprise to the big two, who with Japan and Canada have often negotiated as a "quad" group. In some cases, the unexpected power of smaller countries has resulted from the consensus-driven nature of multilateral bodies originally conceived by the big powers. In the Organisation for Economic Co-operation and Development (OECD) and the WTO, all members have veto power over the biggest. Now, some of them are using it.

Mexico, for example, held up the OECD's new guidelines for foreign investment in June. It was concerned that standards related to labour and the environment were too restrictive. Mexico is also stonewalling on a bilateral agreement with China that it needs to enter the WTO. That accession, as recent months have made clear, is America's top priority in trade policy. And Mike Moore, the WTO's director-general, says that China's entry is "probably more important than a new round."

Another country that is emerging as a heavyweight is Brazil, which has gone through several changes of approach in the past few years. It began as a largely closed economy, known mostly for its skirmishes with Canada over domestic subsidies to makers of regional jets. Then the government decided to revolutionise Brazil's agriculture with a commitment to genetically modified (GM) crops, ripe for export. With the zeal of a convert, Brazil became a cheerleader for a new round of top-level trade talks in the WTO, with standards for GM foods as a headline issue. Brazil's outspoken support for a new round was music to the rich traders' ears. But on second thoughts, Brazil has decided to make an agreement on agriculture, based on access to rich countries' markets, a precondition of a new round.

This closely parallels the line taken by India, a leader of poor countries in trying to ensure that America and Europe deliver on the market-access

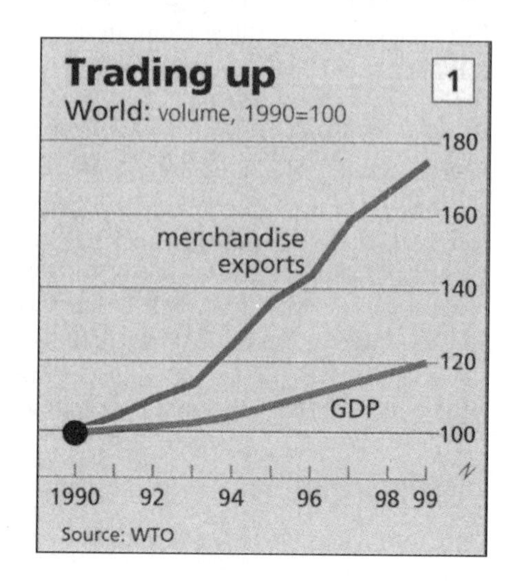

promises they made in the Uruguay round. In exchange for acceptance of international standards for intellectual-property rights, poor countries were meant to get a warm welcome for their exports of labour-intensive goods such as farm products and textiles. That was supposed to include an end to export subsidies, which make crops artificially cheap on world markets, in both America and Europe. But although America has a timetable for eliminating such subsidies, and Europe plans at least to scale them back, neither has proposed to scrap them until long after they had hoped to complete a new round of trade talks. In the meantime, intellectual-property rights have risen up to bite the rich countries back: India, for instance, has decided that knowledge of some plant remedies originated with its folk medics, and is trying to stop western pharmaceutical companies from using the relevant chemicals without paying royalties. This sort of gesture might seem petty, but it demonstrates developing countries' new determination to get what they can from the system.

Egypt and South Africa have also gained in influence. They are not superstars, but they have enough of the right ingredients—developed industries, educated people, relatively strong legal systems and decent infrastructure—to make a difference. Other countries have banded together to find strength in numbers. The Cairns Group, whose membership includes Canada and crop exporters from the Pacific and South America, has followed the Americans and Europeans in putting forward its own comprehensive proposal for agricultural reform. Next week, all of Africa's trade ministers, including the 20 members of the Common Market for Eastern and Southern Africa (COMESA), will meet in Gabon. All of these countries share a single mission: to see to it that rich countries honour past commitments, and to offer alternatives to their proposals in future.

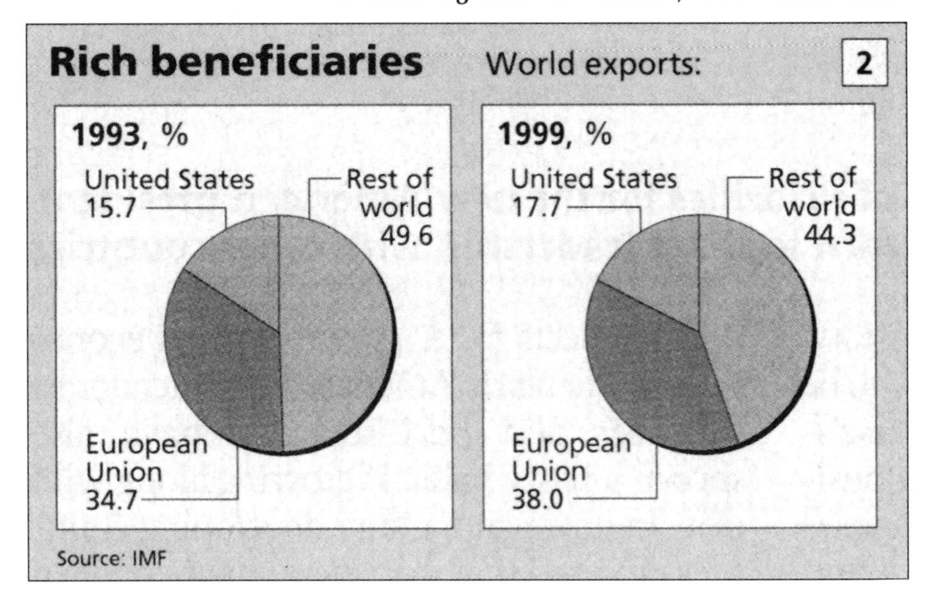

Sleeping giants awaken

Even the most prodigious grumblings and stallings of Brazil, India, Mexico and their cohorts may soon be put to shame. When China enters the WTO, perhaps by the middle of next year, America and Europe will face a contender with the potential to be a heavyweight champion—and a prickly one, to judge by its recent behaviour. Exactly when and on what terms China will join the WTO is still in question, thanks to the country's foot-dragging on technical issues and over the timetable for implementation of trade agreements. China has always wanted to be a part of the next WTO round. In September the prospect of new talks appeared sufficiently distant to merit some backsliding on accession. China is balking at accepting greater commitments to free trade than other developing countries, to which the WTO normally grants special treatment. But China, as the big two have emphasised, is no ordinary developing country.

The latest talks in Geneva this week have yielded agreement on most of the legal requirements of China's accession. Trade bigwigs from America and Europe still insist that China could join the WTO by the end of the year, in time to become part of Bill Clinton's presidential legacy. This optimism may be misplaced, but even a conservative estimate, taking into account technical details yet to be fixed in the multilateral pact, is that China will accede by the third quarter of 2001. One of the surest signs that China is truly close to accession comes from just outside its own borders. Russia, another messy candidate for WTO membership, restarted talks with America, Canada and Europe this week after a period of dormancy in its seven-year-old application. Lagging too far behind China in WTO membership would be embarrassing to Russia, as well as isolating it from a key policymaking unit.

Pretty soon, indeed, the WTO's chamber may look a lot more like the United Nations Security Council; all the juggernauts will be represented, and each will have veto power. Observers of the UN might shudder to think of China and Russia as potential consensus-breakers in yet another big international organisation, but at least in the case of the WTO, all countries will have the same power. As Mr Moore puts it, consensus is both "our strongest point and our weakness."

Given this consensus-based system, and after the Seattle fiasco, it seems bizarre that Charlene Barshefsky, America's trade representative, chose to announce last month that she and Pascal Lamy, Europe's trade commissioner, had nearly agreed on an agenda for a new round of trade talks at the WTO. Closed discussions have continued in Washington over the past week. It may sound like a stitch-up, but Mr Lamy still tries to put the best possible spin on it: "We don't want to give the impression that the rest of the world just has to sign up as well." He has talked to other countries about the agenda, including those he calls his "allies" (Japan, South Korea and the East and Central European countries) and some who do not merit that term (Argentina, Brazil, Chile, Egypt and South Africa). But many other, smaller countries may be left waiting by the telephone. And even those to whom Mr Lamy deigns to speak may not see their wishes heeded; to Brazil's contention that a deal on agriculture must precede a round, his answer is blunt: "That will never work."

The lure of regionalism

To complicate the negotiations, the WTO is no longer the only game in town. Bilateral and regional trade agreements have flourished during the past two decades, to mixed effect. Although deals between small groups of countries can contribute to a climate

Dispute scorecard 3

Main WTO trade disputes involving the European Union and the United States

Plaintiff(s)	Defendant	Issue	Status
United States	European Union	bananas	sanctions in place
United States	European Union	hormone-treated beef	sanctions in place
European Union	United States	foreign sales corporation tax code	under deadline for compliance
European Union	United States	wheat gluten	decision under appeal by defendant
India	European Union	bed linen	decision awaiting appeal by defendant
United States	South Korea	beef	decision awaiting appeal by defendant
Australia, New Zealand	United States	lamb	decision awaiting appeal by defendant
Canada, Japan, European Union	United States	anti-dumping duties given to domestic firms	on the horizon
United States	European Union	electrical circuits	on the horizon
European Union	South Korea	shipbuilding	on the horizon
Brazil, Mexico, European Union	United States	steel	on the horizon
United States	Mexico	telecoms	on the horizon

Sources: WTO; news reports

of liberalisation by fostering trade, they can also damage it by diverting trade away from more efficient producers. Mr Moore, as is his obligation, has consistently criticised countries for circumventing the WTO to draw up their own deals. But both the North American Free-Trade Agreement and the Australia-New Zealand free-trade area have landed on the positive side of the fence (meaning that they seem to have expanded trade inside and outside the blocks), according to Anne Krueger of Stanford University. On the other hand, Mercosur (Argentina, Brazil, Paraguay and Uruguay) has been a cause of trade diversion. Though no data are available yet on Japan's recent spate of bilateral deals, both Ms Barshefsky and Mr Lamy cautiously welcome them as signs of further liberalisation within the context of the WTO's multilateral system.

The most recent bilateral agreement to make news, last month's pact between America and Jordan, promises to create more of a stir. For the first time, America extracted a pledge that its partner would not lower labour and environmental standards in order to reap trade gains. Poor countries see this deal as a worrisome and subtly protectionist precedent; Mr Moore thinks it might drive some wayward souls back into the arms of the multilateral system. But it remains to be seen whether the new president, whoever he is, will persist with this kind of deal.

In any event, he is likely to oversee the genesis of the Free Trade Area of the Americas, perhaps the biggest trading block of all. The FTAA has been founded on the notion that it can exist within the context of the WTO. But, as Ms Krueger points out, the risks to the multilateral system's survival can only mount as the world is increasingly carved up into free-trade blocks. Regionalism in trade, in short, makes it more and not less important to keep the process of WTO trade liberalisation going.

Clashes of the titans

America and Europe also have their own problems to solve, even as they worry about China, the new round and other countries' deals. The past month has seen modest progress on their three biggest disputes: Europe's import regimes for hormone-treated beef and bananas, and America's Foreign Sales Corporation (FSC) tax code, which gives exporters subsidies through tax credits. Although the end may not be in sight for these trade tiffs, the summer's uneasy stalemates have for now been broken.

The long-running dispute over Europe's ban on imports of hormone-treated beef now looks the most likely to be settled. Negotiators appear to have agreed on a framework for a deal: America will drop the beef-related portion of its punitive tariffs on European goods (the "carousel" sanctions) in return for greater access to Europe's market for hormone-free beef. American retaliation, worth $117m a year, would then be phased out over several years to give beef producers time to reduce hormone use.

Talks on Europe's regime for importing bananas have also taken some halting but constructive steps. The latest proposal from Brussels was panned by the United States and its partners in Latin America, but the setback was shortlived; the same seven countries from Latin America turned around two weeks later to back an old proposal from Caribbean producers, mostly former colonies Europe has sought to protect. Another breakthrough came when Dole, the bigger of America's two banana giants, added its support to the Caribbean proposal. But the other big firm, Chiquita, rejected the plan. It is now up to the American government and producers in Africa and the Pacific to decide how to proceed. In the meantime, America continues to impose $191m in punitive tariffs on European goods, in accordance with the WTO's ruling that Europe's regime discriminates unfairly against producers and shippers in the Americas.

Although the beef and banana disputes topped the transatlantic trade agenda over the summer, they faded a little from the limelight as Mr Clinton delayed the announcement of a new carousel of targets for the sanctions. Now the biggest flashpoint is America's system of tax subsidies for its big exporters through FSCs. Europe won a ruling in the WTO that requires America to replace the tax code or make restitution for damage to European companies. Congress missed the initial deadline, October 1st, for passing new legislation. The European Commission extended the deadline to November 1st, but that date has also passed with the House of Representatives and Senate unable to agree on a compromise. The deadline for action within the auspices of the WTO's dispute-settlement body is November 17th. After that, Europe can impose sanctions retroactive to November 1st or, if a new FSC tax code is passed, ask for a review of its compliance with the WTO's rules. In trade policy, however, few deadlines are ever absolute. Mr Lamy simply says, "My options are open."

At the bottom of these and a host of similar trade disputes (see the scorecard above for the main ones), one can usually find political horse-trading with industries seeking protection. Trent Lott, the Senate's majority leader, is about to supply an example. His move to give Chiquita, which has plantations in Latin America, a veto over any settlement of the dispute on bananas, has made many wonder if Congress sees trade as anything more than a political football.

Europe faces some of the same internal concerns. In September, it began to implement an agreement with America, Canada and Japan to grant unrestricted access to its markets to the world's poorest countries. But a proposal by the European Commission in September to end duties and quotas on the world's 48 poorest economies on all goods except arms has run into what Mr Lamy calls "not unexpected difficulties" among member countries. The biggest problem is sugar, which some members want to make an exception to the policy.

Europe and America also face a challenge over their domestic public opinion. GM foods offer just one example. One goal of a new trade round will be to institute WTO-wide standards for importing GM foods. But until definitive proof of their safety is reported by a European authority—the words of foreign watchdogs seem to make little difference—sensationalist fears of strange diseases or mutant species will restrict Europe's ability to make a deal. The artificial protection of farmers in America and Europe is another example. The WTO is determined to eliminate export subsidies throughout its membership, but try telling that to the House of Representatives—or to the French government. Frustration with rich countries' intransigence reaches from grass-roots protesters in Seattle and Prague all the way to the top; even Mr Moore bemoans the snail's pace at which America and Europe have implemented reforms to their markets for agricultural products and textiles. "Sometimes I feel like joining the kids outside," he says. "When they say the system's unfair, they're not always wrong."

Window of opportunity

In constantly juggling the conflicting goals of domestic protection and the opening of new markets, America and Europe have made a habit of offering small carrots—and occasionally big sticks—to prospective trading partners. But as Ms Krueger puts it, "there's a difference between [America's and Europe's] power as agenda-setters and their actually doing something." And emerging economies have given notice that they will no longer be easily appeased. The days when two trading blocks could set trade policy for the world have gone. The big powers' positions, and those of their smallest trading partners, are clear and entrenched. For that reason, it may be the emerging powers who will increasingly take the lead. The new American president and his European colleagues will have to get used to that if they are to preserve and strengthen the world's multilateral trading system. And, given the risk of a downturn in the global economy some time during the next four years, that task is more urgent than ever.

Helping the world's poorest

Jeffrey Sachs, a top academic economist, argues that rich countries must mobilise global science and technology to address the specific problems which help to keep poor countries poor

IN OUR Gilded Age, the poorest of the poor are nearly invisible. Seven hundred million people live in the 42 so-called Highly Indebted Poor Countries (HIPCS), where a combination of extreme poverty and financial insolvency marks them for a special kind of despair and economic isolation. They escape our notice almost entirely, unless war or an exotic disease breaks out, or yet another programme with the International Monetary Fund (IMF) is signed. The Cologne Summit of the G8 in June was a welcome exception to this neglect. The summiteers acknowledged the plight of these countries, offered further debt relief and stressed the need for a greater emphasis by the international community on social programmes to help alleviate human suffering.

The G8 proposals should be seen as a beginning: inadequate to the problem, but at least a good-faith prod to something more useful. We urgently need new creativity and a new partnership between rich and poor if these 700m people (projected to rise to 1.5 billion by 2030), as well as the extremely poor in other parts of the world (especially South Asia), are to enjoy a chance for human betterment. Even outright debt forgiveness, far beyond the G8's stingy offer, is only a step in the right direction. Even the call to the IMF and World Bank to be more sensitive to social conditions is merely an indicative nod.

Jeffrey Sachs is director of the Centre for International Development and professor of international trade at Harvard University. A prolific writer, he has also advised the governments of many developing and East European countries.

A much more important challenge, as yet mainly unrecognised, is that of mobilising global science and technology to address the crises of public health, agricultural productivity, environmental degradation and demographic stress confronting these countries. In part this will require that the wealthy governments enable the grossly underfinanced and underempowered United Nations institutions to become vibrant and active partners of human development. The failure of the United States to pay its UN dues is surely the world's most significant default on international obligations, far more egregious than any defaults by impoverished HIPCS. The broader American neglect of the UN agencies that assist impoverished countries in public health, science, agriculture and the environment must surely rank as another amazingly misguided aspect of current American development policies.

The conditions in many HIPCS are worsening dramatically, even as global science and technology create new surges of wealth and well-being in the richer countries. The problem is that, for myriad reasons, the technological gains in wealthy countries do not readily diffuse to the poorest ones. Some barriers are political and economic. New technologies will not take hold in poor societies if investors fear for their property rights, or even for their lives, in corrupt or conflict-ridden societies. *The Economist's* response to the Cologne Summit ("Helping the Third World", June 26th) is right to stress that aid without policy reform is easily wasted. But the barriers to development are often more subtle than the current emphasis on "good governance" in debtor countries suggests.

Research and development of new technologies are overwhelmingly directed at rich-country problems. To the extent that the poor face distinctive challenges, science and technology must be directed purposefully towards them. In today's global set-up, that rarely happens. Advances in science and technology not only lie at the core of long-term economic growth, but flourish on an intricate mix of social institutions—public and private, national and international.

Currently, the international system fails to meet the scientific and technological needs of the world's poorest. Even when the right institutions exist—say, the World Health Organisation to deal with pressing public health disasters facing the poorest countries—they are generally starved for funds, authority and even access to the key negotiations between poor-country governments and the Fund at which important development strategies get hammered out.

The ecology of underdevelopment

If it were true that the poor were just like the rich but with less money, the global situation would be vastly easier than it is. As it happens, the poor live in different ecological zones, face different health conditions and must overcome agronomic limitations that are very different from those of rich countries. Those differences, indeed, are often a fundamental cause of persisting poverty.

Let us compare the 30 highest-income countries in the world with the 42 HIPCS (see table below). The rich countries overwhelmingly lie in the world's temperate zones. Not every country in those bands is rich, but a good rule of thumb is that temperate-zone economies are either rich, formerly socialist (and hence currently poor), or geographically isolated (such as Afghanistan and Mongolia). Around 93% of the combined population of the 30 highest-income countries lives in temperate and snow zones. The HIPCS by contrast, include 39 tropical or desert societies. There are only three in a substantially temperate climate, and those three are landlocked and therefore geographically isolated (Laos, Malawi and Zambia).

Not only life but also death differs between temperate and tropical zones. Individuals in temperate zones almost everywhere enjoy a life expectancy of 70 years or more. In the tropics, however, life expectancy is generally much shorter. One big reason is that populations are burdened by diseases such as malaria, hookworm, sleeping sickness and schistosomiasis, whose transmission generally depends on a warm climate. (Winter may be the greatest public-health intervention in the world.) Life expectancy in the HIPCS averages just 51 years, reflecting the interacting effects of tropical disease and poverty. The economic evidence strongly suggests that short life expectancy is not just a result of poverty, but is also a powerful cause of impoverishment.

Different ecologies

1995

	HIPCs* (42)	Rich countries (30)
GDP per person, PPP$†	1,187	18,818
Life expectancy at birth, years†	51.5	76.9
Population by ecozones, % in:		
tropical	55.6	0.7
dry	17.6	3.7
temperate and snow	12.5	92.6
highland	14.0	2.5

Source: J. Sachs *Highly indebted poor countries †Unweighted averages

All the rich-country research on rich-country ailments, such as cardiovascular diseases and cancer, will not solve the problems of malaria. Nor will the biotechnology advances for temperate-zone crops easily transfer to the conditions of tropical agriculture. To address the special conditions of the HIPCS, we must first understand their unique problems, and then use our ingenuity and co-operative spirit to create new methods of overcoming them.

Modern society and prosperity rest on the foundation of modern science. Global capitalism is, of course, a set of social institutions—of property rights, legal and political systems, international agreements, transnational corporations, educational establishments, and public and private research institutions—but the prosperity that results from these institutions has its roots in the development and applications of new science-based technologies. In the past 50 years, these have included technologies built on solid-state physics, which gave rise to the information-technology revolution, and on genetics, which have fostered breakthroughs in health and agricultural productivity.

Science at the ecological divide

In this context, it is worth noting that the inequalities of income across the globe are actually exceeded by the inequalities of scientific output and technological innovation. The chart below shows the remarkable dominance of rich countries in scientific publications and, even more notably, in patents filed in Europe and the United States.

The role of the developing world in one sense is much greater than the chart indicates. Many of the scientific and technological breakthroughs are made by poor-country scientists working in rich-country laboratories. Indian and Chinese engineers account for a significant proportion of Silicon Valley's workforce, for example. The basic point, then, holds even more strongly: global science is directed by the rich countries and for the rich-country markets, even to the extent of mobilising much of the scientific potential of the poorer countries.

The imbalance of global science reflects several forces. First, of course, science follows the market. This is especially true in an age when technological leaps require expensive scientific equipment and well-provisioned research laboratories. Second, scientific advance tends to have increasing returns to scale: adding more scientists to a community does not diminish individual marginal productivity but tends to increase it. Therein lies the origin of university science departments, regional agglomerations such as Silicon Valley and Route 128, and mega-laboratories at leading high-technology firms including Merck, Microsoft and Monsanto. And third, science requires a partnership between the public and private sectors. Free-market ideologues notwithstanding, there is scarcely one technology of significance that was not nurtured through public as well as private care.

If technologies easily crossed the ecological divide, the implications would be less dramatic than they are. Some technologies, certainly those involving the computer and other ways of managing information, do indeed cross over, and give great hopes of spurring technological capacity in the poorest countries. Others—especially in the life sciences but also in the use of energy, building techniques, new materials and the like—are prone to "ecological specificity". The result is a profound imbalance in the global production of knowledge: probably the most powerful engine of divergence in global well-being between the rich and the poor.

Consider malaria. The disease kills more than 1m people a year, and perhaps as many as 2.5m. The disease is so heavily concentrated in the poorest tropical countries, and overwhelmingly in sub-Saharan Africa, that nobody even bothers to keep an accurate count of clinical cases or deaths. Those who remember that richer places such as Spain, Italy, Greece and the southern United States once harboured the disease may be misled into thinking that the problem is one of social institutions to control its transmission. In fact, the sporadic transmission of malaria in the sub-tropical regions of the rich countries was vastly easier to control than is its chronic transmission in the heart of the tropics. Tropical countries are plagued by ecological conditions that produce hundreds of infective bites per year per person.

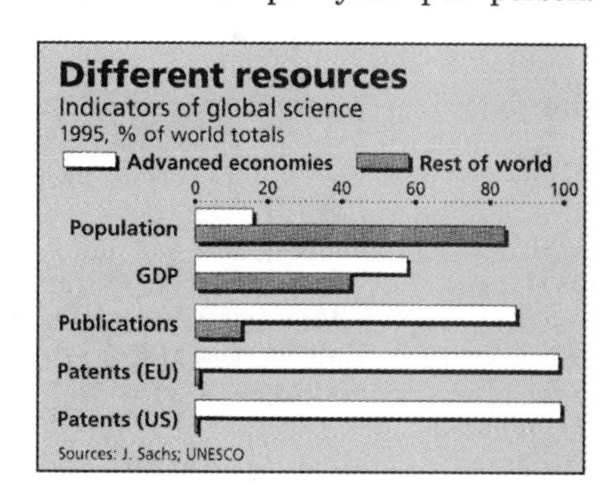

Mosquito control does not work well, if at all, in such circumstances. It is in any event expensive.

Recent advances in biotechnology, including mapping the genome of the malaria parasite, point to a possible malaria vaccine. One would think that this would be high on the agendas of both the international community and private pharmaceutical firms. It is not. A Wellcome Trust study a few years ago found that only around $80m a year was spent on malaria research, and only a small fraction of that on vaccines.

The big vaccine producers, such as Merck, Rhône-Poulenc's Pasteur-Mérieux-Connaught and SmithKline Beecham, have much of the in-house science but not the bottom-line motivation. They strongly believe that there is no market in malaria. Even if they spend the hundreds of millions, or perhaps billions, of dollars to do the R&D and come up with an effective vaccine, they believe, with reason, that their product would just be grabbed by international agencies or private-sector copycats. The hijackers will argue, plausibly, that the poor deserve to have the vaccine at low prices—enough to cover production costs but not the preceding R&D expenditures.

The malaria problem reflects, in microcosm, a vast range of problems facing the HIPCS in health, agriculture and environmental management. They are profound, accessible to science and utterly neglected. A hundred IMF missions or World Bank health-sector loans cannot produce a malaria vaccine. No individual country borrowing from the Fund or the World Bank will ever have the means or incentive to produce the global public good of a malaria vaccine. The root of the problem is a much more complex market failure: private investors and scientists doubt that malaria research will be rewarded financially. Creativity is needed to bridge the huge gulfs between human needs, scientific effort and market returns.

Promise a market

The following approach might work. Rich countries would make a firm pledge to purchase an effective malaria vaccine for Africa's 25m newborn children each year if such a vaccine is developed. They would even state, based on appropriate and clear scientific standards, that they would guarantee a minimum purchase price—say, $10 per dose—for a vaccine that meets minimum conditions of efficacy, and perhaps raise the price for a better one. The recipient countries might also be asked to pledge a part of the cost, depending on their incomes. But nothing need be spent by any government until the vaccine actually exists.

Even without a vast public-sector effort, such a pledge could galvanise the world of private-sector pharmaceutical and biotechnology firms. Malaria vaccine research would suddenly become hot. Within a few years, a breakthrough of profound benefit to the poorest countries would be likely. The costs in foreign aid would be small: a few hundred million dollars a year to tame a killer of millions of children. Such a vaccine would rank among the most effective public-health interventions conceivable. And, if science did not deliver, rich countries would end up paying nothing at all.

Malaria imposes a fearsome burden on poor countries, the AIDS epidemic an even weightier load. Two-thirds of the world's 33m individuals infected with the HIV virus are sub-Saharan Africans, according to a UN estimate in 1998, and the figure is rising. About 95% of worldwide HIV cases are in the developing world. Once again, science is stopping at the ecological divide.

Rich countries are controlling the epidemic through novel drug treatments that are too expensive, by orders of magnitude, for the poorest countries. Vaccine research, which could provide a cost-effective method of prevention, is dramatically underfunded. The vaccine research that is being done focuses on the specific viral strains prevalent in the United States and Europe, not on those which bedevil Africa and Asia. As in the case of malaria, the potential developers of vaccines consider the poor-country market to be no market at all. The same, one should note, is true for a third worldwide killer. Tuberculosis is still taking the lives of more than 2m poor people a year and, like malaria and AIDS, would probably be susceptible to a vaccine, if anyone cared to invest in the effort.

The poorer countries are not necessarily sitting still as their citizenry dies of AIDS. South Africa is on the verge of authorising the manufacture of AIDS medicines by South African pharmaceutical companies, despite patents held by American and European firms. The South African government says that, if rich-country firms will not supply the drugs to the South African market at affordable prices (ones that are high enough to meet marginal production costs but do not include the patent-generated monopoly profits that the drug companies claim as their return for R&D), then it will simply allow its own firms to manufacture the drugs, patent or no. In a world in which science is a rich-country prerogative while the poor continue to die, the niceties of intellectual property rights are likely to prove less compelling than social realities.

There is no shortage of complexities ahead. The world needs to reconsider the question of property rights before patent rights allow rich-country multinationals in effect to own the genetic codes of the very foodstuffs on which the world depends, and even the human genome itself. The world also needs to reconsider the role of institutions such as the World Health Organisation and the Food and Agriculture Organisation. These UN bodies should play a vital role in identifying global priorities in health and agriculture, and also in mobilising private-sector R&D towards globally desired goals. There is no escape from such public-private collaboration. It is notable, for example, that Monsanto, a life-sciences multinational based in St Louis, Missouri, has a research and development budget that is more than twice the R&D budget of the entire worldwide network of public-sector tropical research institutes. Monsanto's research, of course, is overwhelmingly directed towards temperate-zone agriculture.

People, food and the environment

Public health is one of the two distinctive crises of the tropics. The other is the production of food. Poor tropical countries are already incapable of securing an adequate level of nutrition, or paying for necessary food imports out of their own export earnings. The HIPC population is expected to more than double by 2030. Around one-third of all children under the age of five in these countries are malnourished and physically stunted, with profound consequences throughout their lives.

As with malaria, poor food productivity in the tropics is not merely a problem of poor social organisation (for example, exploiting farmers through controls on food prices). Using current technologies and seed types, the tropics are inherently less productive in annual food crops such as wheat (essentially a temperate-zone crop), rice and maize. Most agriculture in the equatorial tropics is of very low productivity, reflecting the fragility of most tropical soils at high temperatures combined with heavy rainfall.

High productivity in the rainforest ecozone is possible only in small parts of the tropics, generally on volcanic soils (on the island of Java, in Indonesia, for example). In the wet-dry tropics, such as the vast savannahs of Africa, agriculture is hindered by the terrible burdens of unpredictable and highly variable water supplies. Drought and resulting famine have killed millions of peasant families in the past generation alone.

Scientific advances again offer great hope. Biotechnology could mobilise genetic engineering to breed hardier plants that are more resistant to drought and less sensitive to pests. Such genetic engineering is stymied at every point, however. It is met with doubts in the rich countries (where people do not have to worry about their next meal); it requires a new scientific and policy framework in the poor countries; and it must somehow generate market incentives for the big life-sciences firms to turn their research towards tropical foodstuffs, in co-operation with tropical research centres. Calestous Juma, one of the world's authorities on biotechnology in Africa, stresses that there are dozens, or perhaps hundreds, of underused foodstuffs that are well adapted to the tropics and could be improved through directed biotechnology research. Such R&D is now all but lacking in the poorest countries.

The situation of much of the tropical world is, in fact, deteriorating, not only because of increased population but also because of long-term trends in climate. As the rich countries fill the atmosphere with increasing concentrations of carbon, it looks ever more likely that the poor tropical countries will bear much of the resulting burden.

Anthropogenic global warming, caused by the growth in atmospheric carbon, may actually benefit agriculture in high-latitude zones, such as Canada, Russia and the northern United States, by extending the growing season and improving photosynthesis through a process known as carbon fertilisation. It is likely to lower tropical food productivity, however, both because of increased heat stress on plants and because the carbon fertilisation effect appears to be smaller in tropical ecozones. Global warming is also contributing to the increased severity of tropical climatic disturbances, such as the "one-in-a-century" El Niño that hit the tropical world in 1997–98, and the "one-in-a-century" Hurricane Mitch that devastated Honduras and Nicaragua a year ago. Once-in-a-century weather events seem to be arriving with disturbing frequency.

The United States feels aggrieved that poor countries are not signing the convention on climatic change. The truth is that these poor tropical countries should be calling for outright compensation from America and other rich countries for the climatic damages that are being imposed on them. The global climate-change debate will be stalled until it is acknowledged in the United States and Europe that the temperate-zone economies are likely to impose heavy burdens on the already impoverished tropics.

New hope in a new millennium

The situation of the HIPCS has become intolerable, especially at a time when the rich countries are bursting with new wealth and scientific prowess. The time has arrived for a fundamental rethinking of the strategy for co-operation between rich and poor, with the avowed aim of helping the poorest of the poor back on to their own feet to join the race for human betterment. Four steps could change the shape of our global community.

First, rich and poor need to learn to talk together. As a start, the world's democracies, rich and poor, should join in a quest for common action. Once again the rich G8 met in 1999 without the presence of the developing world. This rich-country summit should be the last of its kind. A G16 for the new millennium should include old and new democracies such as Brazil, India, South Korea, Nigeria, Poland and South Africa.

Second, rich and poor countries should direct their urgent attention to the mobilisation of science and technology for poor-country problems. The rich countries should understand that the IMF and World Bank are by themselves not equipped for that challenge. The specialised UN agencies have a great role to play, especially if they also act as a bridge between the activities of advanced-country and developing-country scientific centres. They will be able to play that role, however, only after the United States pays its debts to the UN and ends its unthinking hostility to the UN system.

We will also need new and creative institutional alliances. A Millennium Vaccine Fund, which guaranteed future markets for malaria, tuberculosis and AIDS vaccines, would be the right place to start. The vaccine-fund approach is administratively straightforward, desperately needed and within our technological reach. Similar efforts to merge public and private science activities will be needed in agricultural biotechnology.

Third, just as knowledge is becoming the undisputed centrepiece of global prosperity (and lack of it, the core of human impoverishment), the global regime on intellectual property rights requires a new look. The United States prevailed upon the world to toughen patent codes and cut down on intellectual piracy. But now transnational corporations and rich-country institutions are patenting everything from the human genome to rainforest biodiversity. The poor will be ripped off unless some sense and equity are introduced into this runaway process.

Moreover, the system of intellectual property rights must balance the need to provide incentives for innovation against the need of poor countries to get the results of innovation. The current struggle over AIDS medicines in South Africa is but an early warning shot in a much larger struggle over access to the fruits of human knowledge. The issue of setting global rules for the uses and development of new technologies—especially the controversial biotechnologies—will again require global co-operation, not the strong-arming of the few rich countries.

Fourth, and perhaps toughest of all, we need a serious discussion about long-term finance for the international public goods necessary for HIPC countries to break through to prosperity. The rich countries are willing to talk about every aspect except money: money to develop new malaria, tuberculosis and AIDS vaccines; money to spur biotechnology research in food-scarce regions; money to help tropical countries adjust to climate changes imposed on them by the richer countries. The World Bank makes mostly loans, and loans to individual countries at that. It does not finance global public goods. America has systematically squeezed the budgets of UN agencies, including such vital ones as the World Health Organisation.

We will need, in the end, to put real resources in support of our hopes. A global tax on carbon-emitting fossil fuels might be the way to begin. Even a very small tax, less than that which is needed to correct humanity's climate-deforming overuse of fossil fuels, would finance a greatly enhanced supply of global public goods. No better time to start than as the new millennium begins.

Can debt relief make a difference?

Efforts to forgive poor countries their debts are speeding up, but it is not yet obvious that they will be a lasting success

WASHINGTON, DC

HARDLY noticed amid the hullabaloo of the presidential election, America has just given a big (and belated) boost to the international effort to help the world's poorest debtor countries. On November 6th, President Clinton signed legislation that provided $435m in debt relief for HIPC countries (the ugly acronym by which the Heavily Indebted Poor Countries are known). It also gave America's blessing to the IMF's plans to use the proceeds of some limited sales of its gold reserves for further debt relief.

This was a big breakthrough. Stinginess from America's lawmakers, particularly some Republicans, had long stalled the debt-relief effort, because other countries were unwilling to put more money into the pot until America paid its share. Eventually, however, relentless lobbying by a huge coalition from church groups to celebrities had its effect. (Jesse Helms, the crusty chairman of the Senate Foreign Relations Committee was moved to tears during a visit from Bono, a rock star turned debt-relief advocate.)

With the American contribution secured, cash is no longer a constraint to debt relief. At issue now is whether the process is fast and generous enough to satisfy the anti-debt campaigners, while being cautious and conservative enough to ensure that the money is not wasted.

An assessment of the generosity and effectiveness of the HIPC effort depends on how it is framed. By the standards of many international initiatives it has been remarkably quick. Barely five years ago, the World Bank and IMF still refused to accept that the debts owed to them by poor countries should be relieved at all. Only in 1996 did the Bretton Woods institutions launch the first "HIPC initiative", identifying 41 very poor countries and acknowledging that their overall debt burden (including the international institutions' share) should be reduced to a "sustainable" level—so long as the countries showed a record of several years of good economic policy. A sustainable debt burden was defined mainly in terms of the net present value of a country's debt in relation to its exports.

In 1999, at the behest of the G7 group of rich countries (which were in turn reacting to powerful pressure from anti-debt campaigners), the HIPC initiative was dramatically expanded. The debt sustainability criteria were modified (to give more countries more assistance), and the timetables for offering relief accelerated. Countries with good policies were promised faster relief.

Speed limits

This year, in particular, speed has been at the top of the agenda. So far, Uganda is the only country that has finished its entire debt-relief process. But both the IMF and the World Bank have promised to get 20 countries to their "decision points", at which the level of debt forgiveness is determined and countries begin to receive immediate cashflow relief on their debt-service payments, by the end of this year. Including Guyana, whose debt relief was due to be approved by the board of the World Bank this week, 12 countries have so far reached their decision points (see chart).

To fulfil their pledge, the World Bank and IMF must process eight more countries in the next six weeks. The bureaucrats are working frantically on potential candidates, including Guinea Bissau, Zambia, Niger, Gambia, Malawi, Chad, Guinea, Sao Tome and Principe, Madagascar, Ethiopia and Rwanda.

From the officials' perspective, the debt-relief process has been a great success. Once the 20 countries have been processed, they say that debt relief worth $30 billion will have been committed. Moreover, they crow, over the past year the G7 countries have pledged to reduce the debts that HIPC countries owe them bilaterally by 100%. And, says the World Bank, countries

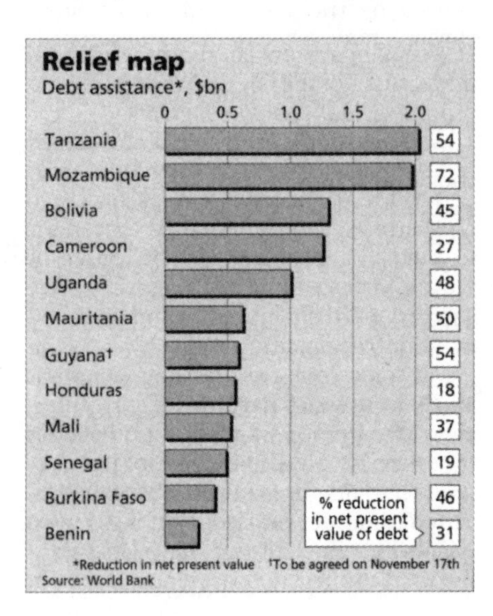

that have received help so far have seen the net present value of their debt burden fall by an average of 40%.

There has also been a big effort to make sure that the poor see the benefits. To qualify, HIPC countries need to prepare a "Poverty Reduction Strategy Paper" (PRSP). Developed in conjunction with non-governmental organisations and other lobbyists for the poor, these blueprints are designed to lay out how a country will fight poverty, and how savings from debt relief will help.

Unfortunately, many of the anti-debt campaigners are not impressed with the rhetoric, or with the record to date. For them, debt relief is not fast enough, generous enough or going in the right direction. Jubilee 2000, the global campaign that was founded in 1996 to demand a total debt write-off for poor countries in the millennium year, reckons that HIPC countries are still suffering under the burden of unpayable debts.

Many NGOs also dispute official claims of generosity. In a recent paper, Oxfam argued that HIPC countries received much less debt relief than the headline figures touted. They argued that some countries could even end up paying more in debt service after the HIPC process than before. In the case of Zambia that is technically true, largely because Zambia has big one-off payments to the IMF looming. But broadly, while it may be right that official figures overstate how much relief HIPC countries will get, it is also true that there has been real progress. Uganda, for instance, has been able to double primary-school enrolment by using the money saved from debt relief. Mozambique expects to save the equivalent of twice its health budget from debt relief. That may not be as much as campaigners have demanded, but it is a lot better than nothing.

A more important question-mark hangs over whether the process is helping poor countries in the long term. Most of them rely permanently on transfers from rich countries. If debt relief results in less aid from individual donors, they might not be better off. Moreover, if the transfers come in the form of cheap loans—the main vehicle through which the World Bank currently doles out money—HIPC countries risk reaching "unsustainable" debt levels yet again. Few people have thought about the financial implications of shifting the World Bank's resources exclusively towards grants.

Equally, the current vogue for speed could come at the expense of good anti-poverty policy. At one level (of great concern to campaigners) there is the danger that efforts to build a national anti-poverty consensus will be sacrificed in the interests of speed. The PRSP will then simply be window-dressing done by bureaucrats.

In some countries—notably Honduras and Bolivia—NGOs have made big contributions to this process, although it is not clear that they have been listened to. But elsewhere there has been minimal consultation. The fear is that, if full debt relief is given too quickly, governments will have less incentive to ensure that more people participate in their poverty strategies.

An even bigger risk, feared above all by those working at the Bretton Woods institutions, is that the pressure for speed will give debt relief to countries with bad economic policies. Here the bureaucrats admit that they are pushing through dubious cases in order to meet the deadline of 20 countries by the end of the year. Pressure from campaigners has helped push the process this far; but such concerns suggest that it might now be time to make haste more slowly.

Unit 3

Unit Selections

Key Points to Consider

- What are the major obstacles to further reductions of nuclear weapons?
- Which countries are most likely to follow the lead of India and Pakistan and test nuclear weapons?
- Do you agree with experts who predict that future Russian leaders will be more likely now than during the cold war to use nuclear weapons in the event of an international crisis? Support your answer.
- Explain why you do/do not support the proposal for the United States to build a ballistic missile defense system.

Links www.dushkin.com/online/

13. **The Bulletin of the Atomic Scientists**
    http://www.bullatomsci.org
14. **ISN International Relations and Security Network**
    http://www.isn.ethz.ch
15. **Terrorism Research Center**
    http://www.terrorism.com

These sites are annotated on pages 4 and 5.

Weapons of Mass Destruction

Proliferating weapons of mass destruction—chemical, biological, and nuclear (CBN)—are an important feature of contemporary international relations. Today scholars and politicians debate theoretical issues related to the magnitude of the threat, how to deter or counter weapons of mass destruction, and whether the spread of CBN weapons encourages or acts as a disincentive to interstate war. Meanwhile, proliferation continues unabated.

Ten years after the collapse of the Soviet Union, nuclear arms control is faring worse in the first days of the twenty-first century than it did in the last days of the cold war and weapons of mass destruction continue to proliferate. During the cold war, four major nuclear arms control regimes were developed: the Moscow-Washington negotiations that led to the Strategic Arms Limitation Treaty (SALT) and the Anti-Ballistic Missile (ABM) Treaty of 1972; the Nonproliferation Treaty (NPT); and the grandfather of them all, the Atmospheric Test Ban Treaty negotiated during the Eisenhower administration. In "The Folly of Arms Control," Jonathan Schell argues that only after the great nuclear powers commit themselves to abolish nuclear weapons will it be possible to control the spread of weapons of mass destruction.

This possibility is unlikely in the foreseeable future. Instead, as faith in arms control weakens, several nation-states are beginning to reconsider their self-imposed moratoriums on nuclear-weapons development. India's decision to test nuclear weapons in May 1998 and Pakistan's decision to follow suit signaled the start of this trend. Faced with U.S. economic sanctions and international diplomatic pressure, Pakistan, which was on the verge of defaulting on outstanding international loans even before the nuclear tests, agreed to sign a treaty banning further nuclear tests. A regime change in Pakistan in 1999, as a military coup replaced an elected government, did not change Pakistan's nuclear policy. India has also agreed in principle to such a treaty. Neither country, however, has yet indicated a willingness to dismantle its nuclear bomb program. The continuing commitment to retain nuclear weapons supports the proposition that more countries now believe that it is important for a country to obtain at least one or a few nuclear bombs.

Joseph Cirincione warns, in "The Asian Nuclear Reaction Chain," that other Asian nations are likely to "go nuclear" in the near-term future. At least 25 countries either have, or are in the process of developing, weapons of mass destruction. Two dozen are researching, developing, or stockpiling chemical weapons. It is difficult to see how the genie of nuclear weapons technology will be kept in the bottle. This dangerous trend could mean a new global arms race that would increase the probability of a war that could engulf the world.

Many security analysts remain focused on potential threats created by the seepage of weapons, materials, and expertise from the former Soviet Union and by "rogue" states who are developing nuclear capabilities. Concerns about the spread of nuclear expertise and capabilities from the former Soviet Union stimulated cooperation between the United States, Russia, and a number of former Soviet states. Since 1991, the United States and Russia have dismantled parts of the old nuclear structure in certain former Soviet republics. In 1992 the ex-Soviet republics of Kazakhstan and Belarus agreed to eliminate nuclear weapons from their territory, and Ukraine eliminated much of its nuclear stockpile by the mid-1990s.

The momentum of diplomatic initiatives slowed in recent years as the economic and political environment changed in the former Soviet Union and in the United States. Several programs designed to improve the security of Russia's deteriorating stockpile of weapons of mass destruction are no longer funded by the United States at their original levels. The funds were cut at the same time that growing economic problems in Russia posed additional threats to the security of Russia's stockpiles of nuclear, chemical, and biological weapons, materials, and human expertise. The ease with which these resources can disappear is a source of increasing worry among Western security analysts.

As the economy, conventional armed forces, and equipment deteriorate, Russia is relying more on nuclear weapons for national defense. The scenario of a future Russian government feeling forced to use nuclear weapons is more credible today than during the cold war. As the preparedness and morale of the troops guarding Russia's weapons of mass destruction decline, weapons stocks deteriorate and the reliability of the country's network of early-warning satellites and computer-based launch facilities degrade.

The slowdown in nuclear arms cooperation and the increased tempo of proliferation was fueled by the failure of the Clinton administration to win support from the U.S. Senate, during the fall of 1999, for the Comprehensive Test Ban Treaty (CTBT) that would impose a worldwide ban on underground testing. This failure triggered wide and highly vocal protests from America's friends and foes.

America's declared intention to build a new missile defense system is creating additional strains between the United States' allies and potential enemies. Due to questions of viability, former President Clinton postponed making a decision about whether to build a missile shield at the end of 2000. This decision will be one of President George W. Bush's most important foreign policy decisions because it is likely to affect U.S. relations with many nation-states. Supporters of an anti-missile defense system argue that it is necessary for America's homeland defense because of the proliferation of ballistic missiles. Critics question the technological feasibility of the system and emphasize the financial and diplomatic costs of the proposed defense system.

The possibility of further erosion in existing international enforcement mechanisms is disturbing because everyone is now a potential victim of a future nuclear, biological, or chemical attack. The realization that weapons of mass destruction are being dispersed throughout the world prompted the United States to ratify the Chemical Weapons Convention (CWC). The United States became one of 100 countries to ratify the CWC in 1997 after a contentious debate in the U.S. Senate. In 1998 the U.S. government also proposed new measures to bolster the 1972 Biological and Toxic Weapons Convention by adding an international inspection system. The new unified American position means that U.S. negotiators are taking a more active role in international talks.

A rash of incidents involving alleged biological and chemical weapons led a recent federal study to warn that authorities in the United States at the federal, state, and local level are not prepared to launch coordinated emergency response measures in the event of a chemical or biological attack on civilians. The high visibility of threatened attacks by international and domestic terrorists and malcontents in the United States fuels concerns among Americans about the possibility of a terrorist attack within the United States.

The Folly of Arms Control

Jonathan Schell

WHY THERE IS NO NUCLEAR MIDDLE GROUND

HISTORY OFTEN places before the world a problem whose solution lies outside the bounds of contemporary political acceptability. Such was the case, for example, in the 1930s, when the rise of Hitler posed a threat to the European democracies that they lacked the resolve to face. To check Nazi aggression, most historians now agree, the democracies would have had to oppose it early and resolutely, as Winston Churchill advocated. But Churchill's prescriptions were beyond the pale of mainstream political thinking at the time, and he was forced "into the wilderness," as he famously put it. Not until the late 1930s did his ideas win political acceptance, and by then the price of stopping Hitler was World War II.

Vietnam offers another example. In retrospect, among the many outcomes under discussion at the time, only two were really possible. One was war without end—the open, unlimited occupation of Vietnam by American forces. The other was withdrawal and defeat. But the political costs of either—on the one hand, of frankly imposing American rule on that country for an indefinite period; on the other, of "losing" Vietnam—were considered prohibitive. Deception and self-deception abounded on all sides. Those who opposed the war counseled withdrawal, but usually without admitting that this meant defeat. Those who supported the war pretended that victory was near—that light was dawning at the end of the proverbial tunnel. Only temporizing, middling policies—first, surreptitious escalation, then "Vietnamization"—that postponed the hard choice were within political bounds. The price was paid by the people of Vietnam and the United States.

A contrast is often drawn between idealistic and realistic policies. But the choices posed by Hitler's rise and the Vietnam War were different. They were between political realism—bound hand and foot by a conventional wisdom out of touch with events—and the reality of those events, which we might call circumstantial reality. The nuclear predicament in the post–Cold War period presents the United States and the world with another choice of this kind. Once again, political reality and circumstantial reality—what Aleksandr Solzhenitsyn once called the "pitiless crowbar of events"—are colliding. The real alternatives—the ones that can actually occur—are at present found politically unacceptable, while the politically acceptable choices are all unreal.

These real alternatives are, on the one hand, the unrestricted proliferation of nuclear weapons—leading to what the late nuclear theorist Albert Wohlstetter some time ago called a "nuclear-armed crowd" and what Harvard's Graham Allison has more recently called "nuclear anarchy"—and, on the other, the abolition of nuclear weapons by international agreement. The current American policy is to try to stop proliferation while simultaneously continuing to hold on to its own nuclear arsenal indefinitely. But these objectives are contradictory. The policy based on them is the equivalent—in the context of the nuclear dilemma as it exists at the opening of the twenty-first century—of appeasement in the 1930s and surreptitious escalation and Vietnamization in the late 1960s and early 1970s. To govern is to choose. The current policy is a way of avoiding choice—a policy without traction in the world as it really is. Meanwhile, as in the earlier dilemmas, both the danger and the cost of dealing with it mount. For in the absence of a decision, events are drifting toward one of the real possible outcomes, namely, uncontrolled proliferation. In politics as in physics, entropy is a recipe for anarchy.

THE CRISIS OF ARMS CONTROL

THE RISE in nuclear danger is already apparent in an across-the-board crisis that has developed in the last two or three years in the regime of nuclear arms control. The fabric of nuclear arms control is woven of four main strands, each the product of decades of negotiation. These were not conceived as parts of a grand design, but over time they came to possess a certain coherence.

The first strand is the Moscow-Washington negotiations—first those that led to the Strategic Arms Limitation Treaty (SALT), then those that have forged the Strategic Arms Reductions Treaties (START I and II)—to reduce the twin mountains of offensive nuclear weapons built up during the Cold War.

Reprinted by permission from *Foreign Affairs*, September/October 2000, pp. 22-46.

Ten years after the Cold War ended, nuclear danger is growing.

The second strand, which is closely entwined with the first, is the attempt to rein in defensive antinuclear systems. Its centerpiece is the Anti-Ballistic Missile (ABM) Treaty of 1972, in which the United States and the Soviet Union each agreed to field no more than one limited-range anti-nuclear missile system. Defensive limits are essential for offensive limits because a defensive buildup can upset any negotiated offensive balance.

The third strand is the nuclear Nonproliferation Treaty (NPT), perhaps the most impressive and successful arms control treaty ever negotiated and the foundation stone of any hope for nuclear sanity in the post–Cold War world. Under its provisions, two classes of nations were created—nations without nuclear weapons that agreed to forego them, and nations that possessed them and were permitted, for a time, to go on possessing them. Today, 182 nations have ratified the NPT as non-nuclear powers, in return for which they have been given access to certain technology for nuclear energy, while five countries—the United States, Russia, China, the United Kingdom, and France—belong to the NPT as nuclear powers. Four countries remain outside the treaty. Three—Israel, India, and Pakistan—have nuclear weapons, and one—Cuba—does not. The NPT does not, however, envision a permanent two-tier system of nuclear haves and have-nots. The nuclear powers are committed under the treaty's Article VI to "pursue negotiations in good faith on effective measures relating to cessation of the nuclear arms race at an early date and to nuclear disarmament, and on a treaty on general and complete disarmament under strict and effective international control."

The fourth strand is the test ban negotiations—the grandfather of arms control measures, dating from the Eisenhower administration. Like the NPT, to which they are a crucial adjunct, the test ban talks are global. The Atmospheric Test Ban was signed and ratified in 1963. Its successor, the Comprehensive Test Ban Treaty (CTBT), would slow arms races since testing is considered necessary for many kinds of nuclear-arms innovations. Companion efforts are the negotiations to ban the production of fissionable materials, the negotiations to tighten restrictions on the spread of missile technology, and the calls to take nuclear weapons off of alert status.

When the Cold War ended, the prospects for a steady strengthening of all four of these strands looked better than ever. The collapse of the Soviet Union in 1991 promised a sharp decline in nuclear danger—the more so as no new global political struggle arose to take the Cold War's place. The mere relaxation of the struggle under Mikhail Gorbachev had given new impetus to START. In the Intermediate-range Nuclear Forces (INF) Treaty signed in 1987, all intermediate-range missiles were banned from the European theater, and under the 1991 START I agreement, strategic warheads were to be reduced to about 7,000 on each side. The START II agreement, which would reduce strategic warheads to 3,000–3,500 on each side, was signed in 1992, and the outlook for early ratification by both sides appeared favorable. The number of countries that had signed the NPT was steadily rising. A positive synergy among the different negotiations seemed to be at work. Success in START and the CTBT promised to secure and strengthen the NPT bargain; a comprehensive test ban would help put a lid on proliferation; and an end to proliferation would encourage the nuclear powers to relinquish their arsenals. The convention banning biological weapons and the negotiations to found a convention banning chemical weapons (ratified by the Senate in 1998) suggested that the world was turning slowly but surely against weapons of mass destruction in general. Above all, the direction was right. Taken in their entirety, the world's nuclear arsenals seemed to be caught in a tightening net of treaties and agreements that, if they did not end nuclear danger altogether, would certainly reduce it radically. Nuclear weapons began to look like a thing of the past, and they all but disappeared from public consciousness.

Ten years later, nuclear danger is growing again, and the net of restrictions is rending. India conducted five tests in May 1998, and Pakistan responded with seven, producing the world's first nuclear confrontation entirely unrelated to the Cold War. In the summer of 1999, an official commission in India, borrowing a leaf from the American playbook of the 1960s, recommended the creation and deployment of a deterrent arsenal based on a triad of forces delivering nuclear bombs from air, land, and sea. North Korea has engaged in on-again, off-again efforts to build nuclear weapons and missiles for their delivery. Saddam Hussein of Iraq, who was forced after the 1991 Gulf War to endure the presence of U.N. weapons inspectors, has thrown them out. Earlier this year, the CIA reported that it was unable to assure Americans that Iran did not already have the wherewithal for building nuclear weapons. The weapons programs in North Korea, Iraq, and Iran have alarmed Congress, which now seeks to deploy an antinuclear national missile defense (NMD) as soon as technically feasible, placing the ABM treaty in jeopardy. The United States has asked Russia to amend the treaty to permit the deployment of NMD, but Russia has refused on the ground that NMD would destabilize the offensive nuclear arms balance. The threat to the ABM treaty in turn threatens START II, whose implementation has been conditioned by Russia on the ABM treaty's integrity. A deployment of antimissile defenses in Taiwan or Japan, which the Clinton administration has discussed with those countries, could lead China to build up its offensive arms. Even the United States' closest allies, the principal members of NATO, are alarmed by the unilateral character of the American decision to deploy defenses when ready. They fear not only that the missile deployment will revive arms races with Russia and China but that the United States, feeling safe behind its shield, will leave Europe to face the renewed danger alone. Meanwhile, Russia's doubtful control over its nuclear weapons and special nuclear materials (control to which the United States has contributed $2.3 billion per year under the Nunn-Lugar legislation) increases the danger that not merely governments but terrorist groups may obtain and use one or more nuclear weapons. Finally, in 1999, the Senate voted down the CTBT.

But the full extent of the jeopardy of arms control does not appear until the interrelationships between these reverses are considered. What if North Korea fires a ballistic missile over Japan and into the Pacific Ocean, as it did in 1998? Forthwith, the Senate votes to deploy NMD, even though it has not yet been shown to be technically feasible, and the administration announces that it will not be stopped from deployment by objections from Russia, which then draws back from implementing START II. These reverses, of course, place new stress on the NPT, whose indefinite renewal in 1995 and 2000 was explicitly conditioned on progress in nuclear disarmament and ratification of the CTBT. Meanwhile, Japan, also alarmed by the North Korean missile test, agrees to share in the expense of developing a missile-defense system, leading China to announce that if Japan (or Taiwan) should deploy such defenses, it might have to engage in an offensive buildup—something it may be in a better position to do thanks to its reported theft of American nuclear secrets pertaining to warhead miniaturization, which is a prerequisite for mounting several warheads on a single missile. That threat, of course, alarms India, which is at work on long-range missiles, and buttresses the American decision to build NMD—and so forth. In short, a single missile test by a small, poverty-stricken nation could touch off a string of consequences that places severe stress on almost every aspect of the global nuclear arms control regime. No longer does an act of nuclear escalation affect only a nearby adversary or two; its repercussions will be felt around the world. Any development of nuclear weapons or their delivery vehicles creates pressure to do likewise throughout what is now a seamless global web of actions and reactions.

WHO'S NEXT?

TEN YEARS after the collapse of the Soviet Union, the startling fact is that nuclear arms control is faring worse in the first days of the twenty-first century than it did in the last days of the Cold War. Then, nuclear danger seemed to be declining. Now, it is on the rise. Then, nuclear arms control agreements were progressing. Now, they are at a stalemate or in danger of unraveling. How has this come about? Why has the end of the global conflict in whose name the great nuclear arsenals were built proved worse for nuclear disarmament than the conflict itself?

Several adverse forces are at work. One is simply the ever-increasing availability of nuclear technology. By convention, the word "proliferation" refers to the actual acquisition of nuclear weapons. But there is also the proliferation of the scientific and technical capabilities on which the construction of nuclear arms is based. "Nuclear capacity" refers to a country's ability to produce nuclear weapons within a definite span of time. Sweden, for example, possesses such a nuclear capacity, though it has no will to build nuclear bombs. Libya, on the other hand, has the will but not the capacity. That this sort of unrealized capacity would proliferate far beyond the number of countries that actually possess nuclear arms was inherent in the nature of nuclear weapons themselves—which are based, of course, on scientific knowledge, which by nature tends to spread. In the early 1940s, for example, only one nation possessed unrealized capacity in this sense: the United States. That is to say, although it had not yet built a bomb, there was every reason to believe that its decision to do so would bear fruit. Today, many dozens of nations have such a capacity. The State Department puts their current number at 44 and, in negotiating the now-rejected CTBT, required that it not come into force until all 44 of them had ratified it. Nuclear technology is old technology. We are in the 55th year of the nuclear age. The secret of the bomb is out; it has been published in magazines. The same holds true for missile technology and chemical and biological weapons technology.

If we think of the NPT as a dam holding back nuclear proliferation, then the spread of nuclear capacity is like water collecting behind the dam. That tide can only rise, increasing the pressure. The world's safety ultimately depends not on the number of nations that want to build nuclear weapons but cannot, but on the number that can but do not. If the spread of nuclear weapons is to be prevented over the long run, it cannot come through restrictions on nations' capacity. Instead, it must come by influencing their will, which entails the use of diplomatic and political means—the very means whose breakdown we are now witnessing.

A second new adverse element is the rise of antinuclear defensive technology. Antinuclear defenses have long been the wild card of nuclear policy, generating almost nonstop intellectual confusion and popular misunderstanding. Most people's visceral response to the idea of defenses in general is positive. The first duty of government is to preserve its citizens' lives, and defenses promise this. The doctrine of nuclear deterrence stood this commonsense appraisal on its head. Under that doctrine, safety depends on the absolute and unchallenged capacity of each side to annihilate the other's population—a capacity that, when recognized by all, is meant to prevent nuclear war from breaking out in the first place. By eroding this vulnerability, defenses destabilize deterrence. Furthermore, they fuel offensive-arms buildups, since a nation whose offensive power is eroded by defenses is likely to try to restore it by building up its offenses. That was why the first achievement of the Strategic Arms Limitation Talks was the treaty banning all but one antiballistic missile system on each side. However sound this reasoning may have been—at least as an adjunct to the deterrence doctrine—the general public probably never grasped it. That may be why President Reagan's proposal for a Strategic Defense Initiative in the 1980s, although technically infeasible, enjoyed such wide popular support.

The collapse of the Soviet Union added fresh layers of confusion to this already bewildering situation. After the extraordinary expenditure of some $60 billion since the early 1980s, a modest NMD program may now have drawn somewhat closer to technical realization. Its goal, though, is to defend the United States not against Russia but against the handful of missiles that might be fired by North Korea, Iran, or some other "rogue" state. Still, Russia has protested and threatened to suspend implementation of START II—for even if the defenses are feasible, neither Russia nor any other country except the United States has the funds or the technical means to build them anytime soon. Antinuclear defenses are not, like nuclear bombs, old technology; they are brand new. (Indeed, they are so new that it is increasingly doubtful that they are feasible even for the United States in the near future; recent antimissile tests have proven embarrassing failures.) If, however, the United States does prove capable of building them, it will be in the position it was in with respect to nuclear weapons in 1943 or 1944—a potential monopoly position—and monopolies, almost by nature, destabilize military balances.

The United States continued its old nuclear deterrence policy even after the Cold War ended.

More important than either the spread of nuclear capacity or the invention of antinuclear defenses is a third adverse element: the decision by the nuclear powers to retain their Cold War nuclear arsenals even in the absence of the Cold War. If I carry a rifle on my shoulder during a war, it means one thing. If I continue to carry the rifle after the war has ended, it means something very different. When the Cold War ended, the United States merely continued with the policy of nuclear deterrence of the Soviet Union/Russia, accompanied by negotiated reductions. Yet this continuation—this doing nothing—constituted one of the most important decisions of the nuclear age. It quietly set a standard for the post–Cold War period.

The negotiated nuclear reductions have now approached the levels specified in START I, which was negotiated mostly with the now-defunct Soviet Union, and implementation of START II is uncertain. What is most important is that the United States, though paying occasional lip service to full nuclear disarmament, has insisted in its negotiations for a START III agreement on a lower limit of 2,500 nuclear weapons. Since no START IV has yet been discussed, the figure of 2,500 nuclear weapons represents the lowest negotiated level to which the United States has, so far, been willing to reduce its arsenal. At the same time, American officials have declared their intention to hold on to that arsenal indefinitely. In late January, for example, Russian negotiators proposed that START III require that the two sides reduce their arsenals to 1,500 nuclear weapons on each side. The United States refused, insisting on keeping a minimum of 2,500. The State Department's then-spokesperson, James Rubin, said, "We can limit the nuclear danger by going down to a level of 2,000 to 2,500 without jeopardizing our interest with respect to nuclear deterrence." In sum, as a matter of actual post–Cold War policy, the United States has consistently declared its intention to remain in a condition of mutual deterrence with Russia—to preserve the capacity of each side to annihilate the other. As Undersecretary of Defense Walter Slocombe explained, "A key conclusion of the administration's national security strategy is [that] the United States will retain strategic nuclear forces sufficient to deter any future hostile foreign leadership with access to strategic nuclear forces from action against our vital interests and to convince it that seeking nuclear advantage would be *futile*."

Whatever one thought about nuclear arms during the Cold War, it did not necessarily follow that because Moscow and Washington had them, everyone else should, too. The double standard provisionally built into the NPT, although obviously inequitable, could be understood. Once the Soviet Union disappeared, however, the foundations of the argument shifted. The Cold War was a special circumstance irrefutably different from any other struggle on earth. Now it appears that the Western nuclear powers believed that no special circumstance was needed to justify nuclear arms. The United States was less threatened militarily than any other nation, but it insisted on retaining nuclear arsenals and switched its first-use policy from its old Cold War rival to what some policymakers called the "generic" target of merely potential dangers that might arise somewhere in the world.

This shift in rationale has been accompanied by a shift in the arsenal's global influence. The American nuclear arsenal is often referred to simply as "our deterrent." But does anyone today seriously maintain that Russia has any thought whatsoever of launching a nuclear strike against the United States and is stopped only by a fear of U.S. retaliation? On the other hand, can anyone doubt that these arsenals, both Russian and American, are a significant goad to proliferation—that they serve, in the words of Indian Foreign Minister Jaswant Singh, as a "nuclear paradigm" emulated by other powers?

PROLIFERANCE

IN THESE CIRCUMSTANCES, there is much more reason to call the American arsenal a "proliferant" than to call it a deterrent. This is not mere word-juggling. A central lesson of deterrence theory is that the psychological effects of nuclear arms are as important as the physical ones. According to the theory, deterrence "works" when the leaderships on both sides of a nuclear standoff so deeply fear the other side's retaliation that they do not dare to strike in the first place. If the weapons are ever used, deterrence has by definition failed. What we may call "proliferance," too, is a psychological effect of nuclear weapons. Proliferance occurs when a country, fearful of a neighbor's nuclear arsenals (and in the age of the intercontinental ballistic missile, who is not, for these purposes, a neighbor?), builds one in response. The difference between deterrence and proliferance is that whereas deterrence stops nations that possess nuclear arsenals from using them, proliferance inspires nations that lack them to get them. In a sense, therefore, the two effects arrive at a common destination: the possession—but not, it is hoped, the use—of nuclear weapons.

Any number of American politicians have stated that nuclear proliferation is the greatest threat to the security of the United States today. In the post–Cold War world, the effects of proliferance are much easier to demonstrate than those of deterrence. Proliferance led India—looking over the Himalayas to China, and beyond China to Russia and the United States—to turn itself into a nuclear power, and proliferance goaded Pakistan to promptly conduct its own nuclear tests. This influence acts both by example (the "nuclear paradigm" cited by Singh) and, even more powerfully, through the direct influence of the terror that is the chief product of nuclear arsenals.

Indeed, the proliferant influence of nuclear terror has been in operation since the earliest days of the nuclear age. The clear lesson of history is that nuclear arsenals breed nuclear arsenals. Even the United States—the first nation to build the bomb—did so, in a sense, *reactively.* Franklin Roosevelt and his advisers were worried that Hitler would get the bomb first. (If there has ever been a good reason for building nuclear weapons, preventing Hitler from having a monopoly on them in the midst of a world war was it.) The Soviet Union then built the bomb in response to the United States; China built it in response to both the United States and Russia; India built it in response to China; and Pakistan built it in response to India. (The cases of the United Kingdom and France, which already enjoyed some protection from the U.S. nuclear umbrella, are less clear. Sheer national prestige appears to have been as important as any immediate security risks. Another murkier case is Israel, which, like the United States in 1945, built its arsenal preemptively but also sought to counter conventional threats from its Arab enemies and deter them from ever dreaming of overrunning it.) Every nuclear arsenal is linked to every other nuclear arsenal in the world by these powerful ties of terror and response. And when the list of nuclear powers grows, the country in question—Iraq? Iran? North Korea? Egypt? —will probably have been inspired by the fear of some nuclear-armed foe. Deterrence is, in fact, the codification and institutionalization of this reactive cycle. Indeed, deterrence teaches that the way to avoid destruction by a rival is to possess nuclear weapons yourself. If this is not an invitation to proliferation, what would be?

Whereas in the Cold War, deterrence was the dominant effect, now proliferance is. Consider the increasing danger of nuclear terrorism. The continued possession by many nations of nuclear arms makes the diversion of nuclear materials or weapons into the hands of terrorist groups more likely. But terrorists, having no nation to lose, cannot be "deterred" by the threat of retaliation. In their case, the proliferant effect of nuclear arsenals is all, the deterrent effect nil. Conversely, the only policy that can seriously hope to sharply reduce (although not entirely eliminate) the danger of nuclear terrorism is abolition, because abolition alone can impose comprehensive global prohibitions on nuclear-weapon technology.

THE EVOLUTION OF STRATEGY

IN THIS SCENE of growing nuclear danger, no single actor, of course, is solely to blame. It is the essence of the new situation that the number of actors on the nuclear stage is growing. India, for example, bears a clear responsibility for nuclearizing South Asia with its May 1998 tests. But by signaling that the earth would remain nuclearized indefinitely even after the Cold War, Washington, Moscow, and Beijing also plainly incurred responsibility. If in the early 1990s the existing nuclear powers had committed themselves to the elimination of nuclear weapons and had by 1998 traveled some of the distance to that goal, it is hard to believe that South Asia would be engaged in a nuclear arms race today.

Nuclear abolition was seen not so much as difficult as undesirable.

If, however, we invert the question and, instead of asking who is to blame for the crisis of arms control, ask which country has the greatest power to tackle the crisis, our attention must turn to the United States. Whether the situation can be retrieved at all remains an open question. But without American leadership, any effort must fail. The question of why the United States plans to hold on to its nuclear arsenal indefinitely is, accordingly, highly important. The answer must be sought at many levels—the moral, the psychological, and the cultural, as well as the political and the military—yet because of the dominant influence of the strategists in preserving the continuity of policy as the Cold War ended, the importance of nuclear strategic doctrine cannot be overlooked.

Four stages in the development of strategic thinking about nuclear abolition can be distinguished. In the first, American policy sought to head off a nuclear arms race by negotiating the abolition of nuclear weapons. In 1946, President Truman's representative for nuclear disarmament to the United Nations, Bernard Baruch, proposed that all nuclear weapons be eliminated and all nuclear technology placed under an international authority. In retrospect, the plan never had much chance. The Soviet Union was well into its own project to build the bomb (thanks in good measure to its outstanding spying on the American effort), and Stalin, according to the historian David Holloway, had no wish to barter away the Soviet Union's capacity to build a bomb before it had even tested one. Former National Security Adviser McGeorge Bundy was probably right when, after examining the abolition proposals of that time, he concluded, "The bitter truth is . . . that what we have just reviewed was not at any time a serious negotiation on either side."

In the second stage of the evolution of nuclear policy—during the late 1950s and the early 1960s, after both powers had developed not only atomic bombs but hydrogen bombs as well—the earlier obstacles to full nuclear disarmament were, increasingly, publicly acknowledged as insurmountable. It was no longer enough, even politically, to make fine-sounding proposals for abolition that everyone knew must fail. So if nuclear disarmament was impossible, nuclear arsenals would have to be accepted for at least as long as the struggle with the Soviet Union lasted. The strategic form that that acceptance took was the doctrine of nuclear deterrence, with its teaching that the way to avoid nuclear war is to strike a nuclear balance.

In this new nuclear dispensation, there was still a role for nuclear disarmament. Its goals, however, would be different from what they had been in the time of Baruch. Instead of aiming for abolition, negotiations would seek to "stabilize" the nuclear stalemate. Accepting the inevitability of nuclear possession, these negotiations sought to diminish the possibility of *use* in two ways. First, they would mutually restrict the development of "first-strike" forces, which otherwise might tempt one side or the other to launch a nuclear war. Second, they would place a numerical, mutually agreed-upon cap on offensive nuclear weapons.

The negotiations based on these principles were called arms control, as distinct from nuclear disarmament. The shift was presented as a victory for realism, in which the surrender of the unachievable goal of abolition prepared the ground for the more modest and achievable goals of limiting and stabilizing the nuclear balance of terror. In practice, however, the modest goals proved almost as elusive as abolition had been.

For one thing, the temptation to build first-strike forces regularly got the better of the hope for stability. Each side habitually saw itself as lagging behind. Cries of alarm and appeals to catch up—to close a "bomber gap," a "missile gap," a "throw-weight gap," a "window of vulnerability"—sounded through the halls of Congress as well as the hidden precincts of the Politburo. Nuclear terror, it turned out, was harder to control than theory had predicted. The hope for stability coexisted uneasily at best with the readiness for prompt mutual annihilation, and the very terror that was the mothers' milk of deterrence spawned nightmares that tended constantly to upset the whole arrangement. In the words of Yale's Paul Bracken, "Once the two sides understood the mechanism of deterrence, there would appear to have been little reason to keep piling up additional weapons. But that is exactly what happened: just as deterrence stabilized in the late 1960s, each side began a huge building program." Not until Gorbachev came to power did significant reductions occur.

As the doctrine of deterrence became entrenched in official circles, attitudes toward nuclear disarmament underwent a subtle but deep transition. During the first two decades of the Cold War, the most intractable obstacles to abolition, in American eyes, stemmed from the totalitarian character of the Soviet Union, which both posed the global threat that justified nuclear arms and, owing to its extreme secretiveness, ruled out the kind of inspections essential to a reliable nuclear-disarmament agreement. Over time, however, the particular reference to the Soviet Union began to give way. Arguments based on the nature of the Soviet Union might be called the limited theory of the impossibility of nuclear disarmament. In the new explanation, which we might call the general theory of the impossibility of nuclear disarmament, it was not particular problems caused by Soviet totalitarianism that were cited but a set of difficulties seen as intrinsic to the nuclear dilemma, whatever regimes might be involved. Nations in general, the argument now ran, would be able to cheat on any abolition agreement; they would have good reason to cheat; they would cheat; and then they would use their sudden nuclear monopoly to bully the world.

In this more generalized view, the very fact that nuclear weapons had been invented was reason enough to believe that they could not be eliminated as long as lambs declined to lie down with lions. For even if the nuclear hardware were destroyed, the know-how would remain in people's minds, and someone would build them again. These views were expressed, to give one prominent example, in the 1983 Harvard-sponsored book *Living with Nuclear Weapons,* which posed the question, "Why not abolish nuclear weapons?" and answered simply, "Because we cannot," explaining that "mankind's nuclear innocence, once lost, cannot be regained." In these circumstances—now regarded as immutable—abolition was seen not so much as difficult to achieve but as actually undesirable. A world free of nuclear weapons was intrinsically a less-safe, less-stable place than a world armed with nuclear weapons. In the words of *Living with Nuclear Weapons,* "If the political pre-conditions of trust and consensus are missing, complete disarmament is inherently unstable. In a disarmed world, the first nation to acquire a few arms would be able to influence events to a much greater extent than it could in a heavily armed world. Nuclear weapons greatly magnify this effect."

If deterrence was proven a success during the Cold War, some ask, why give it up now?

As this general theory of the impossibility of nuclear disarmament won official acceptance, a change in the valuation of nuclear weapons occurred. The deeper, less-qualified embrace of deterrence (and of the nuclear arsenals the doctrine justified) opened the way to the idea that nuclear weapons, instead of being a necessary evil, were a positive benefit to the world—not so much a problem as a solution. They provided, thanks to the policy of deterrence, the only imaginable solution to themselves: they prevented nuclear war. Moreover, they prevented even conventional war—no mean achievement, considering what two world wars had done to the globe in the twentieth century.

There matters stood when the Cold War ended, opening a third stage in the development of American strategy. The policymakers might have reasoned as follows: We built up nuclear arsenals to contain the Soviet Union, whose secretive character stood in the way of nuclear disarmament, but now, with the Soviet Union gone, should we not consider the abolition of these weapons? If in 1946 the Soviet regime had been like the one in Moscow today, wouldn't Baruch's plan have had every chance of acceptance? Shouldn't something like it be possible today?

Unfortunately, what prevailed in the conventional wisdom was not the limited theory of the impossibility of nuclear disarmament but the general theory, and this has dictated a very nearly opposite response to the one sketched above. Nuclear deterrence, the policymakers said, worked during the Cold War; abolition, owing to the intrinsic nature of the nuclear dilemma, remained impossible; therefore the sensible course was to hold on to nuclear arsenals (albeit at reduced levels, in recognition of the improved political climate). Such was the conclusion of the "bottom-up" review of nuclear policy carried out in the early 1990s by the Clinton administration, and it has never been challenged since. Instead of saying to themselves, "During the protracted emergency that was the Cold War, we made a calculated gamble with the survival of the human race in the name of its freedom and were lucky enough to have survived to tell the story," the policymakers in effect said, "During the Cold War, we perfected a confidence-inspiring system for the management of nuclear weapons that should serve as our model for any future contingency." If deterrence, road-tested during the great U.S.-Soviet conflict, was a proven success, then why give it up now? Didn't "the long peace" of the Cold War demonstrate that the world was better off with nuclear weapons than without them? In Undersecretary of Defense Slocombe's words, "It is a remarkable fact that for almost half a century, the U.S. and its allies faced the U.S.S.R. and its coerced auxiliaries in the division over ideology, power, culture, and the very definition of man, the state, and the world, and did so armed to the greatest extent huge sacrifice would afford, and yet did not fight a large-scale war. No one can say for sure why that success was achieved for long enough for communism to collapse of its own internal weakness. But can anyone really doubt that nuclear weapons had a role?"

Thus, at just the moment that a revolution in the international sphere seemed to call for a full-scale reappraisal of nuclear policy, the previous policy was reaffirmed with fewer reservations than ever before. Others embraced the positive role of nuclear weapons in even stronger terms. In the words of the nuclear theorist James May, "Nuclear weapons are not all that is needed to make war obsolete, but they have no real substitute." Because they "cheaply and predictably destroy whatever both sides are fighting for" and "destroy the battlefield as well as the enemy," they "are essential" for maintenance of global peace.

American thinking had come full circle. Preventing war, of course, had been the great unrealized goal of both Woodrow Wilson's beloved League of Nations and the United Nations. The new view, which might be called nuclear Wilsonianism, was that nuclear weapons could accomplish what these ambitious global institutions had not—the abolition of war (or, at least, of world war). Thus, in brief, did the United States, in the 46 years between Hiroshima and the end of the Cold War, make the passage from abolitionism to its current profound and complacent belief in the virtue of nuclear arms.

The post–Cold War nuclear policies of the United States have been easy to misunderstand. Both President Bush and President Clinton have been given to claiming that nuclear danger is a thing of the past—that, as Clinton has said, "for the first time since the dawn of the nuclear age, the children of [pick your state] are not at risk of nuclear war." Both presidents also were committed to the policy of gradual reductions. Clinton has continued to pay the lip service to abolition required by Article VI of the NPT, but as a matter of actual policy, the United States has remained committed to retaining arsenals of thousands of warheads indefinitely.

In the early 1990s, the damaging consequences of this decision were hidden. The non-Russian republics that succeeded the Soviet Union were persuaded to surrender the nuclear weapons that had wound up on their soil, and South Africa's apartheid regime, anticipating majority rule, dismantled its nuclear-weapons program. France began a series of tests but curtailed them in the face of intense public condemnation. Not until the latter half of the decade did the damage become apparent.

Under these conditions, the third stage of American strategic thinking—in which deterrence won previously unequalled support and policymakers sought to reconcile it with a policy of nonproliferation—has begun to break apart, and a fourth stage has begun to loom. In this stage, the decision between possession (justified by deterrence) and nonproliferation will have to be made. The fissures dividing the two courses are already deep and wide. They appeared, for instance, in the world's reaction to India's nuclear tests. The United States and a few other countries promptly announced sanctions. But their resolve was weak, the sanctions were soon badly eroded, and Clinton, the leader of the drive for sanctions, soon made the first state visit to India by an American president in nearly a quarter-century. The recent history of relations with Iraq tells the same story. The United States sought to prevent Iraq from acquiring nuclear weapons—first by requiring Iraq to accept U.N. weapons inspectors and then by the direct use of air strikes. Iraq remained defiant, and now the international community has no reliable instruments for the achievement of its goal. The lesson is clear: Countries that possess nuclear weapons and mean to keep them are in an inherently weak position when they face countries determined to develop these same arms. The possessor nations not only cannot control the debate; they can scarcely get into the conversation.

NUCLEAR WILSONIANISM

IN RESPONSE to the crisis of this fourth stage, some have frankly decided to resolve the contradiction in favor of proliferation. The political scientist Kenneth Waltz, for example, has argued in detail that it is a mistake to suppose that "new nuclear states will be less responsible and capable of self-control than old ones have been." Hence, he writes, "the gradual spread of nuclear weapons is more to be welcomed than feared." A world "with more nuclear states" will have a more "promising future." And John Mearsheimer of the University of Chicago has called for "managed proliferation" and would welcome acquisition of the bomb by Germany, Japan, and one or more eastern European countries. In the third stage of the development of nuclear strategy, deterrence was embraced, but only for a few major powers. Just as we can distinguish between a limited and a general theory of impossibility of nuclear disarmament, so we can distinguish between a limited nuclear Wilsonianism and a general nuclear Wilsonianism. The former school holds that nuclear weapons were a benefit—but only for ourselves and a few privileged friends and adversaries. The latter school, to which Waltz and Mearsheimer belong, holds that nuclear weapons are good for all who feel the need for them. A policy shift from limited nuclear Wilsonianism to general nuclear Wilsonianism would parallel the early shift from Baruch's policy of abolition to the policy of deterrence. Just as, in the earlier period, the American government, despairing of abolition, embraced the more modest goal of arms control, so now the government, in despair of repairing the broken policy of nonproliferation, would embrace global nuclearization. Giving up on a goal whose achievement it sees as impossible—nonproliferation—Washington would aim at the more modest but supposedly achievable goal of superintending a stable transition to a nuclearized world. At that point, the United States' embrace of nuclear weapons, having proceeded step by imperceptible step from 1946 down to the present, would have reached its logical destination. Living with nuclear weapons would then mean living with nuclear weapons on an equal basis with all other nations that wished to have them. This position has the merit, at least, of being attainable. An international order "with more nuclear states" can certainly be achieved and is, in fact, the destination toward which the world is drifting. Doing nothing will be sufficient to bring it about.

Those, however, who find the uncontrolled spread of nuclear weapons (together, almost certainly, with other weapons of mass destruction) terrifying and wish to persevere in the more active and difficult policy of nonproliferation will have to accept that it is fundamentally inconsistent with nuclear possession—and then embrace nuclear abolition. A policy that seeks to marry possession with nonproliferation lacks coherence—in the first place morally, but also militarily, diplomatically, and legally. It is a policy divided against itself. Its moving parts work against each other. Its deeds rise up to knock down its words. For the adverse factors that are breaking down nuclear arms control agreements form a vicious circle. Possession by the current nuclear powers breeds proliferation by new powers; proliferation by new powers breeds defenses in the old ones and undercuts the nuclear test ban; defenses upset the balance of nuclear terror and stalemate arms control; the stalemate of arms control confirms the nuclear powers in their possession of nuclear arsenals; confirmed possession breeds proliferation; and so on.

There are, it is true, countervailing tendencies. In many parts of the world, a steady undertow of nuclear sanity has impeded and slowed what otherwise might already have been a global scramble to obtain nuclear arms. The entire continent of South America, for example, is, in accord with the treaty of Tlatelolco, free of nuclear weapons. Brazil and Argentina—two fully nuclear-capable nations that were the last to join that treaty—proceeded quite far down the path to nuclear armament before turning back. The Cold War and its nuclear balance of terror held no attraction as a model in their eyes. They saw greater safety in the continent-wide abolition of nuclear arms. Africa and the South Pacific have made the same decision. The norm in the family of nations is to be nuclear weapon free, not nuclear armed.

Another broad tendency of the post–Cold War period—democratization—might seem to offer help in reducing nuclear danger. Over the long run, the benefits may appear, but the record so far does not, unfortunately, sustain these hopes. On the evidence, democracy offers no immunity to the nuclear temptation. The world's first nuclear power was, of course, a democracy. Today, six of the world's eight nuclear powers—the United States, the United Kingdom, France, Russia, India, and Israel—are democracies. The democratization of Russia, as noted, did not inspire its democratic adversary, the United States, to seek to liquidate their balance of nuclear terror. In South Asia, democratic India led the way to the nuclearization of the subcontinent.

Great nuclear powers that had committed themselves to abolition would take a dim view of proliferators.

Modest successes in one strand or another of nuclear arms control are still possible. Perhaps the Senate will reverse itself and pass the CTBT. Conceivably, Russia, yielding to financial need and U.S. pressure, will accept some modification of the ABM treaty and implement START II. Yet it is getting harder by the day to imagine, given the tight connections between possession and proliferation, that the deterioration and even collapse of the fabric of nuclear arms control can be stopped absent a commitment to abolition. The bare existence of the world's present nuclear arsenals poses the ever-present danger of unimaginable catastrophe. Amid the legitimate concern regarding proliferation, it is easy to forget that nuclear peril flows from the nations that possess nuclear weapons, not from those that don't.

DANGER AND SURVIVAL

BUT WOULD EVEN a commitment by the nuclear powers to abolition serve to stop proliferation? Or has the world, perhaps without realizing it, proceeded so far down the path of nuclearization that a reversal is impossible, as the nuclear Wilsonians argue?

Even if the will were present, the practical obstacles would be immense. Basic security policies of half a century would have to undergo authentic "bottom-up" reviews in all the great powers. The conventional balances among them would have to be readjusted all over the world. There are few areas of actual or potential regional conflict—for example, East Asia, the Middle East, South Asia—in which the consequences would not be profound. The technical and diplomatic arrangements necessary to undergird abolition would be even more complex than those surrounding current arms negotiations. The inspections regime alone would have to be a masterpiece of science, diplomacy, and statecraft.

We must distinguish, however, between the achievement of the goal—destruction of the world's very last nuclear warhead—and the commitment to the goal. To reverse proliferation and start immediately to radically reduce nuclear danger, the destruction of the last warhead is not necessary. But the commitment by the nuclear powers to do so is. Figures of 2,500 and 1,500 nuclear weapons are already on the Russian-American negotiating table. The stages below these figures should, after suitable study, be delineated. A moment should be identified at which the lesser nuclear powers would be expected to join in the negotiations and begin to draw down their own arsenals. Qualitative steps, beginning with taking nuclear arsenals off their states of alert, would be planned. The expectations that the nuclear powers—once thoroughly embarked on their historic course—had of other nations, including those otherwise inclined to proliferate, would be specified. For example, from the outset, a sort of global freeze might go into effect, under which all countries with nuclear weapons would commit themselves to a process leading to abolition, and countries without nuclear weapons would be required to persevere in their vow not to acquire them. Increasingly severe transparency, inspections, and provisions to control nuclear-weapon materials such as enriched uranium and plutonium could be negotiated promptly. The countries that had embarked on nuclear disarmament would agree on steps to take if proliferation was discovered.

Only by imagining this scene of comprehensively transformed expectations does the power of a policy of committing the world to nuclear abolition emerge—not as a remote vision but as an active force from the moment the commitment is made. Great nuclear powers that had committed themselves to nuclear abolition and taken serious steps toward that goal would have a far different attitude toward proliferators than those who plan to depend indefinitely on nuclear weapons for their ultimate security. They would possess a degree of will to enforce nonproliferation that the U.N. Security Council quite lacks at present. Under the above new conditions, a non-nuclear nation seeking openly to build a nuclear arsenal would arouse the anger and retaliation of the world. Consider again the case of Iraq. Saddam Hussein's strategy has been to kick out the U.N. inspectors at his pleasure and then play one great power off against another—for instance, Russia and France against the United States and the United Kingdom—as they attempt to reintroduce controls. Such tactics would be at an end if all of these countries had made the commitment to eliminate their nuclear arsenals. Nuclear powers that had jointly agreed to abolish their arsenals and were in the midst of so doing would be planning to rely on that agreement for their security to the same extent that they now rely on their nuclear arsenals. Would they let Saddam have what they were renouncing? They would possess an implacable will, based on the most elemental national interest, to stop proliferation, and they would possess the wherewithal to do it—including, certainly, the resolve and means to defeat and overthrow the offending regime. Curiously, today, it is just because the nuclear powers rely for their security on their own nuclear arsenals that they lack the will to eliminate Saddam's nuclear, chemical, and biological weapons programs.

The path to solving the nuclear dilemma runs through U.S. politics.

Is the argument circular? Does it say that countries would have the will to stop proliferation if only they had the will to stop proliferation? Not at all. Political will, where it exists, is a reality. The resolve to proceed to a world without nuclear weapons would be a dominant fact in the life of the world, from which dramatic consequences would flow long before abolition was achieved.

How, though, can the commitment by the United States and the other nuclear powers be signaled, and why should nations that lack nuclear arsenals but think they might eventually need them believe that commitment? Every now and then, a U.S. official will say that the United States wishes to eliminate all nuclear weapons. Remarks of this kind scarcely assure the world that the destination is in sight. Nor, of course, should they. A policy is not a dream. A policy is a plan of action that you believe can happen and that you intend to make happen. A president who intends to commit the United States to a policy of negotiating the abolition of nuclear weapons would not announce the fact in answer to a question at a press conference or in the peroration to some speech on an unrelated subject. Abolition is not a goal at which the world will arrive (to paraphrase the old saying about Britain's acquisition of its empire) through a fit of absence of mind. (Only proliferation can be achieved through absent-mindedness.) For such a commitment to be real—credible, to adapt a key word from nuclear strategy—a number of things would have to happen. A president who meant to embark on this path would have to make abolition an issue in the election campaign to acquire a public mandate. Without this, the destination could not possibly be reached in a democracy. Upon being elected, the new president would choose, among others, secretaries of state and defense who publicly agreed with the abolition policy, and would battle to win their confirmation in the Senate. The president would give a solemn address to the nation—the first of many on the subject—announcing the initiative. This president would then launch an interagency review—or perhaps, first, a presidential commission—to study the feasibility and the precise features, in all their immense complexity, of a nuclear-weapon-free world. The president would then consult with the United States' allies and approach the two next-greatest nuclear powers, Russia and China, and would, at the same time, seek bipartisan support, without which the initiative could never succeed and probably should not be launched. To paraphrase the old saying about revolution, nuclear abolition is not a tea party, and anything less than a full-scale effort backed by the nation as a whole would be stillborn.

The path to a solution of the nuclear dilemma passes first through domestic politics. The public must give its permission and support. As it happens, the Senate's rejection of the CTBT and a furor over NMD have intruded the nuclear question into the current presidential race. Governor George W. Bush of Texas has taken the initiative with a bold if vague proposal. He has made the welcome statement that "our mutual security need no longer depend on a nuclear balance of terror." Today's large arsenals, he has said, "are the expensive relics of dead conflicts. And they do nothing to make us more secure." He would cut them to an unspecified "lowest possible number." At the same time, though, he would deploy missile defenses far more ambitious than even those favored by the Clinton administration. The problem with Bush's program is that his plans for reductions collide with his plans for missile defense. He will not be able to get to his low number if missile defenses stoke nuclear buildups in Russia and China. On the Democratic side, Vice President Al Gore supports the Clinton policies—that is, pursuing reductions, but not below the floor of 2,500 nuclear warheads on the U.S. side. The problems with the Gore approach are the problems with the Clinton policy; an indefinitely held arsenal of thousands of nuclear weapons is a recipe for proliferation. The way to make sense of both positions is the same: a commitment to abolition. If Bush's "lowest possible number" is zero for all nations, his defenses will no longer be destabilizing. Whether possessed by the United States alone or, as Reagan suggested, shared with Russia and other nations, missile defenses could help safeguard a world free of nuclear weapons against secret or open nuclear re-armament. If Gore embraces zero, he will have in his hand the basis for a program that can truly deal with what he calls the greatest threat to American security, nuclear proliferation.

But even a president's intentions alone would not suffice. The nation would have to respond positively. A full-scale debate in the news media, universities, and civil society would have to ensue. Is safety to be found in nuclear arms or in their elimination? Can inspection of an abolition agreement be adequate? What should be the disposition of conventional forces—American and other? Would defense spending rise or fall? What should be done if a country violates the agreement? These and many other questions of similar importance have not been answered. They have not, in any national debate worthy of the name, even been asked.

JONATHAN SCHELL is the author of *The Fate of the Earth, The Abolition,* and *The Gift of Time.* He is a former staff writer for *The New Yorker.*

The Asian Nuclear Reaction Chain

by Joseph Cirincione

Even the casual observer, more concerned with markets than missiles, will have noticed the faltering of global efforts to stop the spread of weapons of mass destruction. Hardly a day passes without a new story about the threat of nuclear war in South Asia, North Korea's ballistic missile program, Russia's unsecured nuclear arsenal, Chinese nuclear espionage, or worries over nascent Iranian and Iraqi efforts to develop nuclear, chemical, and biological weapons.

Such dismal headlines are a far cry from the optimism that prevailed in 1993 when the United States and Russia signed the second Strategic Arms Reduction Treaty (START II)—Boris Yeltsin called it "the treaty of hope"—and spoke of further reductions in nuclear arsenals worldwide. Subsequent events gave an added boost to global arms control efforts. World leaders lined up to renew the Nuclear Non-Proliferation Treaty (NPT) and sign the Comprehensive Test Ban Treaty (CTBT). Nations throughout Africa and Southeast Asia declared themselves Nuclear-Weapon-Free Zones. In the United States, some policy makers spoke earnestly of eliminating nuclear weapons altogether.

Today, not only does the world seem a more dangerous place, but Washington is locked in a contentious debate about what will make it safer. A broad, if rough-hewn, cold war consensus on the importance of negotiated threat reduction has dissolved into a free-for-all tangle over differing assessments of American vulnerabilities, defense spending, and the nature of U.S. global engagement. The U.S. Senate stunned the world when it rejected the test ban treaty last year. Now it seems probable that the Anti-Ballistic Missile (ABM) Treaty is the next pact headed for the chopping block.

There is plenty of blame to go around for the unraveling of arms control. The Russian Duma has dragged out ratification of START II for more than seven years. The British and French insisted on onerous provisions that handicapped the CTBT at birth. Militant Hindu nationalism ignited an Indian-Pakistani arms race with a single atomic blast. The Chinese and North Koreans persist in making political statements via missiles instead of missives. And, of course, America's favorite villain, Saddam Hussein, is still in power and still developing his lethal arsenal of secret chemical, biological, and possibly nuclear weapons.

The United States may not be responsible for this current state of affairs, but its failed leadership is making matters worse. The Clinton administration, through inattention and indecision, squandered priceless opportunities to lock in its initial successes and move quickly beyond them. The door was left open for die-hard opponents of arms control in Congress to step in and dominate the debate over how best to respond to the challenges posed by today's would-be weapons states. Treaties lull the country into a false sense of security, they say, as America keeps to them while other nations cheat. Worse still, multilateral arrangements weaken America like "Gulliver in the land of Lilliputians, stretched out, unable to move, because he has been tied down by a whole host of threads," as Senator Jeff Sessions warned his colleagues during the debate over the test ban treaty. The Senate defeat of the CTBT crystallized the arms control mantra now popular among conservatives: Distrust treaties, increase defenses, and assert American authority.

The rethinking and rejection of arms control is not just the work of a few right-wing congressmen. Senator Rich-

Back on the Brink

An excerpt from "**Half Past India's Bang**," by Lewis A. Dunn (FOREIGN POLICY, Fall 1979):

Just over five years have passed since India exploded a nuclear device in May 1974. Seen by many observers as auguring the spread of nuclear weapons to politically unstable, less developed countries in the 1980s and 1990s, that test helped awaken high-level policy concern in the United States about nuclear proliferation. While some developments since then have decreased the prospects for proliferation, other factors suggest that the current equilibrium is actually quite unstable. . . .

The most important proliferation firebreak in Asia is clearly between the covert or overt acquisition of nuclear weapons by either Taiwan or South Korea and the development of such weapons by Japan. Strengthening that firebreak will require the preservation of the remaining American security connection with each country even after its acquisition of nuclear weapons. Eliminating the security commitment out of either concern about the risks of continued ties or the desire to make an example of the new proliferator would have to be avoided. For such action and its potential consequences—ranging from a Chinese preemptive strike against Taiwan's new nuclear force to nuclear conflict on the Korean peninsula—would further disrupt the Asian strategic-political order, unsettle Japanese calculations, and reinforce doubts in Japan about the U.S. commitment to its security. This might just trigger rapid rearmament by Japan and could even result in a Japanese nuclear-weapons program. . . .

The Asian situation is particularly striking because it illustrates the occasional tension between nonproliferation policy as usually defined and attempts to build firebreaks. A major factor restraining Taiwan and South Korea from developing nuclear-weapons capabilities is the fear that the United States will sever its security ties with them in reaction. But if either country became convinced that the United States would instead seek to integrate that country's new nuclear program into a broader Asian security structure to avoid the even more unsettling event of Japanese nuclearization, that country's estimation of the risks of going nuclear would change drastically.

ard Lugar—one of the architects of the program that helped denuclearize Ukraine, Belarus, and Kazakhstan after those nations inherited thousands of nuclear weapons from the Soviet Union—voted against the test ban. Henry Kissinger—the strategist behind the ABM Treaty and the first Strategic Arms Limitation Treaty, or SALT I—epitomizes the new centrist-conservative thinking. He says that he is not against arms control, just bad arms control, such as the test ban and the ABM Treaty today. He believes we can pick and choose the arms control agreements we like, such as the Non-Proliferation Treaty (by which 182 nations have agreed not to develop nuclear weapons), the Missile Technology Control Regime (which restricts exports of missile technology), and the Australia Group (which restricts chemical and biological exports).

Many arms control critics reject the very idea of negotiated arms reductions as a cold war relic, unsuited for the current era. Now that superpower conflict is over, the logic holds, our strategy needs to change to accommodate "a world of terror and missiles and madmen," to borrow a phrase from presidential candidate George W. Bush.

Those who claim to be reinventing arms control for the future are, in fact, turning their backs on history. Nuclear proliferation among so-called rogue states is not the primary problem. As far back as the early 1960s, policy makers recognized the greatest threat to U.S. security was not that Third World despots might acquire the bomb, but that advanced industrial countries might do so. Few people recall that President John F. Kennedy's oft-quoted warning that "fifteen or twenty or twenty-five nations may have [nuclear] weapons" in the next decade was directed at Japan, Italy, Germany, Sweden, and other European nations that were developing weapons programs. Nuclear weapons in "the hands of countries large and small, stable and unstable," Kennedy worried, would create "the increased chance of accidental war, and an increased necessity for the great powers to involve themselves in what otherwise would be local conflicts."

Kennedy's arms control vision, negotiated by President Lyndon Johnson and implemented by President Richard Nixon, has proved to be a global success story. Since the signing of the NPT in 1968, the treaty regime has greatly restricted the spread of weapons of mass destruction. But Kennedy's legacy is now under siege, and the nonproliferation clock may be set back to the 1960s. If the United States disassembles diplomatic restraints, shatters carefully crafted threat reduction arrangements, and moves from builder to destroyer of the nonproliferation regime, then there will be little to prevent new nations from concluding that their national security requires nuclear arms. Taking elements we don't like out of the regime structure starts a dangerous round of *Jenga,* the tabletop game where blocks are sequentially removed from a wooden tower until the whole structure collapses.

The blocks would fall quickest and hardest in Asia, where proliferation pressures are already building more quickly than anywhere else in the world. If a nuclear breakout takes place in Asia, then the international arms control agreements that have been painstakingly negotiated over the past 40 years will crumble. Moreover, the United States could find itself embroiled in its fourth war on the Asian continent in six decades—a costly rebuke to those who seek the safety of Fortress America by hiding behind national missile defenses.

Consider what is already happening: North Korea continues to play guessing games with its nuclear and missile programs; South Korea wants its own missiles to match Pyongyang's; India and Pakistan shoot across borders while running a slow-motion nuclear arms race;

Associated Press

Honk if you want war: India's Agni-2 missile, which can carry conventional or nuclear warheads, is capable of striking targets within Pakistan and China.

China modernizes its nuclear arsenal amid tensions with Taiwan and the United States; Japan's vice defense minister is forced to resign after extolling the benefits of nuclear weapons; and Russia—whose Far East nuclear deployments alone make it the largest Asian nuclear power—struggles to maintain territorial coherence.

Five of these states have nuclear weapons; the others are capable of constructing them. Like neutrons firing from a split atom, one nation's actions can trigger reactions throughout the region, which in turn, stimulate additional actions. These nations form an interlocking Asian nuclear reaction chain that vibrates dangerously with each new development.

If the frequency and intensity of this reaction cycle increase, critical decisions taken by any one of these governments could cascade into the second great wave of nuclear-weapon proliferation, bringing regional and global economic and political instability and, perhaps, the first combat use of a nuclear weapon since 1945.

Approaching Critical Mass

The threat of nuclear breakout in Asia has been around for years. South Korea and Taiwan, for example, flirted with nuclear-weapon programs in the 1970s but backed down under U.S pressure. India detonated a "peaceful nuclear device" in 1974, but then eschewed further tests or development [see box Back on the Brink]. There are, however, two new developments that make the current situation so volatile. First, technologies and capabilities have advanced to the point where more nations could proceed rapidly to nuclear-weapon status, if they reached the political decision to do so. Second, the United States is backing away from its commitments to the international nonproliferation regime and undertaking actions—such as the deployment of missile defense systems—that could catalyze the reaction chain.

Developments within Japan illustrate how these two dynamics interact in new and dangerous ways. In 1998, Japan was caught by surprise when the Indian-Pakistani tit-for-tat nuclear tests suddenly doubled the number of Asian nuclear-weapon states. Many Japanese were then disturbed by how quickly the world accepted India and Pakistan's de facto status as new nuclear powers. This was not the bargain the Japanese had agreed to when—after a lengthy internal debate—they joined the NPT in 1976. North Korea's launch of a long-range Taepo Dong missile further agitated the Japanese public and political leaders, stirring new debates about Japan's military and nuclear policies. "Japan must be like NATO countries," declared then Vice Defense Minister Shingo Nishimura. "We ought to have aircraft carriers, long-range missiles, long-range bombers. We should even have the atomic bomb." Nishimura was forced to resign over his comments, but he is not alone in his sentiment, nor is South Asia the only concern in Japan. "If North Korea obtains nuclear weapons," warned Yoshifuni Okamura, the former deputy director of the Nuclear Division of the Foreign Ministry of Japan, "this could weaken our commitment to the NPT."

If tensions rise and nuclear-weapon deployments increase in Asia, Japan may well conclude that its security is best served not by relying on the U.S. nuclear umbrella, but by building its own nuclear arsenal. Japan's withdrawal from the NPT would almost certainly trigger the collapse of the treaty. Some in Asia might soon decide to follow Japan's lead, while others might hedge their bets and begin nuclear-weapon research programs. Iran and Iraq, among others, would likely openly accelerate their programs.

Japan has powerful reasons for remaining a non-nuclear-weapon state, and it is unlikely to act precipitously. However, the primary barriers to a Japanese nuclear-weapon program are political and psychological, not technical. If the political dynamics in Asia continue to shift, Japan could move quickly.

Japan's plutonium-based nuclear-energy infrastructure has produced a large stockpile of plutonium that could be utilized in a rapid nuclear buildup. Through plutonium reprocessing contracts with Great Britain and France, Japan had acquired approximately 24.1 metric tons of separated, reactor-grade plutonium as of 1997. It has been estimated that 7 kilograms of reactor-grade plutonium are necessary to build an explosive device of about 20 kilotons (as a point of reference, the atomic bomb dropped on Hiroshima exploded with the force of about 15 kilotons). An advanced warhead design—well

Japan

Vital Statistics:
Population (Millions): 126.5
GDP (Billions of U.S.$): 3,800.0
Defense Expenditures
(Billions of U.S.$): 37.7
Defense Expenditures
(As Percent of GDP): 1.0

Nuclear Notes:
- Massive civilian nuclear-power program possessed 24.1 tons of plutonium by 1997; amount could grow to 80 tons by 2010.
- Developing advanced laser-isotope uranium enrichment techniques.
- Highly developed scientific infrastructure could produce a nuclear warhead in a few months.
- Advanced space launchers could quickly be converted into ballistic missiles.

"There is no doubt that Japan is technically and financially capable of building a bomb."

-Tsutomu Hata, then prime minister, 1994

Source for spending data: International Institute for Strategic Studies, *The Military Balance 1999/2000* (London: Oxford University Press, 1999). All figures in 1998 dollars.

within reach of Japan's technical abilities—could reduce the amount to 4 kilograms or less.

Japan's sophisticated space-launch vehicles could quickly be converted into ballistic missiles. Its M-5 rocket compares roughly in thrust and payload capacity with the intercontinental MX Peacekeeper of the U.S. arsenal. Technical failures recently forced Japan to abandon its $4 billion H-2 space-launcher program, but it is now proceeding with the H-2A, which has a more advanced engine and more power than its predecessors.

As long as countries such as Japan possess the capabilities to develop a nuclear arsenal, it is critical that the political and diplomatic deterrents to the spread of weapons of mass destruction remain strong and viable. Japan will seriously consider its nuclear options if it comes to believe that the United States and other nuclear-weapon states no longer have any intention of pursuing "effective measures relating to cessation of the nuclear arms race at an early date and to nuclear disarmament," as required under Article VI of the NPT.

Nuclear Dominoes

Japan will carefully watch South Asia—the area of the world most likely to see a nuclear weapon used in combat. Here, for the first time, two nuclear-armed nations share a common border and a history of armed conflict. Shamshad Ahmed, the Pakistani foreign secretary, has declared: "If India operationalizes its nuclear weapons, then Pakistan will be obliged to follow suit." Both nations are developing new missiles and crafting nuclear-deployment doctrines. Political instability and underdeveloped command and control systems in both nations raise serious concerns about the ability of either country to implement adequate nuclear safeguards and controls. India and Pakistan's 1999 summer clash over Kashmir came "very close" to a nuclear exchange, according to one diplomatic source. The disputed mountain region, which has been the cause of two past wars between India and Pakistan, remains a frightening flash point.

But the Asian reaction chain is more than a South Asian rivalry gone nuclear. India's nuclear tests and current deployment plans have much more to do with China and the United States than Pakistan. Most experts date the beginning of the Indian nuclear program to China's 1964 test.

China, in turn, says it was forced to develop its nuclear weapons to counter the United States. Historians on both sides of the Pacific detail at least five specific instances of threats by the United States to use nuclear weapons against China at times when China possessed no such capability. During the Korean War, for example, General Douglas MacArthur wanted to use atomic bombs and artillery to decimate Chinese forces and drive them from Korea, and then lay down "fields of suitable radio-active materials" to keep the Chinese off the peninsula for centuries to come.

China

Vital Statistics:
Population (Millions): 1,244.0
GDP (Billions of U.S.$): 703.0
Defense Expenditures
(Billions of U.S.$): 37.5
Defense Expenditures
(As Percent of GDP): 5.3

Nuclear Notes:
- Third-largest nuclear power, with approximately 450 nuclear weapons.
- Could build over 2,700 nuclear weapons with existing fissile material stockpiles.
- Deployed approximately 20 Dong Feng-5 nuclear missiles that could reach the West Coast of the United States.
- Gradually modernizing ballistic missile fleet.

"Any amendment, or abolishing of the [ABM] Treaty will lead to disastrous consequences."

-Sha Zukang, arms control director, Chinese Foreign Ministry, November 1999

Source for spending data: International Institute for Strategic Studies, *The Military Balance 1999/2000* (London: Oxford University Press, 1999). All figures in 1998 dollars.

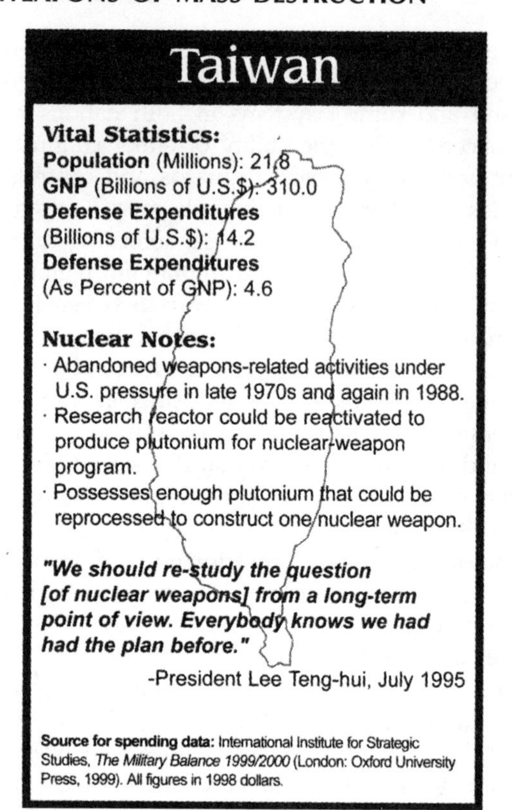

China's leaders concluded that they needed to develop their own nuclear weapons. Their logic is summarized in the famous "Los Angeles" quote, which former U.S. Ambassador Chas Freeman says he has been trying to correct ever since it came out in garbled form in the *New York Times.* Freeman reports that at the end of a heated discussion over China's pressure tactics on Taiwan, a Chinese general told him: "you do not have the strategic leverage that you had in the 1950s when you threatened nuclear strikes on us. You were able to do that because we could not hit back. But if you hit us now, we can hit back. So you will not make those threats. In the end you care more about Los Angeles than you do about Taipei." Rather than a threat, which is how the statement has been portrayed in the United States, the full statement illustrates China's view that it is just reacting to U.S. provocations.

The Chain Grows

The United States, already worried by Chinese threats to Taiwan and (in some quarters) about the rise of a potentially powerful Asian competitor, is advancing what seems to many a perfectly reasonable response: missile defense systems. Pushed by domestic politics and new proliferation threat assessments, the United States both promotes such deployments and seeks Japanese and Taiwanese cooperation. "Only effective missile defenses, not unenforceable arms control treaties," Senate Majority Leader Trent Lott said after the South Asian nuclear tests, "will break the offensive arms race in Asia and provide incentives to address security concerns without a nuclear response." Missile defenses, however, have a dual nature. Although they promise an alluring technological solution to one type of mass destruction delivery system, mere talk of their introduction stimulates the very arsenals they hope to deter.

Taiwan and Japan both initially dismissed missile defense as technically unfeasible and financially debilitating. Taiwan's political leaders, however, now embrace joint defense efforts as a way to bind the United States closer to Taiwan's security. Japan, spurred by North Korea's launch of a Taepo Dong missile and seeking to demonstrate its strategic value to the United States, has now agreed to help finance and develop a new theater missile defense system. Although such systems are unlikely to provide much military capability, talk of deployments has provoked a sharp reaction from the Chinese, who fear both the intentions of a newly assertive Japan and the neutralization of their own nuclear-deterrent force. "First the shield, then the sword," China warns (with living memories of the Japanese occupation). An editorial in *China Daily* is typical, finding it "difficult to believe that [North Korea] constitutes a substantial security threat to Japan" and accusing conservative politicians of using "nonexistent" military threats "to override Japan's Pacifist Constitution and to expand Japan's political influence on the international stage."

North Korea

Vital Statistics:
Population (Millions): 21.5
GNP (Billions of U.S.$): 14.0
Defense Expenditures
(Billions of U.S.$): 2.0
Defense Expenditures
(As Percent of GNP): 14.3

Nuclear Notes:
- Reprocessed enough plutonium by early 1990s to construct one to two nuclear weapons.
- Current spent fuel stocks could yield four or five nuclear weapons if reprocessed.
- In 1994, agreed to freeze nuclear program and relinquish spent fuel stocks in exchange for two light water reactors from the United States and South Korea.
- Deployed No Dong missile that can strike Japan; developing Taepo Dong-2 missile that could reach Alaska.

"We are fully ready to mercilessly annihilate the U.S. imperialists and the South Korean rulers who are keen on invading the D.P.R.K.."

-KCNA News Agency,
November 24, 1999

Source for spending data: International Institute for Strategic Studies, *The Military Balance 1999/2000* (London: Oxford University Press, 1999). All figures in 1998 dollars.

India

Vital Statistics:
Population (Millions): 1,000.0
GDP (Billions of U.S.$): 469.0
Defense Expenditures
(Billions of U.S.$): 14.1
Defense Expenditures
(As Percent of GDP): 3.0

Nuclear Notes:
- Tested five nuclear devices in 1998.
- May possess enough weapons-grade plutonium for 40-90 nuclear weapons.
- Has tested Agni-2 ballistic missile, capable of striking Pakistan and southwestern China.
- Not a member of Non-Proliferation Treaty regime.

"We certainly have tensions and disputes with Pakistan, but for a country like India, Pakistan is not our biggest threat. The biggest threat is China."

-George Fernandes, Indian defense minister, following the 1998 nuclear tests

Source for spending data: International Institute for Strategic Studies, *The Military Balance 1999/2000* (London: Oxford University Press, 1999). All figures in 1998 dollars.

Similarly, neither China nor Russia believes that the United States needs a national missile defense system to protect itself from North Korean missiles. Both see missile defense deployments as part of a strategy to allow the United States to launch a first strike at their nuclear weapons and then use missile defenses to minimize the damage from a retaliatory strike. Missile defense deployment plans have played a major role in derailing Russian Duma ratification of the START II nuclear-reduction agreement and planned START III negotiations. China recently announced it would spend an additional $9.7 billion to upgrade its nuclear-forces modernization program to allow for "a vigorous counterattack once hegemonists and their military alliance use nuclear weapons to make a surprise attack on China," according to General Zhang Wannian of the People's Liberation Army. Pressure from military leaders to enlarge further the nuclear arsenal will increase if India deploys significant numbers of nuclear weapons.

Nuclear Wild Cards

As if matters weren't bad enough, there are two entirely new Asian risks emerging: the possible fragmentation of Russia into separate, nuclear-armed states and the possible unification of Korea as a country with nuclear capabilities and ambitions. The final outcome of these scenarios will depend a great deal on what the rest of the world is doing. If the international community moves toward reducing and eliminating nuclear weapons, then these new nations will likely follow the lead of Ukraine and South Africa, which gave up their nuclear weapons in the early 1990s as their governments changed. If these new nations find themselves in a world with an increasing number of nuclear-weapon states, they may well opt to join the club.

In 1991, Ukraine, Belarus, and Kazakhstan inherited thousands of nuclear weapons after the breakup of the Soviet Union. Dedicated and skilled diplomacy by the United States resulted in one of the greatest arms control achievements of the post-cold-war era: the partial dismantlement and return of all those warheads to Russia and the accession of these three nations to the NPT as non-nuclear-weapon states. The world breathed a sigh of relief. But it may have exhaled too soon; the disintegration of the former Soviet Union may not be over. Many of Russia's states are becoming increasingly independent of Moscow's rule, especially the Asian regions. There are more than 4,100 nuclear weapons in the Ural, Siberian, Transbaikal, and Far Eastern Military Districts of Asian Russia. The soldiers and sailors operating and controlling these weapons depend more and more on local governments for their food, fuel, and shelter.

As Moscow's control weakens, regional leaders are beginning to assert their authority. In 1998, Alexander Lebed, the retired general and now governor of the Krasnoyarsk region in Siberia, informed then Prime Min-

Pakistan

Vital Statistics:
Population (Millions): 144.4
GDP (Billions of U.S.$): 61.0
Defense Expenditures
(Billions of U.S.$): 4.0
Defense Expenditures
(As Percent of GDP): 6.5

Nuclear Notes:
- Tested five or six nuclear devices in 1998.
- May possess enough weapons-grade uranium for 22-43 nuclear weapons.
- Has tested Ghauri-2 ballistic missile, capable of striking anywhere in India.
- Not a member of Non-Proliferation Treaty regime.

"If India operationalizes its nuclear weapons, then Pakistan will be obliged to follow suit."

-Shamshad Ahmed, Pakistani foreign secretary, August 1999

Source for spending data: International Institute for Strategic Studies, *The Military Balance 1999/2000* (London: Oxford University Press, 1999). All figures in 1998 dollars.

ister Sergei Kiriyenko that he was considering taking control of the nuclear weapons stationed in his province. The officers of a nuclear unit in his province were "hungry and angry," he said, after months without pay. "We in Krasnoyarsk are not rich yet," he warned, "but in exchange for the status of a nuclear territory, we could feed the formation and become a headache for the world community along with India and Pakistan."

Korea adds another complicating variable. In response to missile deployments to its north, South Korea has demanded not defenses, but its own missiles. "Without a retaliatory missile capability, South Korea's deterrence strategy is nonexistent and its defense insufficient," concludes Kim Tae-woo, director of the Policy Research Office of the United Liberal Democratic Party in Seoul. Whereas North Korea has deployed large numbers of Scud-B and Scud-C missiles (300- and 500-km range), fielded a few No Dong missiles (1,000-km range), and test-fired the Taepo Dong-1 missile (1,500–2,000-km range), South Korea fields only short-range missiles of a 180-km range or less—the maximum range allowed by the informal agreement signed by the Republic of Korea (ROK) and the United States in 1979, which gives the United States control over missile development. South Korean conservatives increasingly chafe at these restrictions and are pressing for 300- and 500-km systems.

If the United States agreed to assist Seoul, it would violate the Missile Technology Control Regime, which bans the transfer or sale of missiles with a range greater than 300 km and carrying a warhead of more than 500 kilograms. Not waiting for U.S. approval, the South Korean government is pressing ahead with plans for a satellite-launch facility to be completed by 2005. "We plan to put the satellite into a low-altitude orbit by then," explained Lee Sang-Mok, chief of the strategic technology development division of the Science and Technology Ministry. Of course, this is exactly what the North Koreans said they were doing with the Taepo Dong launch that triggered harsh Asian and international reactions. How can the United States object to the launch of a Taepo Dong-2 (now on hold pending the results of talks between the United States and North Korea) if South Korea wants to do the same?

Finally, the solution many hope for in Korea—unification—might resolve one set of problems, but usher in new ones. The Korean peninsula has a painful history of repeated invasions from China and Japan. When southern manufacturing expertise unites with northern experience in missile and plutonium production, the Koreans may be tempted to conclude that in a region of nuclear-armed and nuclear-capable states, their security can best be secured through their own nuclear programs. According to the results of a survey conducted by retired Korean General Kim Sang-ho, 96 percent of 300 former ROK generals believe that, following unification, Korea should acquire nuclear weapons, or develop the ability to produce them rapidly.

BREAKING THE CHAIN

Some scholars suggest that Asians are culturally hard-wired to reject arms control agreements. Harvard University's Samuel Huntington and, more recently, Yale University's Paul Bracken, say that the West naively assumed that as these nations liberalized economically they would also adopt Western values—including the stigmatizing of weapons of mass destruction. The West "promotes nonproliferation as a universal norm and nonproliferation treaties and inspections as means of realizing that norm," notes Huntington. "The non-Western nations, on the other hand, assert their right to acquire and to deploy whatever weapons they think necessary for their security," seeing weapons of mass destruction "as the potential equalizer of superior Western conventional power."

India, China, Japan, Indonesia, and other Asian states do not necessarily disagree with Western nonproliferation goals. However, they resent the hypocrisy of the "do as we say, not as we do" sermon. If China modernizes its nuclear arsenal, it is labeled a threat; when the United States does the same, it is said to be necessary for national security. India's nuclear tests prompted President Clinton to declare that nuclear-weapon capability "is not necessary to peace, to security, to prosperity, to national greatness or personal fulfillment," but on NATO'S 50th anniversary the alliance adopted a new security concept that still found U.S. nuclear weapons "vital to the security of Europe." India has gone so far as to denounce the NPT as "nuclear apartheid."

Not a single country that had nuclear weapons when the NPT was signed has given them up. It has also not gone unnoticed in Asia that the United States has been quietly redefining the mission of nuclear weapons to counter all weapons of mass destruction. Ramesh Thakur, vice rector of the United Nations University in Tokyo, echoed the opinion of many Asian strategists when he observed: "If nuclear weapons come to be accepted as having a role in countering biological-chemical warfare, then by what logic can the United States deny a nuclear weapons capability to a country like Iran, which has actually suffered chemical weapons attacks within recent memory?"

A 1995 international conference extended the NPT indefinitely. But the permanence of the treaty was linked to progress toward specific goals, including a test ban and continued reduction in existing arsenals. United Nations Under Secretary-General for Disarmament Affairs Jayantha Dhanapala, who presided over the conference, now sees serious threats arising not just from outside countries but from inside the regime as well, warning that the "permanence of the Treaty does not represent a permanence of unbalanced obligations . . . non-proliferation and disarmament can be pursued only jointly, not at each other's expense." The Spring 2000 NPT Review

Conference is likely to be a contentious affair that will weaken, not strengthen, international norms.

A great deal depends on U.S. policy choices. The United States remains the one nation with the resources, status, and potential leadership capable of galvanizing international nonproliferation efforts. Unless the United States does so, the next president may find himself re-reading and re-issuing Kennedy's apocalyptic warning.

The response has to be more than the arms control a la carte strategy idealistically advocated by Kissinger and others, which would fail miserably to stem these dangers. This approach harkens back to the embryonic strategy of the 1950s, when the United States and a few other nations thought they could stop the spread of weapons of mass destruction by forming supplier groups to contain key technologies, while developing nuclear, biological, chemical, and missile arsenals for themselves. It was precisely the failure of this piecemeal method that brought about the current nonproliferation regime.

But the regime only works as an integrated whole. Without the test ban treaty and serious reductions in U.S. and Russian arsenals, the Non-Proliferation Treaty will lose credibility, suffering a death by lack of interest if not outright defection. Deployment of missile defenses could weaken the Missile Technology Control Regime, thereby encouraging the proliferation of missiles and defensive countermeasures. For those without nuclear-weapon production capabilities, chemical and biological weapons will hold new appeal. As legal, diplomatic, and political deterrents weaken, it will become easier for a nation to shatter the barriers, triggering a global crisis. And such crises are likely to result in more than just diplomatic emergency meetings. Nuclear insecurities and regional tensions could freeze foreign investments, strangling economic growth both regionally and globally.

It would be foolish to let nonproliferation treaties unravel and thereby disarm the United States of its most effective weapons for fighting these threats. Worse, provocative U.S. actions, however defensively intended, could well prove to be the catalyst that sets in motion a chain of events that diplomacy will be powerless to stop. Only by increasing the understanding of the regional dynamics, expanding the national resources devoted to regional and international negotiations, and having the courage to lead by example in reducing nuclear dangers can the United States hope to prevent a nuclear tsunami from sweeping out of Asia.

WANT TO KNOW MORE?

The outlook for arms control and nonproliferation is discussed in Joseph Cirincione, ed., Repairing the Regime: Preventing the Spread of Weapons of Mass Destruction (Washington: Routledge, April 2000) and in Cirincione's article **"The Assault on Arms Control"** (Bulletin of the Atomic Scientists, January/February 2000). Facts and figures on nuclear developments in Asia and around the world are detailed by Rodney W. Jones and Mark G. McDonough, with Toby F. Dalton and Gregory D. Koblentz, in **Tracking Nuclear Proliferation: A Guide in Maps and Charts, 1998** (Washington: Carnegie Endowment for International Peace, 1998). In their article **"National Missile Defense: An Indefensible System"** (FOREIGN POLICY, Winter 1999–2000), George Lewis, Lisbeth Gronlund, and David Wright warn that a U.S. decision to deploy a national missile defense system could undermine nonproliferation efforts worldwide.

The potential for nuclear proliferation in East Asia and its consequences are assessed in Paul J. Bracken's ***Fire in the East: The Rise of Asian Military Power and the Second Nuclear Age*** (New York: HarperCollins, 1999) and Kent E. Calder's ***Pacific Defense: Arms, Energy, and America's Future in Asia*** (New York: William Morrow and Co., 1996). Selig S. Harrison reviews the nuclear potential of Japan in ***Japan's Nuclear Future: The Plutonium Debate and East Asian Security*** (Washington: Carnegie Endowment for International Peace, 1996). Not all of the literature is so bleak: Mitchell Reiss considers the options of various non-Asian countries to forgo nuclear weapons in ***Bridled Ambition: Why Countries Constrain Their Nuclear Capabilities*** (Washington: Woodrow Wilson Center Press, 1995).

Daniel Morrow and Michael Carriere examine economic sanctions as an instrument of nonproliferation in **"The Economic Impacts of the 1998 Sanctions on India and Pakistan"** (*Nonproliferation Review,* Fall 1999). John Wilson Lewis and Xue Litai consider the decisions that drove the creation of China's nuclear program in ***China Builds the Bomb*** (Stanford: Stanford University Press, 1988), and George Perkovich undertakes the same task for India in ***India's Nuclear Bomb: The Impact on Global Proliferation*** (Berkeley: University of California Press, 1999). Perkovich argues that domestic political factors often compel nations to obtain nuclear weapons in his article ***"Think Again: Nuclear Proliferation"*** (FOREIGN POLICY, Fall 1998).

A large set of proliferation-related resources can be found on the Internet. The site of the **Non-Proliferation Project of the Carnegie Endowment for International Peace** provides a useful compilation of the best the Web has to offer, including online chapters from ***Tracking Nuclear Proliferation, 1998.***

For links to this and other relevant Web sites, as well as a comprehensive index of related FOREIGN POLICY articles, access **www.foreignpolicy.com.**

JOSEPH CIRINCIONE *is director of the Non-Proliferation Project at the Carnegie Endowment for International Peace.*

MISSILE DEFENCES

A shield in space

America wants to build a new system of missile defences. This is not popular with others, whether allies or potential foes

LATE next spring, when the ice melts and the wind subsides to a moderate gale, barges based in Seattle may well be making the 3,000-mile voyage to deliver building materials to an Alaskan island called Shemya. The erection of an ultra-sensitive radar installation on this unforgiving terrain, where building is possible only for a few weeks every summer, would mark the first step in a crash programme to provide the United States with a shield against certain limited types of rocket attack.

Although the Pentagon has already embarked on half-a-dozen other programmes designed to stop missiles in mid-flight, this will be the first time a nuclear power has openly set out to defend its entire territory from such attacks. But before the barges can start plying the north Pacific, a big change will have occurred, for better or worse, in international diplomacy. From the moment the first concrete is poured into Shemya's soil, the United States will be in breach of the current terms of the 1972 Anti-Ballistic Missile (ABM) treaty, under which America and the Soviet Union agreed that neither would build a comprehensive defence against the other's long-range nuclear arsenal.

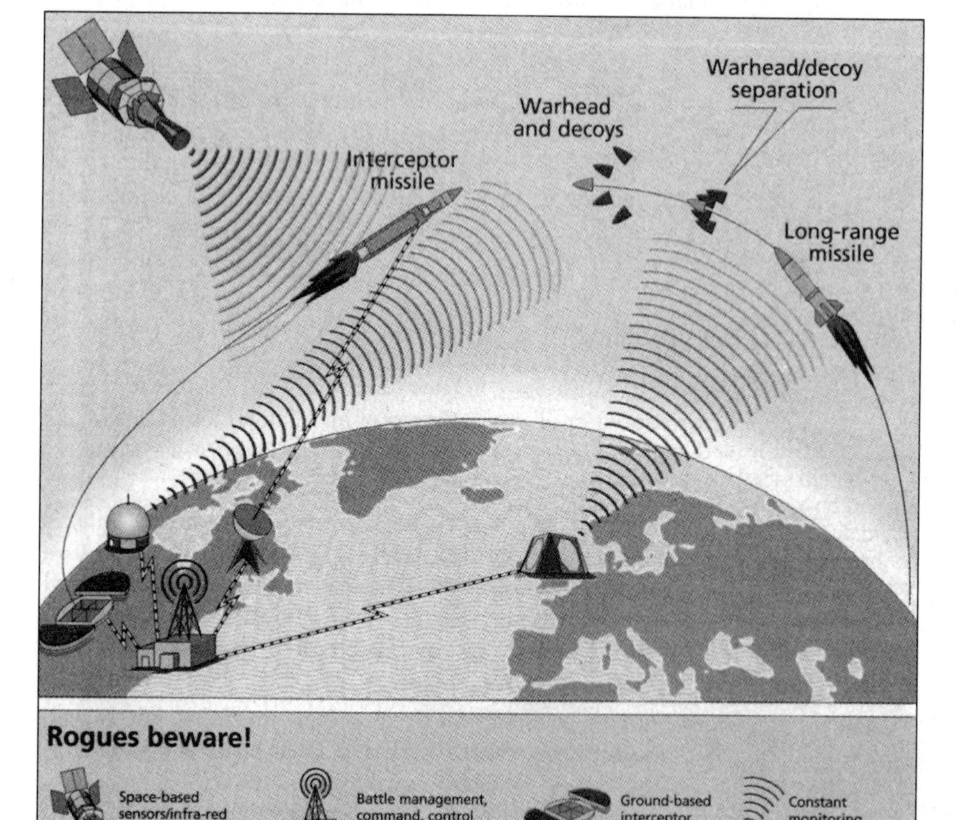

SOURCE: PENATAGON (adapted from Ballistic Missile Defence Organisation).

That accord, designed as a guarantee against a "first strike" by either side, has been widely criticised, especially on America's political right, as a hangover from the cold war that is no longer useful in a world where any rogue state can acquire deadly missiles. Russia and China, on the other hand, have expressed horror at the idea of abrogating the treaty. They fear (plausibly in China's case, less so in Russia's) that their own nuclear arsenals could be rendered useless by an American shield—while America could still use its rockets with impunity.

Among the main provisions of the treaty are strict curbs on the construction of radars powerful enough to track incoming missiles in space. So, before starting to build the $500m radar in Alaska, the American government must do one of two things. It could exercise its option to withdraw from the ABM treaty on six months' notice—which would delight Republicans in Congress, but could plunge relations with Russia and China into crisis and strain the Atlantic alliance.

The alternative course, which President Bill Clinton hopes to follow during his final months in office, is to negotiate with Russia the changes to the treaty that would be needed to make a limited national missile defence (NMD) system possible. In order to do this, America must convince Russia that its proposed anti-missile shield is designed to ward off a handful of rockets from a North Korea or an Iran—not a massed attack from the still-formidable Russian arsenal.

The treaty changes America is now proposing are only the bare minimum required to allow work in Alaska to begin. Broader changes would be needed before implementing in full the Pentagon's current plan for an anti-missile system with a second interceptor site, in North Dakota, and super-high-frequency radar stations in Greenland, Britain and possibly South Korea as well as other parts of the United States. The immediate plan is to deploy 20 interceptors, able to stop a few crude missiles, in Alaska by 2005; but by the end of the decade there could be as many as 250 interceptors, capable of knocking out a "few dozen" missiles.

Reassuring Russia

American diplomats are working hard to convince the Russians that, even at its maximum stretch, such a shield would not render Russia's nuclear deterrent ineffective. This would still be true, they say, even if, as Russia has proposed, a new agreement were to cut the number of warheads deployed by America and Russia to 1,500 each. Under the Start-2 accord, each side's total will come down to 3,500 by 2007. Follow-on Start-3 talks aim to cut to 2,000–2,500 warheads. The Pentagon said last week it would be "uncomfortable" about going lower than that.

Even if it successfully deploys a limited shield, and both sides' arsenals are slashed, the United States would still not be able to strike Russia with impunity, American officials have assured their Russian counterparts. The Pentagon would have to assume that Russia still had a huge number of warheads, based on land and sea, primed for "launch on warning" of an American attack. By sending this message of reassurance, the Clinton administration has exposed itself to the charge that it is positively encouraging its cold-war foe to maintain a large, sophisticated arsenal on hair-trigger alert.

In any case, Russia's new president, Vladimir Putin, whom Mr Clinton will be meeting on June 4th, seems so far to be unimpressed. Senior American officials admit that Russia is not yet convinced of the need to amend the ABM treaty, so the presidents will also focus on other arms-control measures, such as a deal to destroy large amounts of plutonium.

If the two presidents find they disagree sharply over ABM issues, the stage could be set for a hot diplomatic summer. America's European allies have concerns of their own about the proposed missile shield. Their biggest worry is that the ABM issue will cause a general downturn in relations with Russia and China, whose consequences would be felt in Europe. "Quitting the ABM treaty would send an unfortunate signal about America's readiness to play by agreed rules rather than unilaterally," says François Heisbourg, a French security analyst.

Mr Clinton's room for manoeuvre in this political and diplomatic game is small. The Pentagon says a decision to start the NMD programme must be made by this autumn; otherwise it will be impossible to start work in Alaska next year, and there will be no hope of meeting the goal of erecting a modest anti-missile shield by 2005.

According to the White House, the timetable is based on estimates that North Korea could have developed a missile capable of hitting the United States in five years' time, if not sooner. But Zbigniew Brzezinski, a former national security adviser, believes one aim of the timetable is to shield Vice-President Al Gore from charges that he would be less keen on "defending American families" than his Republican rival, George W. Bush. Mr Bush said last week that, as president, he would deploy anti-missile defences as soon as possible. But he questioned the need for an immediate decision.

In political terms, the anti-missile network proposed by Mr Clinton, calling for the eventual deployment of 250 interceptors, is nowhere near robust enough to satisfy the keenest supporters of anti-missile defence on the Republican side. They want to withdraw from the ABM treaty immediately and start constructing a multi-layered system of interceptors, based at sea and in space as well as on land.

Meanwhile, American citizens—and the rest of the world—are left wondering whether they will be safer or in greater danger if work starts on anti-missile defences. They want to know whether the perceived threat from rogue missiles is real, whether the proposed shield would work and what the economic and diplomatic costs will be.

The real threat

The strongest arguments in favour of developing anti-missile defences have to do with the proliferation of ballistic missiles—and of the know-how needed to tip them with nuclear, chemical or biological warheads, which are lumped together under the catch-all term of "weapons of mass destruction" (WMD). General Ronald Kadish, the head of the Pentagon's ballistic-missile-defence programme, has said that at least 20 countries possess either short- or medium-range ballistic missiles, while "two dozen" either have developed or can develop a WMD capacity. Because countries like North Korea will sell rocket technology to anybody who has the money, the pace of proliferation has been accelerating. "Co-operation between rogues is getting deeper and wider all the time," according to Ranger Associates, a Washington missile consultancy.

But how many of these regional pariahs could develop missiles of long enough range to threaten the United States with non-conventional weapons? Only a handful. The Central Intelligence Agency has projected that over the next 15 years, in addition to the existing arsenals of Russia and China, America is "likely" to face a missile threat from North Korea. Such a threat is "probable" from Iran and "possible" from Iraq.

Regimes may change for the better, of course. Still, the pace at which anti-American regimes can develop ballistic-missile technology has often been underestimated by western experts. North Korea's launch in August 1998 of a three-stage rocket shocked the world; since last autumn it has been observing a freeze on new flight tests, although it is believed to be pursuing other research.

But would such rockets ever be fired against the United States? It would seem suicidal. It is possible, nonetheless, to imagine a regional crisis in which America's freedom to support local allies would be hampered by the knowledge that its territory could, however hypothetically, be attacked with missiles. Yet for the Pentagon to feel that the homeland was immune, it would need to be sure that its shield would be able to stop all-comers; and that degree of certainty has still not been reached.

There are also more immediate dangers: the use of crude short-range missiles in regional conflicts, against American bases or American allies; or a non-conventional attack on the United States by some means other than long-range ballistic missiles, such as truck bombs or even sea-launched rockets. This has prompted some defence specialists, not all of them doves,

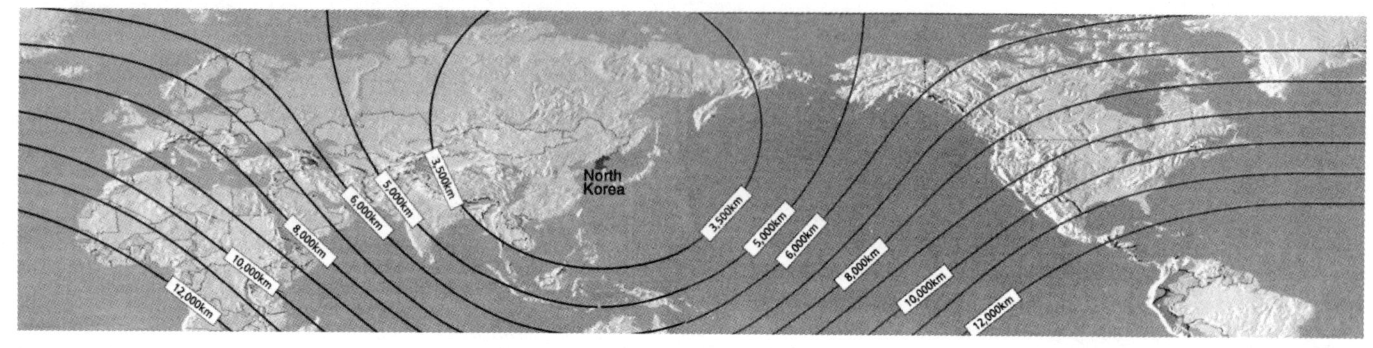

Source: Department of Defence

to suggest that the NMD programme involves spending far too much money, and incurring huge diplomatic costs, for a threat which is by no means the most acute.

How it would work

The cost of Mr Clinton's proposed system—estimated by the Pentagon at $27 billion over 20 years for a single interceptor site, plus radars—looks small compared with some other defence programmes. The Congressional Budget Office reckons the full system, without extra satellites, could cost $50 billion. Obviously the more complex the defences attempted, the higher the price tag.

How would Mr Clinton's proposed NMD system deal with a rocket attack? The idea is that far above the atmosphere, near the top of its flight path, the rogue rocket would be stopped in its tracks. An American missile, guided by one of the most powerful radar systems ever built, and equipped with detectors of its own, would home in on the intruder—by this stage a cone-shaped object, five feet long—and smash it to pieces.

The hostile launch would first have been detected by space-based sensors. Then a network of ground-based radars would erect "search fences" to detect the intruder and consider how to stop it. The powerful X-band radar, based initially at Shemya, would follow the attacker as it soared above the atmosphere, while a command centre deep in Colorado's Cheyenne mountains directed the launch of an interceptor. Once the interceptor or "kill vehicle" got close enough to the target, it would start using its own sensors to tell the real rocket from any decoys.

So far, the Pentagon has tried out the concept with two attempted intercepts, each costing about $100m. One, last October, was a success (although its terms of reference were restricted), while the second, in January, narrowly failed. As a result of this failure, a third test (of a total of 19) has been postponed from April to July. The Pentagon is then due to give the president an estimate of whether the system can be deployed in five years' time. General Kadish describes the 2005 timetable as "high risk", because five very sophisticated components have to be developed concurrently and then tied together, much faster than military planners would like.

Decoys and alternatives

One of the strongest arguments put forward by the sceptics (on both right and left) is that the system currently proposed would be too vulnerable to counter-measures. A report issued in April by the Union of Concerned Scientists argued that any country clever enough to design ballistic missiles would also be able to make decoys of sufficient sophistication to fool the interceptors. According to the UCS, decoys can be particularly effective outside the atmosphere, where there is no resistance from the air, and where objects of different weights and shapes behave in the same way.

One technique would be to wrap the warhead in a material called aluminised mylar and simultaneously to release balloons coated with the same substance; another would be to cool the warhead with a shroud of liquid nitrogen, making it harder for the interceptor to home in. If a rogue wanted to tip his rockets with chemical or biological warheads, they would almost certainly be split up into "bomblets" or sub-munitions which, the UCS believes, would be too numerous for interceptors to stop.

In short, it would be hard to stop missiles in space with land-based interceptors. So why not stop them earlier in their flight, from the sea?

The main argument against sea-based defences is that these would require a much more radical rewriting of the ABM treaty. In other words, they would be harder to sell to the Russians. Already the Pentagon's effort to develop a sea-based shield against medium-range missiles, known as Navy Theatre Wide, has been limited in scope—or as critics would say, "dumbed down"—in order to reassure Russia that it will not be used as a proxy for a system to defend America.

The advantage of a system like Navy Theatre Wide, which should be operational by 2007, is that it aims, ideally, to stop missiles in their ascent phase—in other words, before they reach their highest point. This makes it harder for the enemy to use counter-measures, although the ships themselves would be vulnerable to attack.

Better still, in theory, would be a system that knocked out enemy missiles in their boost phase, a few minutes after being launched. The only Pentagon effort that is explicitly designed to achieve that purpose is the air force's Airborne Laser programme, which is probably a decade away from deployment. Tantalising as it sounds, the success of this effort is far from assured—and it would be anathema to the Russsians.

The diplomatic costs

The diplomatic, economic and military consequences of the American decision are already being felt in many different parts of the world. In Greenland, local politicians are worried that the upgrading of an American radar station, as part of the NMD network, will make the vast, icy landmass a target for enemy attack. In Canada, which might well have a role to play in tracking incoming missiles, officials are furious about a remark, by an American admiral, that a missile heading towards Ottawa might not be stopped unless Canada joins the shield. In NATO capitals, diplomats are fretting over the "decoupling" of the United States, protected by an anti-missile shield, from its European allies.

In China, which has threatened to accelerate its own strategic arms build-up in response to the American shield, officials are convinced that the shield is directed against them; they speak ominously about a new cold war. Although the Chinese are not party to the ABM treaty, they are—like the other minor nuclear powers—a beneficiary of its curbs on anti-missile defences. They have suggested that playing about with the treaty could wreck the fabric of arms control. Such talk is a veiled threat that China would not only boost its own arsenal but withdraw promises to stop exporting dangerous defence technology.

On Capitol Hill, meanwhile, Republican hawks such as Senator Jesse Helms have given warning that any deal with Russia to keep the ABM treaty, and prevent America building a more ambitious anti-missile shield, will be "dead on arrival" in Congress.

All this has prompted supporters of missile defences to suggest that more imaginative ways ought to be found of maintaining Russian confidence, while giving America a free hand to defend itself. Russia itself has put forward proposals for countering the threat of rogue missiles, and for reducing the risk of an accidental nuclear exchange.

The Russian proposals include "broad international participation" in an arrangement to swap information about missile launches; and a set of incentives designed to encourage rogue missile-makers to abandon their efforts by offering them commercial space technology, and security guarantees.

America rejects the idea of security guarantees and is wary of any formal system of incentives, available to any country that starts making rockets and then stops. Moreover, help for space programmes could be misused to develop longer-range missiles. But the Americans have not ruled out extending an information-sharing regime beyond Washington and Moscow.

What about bolder initiatives from the American side, designed to reassure Russia while ensuring greater freedom of action for the Pentagon? Ever since the "star wars" programme of the 1980s, advocates of anti-missile defence have insisted that it should be possible to break the "balance of terror" logic without alienating Russia. In practice, it is hard to think how this might safely be done. But unless it can, America could find itself in the worst of all worlds: incurring the huge diplomatic cost of withdrawal from the ABM treaty, without any real guarantee that rogue missiles could be stopped.

Unit 4

Unit Selections

Key Points to Consider

- How much money should the United States spend on foreign policy?
- What are the most important national interests of the United States today?
- What type of event or trend might cause Americans to pay more attention to foreign affairs?
- Explain why you agree or disagree with the proposition that America will support the loss of American lives in a military operation overseas if the operation promises to be a success.
- Will Canada continue to scale back its troop commitments to future international peacekeeping missions?
- How likely is it that conflicts over water will increase tensions between the United States and Canada?

Links **www.dushkin.com/online/**

16. **The Henry L. Stimson Center**
    http://www.stimson.org
17. **The North American Institute**
    http://www.santafe.edu/~naminet/index.html

These sites are annotated on pages 4 and 5.

President Clinton completed his second term in office without accomplishing many of his foreign policy goals. The resumption of violence between Israel and the Palestinians meant that Clinton left office without having achieved the brokering of a lasting peace agreement in the Middle East. Despite the success of NATO's military campaign in Kosovo—to accomplish its mission without the loss of American active duty military personnel, and the subsequent peaceful ousting of President Milosevic via elections in Serbia—many Americans continue to display an unwillingness to support new U.S. commitments abroad. Meanwhile, international trends suggest that political and economic power will continue to diffuse in an international system that is in transition towards a multipower system. In "The One Percent Solution," Richard Gardner explains why a successful U.S. foreign policy cannot be carried out with barely one percent of the federal budget. He emphasizes that this dangerous charade must be ended.

After a contentious period, George W. Bush was declared the winner of the 2000 U.S. presidential election. In "Promoting the National Interest," his national security adviser, Condoleezza Rice, outlines the foreign policy priorities of the new Republican administration. These priorities include building a military that is ready to ensure American power, extending free trade, promoting a stable international monetary system, renewing relationships with allies, Russia, and China, and dealing decisively with the threat of rogue regimes and hostile powers.

It is too early to gauge how historians will rate Clinton's foreign policy legacy. Current views on Clinton's record as a world leader remain sharply divided. Where supporters see pragmatic leadership and bold innovation, critics see improvised initiatives that left America adrift.

Many observers now emphasize the importance of the foreign policy decisions made by senior officials of the Bush administration during the first few years of the new administration for continuing the United States' role as a superpower. In contrast, Robert Daniels, in "Home Alone," criticizes much of the recent triumphalist talk since the end of the cold war. While America is in a position without precedent since the Roman Empire, Daniels emphasizes the fact that the nation's political leadership cannot agree on what to do with this power. Moreover, the American public may not be willing or able to sustain it. The contradictions and existing divisions in the national political psyche about the role of America in the world are apparent in the current debate over the proposed Missile Defense Initiative.

After the success of the U.S. air war against Serbia, several analysts claimed that Americans will no longer tolerate U.S. involvement in foreign conflicts if this involvement leads to the death of American soldiers. Many U.S. leaders now believe that Americans will lose their stomach for combat when the body bags come home. But some recent public opinion polls indicate that this view is wrong. Instead, recent polls suggest that Americans will accept combat deaths so long as the mission has the potential to be successful. Despite the growth of noninterventionist sentiments among some U.S. politicians and members of the public, the United States continues its commitment to European integration and increased military capabilities of member-states in an expanded NATO. These goals are being pursued at the same time that the United States is encouraging Central and Eastern European countries' and Russia's integration with Europe.

Despite the continuing importance of Europe in U.S. foreign policy priorities, defense planners are quietly shifting U.S. military forces away from its traditional focus on Europe. China is viewed in U.S. Defense Department planning documents as a potential future adversary. Pentagon planners are looking toward Asia as the most likely arena for future conflict, or, at least, competition. This change carries huge implications for the shape of the armed forces and high stakes for U.S. foreign policy. The need to modernize conventional forces, retain skilled military personnel, and fund a new strategic defense initiative will require the Bush administration to make major changes in current U.S. defense doctrine after winning support for increased defense spending from Congress and the U.S. public. It is too early to tell how many of these proposed changes the new administration be willing to tackle.

The Bush administration must continue the United States commitment to promoting democracy and human rights worldwide. However, the specific policies that will be pursued to promote these foreign policy goals will only be evident over time.

Despite its middle-level status, Canada has maintained an activist foreign policy while reducing military expenditures and increasing trade links. In 1999, the House of Commons Foreign Affairs and International Trade Committee recommended that NATO adopt a policy stating that it would not be the first to use nuclear weapons in a conflict.

Canada maintains an activist profile by pursuing "niche" diplomacy that includes taking a leading role in sponsoring the international landmine treaty and participation in UN international peacekeeping missions. The approach permits Canada to play a large role in world affairs with limited resources. However, the cost of this activist role is currently straining the resources of the federal government. The staff writers for *The Economist* describe, in "Canada Battles with Its Vision of Peace," how the number of Canadian troops committed to peacekeeping operations during 2000 declined. Although Canada has prided itself on having invested heavily in modern peacekeeping since 1956, Canada is only contributing a few military observers and some money to disarm child soldiers in peacekeeping missions in Sierra Leone and Congo. At the same time Canada is embarking on a military hardware spending spree, partly in response to demands of its mighty neighbor, and implementing new tax cuts. These trends suggest declining support for foreign minister Lloyd Asworthy's "soft power," the idea that the world's mightier countries should worry less about their own security and more about that of the world's poor.

Although the United States and Canada have managed to pursue peaceful relations throughout their history, water issues have always been a source of conflict between the two countries, especially among western provinces in Canada and western states in the United States. Water issues promise to continue to be a source of tension between the two states in future decades. As writers for *The Economist* note in "Canada's Water: Hands Off," water is increasingly viewed as "blue gold" by federal officials in Ontario. As this abundant Canadian natural resource becomes more valuable to nation-states with water-scarce regions, the federal government is moving to regulate provinces' right to sell water to the United States and other customers worldwide.

The One Percent Solution

SHIRKING THE COST OF WORLD LEADERSHIP

Richard N. Gardner

A dangerous game is being played in Washington with America's national security. Call it the "one percent solution"—the fallacy that a successful U.S. foreign policy can be carried out with barely one percent of the federal budget. Unless the next president moves urgently to end this charade, he will find himself in a financial straitjacket that frustrates his ability to promote American interests and values in an increasingly uncertain world.

Ultimately, the only way to end the dangerous one percent solution game is to develop a new national consensus that sees the international affairs budget as part of the national security budget—because the failure to build solid international partnerships to treat the causes of conflict today will mean costly military responses tomorrow. Those who play the one percent solution game do not understand a post–Cold War world in which a host of international problems now affects Americans' domestic welfare, from financial crises and the closing of markets to global warming, AIDS, terrorism, drug trafficking, and the spread of weapons of mass destruction. Solving these problems will require leadership, and that will cost.

MONEY CHANGES EVERYTHING

If this all sounds exaggerated, consider the way the one percent solution game is being played this year, when America has a GDP of nearly $10 trillion and a federal budget of over $1.8 trillion. Secretary of State Madeleine Albright asked the Office of Management and Budget (OMB) for $25 billion in the budget for fiscal year (FY) 2001, which begins October 1, for the so-called 150 Account, which covers the nonmilitary costs of protecting U.S. national security. OMB cut that figure to $22.8 billion to fit President Clinton's commitment to continued fiscal responsibility and limited budgetary growth. The congressional budget committees cut it further to $20 billion, or $2.3 billion less than the $22.3 billion approved for FY 2000. At the same time, the budget committees raised defense spending authority for FY 2001 to $310.8 billion—$4.5 billion more than the administration requested.

Clinton and Albright strongly protested the congressional cuts. They will undoubtedly protest even more when the appropriations committees of the Senate and the House divide up the meager 150 Account pie into inadequate slices for essential foreign affairs functions. At the end of this congressional session, $1 billion or so of the foreign affairs cuts may be restored if Clinton threatens to veto the appropriation bills—not easy to do in an election year. Of course, the next president could make another familiar move in the one percent solution game—ask for a small supplemental appropriation to restore the previous cuts. But if the past is any guide, Congress will do its best to force the next administration to accommodate most of its supplemental spending within the existing budget. (This year, for instance, Congress resisted additional spending to pay for the U.S. share of multilateral projects such as more U.N. peacekeeping and debt reduction for the poorest countries.)

Even more discouraging for the next president are the projections for the 150 Account that the Clinton administration and the budget committees have presented as spending guidelines until 2005. The president's projected foreign affairs spending request of $24.5 billion for 2005 hardly keeps up with inflation, and the budget committees' target of $20 billion means a decrease of nearly 20 percent from FY 2000, adjusted for inflation. By contrast, the administration's projected defense spending authority goes up to $331 billion in

FY 2005; the budget committees' defense projection is comparable. Thus the ratio of military spending to foreign affairs spending would continue to increase in the next few years, rising to more than 16 to 1.

The percentage of the U.S. budget devoted to international affairs has been declining for four decades. In the 1960s, the 150 Account made up 4 percent of the federal budget; in the 1970s, it averaged about 2 percent; during the first half of the 1990s, it went down to 1 percent, with only a slight recovery in FYS 1999 and 2000. The international affairs budget is now about 20 percent less in today's dollars than it was on average during the late 1970s and the 1980s.

A nation's budget, like that of a corporation or an individual, reflects its priorities. Both main political parties share a broad consensus that assuring U.S. national security in the post–Cold War era requires a strong military and the willingness to use it to defend important U.S. interests and values. The Clinton administration and Congress have therefore supported recent increases in the defense budget to pay for more generous salaries and a better quality of life in order to attract and retain quality personnel; fund necessary research, training, and weapons maintenance; and procure new and improved weapons systems. Politicians and military experts may differ on the utility and cost-effectiveness of particular weapons, but after the catch-up defense increases of the last several years, Washington appears to be on an agreed course to keep the defense budget growing modestly to keep up with the rate of inflation.

Why then, at a time of unprecedented prosperity and budget surpluses, can Washington not generate a similar consensus on the need to adequately fund the nonmilitary component of national security? Apparently spending on foreign affairs is not regarded as spending for national security. Compounding the problem is Washington's commendable new commitment to fiscal responsibility after years of huge budget deficits—a commitment reflected in the tight cap that Congress placed on discretionary spending in 1997. Even though that cap is already being violated and will undoubtedly be revised upward this year, the new bipartisan agreement to lock up the Social Security surplus to meet the retirement costs of the baby boomers will continue to make for difficult budget choices and leave limited room for increased spending elsewhere, foreign affairs included.

The non–Social Security surplus—estimated at something more than $700 billion during the decade 2000–2010—will barely cover some modest tax cuts while keeping Medicare solvent and paying for some new spending on health care and education. Fortunately, higher-than-expected GDP growth may add $20–30 billion per year to the non-Social Security surplus, affording some additional budgetary wiggle room. Even so, that windfall could be entirely eaten up by larger tax cuts, more domestic spending, or unanticipated defense budget increases—unless foreign affairs spending becomes a higher priority now.

More money is not a substitute for an effective foreign policy, but an effective foreign policy will simply be impossible without more money. Foreign policy experts therefore disdain "boring budget arithmetic" at their peril.

The State Department recently set forth seven fundamental national interests in its foreign affairs strategic plan: national security; economic prosperity and freer trade; protection of U.S. citizens abroad and safeguarding of U.S. borders; the fight against international terrorism, crime, and drug trafficking; the establishment and consolidation of democracies and the upholding of human rights; the provision of humanitarian assistance to victims of crisis and disaster; and finally, the improvement of the global environment, stabilization of world population growth, and protection of human health. This is a sensible list, but in the political climate of today's Washington, few in the executive branch or Congress dare ask how much money will really be required to support it. Rather, the question usually asked is how much the political traffic will bear.

Going on this way will force unacceptable foreign policy choices—either adequate funding for secure embassies and modern communications systems for diplomats or adequate funding for U.N. peacekeeping in Kosovo, East Timor, and Africa; either adequate funding for the Middle East peace process or adequate funding to safeguard nuclear weapons and materials in Russia; either adequate funding for family planning to control world population growth or adequate funding to save refugees and displaced persons. The world's greatest power need not and should not accept a situation in which it has to make these kinds of choices.

THE STATE OF STATE

Ideally, a bipartisan, expert study would tell us what a properly funded foreign affairs budget would look like. In the absence of such a study, consider the following a rough estimate of the increases now required in the two main parts of the 150 Account. The first part is the State Department budget, which includes not only the cost of U.S. diplomacy but also U.S. assessed contributions to international organizations and peacekeeping. The second part is the foreign operations budget, which includes bilateral development aid, the bilateral economic support fund for special foreign policy priorities, bilateral military aid, and contributions to voluntary U.N. programs and multilateral development banks.

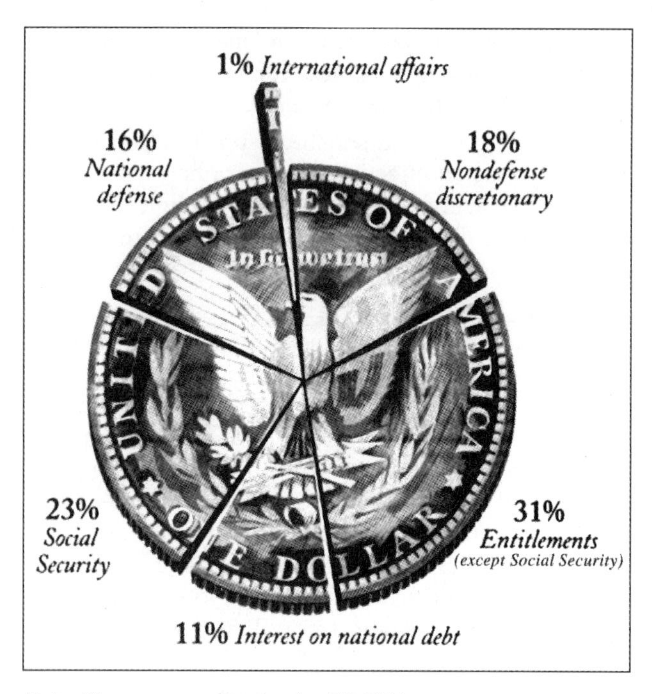

Note: Figures are estimates for FY 2001.

Take State's budget first. The United States maintains 250 embassies and other posts in 160 countries. Far from being rendered less important by the end of the Cold War or today's instant communications, these diplomatic posts and the State Department that directs them are more essential than ever in promoting the seven fundamental U.S. foreign policy interests identified above.

Ambassadors and their staffs have to play multiple roles today—as the "eyes and ears" of the president and secretary of state, advocates for U.S. policies in the upper reaches of the host government, resourceful negotiators, and intellectual, educational, and cultural emissaries in public diplomacy with key interest groups, opinion leaders, and the public at large. As Albright put it in recent congressional testimony, the Foreign Service, the Civil Service, and the foreign nationals serving in U.S. overseas posts contribute daily to the welfare of the American people "through the dangers they help contain; the crimes they help prevent; the deals they help close; the rights they help protect; and the travelers they just plain help."

Following the tragic August 1998 bombings of American embassies in Nairobi and Dar es Salaam, the secretary of state, with the support of the president and Congress, established the Overseas Presence Advisory Panel (OPAP), composed of current and former diplomats and private-sector representatives, to recommend improvements in America's overseas diplomatic establishment. "The United States overseas presence, which has provided the essential underpinnings of U.S. foreign policy for many decades, is near a state of crisis," the panel warned. "Insecure and often decrepit facilities, obsolete information technology, outmoded administrative and human resources practices, poor allocation of resources, and competition from the private sector for talented staff threaten to cripple America's overseas capability, with far-reaching consequences for national security and prosperity."

The OPAP report focused more on reforms than on money, but many of its recommendations have price tags. The report called for $1.3 billion per year for embassy construction and security upgrades—probably $100 million too little, since an earlier and more authoritative study by the Accountability Review Boards under former Joint Chiefs of Staff Chair William Crowe proposed $1.4 billion annually for that purpose. OPAP also called for another $330 million over several years to provide unclassified and secure Internet and e-mail information networks linking all U.S. agencies and overseas posts.

Moreover, OPAP proposed establishing an interagency panel chaired by the secretary of state to evaluate the size, location, and composition of America's overseas presence. Visitors who see many people in U.S. embassies often do not realize that the State Department accounts for only 42 percent of America's total overseas personnel; the Defense Department accounts for 37 percent, and more than two dozen other agencies such as the Agency for International Development and the departments of Commerce, Treasury, and Justice make up the rest. If one includes the foreign nationals hired as support staff, State Department personnel in some large U.S. embassies are less than 15 percent of the employees, and many of them are administrators.

The State Department's FY 2001 budget of $6.8 billion provides $3.2 billion for administering foreign affairs. Of that, even after the East Africa bombings, only $1.1 billion will go toward embassy construction and security upgrades, even though $1.4 billion is needed. Moreover, only $17 million is provided for new communications infrastructure, although $330 million is needed. Almost nothing is included to fill a 700-position shortfall of qualified personnel. The State Department therefore requires another $500 million just to meet its minimal needs.

The FY 2001 State Department budget contains a small but inadequate increase—from $204 million in FY 2000 to $225 million—for the educational and cultural exchanges formerly administered by the U.S. Information Agency. Most of this money will go to the Fulbright academic program and the International Visitors Program, which brings future foreign leaders in politics, the media, trade unions, and other nongovernmental organizations (NGOs) to meet with their American counterparts. These valuable and cost-effective exchanges have been slashed from their 1960s and 1970s heights. A near-doubling of these programs' size—with disproportionate increases for exchanges with especially important countries such as Russia and China—would clearly serve U.S. national security interests. A sensible annual budget increase for educational and cultural exchanges would be $200 million.

The budget includes $946 million for assessed contributions to international organizations, of which $300 million is for the U.N. itself and $380 million more is for U.N.-affiliated agencies such as the International Labor Organization, the World Health Organization, the International Atomic Energy Agency, and the war crimes tribunals for Rwanda and the Balkans. Other bodies such as NATO, the Organization for Economic Cooperation and Development (OECD), and the World Trade Organization (WTO) account for the rest.

Richard Holbrooke, the able American ambassador to the U.N., is currently deep in difficult negotiations to reduce the assessed U.S. share of the regular U.N. budget and the budgets of major specialized U.N. agencies from 25 percent to 22 percent—a precondition required by the Helms-Biden legislation for paying America's U.N. arrears. If Holbrooke succeeds, U.S. contributions to international organizations will drop slightly.

But this reduction will be more than offset by the need to pay for modest U.N. budget increases. The zero nominal growth requirement that Congress slapped on U.N. budgets is now becoming counterproductive. To take just one example, the U.N. Department of Peacekeeping Operations is now short at least 100 staffers, which leaves it ill-prepared to handle the increased number and scale of peacekeeping operations. If Washington could agree to let U.N. budgets rise by inflation plus a percent or two in the years ahead and to channel the increase to programs of particular U.S. interest, America would have more influence and the U.N. would be more effective. Some non-U.N. organizations, such as NATO, the OECD, and the WTO, also require budget increases beyond the rate of inflation to do their jobs properly. Moreover, America should rejoin the U.N. Educational, Scientific, and Cultural Organization (UNESCO), given the growing foreign policy importance of its concerns and the role that new communications technology can play in helping developing countries. The increased annual cost of UNESCO membership ($70 million) and of permitting small annual increases in the U.N.'s and other international organizations' budgets ($30 million) comes to another $100 million.

Selling this will take leadership. In particular, a showdown is brewing with Congress over the costs of U.N. peacekeeping. After reaching a high of 80,000 in 1993 and then dropping to 13,000 in 1998, the number of U.N. peacekeepers is rising again to 30,000 or more as a result of new missions in Kosovo, East Timor, Sierra Leone, and the proposed mission in the Democratic Republic of the Congo (DRC). So the State Department had to ask Congress for $739 million for U.N. peacekeeping in the FY 2001 budget, compared to the $500 million it received in FY 2000. (The White House also requested a FY 2000 budget supplement of $143 million, which has not yet been approved.) But even these sums fall well short of what Washington will have to pay for peacekeeping this year and next. In Kosovo, the mission is seriously underfunded; the U.N. peacekeeping force in southern Lebanon will have to be beefed up after an Israeli withdrawal; and new or expanded missions could be required for conflicts in Sierra Leone, Ethiopia-Eritrea, and the DRC. So total U.N. peacekeeping costs could rise to $3.5–4 billion per year. With the United States paying for 25 percent of peacekeeping (although it is still assessed at the rate of 31 percent, which is unduly high), these new challenges could cost taxpayers at least $200 million per year more than the amount currently budgeted. Washington should, of course, watch the number, cost, and effectiveness of U.N. peacekeeping operations, but the existing and proposed operations serve U.S. interests and must be adequately funded.

Add up all these sums and one finds that the State Department budget needs an increase of $1 billion, for a total of $7.8 billion per year.

A DECENT RESPECT

The Clinton administration has asked for $15.1 billion for the foreign operations budget for FY 2001—the second part of the 150 Account. Excluding $3.7 billion for military aid and $1 billion for the Export-Import Bank, that leaves about $10.4 billion in international development and humanitarian assistance. This includes various categories of bilateral aid: $2.1 billion for sustainable development; $658 million for migration and refugee assistance; $830 million to promote free-market democracies and secure nuclear materials in the countries of the former Soviet Union; and $610 million of support for eastern Europe and the Balkans. It also covers about $1.4 billion for multilateral development banks, including $800 million for the International Development Association, the World Bank affiliate for lending to the poorest countries. Another $350 million goes to international organizations and programs such as the U.N. Development Program ($90 million), the U.N. Children's Fund ($110 million), the U.N. Population Fund ($25 million), and the U.N. Environment Program ($10 million).

The $10.4 billion for development and humanitarian aid is just 0.11 percent of U.S. GDP and 0.60 percent of federal budget outlays. This figure is now near record lows. In 1962, foreign aid amounted to $18.5 billion in current dollars, or 0.58 percent of GDP and 3.06 percent of federal spending. In the 1980s, it averaged just over $13 billion a year in current dollars, or 0.20 percent of GDP and 0.92 percent of federal spending. Washington's current 0.11 percent aid-to-GDP share compares

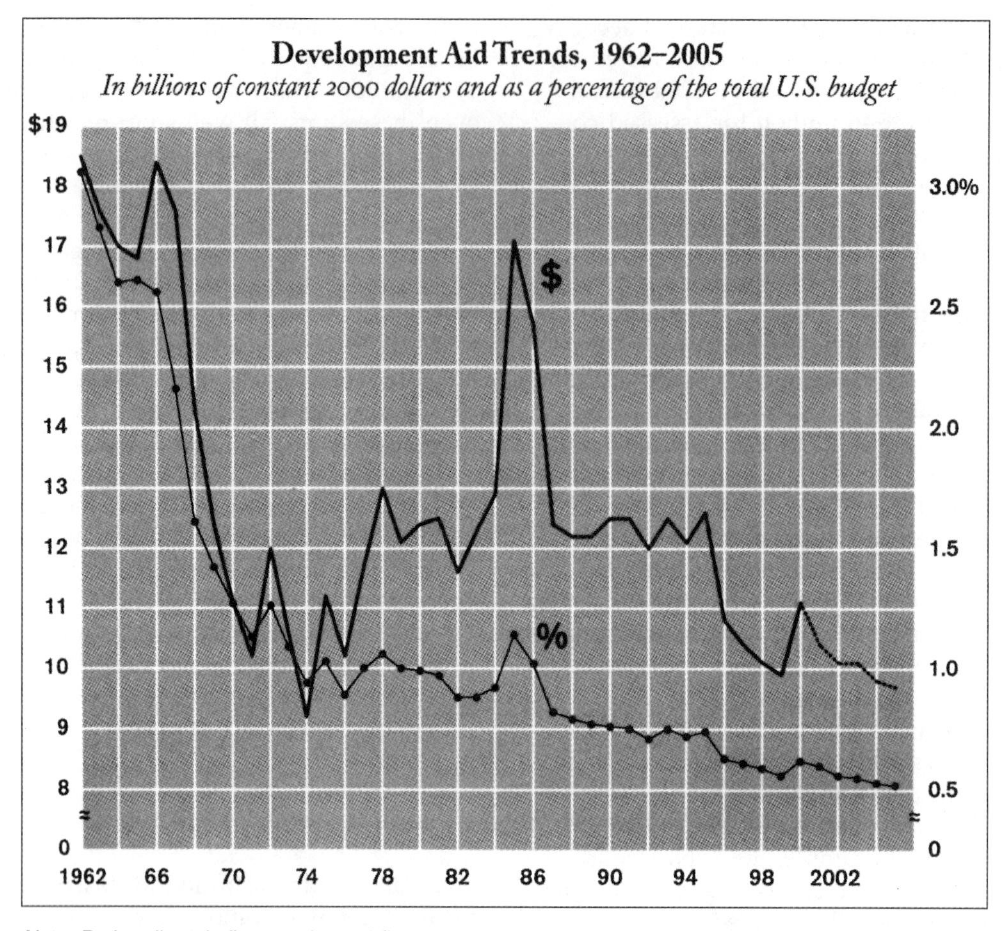

Note: Broken lines indicate estimated figures.
Source: Center on Budget and Policy Priorities analysis of Office of Management and Budget data.

unflatteringly with the average of 0.30 percent in the other OECD donor countries. On a per capita basis, each American contributes about $29 per year to development and humanitarian aid, compared to a median of $70 in the other OECD countries. According to the Clinton administration's own budget forecasts, the FY 2001 aid figure of $10.4 billion will drop even further in FY 2005, to $9.7 billion. Congress' low target for total international spending that year will almost certainly cut the FY 2005 aid figure even more.

Considering current economic and social trends in the world's poor countries, these low and declining aid levels are unjustifiable. World Bank President James Wolfensohn is right: the global struggle to reduce poverty and save the environment is being lost. Although hundreds of millions of people in the developing world escaped from poverty in recent years, half of the six billion people on Earth still live on less than $2 a day. Two billion are not connected to any energy system. One and a half billion lack clean water. More than a billion lack basic education, health care, or modern birth control methods.

The world's population, which grows by about 75 million a year, will probably reach about 9 billion by 2050; most will live in the world's poorest countries. If present trends continue, we can expect more abject poverty, environmental damage, epidemics, political instability, drug trafficking, ethnic violence, religious fundamentalism, and terrorism. This is not the kind of world Americans want their children to inherit. The Declaration of Independence speaks of "a decent respect for the opinion of mankind." Today's political leaders need a decent respect for future generations.

To be sure, the principal responsibility for progress in the developing countries rests with those countries themselves. But their commitments to pursue sound economic policies and humane social policies will fall short without more and better-designed development aid—as well as more generous trade concessions—from the United States and its wealthy partners. At the main industrialized nations' summit last year in Birmingham, U.K., the G-8 (the G-7 group of highly industrialized countries plus Russia) endorsed such U.N.-backed goals as halving the number of people suffering from illiteracy, malnutrition, and extreme poverty by 2015.

Beyond these broad goals, America's next president should earmark proposed increases in U.S. development aid for specific programs that promote fundamental American interests and values and that powerful domestic constituencies could be mobilized to support. These would include programs that promote clean energy technologies to help fight global warming; combat the spread of diseases such as AIDS, which is ravaging Africa; assure primary education for all children, without the present widespread discrimination against girls; bridge the "digital divide" and stimulate development by bringing information technology and the Internet to schools, libraries, and hospitals; provide universal maternal and child care, as well as family planning for all those who wish to use it, thus reducing unwanted pregnancies and unsafe abortions; support democracy and the rule of law; establish better corporate governance, banking regulations, and accounting standards; and protect basic worker rights.

What would the G-8 and U.N. targets and these specific programs mean for the U.S. foreign operations budget? Answering this question is much harder than estimating an adequate State Department budget. Doing so requires more information on total requirements, appropriate burden-sharing between developed and developing countries, the share that can be assumed by business and NGOs, the absorptive capacity of countries, and aid agencies' ability to handle more assistance effectively.

Still, there are fairly reliable estimates of total aid needs in many areas. For example, the 1994 Cairo Conference on Population and Development endorsed an expert estimate that $17 billion per year is now required to provide universal access to voluntary family planning in the developing world, with $5.7 billion of it to be supplied by developed countries. Were the United States to contribute based on its share of donor-country GDP, U.S. aid in this sector would rise to about $1.9 billion annually. By contrast, U.S. foreign family-planning funding in FY 2000 was only $372 million; the Clinton administration has requested $541 million for FY 2001.

We already know enough about aid requirements in other sectors to suggest that doing Washington's fair share in sustainable-development programs would require about $10 billion more per year by FY 2005, which would bring its total aid spending up to some $20 billion annually. This would raise U.S. aid levels from their present 0.11 percent of GDP to about 0.20 percent, the level of U.S. aid 20 years ago. That total could be reached by annual increases of $2 billion per year, starting with a $1.6 billion foreign-aid supplement for FY 2001 and conditioning each annual increase on appropriate management reforms and appropriate increases in aid from other donors.

An FY 2005 target of $20 billion for development and humanitarian aid would mean a foreign operations budget that year of about $25 billion; total foreign affairs spending that year would be about $33 billion. This sounds like a lot of money, but it would be less than the United States spent on foreign affairs in real terms in 1985. As a percentage of the FY 2005 federal budget, it would still be less than average annual U.S. foreign affairs spending in the late 1970s and 1980s.

STICKER SHOCK

For a newly elected George W. Bush or Al Gore, asking for $2.6 billion in additional supplemental funds for FY 2001 on top of reversing this year's budget cuts—thus adding $1 billion for the State Department and $1.6 billion more for foreign operations—would produce serious "sticker shock" in the congressional budget and appropriations committees. So would seeking $27 billion for the 150 Account for FY 2002 and additional annual increases of $2 billion per year in order to reach a total of $33 billion in FY 2005. How could Congress be persuaded?

The new president—Democrat or Republican—would have to pave the way in meetings with congressional leaders between election day and his inauguration, justifying the additional expenditures in national security terms. He would need to make the case with opinion leaders and the public, explaining in a series of speeches and press conferences that America is entering not just a new century but also a new era of global interaction. He would need to energize the business community, unions, and the religious and civic groups who are the main constituencies for a more adequate foreign affairs budget. Last but not least, he would need to emphasize reforms in the State Department, in foreign-aid programs, and in international agencies to provide confidence that the additional money would be spent wisely.

Starting off a presidency this way would be a gamble, of course. But most presidents get the benefit of the doubt immediately after their first election. Anyway, without this kind of risk-taking, the new commander in chief would be condemning his administration to playing the old one percent solution game, almost certainly crippling U.S. foreign policy for the remainder of his term. The one percent solution is no solution at all.

RICHARD N. GARDNER, Of Counsel to Morgan, Lewis, and Bockius and Professor of Law and International Organization at Columbia University, has been U.S. Ambassador to Italy and Spain and Deputy Assistant Secretary of State for International Organization Affairs. Last year, he served on the Secretary of State's Overseas Presence Advisory Panel, which made recommendations on the reform and funding of U.S. diplomacy.

Campaign 2000

Promoting the National Interest

Condoleezza Rice

LIFE AFTER THE COLD WAR

THE UNITED STATES has found it exceedingly difficult to define its "national interest" in the absence of Soviet power. That we do not know how to think about what follows the U.S.-Soviet confrontation is clear from the continued references to the "post-Cold War period." Yet such periods of transition are important, because they offer strategic opportunities. During these fluid times, one can affect the shape of the world to come.

The enormity of the moment is obvious. The Soviet Union was more than just a traditional global competitor; it strove to lead a universal socialist alternative to markets and democracy. The Soviet Union quarantined itself and many often-unwitting captives and clients from the rigors of international capitalism. In the end, it sowed the seeds of its own destruction, becoming in isolation an economic and technological dinosaur.

But this is only part of the story. The Soviet Union's collapse coincided with another great revolution. Dramatic changes in information technology and the growth of "knowledge-based" industries altered the very basis of economic dynamism, accelerating already noticeable trends in economic interaction that often circumvented and ignored state boundaries. As competition for capital investment has intensified, states have faced difficult choices about their internal economic, political, and social structures. As the prototype of this "new economy," the United States has seen its economic influence grow—and with it, its diplomatic influence. America has emerged as both the principal benefactor of these simultaneous revolutions and their beneficiary.

The process of outlining a new foreign policy must begin by recognizing that the United States is in a remarkable position. Powerful secular trends are moving the world toward economic openness and—more unevenly—democracy and individual liberty. Some states have one foot on the train and the other off. Some states still hope to find a way to decouple democracy and economic progress. Some hold on to old hatreds as diversions from the modernizing task at hand. But the United States and its allies are on the right side of history.

In such an environment, American policies must help further these favorable trends by maintaining a disciplined and consistent foreign policy that separates the important from the trivial. The Clinton administration has assiduously avoided implementing such an agenda. Instead, every issue has been taken on its own terms—crisis by crisis, day by day. It takes courage to set priorities because doing so is an admission that American foreign policy cannot be all things to all people—or rather, to all interest groups. The Clinton administration's approach has its advantages: If priorities and intent are not clear, they cannot be criticized. But there is a high price to pay for this approach. In a democracy as pluralistic as ours, the absence of an articulated "national interest" either produces a fertile ground for those wishing to withdraw from the world or creates a vacuum to be filled by parochial groups and transitory pressures.

THE ALTERNATIVE

AMERICAN FOREIGN POLICY in a Republican administration should refocus the United States on the national interest and the pursuit of key priorities. These tasks are

- to ensure that America's military can deter war, project power, and fight in defense of its interests if deterrence fails;
- to promote economic growth and political openness by extending free trade and a stable international monetary system to all committed to these principles, including in the western hemisphere, which has too often been neglected as a vital area of U.S. national interest;
- to renew strong and intimate relationships with allies who share American values and can thus share the burden of promoting peace, prosperity, and freedom;
- to focus U.S. energies on comprehensive relationships with the big powers, particularly Russia and China, that can and will mold the character of the international political system; and
- to deal decisively with the threat of rogue regimes and hostile powers, which is increasingly taking the forms of the potential for terrorism and the development of weapons of mass destruction (WMD).

INTERESTS AND IDEALS

POWER MATTERS, both the exercise of power by the United States and the ability of others to exercise it. Yet many in the United States are (and have always been) uncomfortable with the notions of power politics, great powers, and power balances. In an extreme form, this discomfort leads to a reflexive appeal instead to notions of international law and norms, and the belief that the support of many states—or even better, of institutions like the United Nations—is essential to the legitimate exercise of power. The "national interest" is replaced with "humanitarian interests" or the interests of "the international community." The belief that the United States is exercising power legitimately only when it is doing so on behalf of someone or something else was deeply rooted in Wilsonian thought, and there are strong echoes of it in the Clinton administration. To be sure, there is nothing wrong with doing something that benefits all humanity, but that is, in a sense, a second-order effect. America's pursuit of the national interest will create conditions that promote freedom, markets, and peace. Its pursuit of national interests after World War II led to a more prosperous and democratic world. This can happen again.

So multilateral agreements and institutions should not be ends in themselves. U.S. interests are served by having strong alliances and can be promoted within the U.N. and other multilateral organizations, as well as through well-crafted international agreements. But the Clinton administration has often been so anxious to find multilateral solutions to problems that it has signed agreements that are not in America's interest. The Kyoto treaty is a case in point: whatever the facts on global warming, a treaty that does not include China and exempts "developing" countries from tough standards while penalizing American industry cannot possibly be in America's national interest.

Similarly, the arguments about U.S. ratification of the Comprehensive Test Ban Treaty are instructive. Since 1992, the United States has refrained unilaterally from testing nuclear weapons. It is an example to the rest of the world yet does not tie its own hands "in perpetuity" if testing becomes necessary again. But in pursuit of a "norm" against the acquisition of nuclear weapons, the United States signed a treaty that was not verifiable, did not deal with the threat of the development of nuclear weapons by rogue states, and threatened the reliability of the nuclear stockpile. Legitimate congressional concerns about the substance of the treaty were ignored during negotiations. When faced with the defeat of a bad treaty, the administration attacked the motives of its opponents—incredibly branding long-standing internationalists like Senators Richard Lugar (R-Ind.) and John Warner (R-Va.) as isolationists.

Certainly, Republican presidents have not been immune to the practice of pursuing symbolic agreements of questionable value. According to the Senate Foreign Relations Committee, some 52 conventions, agreements, and treaties still await ratification; some even date back to 1949. But the Clinton administration's attachment to largely symbolic agreements and its pursuit of, at best, illusory "norms" of international behavior have become an epidemic. That is not leadership. Neither is it isolationist to suggest that the United States has a special role in the world and should not adhere to every international convention and agreement that someone thinks to propose.

Even those comfortable with notions of the "national interest" are still queasy with a focus on power relationships and great-power politics. The reality is that a few big powers can radically affect international peace, stability, and prosperity. These states are capable of disruption on a grand scale, and their fits of anger or acts of beneficence affect hundreds of millions of people. By reason of size, geographic position, economic potential, and military strength, they are capable of influencing American welfare for good or ill. Moreover, that kind of power is usually accompanied by a sense of entitlement to play a decisive role in international politics. Great powers do not just mind their own business.

Some worry that this view of the world ignores the role of values, particularly human rights and the promotion of democracy. In fact, there are those who would draw a sharp line between power politics and a principled foreign policy based on values. This polarized view—you are either a realist or devoted to norms and values—may be just fine in academic debate, but it is a disaster for American foreign policy. American values are universal. People want to say what they think, worship as they wish, and elect those who govern them; the triumph of these values is most assuredly easier when the international balance of power favors those who believe in them. But sometimes that favorable balance of power takes time to achieve, both internationally and within a society. And in the meantime, it is simply not possible to ignore and isolate other powerful states that do not share those values.

The Cold War is a good example. Few would deny that the collapse of the Soviet Union profoundly transformed the picture of democracy and human rights in eastern and central Europe and the former Soviet territories. Nothing improved human rights as much as the collapse of Soviet power. Throughout the Cold War, the United States pursued a policy that promoted political liberty, using every instrument from the Voice of America to direct presidential intervention on behalf of dissidents. But it lost sight neither of the importance of the geopolitical relationship with Moscow nor of the absolute necessity of retaining robust American military power to deter an all-out military confrontation.

In the 1970s, the Soviet Union was at the height of its power—which it was more than willing to use. Given its weak economic and technological base, the victories of that period turned out to be Pyrrhic. President Reagan's challenge to Soviet power was both resolute and well timed. It included intense substantive engagements with Moscow across the entire range of issues captured in the "four-part agenda" (arms control, human rights, economic issues, and regional conflicts). The Bush administration then focused greater attention on rolling back Soviet power in central and eastern Europe. As the Soviet Union's might waned, it could no longer defend its interests and gave up peacefully (thankfully) to the West—a tremendous victory for Western power and also for human liberty.

SETTING PRIORITIES

THE UNITED STATES has many sources of power in the pursuit of its goals. The global economy demands economic liberalization, greater openness and transparency, and at the very least, access to information technology. International economic policies that leverage the advantages of the American economy and expand free trade are the decisive tools in shaping international politics. They permit us to reach out to states as varied as South Africa and India and to engage our neighbors in the western hemisphere in a shared interest in economic prosperity. The growth of entrepreneurial classes throughout the world is an asset in the promotion of human rights and individual liberty, and it should be understood and used as such. Yet peace is the first and most important condition for continued prosperity and freedom. America's military power must be secure because the United States is the only guarantor of global peace and stability. The current neglect of America's armed forces threatens its ability to maintain peace.

The Bush administration had been able to reduce defense spending somewhat at the end of the Cold War in 1991. But the Clinton administration witlessly accelerated and deepened these cuts. The results were devastating: military readiness declined, training suffered, military pay slipped 15 percent below civilian equivalents, morale plummeted, and the services cannibalized existing equipment to keep airplanes flying, ships afloat, and tanks moving. The increased difficulty in recruiting people to the armed forces or retaining them is hardly surprising.

Moreover, the administration began deploying American forces abroad at a furious pace—an average of once every nine weeks. As it cut defense spending to its lowest point as a percentage of GDP since Pearl Harbor, the administration deployed the armed forces more often than at any time in the last 50 years. Some of the deployments themselves were questionable, such as in Haiti. But more than anything it was simply unwise to multiply missions in the face of a continuing budget reduction. Means and mission were not matched, and (predictably) the already thinly stretched armed forces came close to a breaking point. When all these trends became so obvious and embarrassing that they could no longer be ignored, the administration finally requested increased defense spending. But the "death spiral," as the administration's own undersecretary of defense called it—robbing procurement and research and development simply to operate the armed forces— was already well under way. That the administration did nothing, choosing instead to live off the fruits of Reagan's military buildup, constitutes an extraordinary neglect of the fiduciary responsibilities of the commander in chief.

Now the next president will be confronted with a prolonged job of repair. Military readiness will have to take center stage, particularly those aspects that affect the living conditions of the troops—military pay, housing—and also training. New weapons will have to be procured in order to give the military the capacity to carry out today's missions. But even in its current state, the American military still enjoys a commanding technological lead and therefore has a battlefield advantage over any competitor. Thus the next president should refocus the Pentagon's priorities on building the military of the 21st century rather than continuing to build on the structure of the Cold War. U.S. technological advantages should be leveraged to build forces that are lighter and more lethal, more mobile and agile, and capable of firing accurately from long distances. In order to do this, Washington must reallocate resources, perhaps in some cases skipping a generation of technology to make leaps rather than incremental improvements in its forces.

The other major concern is a loss of focus on the mission of the armed forces. What does it mean to deter, fight, and win wars and defend the national interest? First, the American military must be able to meet decisively the emergence of any hostile military power in the Asia-Pacific region, the Middle East, the Persian Gulf, and Europe—areas in which not only our interests but also those of our key allies are at stake. America's military is the only one capable of this deterrence function, and it must not be stretched or diverted into areas that weaken these broader responsibilities. It is the role that the United States played when Saddam Hussein threatened the Persian Gulf, and it is the power needed to deter trouble on the Korean Peninsula or across the Taiwan Strait. In the latter cases, the goal is to make it inconceivable for North Korea or China to use force because American military power is a compelling factor in their equations.

Some small-scale conflicts clearly have an impact on American strategic interests. Such was the case with Kosovo, which was in the backyard of America's most important strategic alliance: NATO. In fact, Yugoslav President Slobodan Miloševic's rejection of peaceful coexistence with the Kosovar Albanians threatened to rock the area's fragile ethnic balance. Eastern Europe is a patchwork of ethnic minorities. For the most part, Hungarians and Romanians, Bulgarians and Turks, and even Ukrainians and Russians have found a way since 1991 of preventing their differences from exploding. Miloševic has been the exception, and the United States had an overriding strategic interest in stopping him. There was, of course, a humanitarian disaster looming as well, but in the absence of concerns based on the interests of the alliance, the case for intervention would have been more tenuous.

The Kosovo war was conducted incompetently, in part because the administration's political goals kept shifting and in part because it was not, at the start, committed to the decisive use of military force. That President Clinton was surprised at Miloševic's tenacity is, well, surprising. If there is any lesson from history, it is that small powers with everything to lose are often more stubborn than big powers, for whom the conflict is merely one among many problems. The lesson, too, is that if it is worth fighting for, you had better be prepared to win. Also, there must be a political game plan that will permit the withdrawal of our forces—something that is still completely absent in Kosovo.

But what if our values are attacked in areas that are not arguably of strategic concern?

Should the United States not try to save lives in the absence of an overriding strategic rationale? The next American president should be in a position to intervene when he believes, and can make the case, that the United States is duty-bound to do so. "Humanitarian intervention" cannot be ruled out a priori. But a decision to intervene in the absence of strategic concerns should be understood for what it is. Humanitarian problems are rarely only humanitarian problems; the taking of life or withholding of food is almost always a political act. If the United States is not prepared to address the underlying political conflict and to know whose side it is on, the military may end up separating warring parties for an indefinite period. Sometimes one party (or both) can come to see the United States as the enemy. Because the military cannot, by definition, do anything decisive in these "humanitarian" crises, the chances of misreading the situation and ending up in very different circumstances are very high. This was essentially the problem of "mission creep" in Somalia.

The president must remember that the military is a special instrument. It is lethal, and it is meant to be. It is not a civilian police force. It is not a political referee. And it is most certainly not designed to build a civilian society. Military force is best used to support clear political goals, whether limited, such as expelling Saddam from Kuwait, or comprehensive, such as demanding the unconditional surrender of Japan and Germany during World War II. It is one thing to have a limited political goal and to fight decisively for it; it is quite another to apply military force incrementally, hoping to find a political solution somewhere along the way. A president entering these situations must ask whether decisive force is possible and is likely to be effective and must know how and when to get out. These are difficult criteria to meet, so U.S. intervention in these "humanitarian" crises should be, at best, exceedingly rare.

This does not mean that the United States must ignore humanitarian and civil conflicts around the world. But the military cannot be involved everywhere. Often, these tasks might be better carried out by regional actors, as modeled by the Australian-led intervention in East Timor. The U.S. might be able to lend financial, logistical, and intelligence support. Sometimes tough, competent diplomacy in the beginning can prevent the need for military force later. Using the American armed forces as the world's "911" will degrade capabilities, bog soldiers down in peacekeeping roles, and fuel concern among other great powers that the United States has decided to enforce notions of "limited sovereignty" worldwide in the name of humanitarianism. This overly broad definition of America's national interest is bound to backfire as others arrogate the same authority to themselves. Or we will find ourselves looking to the United Nations to sanction the use of American military power in these cases, implying that we will do so even when our vital interests are involved, which would also be a mistake.

DEALING WITH THE POWERFUL

ANOTHER CRUCIAL TASK for the United States is to focus on relations with other powerful states. Although the United States is fortunate to count among its friends several great powers, it is important not to take them for granted—so that there is a firm foundation when it comes time to rely on them. The challenges of China and North Korea require coordination and cooperation with Japan and South Korea. The signals that we send to our real partners are important. Never again should an American president go to Beijing for nine days and refuse to stop in Tokyo or Seoul.

There is work to do with the Europeans, too, on defining what holds the transatlantic alliance together in the absence of the Soviet threat. NATO is badly in need of attention in the wake of Kosovo and with the looming question of its further enlargement in 2002 and beyond. The door to NATO for the remaining states of eastern and central Europe should remain open, as many are actively preparing to meet the criteria for membership. But the parallel track of NATO's own evolution, its attention to the definition of its mission, and its ability to digest and then defend new members has been neglected. Moreover, the United States has an interest in shaping the European defense identity—welcoming a greater European military capability as long as it is within the context of NATO. NATO has a very full agenda. Membership in NATO will mean nothing to anyone if the organization is no longer militarily capable and if it is unclear about its mission.

For America and our allies, the most daunting task is to find the right balance in our policy toward Russia and China. Both are equally important to the future of international peace, but the challenges they pose are very different. China is a rising power; in economic terms, that should be good news, because in order to maintain its economic dynamism, China must be more integrated into the international economy. This will require increased openness and transparency and the growth of private industry. The political struggle in Beijing is over how to maintain the Communist Party's monopoly on power. Some see economic reform, growth, and a better life for the Chinese people as the key. Others see the inherent contradiction in loosening economic control and maintaining the party's political dominance. As China's economic problems multiply due to slowing growth rates, failing banks, inert state enterprises, and rising unemployment, this struggle will intensify.

It is in America's interest to strengthen the hands of those who seek economic integration because this will probably lead to sustained and organized pressures for political liberalization. There are no guarantees, but in scores of cases from Chile to Spain to Taiwan, the link between democracy and economic liberalization has proven powerful over the long run. Trade and economic interaction are, in fact, good—not only for America's economic growth but for its political aims as well. Human rights concerns should not move to the sidelines in the meantime. Rather, the American president should press the Chinese leadership for change. But it is wise to remember that our influence through moral arguments and commitment is still limited in the face of Beijing's pervasive political control. The big trends toward the spread of information, the access of young Chinese to American values through educational exchanges and training, and the growth of an entrepreneurial class that does not owe its livelihood to the state are, in the end, likely to have a more powerful effect on life in China.

Although some argue that the way to support human rights is to refuse trade with China, this punishes precisely those who are most likely to change the system. Put bluntly, Li Peng and the Chinese conservatives want to continue to run the economy by state fiat. Of course, there should be tight export controls on the transfer of militarily sensitive technology to China. But trade in general can open up the Chinese economy and, ultimately, its politics too. This view requires faith in the power of markets and economic freedom to drive political change, but it is a faith confirmed by experiences around the globe.

Even if there is an argument for economic interaction with Beijing, China is still a potential threat to stability in the Asia-Pacific region. Its military power is currently no match for that of the United States. But that condition is not necessarily permanent. What we do know is that China is a great power with unresolved vital interests, particularly concerning Taiwan and the South China Sea. China resents the role of the United States in the Asia-Pacific region. This means that China is not a "status quo" power but one that would like to alter Asia's balance of power in its own favor. That alone makes it a strategic competitor, not the "strategic partner" the Clinton administration once called it. Add to this China's record of cooperation with Iran and Pakistan in the proliferation of ballistic-missile technology, and the security problem is obvious. China will do what it can to enhance its position, whether by stealing nuclear secrets or by trying to intimidate Taiwan.

China's success in controlling the balance of power depends in large part on America's reaction to the challenge. The United States must deepen its cooperation with Japan and South Korea and maintain its commitment to a robust military presence in the region. It should pay closer attention to India's role in the regional balance. There is a strong tendency conceptually to connect India with Pakistan and to think only of Kashmir or the nuclear competition between the two states. But India is an element in China's calculation, and it should be in America's, too. India is not a great power yet, but it has the potential to emerge as one.

The United States also has a deep interest in the security of Taiwan. It is a model of democratic and market-oriented development, and it invests significantly in the mainland's economy. The longstanding U.S. commitment to a "one-China" policy that leaves to a future date the resolution of the relationship between Taipei and Beijing is wise. But that policy requires that neither side challenge the status quo and that Beijing, as the more powerful actor, renounce the use of force. U.S. resolve anchors this policy. The Clinton administration tilted toward Beijing, when, for instance, it used China's formulation of the "three no's" during the president's trip there. Taiwan has been looking for attention and reassurance ever since. If the United States is resolute, peace can be maintained in the Taiwan Strait until a political settlement on democratic terms is available.

Some things take time. U.S. policy toward China requires nuance and balance. It is important to promote China's internal transition through economic interaction while containing Chinese power and security ambitions. Cooperation should be pursued, but we should never be afraid to confront Beijing when our interests collide.

RUSSIAN WEAKNESS

RUSSIA PRESENTS a different challenge. It still has many of the attributes of a great power: a large population, vast territory, and military potential. But its economic weakness and problems of national identity threaten to overwhelm it. Moscow is determined to assert itself in the world and often does so in ways that are at once haphazard and threatening to American interests. The picture is complicated by Russia's own internal transition—one that the United States wants to see succeed. The old Soviet system has broken down, and some of the basic elements of democratic development are in place. People are free to say what they think, vote for whom they please, and (for the most part) worship freely. But the democratic fragments are not institutionalized—with the exception of the Communist Party, political parties are weak—and the balance of political power is so strongly in favor of the president that he often rules simply by decree. Of course, few pay attention to Boris Yeltsin's decrees, and the Russian government has been mired in inaction and stagnation for at least three years. Russia's economic troubles and its high-level corruption have been widely discussed in recent months; Russia's economy is not becoming a market but is mutating into something else. Widespread barter, banks that are not banks, billions of rubles stashed abroad and in mattresses at home, and bizarre privatization schemes that have enriched the so-called reformers give Moscow's economy a medieval tinge.

The problem for U.S. policy is that the Clinton administration's embrace of Yeltsin and those who were thought to be reformers around him has failed. Yeltsin is Russia's president and clearly the United States had to deal with the head of state. But support for democracy and economic reform became support for Yeltsin. His agenda became the American agenda. The United States certified that reform was taking place where it was not, continuing to disburse money from the International Monetary Fund in the absence of any evidence of serious change. The curious privatization methods were hailed as economic liberalization; the looting of the country's assets by powerful people either went unnoticed or was ignored. The realities in Russia simply did not accord with the administration's script about Russian economic reform. The United States should not be faulted for trying to help. But, as the Russian reformer Grigori Yavlinsky has said, the United States should have "told the truth" about what was happening.

Now we have a dual credibility problem—with Russians and with Americans. There are signs of life in the Russian economy. The financial crash of August 1998 forced import substitution, and domestic production has increased as the resilient Russian people have taken matters into their own hands. Rising oil prices have helped as well. But these are short-term fixes. There is no longer a consensus in America or Europe on what to do next with Russia. Frustrated expectations and "Russia fatigue" are direct consequences of the "happy talk" in which the Clinton administration engaged.

Russia's economic future is now in the hands of the Russians. The country is not without assets, including its natural resources and an educated population. It is up to Russia to make structural reforms, particularly concerning the rule of law and the tax codes, so that investors—foreign and domestic—will provide the capital needed for economic growth. That opportunity will arise once there is a new government in Moscow after last December's Duma elections and next June's presidential election. But the cultural changes ultimately needed to sustain a functioning civil society and a market-based economy may take a generation. Western openness to Russia's people, particularly its youth, in exchange programs and contact with the private sector and educational opportunities can help that process. It is also important to engage the leadership of Russia's diverse regions, where economic and social policies are increasingly pursued independently of Moscow.

In the meantime, U.S. policy must concentrate on the important security agenda with Russia. First, it must recognize that American security is threatened less by Russia's strength than by its weakness and incoherence. This suggests immediate attention to the safety and security of Moscow's nuclear forces and stockpile. The Nunn-Lugar program should be funded fully and pursued aggressively. (Because American contractors do most of the work, the risk of the diversion of funds is low.) Second, Washington must begin a comprehensive discussion with Moscow on the changing nuclear threat. Much has been made by Russian military officials about their increased reliance on nuclear weapons in the face of their declining conventional readiness. The Russian deterrent is more than adequate against the U.S. nuclear arsenal, and vice versa. But that fact need no longer be enshrined in a treaty that is almost 30 years old and is a relic of a profoundly adversarial relationship between the United States and the Soviet Union. The Anti–Ballistic Missile Treaty was intended to prevent the development of national missile defenses in the Cold War security environment. Today, the principal concerns are nuclear threats from the Iraqs and North Koreas of the world and the possibility of unauthorized releases as nuclear weapons spread.

Moscow, in fact, lives closer to those threats than Washington does. It ought to be possible to engage the Russians in a discussion of the changed threat environment, their possible responses, and the relationship of strategic offensive-force reductions to the deployment of defenses. The United States should make clear that it prefers to move cooperatively toward a new offense-defense mix, but that it is prepared to do so unilaterally. Moscow should understand, too, that any possibilities for sharing technology or information in these areas would depend heavily on its record—problematic to date—on the proliferation of ballistic-missile and other technologies related to WMD. It would be foolish in the extreme to share defenses with Moscow if it either leaks or deliberately transfers weapons technologies to the very states against which America is defending.

Finally, the United States needs to recognize that Russia is a great power, and that we will always have interests that conflict as well as coincide. The war in Chechnya, located in the oil-rich Caucasus, is particularly dangerous. Prime Minister Vladimir Putin has used the war to stir nationalism at home while fueling his own political fortunes. The Russian military has been uncharacteristically blunt and vocal in asserting its duty to defend the integrity of the Russian Federation—an unwelcome development in civil-military relations. The long-term effect on Russia's political culture should not be underestimated. And the war has affected relations between Russia and its neighbors in the Caucasus, as the Kremlin hurls charges of harboring and abetting Chechen terrorists against states as diverse as Saudi Arabia, Georgia, and Azerbaijan. The war is a reminder of the vulnerability of the small, new states around Russia and of America's interest in their independence. If they can become stronger, they will be less tempting to Russia. But much depends on the ability of these states to reform their economies and political systems—a process, to date, whose success is mixed at best.

COPING WITH ROGUE REGIMES

AS HISTORY MARCHES toward markets and democracy, some states have been left by the side of the road. Iraq is the prototype. Saddam Hussein's regime is isolated, his conventional military power has been severely weakened, his people live in poverty and terror, and he has no useful place in international politics. He is therefore determined to develop WMD. Nothing will change until Saddam is gone, so the United States must mobilize whatever resources it can, including support from his opposition, to remove him.

The regime of Kim Jong Il is so opaque that it is difficult to know its motivations, other than that they are malign. But North Korea also lives outside of the international system. Like East Germany, North Korea is the evil twin of a successful regime just across its border. It must fear its eventual demise from the sheer power and pull of South Korea. Pyongyang, too, has little to gain and everything to lose from engagement in the international economy. The development of WMD thus provides the destructive way out for Kim Jong Il.

President Kim Dae Jung of South Korea is attempting to find a peaceful resolution with the north through engagement. Any U.S. policy toward the north should depend heavily on coordination with Seoul and Tokyo. In that context, the 1994 framework agreement that attempted to bribe North Korea into forsaking nuclear weapons cannot easily be set aside. Still, there is a trap inherent in this approach: sooner or later Pyongyang will threaten to test a missile one too many times, and the United

States will not respond with further benefits. Then what will Kim Jong Il do? The possibility for miscalculation is very high.

One thing is clear: the United States must approach regimes like North Korea resolutely and decisively. The Clinton administration has failed here, sometimes threatening to use force and then backing down, as it often has with Iraq. These regimes are living on borrowed time, so there need be no sense of panic about them. Rather, the first line of defense should be a clear and classical statement of deterrence—if they do acquire WMD, their weapons will be unusable because any attempt to use them will bring national obliteration. Second, we should accelerate efforts to defend against these weapons. This is the most important reason to deploy national and theater missile defenses as soon as possible, to focus attention on U.S. homeland defenses against chemical and biological agents, and to expand intelligence capabilities against terrorism of all kinds.

Finally, there is the Iranian regime. Iran's motivation is not to disrupt simply the development of an international system based on markets and democracy, but to replace it with an alternative: fundamentalist Islam. Fortunately, the Iranians do not have the kind of reach and power that the Soviet Union enjoyed in trying to promote its socialist alternative. But Iran's tactics have posed real problems for U.S. security. It has tried to destabilize moderate Arab states such as Saudi Arabia, though its relations with the Saudis have improved recently. Iran has also supported terrorism against America andWestern interests and attempted to develop and transfer sensitive military technologies.

Iran presents special difficulties in the Middle East, a region of core interest to the United States and to our key ally Israel. Iranian weaponry increasingly threatens Israel directly. As important as Israel's efforts to reach peace with its Arab neighbors are to the future of the Middle East, they are not the whole story of stability in the region. Israel has a real security problem, so defense cooperation with the United States—particularly in the area of ballistic missile defense—is critical. That in turn will help Israel protect itself both through agreements and through enhanced military power.

Still, it is important to note that there are trends in Iran that bear watching. Mohammad Khatami's election as president has given some hope of a new course for a country that once hosted a great and thriving civilization—though there are questions about how much authority he exercises. Moreover, Khatami's more moderate domestic views may not translate into more acceptable behavior abroad. All in all, changes in U.S. policy toward Iran would require changes in Iranian behavior.

BUILDING A CONSENSUS FOR THE NATIONAL INTEREST

AMERICA IS BLESSED with an extraordinary opportunity. It has had no territorial ambitions for nearly a century. Its national interest has been defined instead by a desire to foster the spread of freedom, prosperity, and peace. Both the will of the people and the demands of modern economies accord with that vision of the future. But even America's advantages offer no guarantees of success. It is up to America's presidential leadership and policy to bridge the gap between tomorrow's possibilities and today's realities.

The president must speak to the American people about national priorities and intentions and work with Congress to focus foreign policy around the national interest. The problem today is not an absence of bipartisan spirit in Congress or the American people's disinterest. It is the existence of a vacuum. In the absence of a compelling vision, parochial interests are filling the void.

Foreign policy in a Republican administration will most certainly be internationalist; the leading contenders in the party's presidential race have strong credentials in that regard. But it will also proceed from the firm ground of the national interest, not from the interests of an illusory international community. America can exercise power without arrogance and pursue its interests without hectoring and bluster. When it does so in concert with those who share its core values, the world becomes more prosperous, democratic, and peaceful. That has been America's special role in the past, and it should be again as we enter the next century.

CONDOLEEZZA RICE is Senior Fellow at the Hoover Institution and Professor of Political Science at Stanford University. She is also foreign policy adviser to Republican presidential candidate George W. Bush.

Home Alone

Can America Play the Superpower Role?

Robert V. Daniels

IF YOU LISTEN closely, you can hear a hollow ring to all the triumphalist talk about America's superpower monopoly since the end of the cold war. True, it is a position without precedent for any government since the days of the Roman Empire. But the nation's political leadership cannot agree on what to do with this power, and the American public may not be willing or able to sustain it. "The present danger," wrote Robert Kagan and William Kristol in *Foreign Affairs* early this year, "is that the US . . . will shrink its responsibilities," thereby "frittering away the opportunity to strengthen and extend an international order uniquely favorable to the US." But it is not enough just to press for more military spending and a more vigorous doctrine of intervention, as these authors do. One needs to consider Americans' post–cold war "battle fatigue," as Stanley Hoffmann calls it in *World Disorders:* "fatigue with battles, fatigue both with unilateral interventions and with multilateral agencies and operations not controlled by the US." American tradition, already overstrained by the great international tests of the past century, finds it hard to accommodate the country's new, overweening, but nevertheless exposed position.

Survival and Triumph

A good way to understand Americans' uncertainties as they confront their new world role is to recall two formative events in the early history of the American republic that set up paradigms—bundles of assumptions and reflexes—illuminating much in Americans' thinking ever since. One of these was the War of 1812, the "second war of independence," as it came to be known. Rightly or wrongly, that war went down in American history as the quintessential struggle of an infant democracy to preserve its liberty and assert its identity against a threatening world of evil powers. In *The War of 1812: A Forgotten Conflict,* Donald R. Hickey culled some contemporary expressions of this spirit: "We have stood the contest, single-handed, against the conqueror of Europe," boasted Supreme Court Justice Joseph Story, and Representative Charles J. Ingersoll of Pennsylvania declaimed, "Who is not proud to feel himself an American—our wrongs revenged—our rights recognized!" Not for nothing did the national anthem derive from that war: "Then conquer we must, for our cause it is just."

The other early experience that shaped Americans' outlook on the world had a very different direction. This was the so-called Second Great Awakening, the religious revival of the 1820s and 1830s that affirmed evangelical rectitude and stimulated American missionary activity all over the world. "Leaders of the Second Great Awakening," says Robert William Fogel in his new study of American reformism, *The Fourth Great Awakening and the Future of Egalitarianism,* "preached that the American mission was to build God's kingdom on earth."

These paradigms, deriving from 1812 and the Great Awakening respectively, are not to be confused with the familiar realist-idealist debate in American policy making. They are deeply embedded attitudes, largely beyond consciousness of their origins. For generations they have governed popular responsiveness to competing political appeals, and they still give Americans two almost opposite ways of looking at their international environment.

In the 1812 view, the outside world is a perpetual threat, not only to the country's values but to its very existence. Here is the basis for the philosophy of isolationism: "the original tradition that all subsequent ones purported to serve: *Liberty at home,*" as Walter A. McDougall recently put it in *Promised Land, Crusader State.* Alliances are suspect, in the spirit of George Washington's Farewell Address, particularly if the United States is not in command. The spirit of 1812 encourages Americans not to make sacrifices unless they are directly threatened.

According to the Great Awakening outlook, by contrast, the outside world is not so much a threat as a calling, an opportunity to save the benighted foreigners by exporting the American Way. This is the model for American self-righteousness and moralistic intervention in international affairs, "America's self-assigned role in the world, the . . . democratizing mission," according to Tony Smith in *America's Mission: The United States and the Worldwide Struggle for Democracy in the Twentieth Century,* or simply the "Wilsonian vision of saving the world," in McDougall's words. Although this national mission was at first conceived of in religious terms, as time went on it became progressively secularized into crusades for democracy and now for what passes as the free market.

At the time of the two world wars and during the cold war, the two paradigms more or less converged around their common presumption of American moral superiority. The 1812 sense of a struggle for survival fused with the Great Awakening spirit of saving the world from the devil. Kagan and Kristol quote the future defense secretary James Forrestal at the moment of U.S. entry into World War II: "America must be the dominant power of the twentieth century." According to Henry Luce, the nation would build "an international moral order."

In Americans' post–cold war triumphalism, the combined 1812 and Great Awakening paradigms have generated a new outburst of national hubris. Joshua Muravchik, for example, titled his exculpatory history of American political warfare during the cold-war era *Exporting Democracy: Fulfilling America's Destiny.* Looking to a "Pax Americana" based on "the humane idea born in the American experiment," Muravchik writes, "we would stand triumphant . . . achieving by our model and our influence the visionary goal stamped by the founding fathers on the seal of the United States: *novus ordo seclorum,* a new order of the ages." Even more pointedly, William Shawcross (in *Deliver Us from Evil: Peacekeepers, Warlords and a World of Endless Conflict*) cites the former chair of the Joint Chiefs of Staff General John Shalikashvilli's justification of NATO action outside Western Europe: "This is no longer a world where you limit yourself to vital interests. Today, we protect our interests when they are threatened in order to shape the environment to ensure that what develops is in accord with our goals, using American military forces in situations when lesser interests are threatened so they don't grow." These sentiments verge on what the late Senator J. William Fulbright, in his book by that title, called "the arrogance of power."

Hegemony and its Limits

All this confidence notwithstanding, there are internal limits to America's exercise of global hegemony that the superpower triumphalists fail to appreciate. The problem is not material but psychological. Changes in the interests and attitudes of the American public are undercutting all the main elements in the country's superior power—military, economic, and technological.

Although the American economy appears at the moment beyond challenge, with a commanding position in world business and in international financial institutions, a longer term view gives concern. Americans are obsessed with immediate gratification and this year's bottom line; net savings have vanished, private debt continues to mount, and tax-cutting demands defy a still formidable public debt. The nation's chronic and growing trade deficit depends on foreign financing and compounds the de-industrialization of America that has been going on for the last two decades. These trends are not marks of a superpower.

Technologically, the future is at risk because American students don't want to study hard subjects. Engineering schools fill half their ranks with foreign students, and high-tech business is desperate to import the skills it needs—adding a brain imbalance to the nation's chronic trade imbalance. Worse, in this age of competition for technological superiority, the United States suffers from what can only be called mental backwardness. Pop culture based on sensory overexcitement displaces educational accomplishment. Religious fundamentalism and the superstitiousness abetted by mass media entertainment stand in the way of scientific thinking. If there is change underway in this respect, it is only toward newer or revived forms of mysticism:

people know more about astrology than about astronomy.

For this deficiency of knowledge and attitude, American education is the culprit. To be sure, at the pinnacle of graduate training in elite universities, education and research are still second to none, but the base of the pyramid is porous and shaky. Even at the college level, American students are notorious for their ignorance of basic geography and history. Foreign travel may be up, but foreign language study is in critical decline. In his *Public Opinion and American Foreign Policy,* Ole R. Holsti reports, "The most consistent finding [is that] Americans are poorly informed about most aspects of international affairs." Whatever may be thought about trends in American education in the last half-century, the system has failed to equip the bulk of its students to be citizens of a superpower.

There is a vicious, three-way interaction between education, popular interests, and the media. Interest is dulled by deficient educational background about the world. Short of momentary crises and sensations, the media shy away from what the public lacks interest in—scan the front page of any small-town daily to see this. There are, as in education, niche exceptions for the devoted few, but the media intake of most Americans dilutes their understanding of world affairs even more, and their interest evaporates accordingly. America has become a nation of complacent, even mindless, self-indulgence. We have come a long way from John Kennedy's "pay any price. . . . ask what you can do for your country."

The contradiction between self-indulgence and global power is nowhere clearer than in the new American attitude toward military action. Americans, as their political leaders read them, are unwilling to back any overseas projection of the nation's power that might involve combat fatalities. People still seem to regard their military as citizen draftees rather than professionals paid to risk their lives. Television images prompt demands for American to do something about every interethnic outbreak around the globe (a latter-day reflex of the Great Awakening paradigm), but at the same time they have brought home to a comfortable and risk-averse populace the horror of warfare even on the smallest scale. The Gulf War, tightly censored by the military even though the superiority of the American-led alliance made the defeat of Saddam Hussein a walkaway, stands as the last real military conflict in which the United States engaged voluntarily. Then came the Somalia debacle and the Post-Somalia Syndrome, when television images of a few American bodies being dragged through the streets of Mogadishu soured the American public on armed intervention anywhere. The extraordinarily cautious management of NATO intervention in Kosovo, so that no American would get scratched in combat, proves the point.

This fear of fighting comes on top of demographic changes in modern industrial societies where, as Edward Luttwak in particular has pointed out, families are no longer large enough to accept the risk of their sons' getting killed. The inclusion of women in all roles in the armed forces has made the commitment of troops in real battle even more problematic. The American superpower has, in effect, ruled out the employment of its own military to exert this power, unless the use of force can be sanitized by technological quick fixes.

As the sole superpower, the United States presumes that it is exercising global leadership. Americans are still encouraged in the smug self-image that they lead the world in all the things that American tradition (however inconsistently) holds dear—democracy and prosperity, spirituality and morality, science and technology. In fact, by most measurable indicators of political and material progress, Western Europe has caught up, as has Japan, while Scandinavia has forged ahead. On the newer goals set by the revolution of the 1960s, notably tolerance for ethnic pluralism and the equality of women, the United States took the lead, but once again Europe has largely caught up. In the youth revolt against the authority of experts and educators, Europe led the way in the uprisings of 1968, but the movement has pushed much further in America, with disturbing consequences for the nation's educational system and its competitiveness in the knowledge market. America's leading export, after wheat and airplanes, is mass culture, a commodity that policy-making elites practically everywhere else find revolting. And on basic indicators of social health—crime, life expectancy, child poverty—the United States now lags perceptibly among industrialized countries, thanks above all to its failure to address problems of inequality in the modern economy.

The Two Paradigms

Against this backdrop of a deteriorating power base at home, the end of the cold war has opened up the old divisions in the nation's political psyche. There is a new cleavage between the two paradigms about the outside world, corresponding to the national division in the 1930s when the two major parties were polarized between the isolationist camp on one side and the interventionists on the other. The difference now is that the nation is not merely maneuvering in a multipower environment, but swings the clout of a superpower, whichever paradigm it heeds. Sean Kay of Ohio Wesleyan University, writing in *Problems of Post-Communism* ("What Is a Strategic Partnership?" May–June 2000), speaks of "two competing national grand strategies, primacy and balancing."

Under the pull of the 1812 assumptions, fortified by America's new power, the Republicans now incline toward global unilateralism—no one dare try to tell us what to do, while we tell everyone else what to do. As exemplified by George W. Bush's foreign policy adviser Condoleeza Rice in the January–February *Foreign Affairs,* they want to put an end to Wilsonian idealism and set the "national interest" ahead of any "humanitarian interest" or "international community." They don't define "national interest," because, to put it crassly, the national interest boils down to making the world safe for the multinational corporations.

Outside of corporate economics, talk of the "national interest" reflects not world leadership but a determination to use America's superpower status to wall the nation off from the world. Seeking security behind the nuclear shield, the 1812ers went so far last year as to reject the Comprehensive Nuclear Test Ban Treaty, confident that America could keep the technological lead in arms. Shortly after that, the Stanley Foundation's UN Issues Conference warned, "Increasing US tendencies toward exceptionalism and unilateral action are reducing the effectiveness of multilateral organization."

Designedly so. The 1812ers have always harbored a deep antipathy toward the UN and any semblance of international authority to which the United States might be subject. They block payment of the country's back dues owed the UN, though they are eager to commit infinitely larger sums to the maintenance of national military power. They carp at support for international peacekeeping operations—though this is one way to play the superpower while minimizing the risk of American casualties. Last April, the House of Representatives was barely dissuaded from defunding American forces in Kosovo. Yet the 1812ers talk tough: Rice's complaint about Kosovo was that "the administration . . . was not, at the start, committed to the decisive use of force."

The Democrats, for their part, remain more sensitive to Great Awakening missions and the politics of balance—let's work together to resolve the world's problems, as long as you acknowledge our leading role. However, under the stress of presidential campaigning, everyone has been drawn further toward the 1812 principle of military power as the guarantee of security for a self-satisfied America. So the Democrats are left to waffle between competing with Republican militarism and defending a rational view of the world.

Whether they are aligned with the 1812 paradigm or the Great Awakening paradigm, Americans have a hard time putting themselves in other nations' shoes. The 1812 devotees of military security cannot grasp how America's preponderance of power could appear to Russia or China not defensive but potentially offensive. The adherents of the secularized Great Awakening cannot comprehend the resentment abroad of America's presumption of moral superiority, though the United States would never accept corresponding missions of religious or political uplift in reverse—note only its rejection of Marxism. What was once the world's most revolutionary country, in the early nineteenth century, had become a century later the most counterrevolutionary.

For all the talk of allies and cooperation, Americans refuse to accept full reciprocity of responsibilities and obligations. Though ever since Nuremberg it has been a vigorous advocate for international justice, the American government rejects any jurisdiction over its own military forces on the part of international judicial bodies. It goes without saying that American troops can never be allowed to operate under foreign command. Indeed, an early blunder in cold-war alliance politics was the U.S. reluctance to rotate the military command of NATO and give the French the second crack at it following General Dwight D. Eisenhower.

Star Wars II

All the contradictions in America's stance toward the outside world come together in the so-called National Missile Defense (NMD) or "Star Wars II." This resurrection of Ronald Reagan's celestial dream has been seized upon by the Republicans, with encouragement from the military contractors, to embarrass the Democrats. To protect its political right flank, the Clinton administration has felt driven to follow suit with its own version of the scheme, regardless of doubts about its cost and effectiveness. It seems that the national psyche cannot manage without a substitute for the cold war.

NMD is a perfect embodiment of the 1812 paradigm. It is, after all, a project for "defense," to ward off threats from the "rogue nations" who have conveniently popped up to take the place of the Soviet menace. It is "national," aiming first of all to protect the United States. And it is "missile," that is, a resort to technological superiority to substitute for the two oceans in guaranteeing America's security against the evil forces "out there" who plot to do the United States in, notwithstanding its overwhelming preemptive and retaliatory power. The cocoon of miracle technology that Americans spin about themselves will presumably suffice to shield them from the rogue devils, allowing the leaders of both parties to display maximum toughness toward outsiders without risking the blood of a single American soldier.

Why one of these pipsqueak adversaries would attempt a suicidal nuclear missile attack on the United States, if it ever could, has never been figured out. America seems to be driven by a psychology of chagrin, coupled with the "threat exaggeration" analyzed by Robert H. Johnson (*Improbable Dangers: U.S. Conceptions of Threat in the Cold War and After*). The alleged "rogues" are all weak, mostly Muslim countries that have piqued the United States by successful acts of defiance in the past, so they must be treated as enemies to the death. "Rogue states," said Secretary of State Madeleine Albright three years ago, "are there with the sole purpose of destroying . . . the international system." Condoleeza Rice worries, preposterously, that "fundamentalist Islam" would try to undo the whole American-dominated "international system based on markets and democracy."

The rogue-nation panic reflects the 1812 paradigm at work in American thinking. If nuclear attack by a rogue state were a real danger, it would be logical to develop a broad international response. Yet until the current presidential campaign prompted extension of projected missile defense coverage to America's skeptical allies, the scheme has been couched in strictly American terms.

The question of whether NMD would work, or by any stretch of the imagination justify its probable cost, any more than its ancestor the Strategic Defense Initiative–Star Wars is not as important as the political and economic interests that are served in attempting it anyway. The fact that NMD would upset arms control treaties with Russia, antagonize China, and strain relations with America's European allies matters not to the 1812ers. They are tired of conciliating allies and putting up with treaty restrictions on America's ability to defend itself. Even more to the point, as the *Washington Post* showed (June 4, 2000), NMD has been vigorously promoted by the same industrial interests that would get the lion's share of the contracts to build the system. NATO expansion was similarly driven—American arms and planes could be sold to the new member countries in Eastern Europe, paid for ultimately by American taxpayers. At the governmental level there is little resistance to such pressures, given the political need to appear to stand tough against foreign enemies. Economic and political interests neatly dovetail.

Superpower is not total power, the triumphalists notwithstanding, and it will not last forever, if only because of the potential among other major countries (not just the alleged "rogues") to combine their demographic weight with military know-how and conclude countervailing alliances. The United States cannot indefinitely function as a world policeman nor even as a "reluctant sheriff," as Richard Haas put it in his recent book of that title, nor can it use its power to impose American "interests" without stimulating wide reactions against American hegemony. On the other hand, when a superpower begins behaving as if it were a beleaguered outpost with the world against it, its suspicions are likely to become a self-fulfilling prophecy. The future holds unpredictable hazards, as the world comes to see that the American superpower has neither the political will nor the psychological stamina to sustain the role it has been cast in.

ROBERT V. DANIELS, professor emeritus of history at the University of Vermont, is author of *Russia: The Roots of Confrontation* and *The End of the Communist Revolution*.

NO-FIRST-USE FOR NATO?

In December the House of Commons Standing Committee on Foreign Affairs and International Trade issued a report recommending, among other things, that NATO adopt a policy of no-first-use of nuclear weapons. Last month, Policy Options editor ***William Watson*** *asked the chairman of the committee, the Hon.* ***Bill Graham,*** *and* ***Frank Gaffney,*** *founder and director of the Washington-based Center for Security Policy and Deputy Assistant Secretary of Defense for Nuclear Forces and Arms Control Policy in the Reagan administration, to discuss this proposal by conference call. Here is an edited transcript of their conversation.*

Mr. Graham, last December your committee published a report recommending, among other things, that NATO consider adopting a policy of no-first-use of nuclear weapons. What's your reason for wanting to change NATO's current policy, which is that nuclear weapons are a weapon of last resort?

Bill Graham: Let me make two points. The report clearly says that for NATO to conduct a strategic review and not to review the nuclear component of its strategy just doesn't make sense, and, therefore, the nuclear review should take place as a part of the overall strategic review by NATO. Others, particularly in the defense department in the United States, feel strongly that this subject shouldn't even be talked about. So, really, there are two conversations here. One is, is it appropriate to have a review as a part of NATO's review and, two, if you do, then what's your point of view of what the policy should [be]? Should it be no-first-use, should it be the status quo, or what? The committee's conclusion, and certainly my own, is that the important thing is that this be on the agenda for discussion, that the strategic review of NATO will lack credibility if it doesn't discuss this issue, even if, in the end, the allies together come to the conclusion that the status quo is the appropriate place to be.

That said, you can then go on and say, "Where would you be if you were in that debate?" and I personally would lean towards those that would say, "Well, I think there's a momentum now for NATO to consider a no-first-use policy," but that's another discussion and that was not the recommendation of the report.

Could you explain why you do lean in the direction of no-first-use?

Bill Graham: I want to make it clear that I am not a nuclear policy expert in any way. I came to this as someone whose job was to hear Canadians and try to understand their position *vis-à-vis* that of our allies and those others outside of Canada that we were able to talk to, in the context of considering this issue and then referring this matter to the government for a response, which they will give in the House of Commons to the recommendations of the report. So, with that caveat, what we heard was that the first-use policy of NATO first came about as a deterrence factor at a time when NATO forces in Europe had a conventional disparity *vis-á-vis* the Soviet Union. In fact, the Warsaw Pact had an enormous superiority. That is no longer the case and that in itself, I think, has changed one's views.

We heard the US National Academy of Sciences, and the Canberra Commission, and General George Lee Butler, commander of the United States Strategic Command from 1992 to 1994, and the Pugwash Conference, and statements by people like Paul Nitze and retired General Andrew Goodpastor and former Secretary of Defense Robert McNamara. Most of those highly qualified people are saying, "Now is the time to go for no-first-use." The persuasive thing for me is that it moves the agenda along in trying to persuade other countries that they have to give up the idea of developing nuclear weapons. We have to deal with a nuclear Israel, we have to deal now with a nuclear Pakistan and a nuclear India. I was just on a trip to

Iran. If the West doesn't have any credibility in bringing nuclear weapons down and reducing their availability and their usefulness, then the other states are going to be driven to acquiring them.

Frank Gaffney: I believe it's a bit disingenuous, frankly, to suggest that we're only interested in talking about it. People who are interested in having this idea on the agenda clearly have in mind bringing pressure to bear on the United States, and the NATO alliance more generally, to adopt a policy that NATO has for the better part of its 50 years of existence deemed unacceptable. I am among those supporters of NATO who think that even in a post-Cold War world the NATO alliance is an important instrument for peace, both in its own immediate region and, to some extent, more generally. Anything which contributes to divisiveness and the perception that NATO is driven by internal strife in one form or another is counterproductive. And it's particularly unhelpful when the alliance is supposedly trying to celebrate its half century of success. So I would be opposed to talking about it unless people are serious about changing the policy. To suggest that the proponents of this are not serious about changing the policy is either misleading or suggests that the whole exercise would be counterproductive.

If the West doesn't have any credibility in bringing nuclear weapons down and reducing their availability and their usefulness, then other states will be driven to acquire them.

But the bigger problem is, why would you change this policy? I do consider myself something of a nuclear policy expert, even if Bill chooses to describe his credentials as otherwise. In 25 years of work in this field, I've seen a lot of ideas, nostrums and notions advanced. And one of the hoariest is that if only we behave in such and such a fashion, countries around the world like Iran will see the wisdom of eschewing nuclear weapons. This is, on the face of it, laughable. I must say with all due respect that it is laughable to suggest that Iran is motivated in its pursuit of nuclear weapons—or for that matter chemical weapons or biological weapons or the long-range ballistic missiles with which to deliver them or any form of weaponry—by what they think is the declaratory policy of the United States government or NATO or some other country that might be setting some sort of high moral tone.

Finally, and I know this does not sit well with my Canadian friends, but in the interest of candour and a frank and therefore constructive relationship between our two countries I think it best to say: It is deeply distressing to me that in this area a country that is currently bearing very little of the share of the burden of providing for its own security, let alone anybody else's security, is insisting on dictating, or at least instructing, the country that is principally providing for its security as to the terms and conditions under which that security will be provided. As a case in point, I know that I'm wearing the scars of what I consider to be an extremely counterproductive and dangerous Canadian initiative on banning landmines. It is the height of irresponsibility, in my judgment, for the United States to be coerced, pressured, cajoled, intimidated, choose your verb, by its Canadian ally, among others of course, into giving up weapons that are deemed by our military to be essential to providing for the security of our own troops and those that they are in places around the world to protect, which I suggest includes Canadian interests broadly defined as well.

Bill Graham: I certainly don't mean to be disingenuous. What I do say, though, is that I believe strongly that this matter should be debated. But it is the governments in NATO that will debate it, so it is in no way Canada dictating anything to anybody, including the United States. We're talking about NATO here. The United States can keep any policy it wants. It has that sovereign right. Nobody is saying the United States should give up its no-first-use policy, that's its internal debate. But we are a participant in NATO, and Germany is a participant in NATO, too. If American strategists are concerned about NATO cohesion, well, I think the genie is out of the bottle, and to try to suppress it at this point would be much more dangerous. If you look at the vote in the United Nations on the new agenda, it was very clear that the majority of the United States' and our NATO allies abstained along with us on that resolution, clearly indicating that within NATO itself there's a strong push. Even if it were just Germany alone, but with Germany, Canada and various other countries dealing with this, I think it has to be debated in NATO.

If this ends up causing a change in policy, then we'd have to look at whether that change is desirable or not. But I would have thought that if Frank's position is as well-founded in policy as he puts it, he has nothing to fear from an open debate, and he can give the back of his hand to the National Academy of Sciences, the Canberra Commission, General Butler, General Goodpastor and everybody else and tell them they're out to lunch. But that will have to be a debate that takes place within that NATO context.

How about the argument that Iraq or Iran will not pay any attention to what the NATO declaration says?

Bill Graham: As I say I've just come back from Iran—that hardly makes me an expert on Iran—but one of the problems is that when you talk to people, they say, "Well, Israel's there, they've got the nuclear weapons, they haven't signed the non-proliferation treaty, we've signed the non-proliferation treaty." They say, "We don't trust you, we don't care what you say, you're going to do whatever you're going to do."

At some point, we have to work towards constraining people from access to nuclear weapons. We do that through our policies in the various forums where we control access to nuclear technology, and so on. But I think we have to try and draw people in as well where they believe there is some greater form of greater disarmament that is taking place by the major powers. I mean, India said, "Well, look we've developed a nuclear weapon because we will not be dictated to by the other countries as to whether we should have one or not, they themselves are making no serious disarmament moves." I disagree with that by the way. I think the United States and the Soviet Union have made some enormously serious moves in disarmament. So that's an exaggerated position, but it is a position we have to be able to deal with.

Frank Gaffney: It is a fraud. It is an excuse designed to induce, on the part of Westerners, a sense of responsibility for behaviour that these countries are pursuing for their own reasons that have nothing to do with policies or positions of the United States or others. You might argue that the Indians are pursuing it because of the Pakistanis or the Chinese, but the United States could become a zero nuclear weapons state and I daresay it would be an inducement to the Iranians and the Indians and these other characters to proceed apace because then they become bigger fish than otherwise.

But if I may come back to a point I didn't address in my initial response. We're hearing cited as authorities for a policy that NATO has consistently rejected over the years the Canberra Commission, the Pugwash Conference, the several distinguished former American generals and Secretary of Defense. I think it only fair to point out that these institutions and individuals have associated themselves with the idea of abolishing nuclear weapons. Now I don't know where the government of Canada is on abolishing nuclear weapons. They're certainly following the logic of abolishing landmines. If you believe you can abolish landmines, you certainly can abolish nuclear weapons. But since you can't abolish either, it is nonsense to even discuss it—unless what you really are about is taking huge risks by disarming the country that you know you can disarm, which is of course the United States, and letting the devil take the hindmost with respect to the others, who will not observe international treaty obligations. We know this on the basis of historical experience. These countries will, to the contrary, see this as an opportunity to advance their national agendas, improving their relative positions *vis-à-vis* the United States or for that matter, the United States and its allies, like NATO. My point is that we must not lose sight of the agenda of at least some of the individuals whose advice the committee apparently has taken to heart.

I think it's time to call a spade a spade. They have embarked upon a loony left-wing disarmament agenda, the first step of which is a policy shift that seems relatively innocuous: announcing we no longer will use nuclear weapons first. Another step embraced by many of these organizations is to de-alert our nuclear weapons so they couldn't be used even if the policy were otherwise. But the desired end result is clear. And I think we ought to hear: Does the government of Canada or the parliamentary forces within Canada or Mr. Graham individually believe that in the world we are currently in or are about to enter we can safely abandon or abolish nuclear weapons—or not? And if not, you might want to distance yourself somewhat from the authorities who are now telling you it would also be a splendid idea to announce a no-first-use policy.

Bill Graham: I didn't, quite frankly, get the impression that the people who have been mentioned, while they are seeking to reduce nuclear weapons completely as a long-term goal, are in any way dewy-eyed crazies. They all were talking the language of extreme caution in moving towards that goal, which would be accompanied by appropriate surveillance and international controls. Our committee didn't espouse—and I cannot speak for the government of Canada, but I do believe that when the government of Canada responds to our report in the House of Commons, they will not adopt—some, "Yes, let's just go and get everybody to agree to get rid of everything" without any controls, without the usual steps that we're going through which take an extreme degree of caution and a great deal of surveillance and mutual reductions.

Frank Gaffney: As opposed to landmines.

Bill Graham: No, landmines as well.

If you think you can abolish landmines, you certainly can abolish nuclear weapons. But since you can't abolish either, it is nonsense to even discuss it.

Frank Gaffney: No, there were no controls on landmines. There was none of this caution. It was "Let's go do it right now and make ourselves all feel better."

Bill Graham: We could discuss landmines, but I think that in fact the treaty has been extremely successful and I believe the time will come when the United States signs on.

Frank Gaffney: The landmine ban has not prevented the building or deployment of a single landmine anywhere on the planet.

Bill Graham: I think that your comment about Canada bearing a small security burden really should not go unchallenged. Whether you want to talk about Mr. Axworthy's concept of human security, which a lot of people are very interested in, or whether you look at what Canada is doing in peacekeeping, we're making a contribution to security in a way which I believe helps the United States in its security. When we put our peacekeepers into Haiti and into Bosnia and contribute to these operations, these are coming at no little cost to us. When the allies are talking about the present Kosovo situation, the prime minister has said he will look very favourably at a Canadian contribution. I'm sure that when that matter is debated in the House, I would strongly speak in favour of it. I believe that is the type of operation where we must contribute and also recognize tremendous United States leadership. But that doesn't mean we have to agree on every other single item about where we're going, and nuclear weapons, landmines and a few others are clearly areas where we disagree. But I don't think we should get confused in that sort of debate and say that "You guys are doing nothing." That's an unfortunate exaggeration of the situation.

Frank Gaffney: As to whether people are dewy-eyed crazies who espouse the long-term abolition of nuclear weapons, you can use whatever qualifiers, adjectives, conditions, caveats, you wish. It is dewy-eyed crazy to believe that you can rid the world of nuclear weapons. It is fatuous nonsense. You cannot disinvent the technology. You cannot prevent it from proliferating further. You cannot dissuade people who now have either the means to buy this technology or make it available to themselves from proceeding to get it. I respectfully suggest that it is crazy and really misleading to think that people who can embrace that as a long-term goal are not impeaching their judgment on what seem to be less controversial or less radical but nearer-term steps. This is particularly true since they entail a real danger of increasing the possibilities of war through miscalculation rather than making the world a more peaceful place.

The problem with changing the policy of no-first-use—and the reason for my extreme reluctance to start a debate that, almost inevitably, will try to move NATO toward embracing that policy—is that it may create in the minds of potential aggressors a sense that war is a more doable do, that it is less risky, that it is less deterred than it should be and then I think we have a responsibility to make it. That's the policy that has worked for us for 50 years and I believe it should be perpetuated.

A final point on this: I don't for a minute discount the fact that Canada is contributing to peacekeeping operations and thinks it is contributing to the security of the world by promulgating and promoting these kinds of arms control notions. I am simply saying that what history teaches us is that wars happen. Wars generally happen, certainly in this century, after people embark on this kind of nuttiness, this kind of self-delusion, that "human security" and arms control are going to provide for the physical security of their countries.

What Canada is doing to dissipate what is left of its armed forces and use what remains of those forces in places like Kosovo, which have precious little to do with Canada's security and certainly less with the larger international security than does the question of whether or not we are going to maintain a coherent, viable, credible NATO and a NATO nuclear deterrent. I would prefer to see Canada adopting a different set of priorities than the one which is obviously in place.

NATO has discussed its nuclear strategy in the past and has moved from a doctrine of massive retaliation to flexible response to, in the early nineties, a weapons-of-last-resort doctrine. Haven't we slid down most of the slippery slope already? Why is it that discussion of no-first-use would create an even greater danger? And in what circumstances these days could you imagine first-use?

Frank Gaffney: I believe, based on my study and my own personal involvement as a Defense Department official leading NATO's High Level Group, that nuclear weapons have always been something that American officials and NATO officials would be very reluctant to use. Even during the days when we were facing a great disparity between the armed forces of the Soviet Warsaw Pact and very little conventional capability on the part of the West, there was never any illusion on the part of Western leaders, certainly in the United States, that nuclear weapons would be a very, very unattractive option for the West to have to use in its defense. You'd wind up destroying a good part of the West to save the rest.

The steps that have been taken to this point to refine the kind of weapons we have, the kind of doctrine we have for their employment and the kind of circumstances under which they would be used, all was consistent with *enhancing* deterrence, not undermining it. Our concern and NATO's historical concern and the concern NATO felt even when Andy Goodpastor was SHAPE's commander was that you don't want to take steps that would encourage others to believe that nuclear weapons might not be used at all.

The circumstances under which they would be used, if at all now, would be ones in which vital security interests of NATO were clearly, imminently threatened and as a matter of last resort and in as discriminate a way as possible to try to prevent that threat from materializing. But I think it will help enormously to keep that threat from materializing if we refrain from increasing people's uncertainty as to what would be the consequence if such a threat, in fact, did get used.

Bill Graham: I totally agree that within the NATO circles and amongst the strategy experts, the essence of the debate will turn around the issue of deterrence, because that is the only justifiable use or possession of nuclear weapons. When you look at it, it's hard to imagine any circumstance in which they will be used or could be used. But the fact of the matter is it is a deterrent, and as Mr. Gaffney says, it has served the alliance well in a certain context. Now the question is whether we move into a new phase. Everything in life is a series of tradeoffs. Deterrence is one thing, but if in fact by keeping to the present policies we contribute to the instability of the world and encourage other countries to decide to acquire nuclear weapons because of the fear that they might be used against them first, then of course we've not created a climate of deterrence and security, we've increased the insecurity and created a much more dangerous place. We don't want another 50 nuclear states galloping around the world. I think that perhaps the difference between Mr. Gaffney and myself is that he thinks that anybody who wants to become a nuclear state will do it anyway, regardless of the world conditions because they're all evil and can't be controlled. My view is that we have to set in place some form of international framework within which we can work on these issues and bring them to the position where they recognize that it's not worth their while to get them.

Pakistan and India today are not better off for each having nuclear weapons. Everybody agrees that they're both far worse off from a military and every other point of view. They've just moved it up to the point where a possible Kashmir could be far more destructive than it otherwise was. So this it seems is what we're trying to work toward, this is the debate I'd like to see in NATO.

Frank Gaffney: Well, it remains to be seen whether things are worse on the subcontinent. I think you may, in fact, now see a standoff that perhaps permits a resolution of the Kashmir problem because neither side can afford to have a nuclear exchange over it. We'll see. My point is not that every country in the world is evil but that every country that wants nuclear weapons can get them. It is illusory to think that we will prevent them by exercising restraint and particularly in saying that a policy we felt was critical to NATO's security position for 50 years now is somehow the engine for causing others to proceed in a nuclear armaments program of their own. It hasn't been, it won't be, and we will simply do ourselves harm. The kind of calculation or balance that Mr. Graham is talking about is right but his answer is wrong. The costs that he perceives are not, in fact, the result of the policy that he proposes to change. If we change it, I don't think the result will be a real diminution of the proliferation of nuclear weapons around the world.

Thank you very much for doing this.

Canada battles with its vision of peace

The army is beating a partial retreat from its traditional peacekeeping duties just when Canada faces new American pressures to take on a more controversial military role

OTTAWA

ON SUSSEX DRIVE, the Canadian capital's ceremonial avenue, the newly built American embassy towers above a bronze monument of three soldiers, which depicts the country's long-standing devotion to international peacekeeping. The contrast makes a timely symbol. More than ever before, Canada finds itself torn between two versions of its military responsibility. On the one hand, there is a lingering faith in the country's honourable tradition of helping to police the peace in the world's trouble spots. On the other, a federal budget squeeze in recent years has limited Canada's ability to pay for such participation—and the country is under new pressure to integrate further into the United States' military structures.

Canada has long prided itself on having invented modern peacekeeping. In 1956, Lester Pearson, then its foreign minister, proposed an emergency force for the Sinai to cover the withdrawal of British and French troops from Egypt. Since then, Canadian troops have been found in almost every trouble spot. Their activities reached a peak during the 1990s, when Canadians were at various times engaged in a total of 65 different peacekeeping operations. By mid-1999, there were 4,400 soldiers abroad, and generals were openly complaining that resources were being stretched beyond the limit: five previous years of deficit-cutting budgets had cut the regular armed forces from 75,000 to 60,000, and their civilian staff by almost 40%.

Now, however, Canada's involvement in international peacekeeping is dwindling. By this summer, the number of its soldiers abroad will be down to 3,000, as troops pull out of both East Timor and Kosovo—though Canada's contingent in Bosnia will be reinforced. To the latest call by the United Nations for peacekeeping troops, to go off to Sierra Leone and Congo, Canada is contributing just a few military observers and some money to disarm child soldiers.

Moreover, Canada's confidence in its ability to make peace abroad has been badly shaken in recent years, not least since an inquiry into torture allegations against Canadian soldiers who took part in an operation in Somalia in 1993, which resulted in the disbanding of the country's Airborne Regiment. Many soldiers have suffered from burn-out after hazardous tours of duty. One such was General Romo Dallaire, who was in charge in Rwanda at the start of the 1994 genocide and took lengthy sick leave on his return.

Yet, at the same time as Canada appears to be making a partial retreat from peacekeeping, the country is also embarking on a military-hardware spending spree, partly in response to the demands of its mighty neighbour. Last June, the Department of National Defence published "Defence Strategy 2020", a long-range policy paper containing five-year targets, one of which was to strengthen Canada's military relations with the United States in order "to permit seamless operational integration at short notice". This "inter-operability", the paper declares, will mean adopting equipment compatible with that of Canada's main allies, the United States being the only one named. In short, the country is getting a big military upgrade.

Already, Canada is to acquire from Britain four diesel-electric Upholder-class submarines, whose main uses will be the patrolling of fishing waters and the control of the smuggling of would-be immigrants into North America. In exchange, Britain will get free use of training ranges in the western province of Alberta and in Labrador, on the Atlantic coast.

The new federal budget, announced on February 28th, includes C$2 billion ($1.4 billion) for defence equipment. This will enable Art Eggleton, the defence minister, to make good his frequent promises to buy replacements for the country's naval helicopters, which are now so antique they require dozens of maintenance hours for every hour spent in the air. Leopard tanks, which Canadian troops will take into troubled areas of southern Bosnia, are to be equipped with specially armoured turrets; and the ground-attack CF-18 fighter aircraft, which took part in the bombardment of Serbia last year, are to be fitted with more modern avionics.

In many ways, this upgrade is needed. It comes after a decade of defence cuts. In the last days of the cold war, the Conservative government then in power proposed spending C$8 billion on up to a dozen nuclear-powered submarines of either British or French design. The Liberal Party under Jean Chrétien not only successfully opposed that plan at the time, but, after taking office in 1993, paid a hefty penalty of C$500m to cancel a separate purchase of sophisticated helicopters.

More military controversy lies ahead. The Americans are due to decide later this year whether to press ahead with their plans to install the "national missile defence", a system that will, in theory, enable them to intercept and destroy incoming missiles from countries such as North Korea. The Americans would like to use a joint American-Canadian command structure, set up by the two countries in the 1950s, for the new system. Yet such a system, unless sanctioned by the Russians, would directly contravene the Anti-Ballistic Missile Treaty signed by the Americans and the Russians, which the traditionally peace-minded Canadians consider to be a centrepiece of arms control.

All this comes at a time when other totems of Canadian identity are also being eroded. The budget unveiled this week by Paul Martin, the finance minister, offered a wide range of uncharacteristic income-tax cuts, from which the middle classes will benefit most. Canadians have grown tired of their heavy tax burden, and are increasingly unimpressed with the state social provision it is supposed to finance. The budget also puts a squeeze on overseas aid, another matter about which Canada has been traditionally generous. This will hardly help fortify the crusade of the foreign minister, Lloyd Axworthy, for "soft power": the idea that the world's mightier countries should worry less about their own security and more about that of the world's poor. But a harder kind of power is now the vogue in Ottawa.

Canada's water:

Hands off

OTTAWA

BLUE gold" is the latest catchphrase to gain currency in Canada. It refers to the country's abundant water resources, estimated to amount to one-fifth of the world's total supply of fresh water. Water, declared Terence Corcoran, editor of the Toronto-based *Financial Post,* will be "the oil of the 21st century". As such a well-stocked supplier, Canada would stand to gain handsomely from a boom in demand for fresh water. But the subject is prompting more controversy than glee.

On November 29th and 30th, David Anderson, Canada's environment minister, and his ten provincial counterparts, whose governments jointly own nearly all the country's water, met to discuss water policy. The biggest headache is the prospect of large-scale water exports, for which firms in several provinces are lining up with export applications. The governments are formally against the idea, partly for ecological reasons, and, under pressure from the federal government, each province has now declared a six-month moratorium on approving any licences. Moreover, protest groups have been rallying to the issue, and some gathered this week to block the road bridge to Kananaskis, in the Rocky Mountains, where the ministers were meeting.

The matter has touched a raw nerve in a country deeply protective of its natural environment. In a report on the global water shortage entitled "Blue Gold", published in June, Maude Barlow, who heads the country's biggest pressure group, the Council of Canadians, called Canada's fresh water "our lifeblood". She argued that water should be left where it is wherever possible and called for a "local sources first" policy worldwide. In short: hands off Canada's water. In September, her council sponsored a "water watch summit" of 40 protest groups, which called on both tiers of government to ban the bulk removal and export of water.

The bogeyman, as so often for Canadians, is the United States. To meet the demands of farmers and the growing population of the south-western states, ambitious and hugely controversial schemes have long been floated for diverting Canadian rivers southward. One would divert the Yukon and Mackenzie rivers down the Rocky Mountain Trench; another, which would be equally damaging to the environment, would trap several Quebec rivers inside a dike across James Bay, and flush the water through the Great Lakes. Yet it is the recent flood of far more modest applications to ship out water by the tankerful, not these vast diversion schemes, that have prompted the present calls to ban bulk exports.

Only recently, the Ontario government approved and then rescinded one application to ship water by tanker from Lake Superior to Asia, while the Newfoundland government pulled back from approving a much larger shipment to the Middle East. A Vancouver company hopes to ship Alaska's glacier water to China for bottling, which would skirt the British Columbia government's own ban on bulk exports that dates from 1993. A would-be importing company in California is now suing the British Columbia government for losses under this ban, saying it violates NAFTA rules on free trade in North America.

Ahead of this week's ministerial meeting, the federal government announced changes it wanted made to the Boundary Waters Treaty in order to prevent bulk water exports, and referred the Lake Superior case to the International Joint Commission, which deals with boundary waters. But the Newfoundland and British Columbia cases are outside the commission's mandate. So the federal government has now invited the provinces to sign a deal to ban, for environmental reasons, the bulk withdrawal of water at its source—an attempt at an export ban by other means.

To the fury of the government of British Columbia, there is, however, no mention in this deal of an explicit, water-tight export ban—partly for fear that this might amount to a concession that water is a tradable good, and therefore that it does fall under NAFTA's free-trade rules. Quebec and the prairie provinces also refused this week to sign the accord. A decision is now delayed until May next year, leaving Mr. Anderson to grumble that "contrived indecision" will only make Canada's resources even more sought-after.

Unit 5

Unit Selections

Key Points to Consider

- What are some of the costs and benefits of the North American Free Trade Agreement for America? Canada? Mexico?
- What else might the United States do to stem the tide of drugs and illegal immigrants from Mexico? Colombia?
- What can the United States, Canada, and European countries do to encourage continued democratic and economic reform in Latin America?

Links

www.dushkin.com/online/

18. **Inter-American Dialogue**
    http://www.iadialog.org

These sites are annotated on pages 4 and 5.

For nearly two centuries, the United States viewed Latin America as being within its exclusive sphere of influence. But several countries in the region are developing independent international security policies. In "The International Relations of Latin America and the Caribbean," G. Pope Atkins describes recent regional trends and outlines the reason why democratic development and economic reform are the new overarching norms in hemispheric relations.

Few Americans appreciate that North American Free Trade Association (NAFTA) countries purchase 40 percent of U.S. exports. Today the state of the Canadian and Mexican economies is as important for the continued health of the U.S. economy as are economic trends in large states such as Texas. Growing economic interdependence throughout the Western Hemisphere increases the risk that international contagion may eventually spread to the United States through its closest neighbors and most important trade partners.

In the early 1990s, when free market reforms were adopted, the economic growth rate throughout Central America was approximately 3 percent. This growth plummeted to .8 percent in 1995 after Mexico's crash. The backlash against free trade and government corruption plagued Mexico. There was widespread discontent when the government announced a $62 billion bailout plan in 1998 to help the bankrupt banks. Critics argue that the plan is a public subsidy for those who created the 1994 banking crisis. Continuing government corruption until recently blocked efforts to reform the political process, and facilitated the flow of black market drugs into the United States.

The loss of legitimacy of the long-ruling political party in Mexico led to a historic change in 2000 when the first president from outside the Institutional Revolutionary Party (PRI) was elected. The newly elected president, Vicente Fox, is the first representative from the National Action Party, or PAN, to gain power in 71 years. He must now contend with a Congress that is no longer a rubber stamp because no party holds a majority in either house. These changes represent a fundamentally altered balance of power in Mexico where the president traditionally operated with near omnipotence. For the first time, 100 million Mexicans will have more voice in government through their congressmen. Mexican and U.S. corporations who compete for shares of the $200 billion in annual trade between the two countries will also have to pay attention to legislators who rarely mattered before.

Most analysts hail this recent election as a positive change in efforts to help Mexico avoid a social explosion. Continued American aid and the safety valve for emigration to the United States for unemployed Mexicans are other important factors that have helped to maintain political stability in Mexico. Future American aid, however, will be contingent on how Americans perceive Mexico's role as a source of illegal drugs and immigrants. While only a fraction of the estimated 7 million Mexicans living in the United States are involved in drug operations, drug trafficking into the United States from Mexico is increasing antagonism toward Mexican immigrants in the United States.

Traditionally, Central American states were viewed as "coffee" or "banana republics," but the region's political economy is being reshaped by Asian growth processes. Maquiladora-produced goods and nontraditional agricultural products now comprise approximately 60 percent of all exports from Guatemala, El Salvador, and Costa Rica. Unfortunately, the small size and openness of Central America's economies means that Asia's economic slowdown adversely affected the region's economies at the same time that the countries struggled to recover from the storm-damage caused by Hurricane Mitch during the fall of 1998. Flooding during 1998 was the worst in recent history because the droughts associated with El Niño left little vegetation to stop the floodwater that accompanied the La Niña storms. It may take decades for the region to recover as the losses are estimated in Honduras to be equal to the annual GDP of $4 billion and in Nicaragua to about half of its GDP of $1 billion.

Illegal drugs rather than natural disasters increasingly concern U.S. government officials working to implement the "war on drugs" in Colombia. Martin Hodgson explains, in "The Coca Leaf War," how the United States is attempting to rescue a war-torn country and stop the flow of illegal drugs into the United States. Drug-fighters claim that a combination of repression and social engineering can eliminate coca cultivation and cocaine. However, critics question whether the United States' strategy will accomplish its objective. They charge that the United States' recent "Plan for Colombia" sacrifices more important policy goals in Latin America, such as support for democracy and human rights while pursuing a Vietnamization strategy that is doomed to fail. Concerns about civil rights abuses by the Colombian police and military and the failure of the government to stop right-wing vigilantes has led to increased calls for a halt to U.S. aid. During 2000, the U.S. government ignored these calls and approved increased levels of funding for the war on drugs.

President Clinton's hopes for swift progress toward a Pan-American free-trade area were dashed when Congress refused to renew his administration's fast-track authority to negotiate further tariff and trade restrictions with Mercosur countries. Although the major Latin economies weathered the initial shocks associated with the Asia economic crisis and the reduction in world demand for commodity exports, international confidence in the national currencies continued to decline in part because all countries in the region have balance of payments deficits. Large amounts of international capital were withdrawn from "emerging markets" worldwide after Russia devalued the ruble in August of 1998. Brazil was forced to devalue the national currency, the real, at the beginning of 1999 in response to pressure on its currency even though the country's fundamental economic position was sound. State workers who had not been paid in several months rioted in several areas in Argentina during 1999 as hard times reduced popular support for Carlos Menin's efforts to implement economic reforms. The recent economic slowdown affected economies throughout Latin America. Although the major economic powers of the region are showing signs of recovery, uncertainty remains about whether the recent movement toward free markets and democracy will continue.

In "Is Latin America Doomed to Failure?" Peter Hakim describes how many citizens in Latin American countries appear willing to give up some measure of democracy and accept authoritarian governments that they believe can solve their problems. The recent popularity and success of Hugo Chavez in Venezuela seems to support this proposition. However, Hakim concludes that most countries in the region need to worry more about stagnation than backsliding.

The International Relations of Latin America and the Caribbean: Defining the New Era

G. Pope Atkins

Dr. Atkins is a research fellow at the Institute of Latin American Studies, University of Texas at Austin and professor emeritus of political science, U.S. Naval Academy.

This article focuses on the structure and conditions of the international relations of Latin America and the Caribbean in the current international system. The end of global East-West conflict by the end of the 1980s was combined with Latin America's political and economic transformations away from authoritarian governance and state-dominated economies, which had begun earlier in the decade. The designation of "post-Cold War" indicates the understanding that the old analytic and policy frameworks were no longer valid. The United States abandoned its 180-year-old preoccupation with minimizing what it saw as hostile foreign intrusions in the Western Hemisphere. Consequently, the inter-American agenda was no longer encumbered with fears of Soviet encroachment and communist expansionism. A general consensus emerged that democratic development and economic reform constituted the overarching norms in hemispheric relations. They provided the subtext for the salient issues of human rights, state governance, and civil-military relations; economic integration, trade, and investment; illicit narcotics traffic; immigration and refugee problems; degradation of the physical environment and sustainable development; insurgencies, arms control, and demilitarization; and other matters. President Bush's Enterprise for the American Institute proposed on June 27, 1990 called for a Western Hemispheric free trade area. It has been pursued in a slow and complex manner.

Questions arise about the appropriate "levels of analysis" in contemporary world politics. Many specialists on Latin America are impatient with overall regional parameters and highlight the major countries and subregions. Others emphasize the larger regional Inter-American System of all the states in the Western Hemisphere, and see inter-American cooperation as an important path to international problem-solving. Globalists say that the most important issues today are world-wide in scope and consequently analytic efforts should concentrate on that level, with a view to resolving current issues within global regimes. The debate has been further complicated by the revived importance of globalization and transnationalization—the intertwining of relations at all systemic levels and the elevating of the prominence of nonstate actors and transnational activities. In my view, an accurate picture of Latin America and Caribbean international relations requires that we acknowledge and link national, subregional, regional, hemispheric, and global and extrahemispheric levels of analysis. The nature of the issues and the high stakes involved compel action in all arenas.

THE LATIN AMERICAN-CARIBBEAN REGION

Latin America and the Caribbean comprises an area roughly two-and-one-half times larger than the United States. It is populated by almost 500 million people and mostly occupied by 33 independent states exhibiting great diversity in terms of culture, size, and other aspects. Among them are the 18 Spanish American states, with widely varying stages of development and international capabilities; huge Brazil, which is Portuguese in origin; and tiny Haiti, which has maintained its West African culture to a remarkable degree. These 20 states, all but two of which (Cuba and Panama) gained their independence during the first third of the nineteenth century, together account for some 97 percent of the region's territory and population. Since 1962 an additional 13 Caribbean countries have gained independence; 12 of them had been British colonies and the thirteenth is Suriname, formerly a colony of the Netherlands. In order to recognize the emergence of these new states and distinguish them from the long-existing "traditional" Latin American states, the term "Latin America and the Caribbean" was adopted. This understandable effort is an inadequate adjustment, however, since older Spanish American states had already encompassed most of the Caribbean area's territory and population. Nevertheless, "Latin America and the Caribbean" has become a matter of general usage.

Despite the diversity, a Latin American regional subsystem has always exhibited to some degree an international life of its own. This has been partly reflected in Latin American self-perceptions. Latin Americans have always tended to band together when outsiders intervened or exerted other pressures. They have organized among themselves to achieve common purposes. A few examples illustrate the point. Latin American Groups were created within the United Nations, Third World associations, and the European Community (now the European Union), in order to caucus on a regional basis before confronting the outside world. The 11-member Latin American Free Trade Association (LAFTA), established in 1961 and reorganized in 1980 as the Latin American Integration Association (LAIA), includes all of the large regional economies so that it represents a broadly cross-regional association. The Latin American Parliament was created in 1964; although its decisions are not binding it serves as a focal point for the discussion of region-wide issues. Also in 1964 most Latin American states joined the Special Latin American Coordinating Committee (CECLA) as an informal regional caucusing group. In 1975 the permanent Latin American Economic System (SELA) was created with near-universal regional membership, superseding CECLA and broadening the agenda of purposes. Organized in 1986, the Rio Group expanded to include almost all of the Latin American and Caribbean states and became the leading voice on the new agenda of issues.

These organizations have taken on new significance in the post-Cold War era and given renewed impetus to inter-regional cooperation. Nevertheless, viewing Latin America only in terms of a single unit is insufficient. We also need to highlight those subregions where different conditions obtain.

MEXICO

Mexico stands apart as a large and important state that has intense bilateral relations with the United States. The current reality of the complicated Mexican-U.S. association, in contrast to much of the past, is the existence of a strong mutual dependency. Although the United States is clearly the stronger partner, Mexico has considerable say. Much of the relationship is essentially divorced from the broader Latin American arena. The issues have long been determined by territorial proximity and increasingly integrated economies and societies in terms of trade, investment, migration, tourism, the drug traffic, and a host of border issues.

Mexico and the United States recently reoriented their policies toward each other. Until the latter half of the 1980s, Mexico differed with the United States on such issues as Central American conflict, Cuba, and external debt. Then it began to abandon its historic protectionist investment and trade policies by privatizing government enterprises, liberalizing trade, and attracting U.S. investment. It pressed the United States for a free trade agreement; President Bush responded positively and in 1990 free trade negotiations began. Canada joined the process and the trilateral talks resulted in the North American Free Trade Agreement (NAFTA), which went into effect in January 1992.

The United States is by far Mexico's major trading partner; Mexico is the United States' third largest. Mexico's mutually exacerbating economic, political, and social crises complicated relations with the United States (and with Canada on a smaller scale) and eroded their smooth functioning. Other developments indicated, however, that the Mexican economy and NAFTA were weathering financial and commercial problems. In April 1996 Mexico signed an agreement with the European Union opening the possibility of a free trade arrangement between them.

THE CIRCUM-CARIBBEAN

The circum-Caribbean is a complex geographic and political region. It includes the islands of the Caribbean Sea and those nearby in the Atlantic Ocean, the Central American isthmus, and the north coast of South America extending into the Atlantic Ocean (thus including Colombia, Venezuela, and Suriname). It has its own further subregions, notably the Central American and the Commonwealth Caribbean countries. Throughout the twentieth century the United States pursued a hegemonic presence in the circum-Caribbean, with unilateral military interventions as late as 1983 in Grenada and 1989-1990 in Panama; in 1994 it led a United Nations force in the military occupation of Haiti. The Panama Canal historically loomed large in U.S. calculations; it is still of concern but the canal's strategic and commercial importance has sharply declined. A major challenge to U.S. hegemony arose after 1959 when Cuba became the Soviet Union's first high-priority Latin American interest. After the Nicaraguan Revolution of 1979 the Soviets supported the Sandinistas in Nicaragua and by extension the Farabundo Martí National Liberation Front (FMLN) insurgency in El Salvador.

The Nicaraguan Revolution precipitated general Central American conflict and the United States responded by making it a major Cold War arena. One of the casualties of the conflict was the effort to integrate the isthmian states. The Organization of Central American States

(ODECA), made up of the five traditional isthmian states of Costa Rica, El Salvador, Guatemala, Honduras, and Nicaragua, had gone into effect in 1955. ODECA did not realize its purposes of both political and economic integration; it was unable to settle a variety of disputes between its members and its companion organization, the Central American Common Market (CACM) took the lead in economic integration. The CACM, composed of the same membership, began to function in 1960. The violent Central American conflict beginning in 1979 virtually dissolved the organization (as well as ODECA).

In 1983, Mexico, Venezuela, Colombia, and Panama organized the Contadora Group to offer a multilateral negotiating formula challenging U.S. policies; they were joined by the Contadora Support Group formed by Argentina, Brazil, Peru, and Uruguay. This was followed in 1987 by a multilateral peace plan agreed to by all five Central American states on the initiative of President Oscar Arias of Costa Rica that enjoyed considerable success. (In December 1986 the eight Contadora Group and Support Group met and created the Permanent Mechanism of Consultation and Political Coordination, known informally as the Rio Group. As Central American conflict faded the group expanded its agenda and membership in the context of growing Latin American unity and, as indicated above, became the most important and dynamic Latin American and Caribbean international organization.)

The Soviet role changed dramatically in the post-Cold War era as it ceased weapons transfers to Cuba and Nicaragua and pressured them to end deliveries to insurgents in El Salvador. The February 1990 elections in Nicaragua that ejected the Sandinista government also ended the by-then reluctant Soviet role. In the meantime, the Soviets joined the United States in the UN Security Council to create a peacekeeping force and other missions for electoral and human rights observation and verification that were sent to Central America. With the decline of Soviet power and then the breakup of the Soviet Union itself, commitments to Cuba were virtually canceled. Cuba itself became internationally isolated and increasingly inactive, absorbed with its own internal economic and social problems.

The Central American peace process revived subregional integration and then concentrated on expanding it. In 1987 the Central American presidents signed a treaty creating the Central American Parliament. In 1990 and 1991, as part of the Enterprise for the Americas Initiative, individual Central American states signed framework agreements with the United States committing to negotiations for a free trade agreement—processes that since then have been stalled, primarily by internal U.S. politics. Mexico initiated negotiations with Central America with the view of establishing a free trade area, implying the potential of their being a part of NAFTA. The Central American presidents continued to hold summit meetings and brought in Belize and Panama as participants. In December 1995 the presidents signed two treaties of particular significance and submitted them to the individual states for ratification. One of them extended the terms of the previously adopted Central American Alliance for Sustainable Development. The other, the Democratic Security Treaty of Central America, addressed legal systems, corruption, internationalization of organized crime, drug trafficking, terrorism, and arms smuggling; and stipulations concerning the reduction of national military forces. The European Union continued to hold high-level meetings with the Central American states, a practice begun early in the peace process.

The Commonwealth Caribbean countries are the 18 English-speaking entities in the circum-Caribbean. Of that number, 12 are no longer British dependencies and have become independent states—Antigua and Barbuda, Bahamas, Barbados, Belize, Dominica, Grenada, Guyana, Jamaica, St. Kitts-Nevis, St. Lucia, St. Vincent, and Trinidad and Tobago. One of them (Belize) is on the Central American isthmus, another (Guyana) is on the South American continent, and the remainder are islands in the Caribbean Sea. The non-sovereign countries have a constitutional status of "States in Association with Great Britain." They are self-governing but dependent on the United Kingdom for external affairs. They are Anguilla, Bermuda, British Virgin Islands, Cayman Islands, Montserrat, and the Turks and Caicos Islands.

A number of the Commonwealth Caribbean countries established the Caribbean Free Trade Association (CARIFTA) with an agreement that went into effect in 1968. In 1972 most CARIFTA members drew up a charter establishing the Caribbean Community (CARICOM) that went into effect in 1973 with 13 members (all but one a sovereign state). Three other local states—the Dominican Republic, Haiti, and Suriname, became permanent observers; the Dominican Republic later became a full member. In 1981, seven members formed the Organization of Eastern Caribbean States (OECS) within CARICOM in order to pool economic resources and coordinate foreign policy.

CARICOM was also stimulated by events in the new era. In 1991 it signed a framework agreement with the United States with a view to negotiating a free trade agreement. In 1991 and 1992 the member governments agreed to further elements of their integration structure but progress was slow. The Commonwealth Caribbean countries enjoy trade preferences with the European Community under the Lome convention.

On July 24, 1994, the charter of the Association of Caribbean States (ACS) was signed and went into effect within a year with the purpose of forming a free trade area. The ACS members are divided into subgroups: CARICOM, Central America (including Panama but not Belize, a member of CARICOM), the Group of Three (a formal free trade agreement by Mexico, Colombia, and Venezuela), and Greater Antilles (the informal grouping of Cuba, the Dominican Republic, and Haiti). Provision was made for associate membership by non-sovereign entities. Anguilla, Turks and Caicos, and Guadalupe joined as associate members; eligible were Bermuda, the Caymans, Martinique, the U.S. Virgin Islands, the British Virgin Islands, French Guiana, and Puerto Rico.

SOUTH AMERICA BEYOND THE CARIBBEAN

The third important subregion encompasses South America beyond the Caribbean, most of which are the countries of what is called the Southern Cone. The key states are Argentina, Brazil, and Chile; the others are Uruguay, Paraguay, Bolivia, and Peru. Brazil, like Mexico, can be singled out as forming its own subsystem. It stands apart with its Portuguese cultural heritage, large size, and potential to be a much more influential state in global politics.

The subregion has a number of characteristics that make it dramatically different from the northern half of Latin America. It has not been a sphere of influence of the United States or another state; no outside great power has had the function of international policeman enforcing the peace. The South American states have a broad array of external relationships. They represent a multilateralized trading area, with long-standing cultural and economic ties with Europe, and Japan an important economic actor. The transition away from militarism has been completed, although democracy has been under continuous stress and "partial democracies" more often than not characterize the current situation. Most of the subregion's traditional international rivalries have been muted. Brazil and Argentina have extended a rapprochement begun in 1979 to include extensive bilateral economic and other kinds of policy integration. Argentina and Chile settled their contentious Beagle Channel dispute in 1983. In 1990 Argentina and the United Kingdom reestablished relations broken in 1982 during their war over the Falkland/Malvinas islands.

When the Latin American Free Trade Association (LAFTA) was formed in 1961 it was widely perceived as the initial step toward formation of a Latin American-wide common market. A universal regional organization was not created, however. In fact, both LAFTA and its successor Latin American Integration Association (LAIA) were fragmented by South American-led reform movements. In 1969 certain dissatisfied LAFTA members formed the Andean Common Market, usually known as the Andean Group. They did not withdraw from LAFTA but hoped eventually to reform it. The charter members were Bolivia, Colombia, Chile, Ecuador and Peru; Venezuela joined in 1973 and Chile dropped out in 1976. Thus the Andean Group, with South American Caribbean states in its membership, in fact bridged two Latin American subregions. The Andean Group was able to undertake important reforms but it also suffered from its own political and economic divisiveness. In the new international era the organization managed to overcome much of the differences and in 1995 converted itself to the Andean Community. In 1996 it signed a framework agreement with the European Union opening the possibility of free trade.

In 1991 another new organization was organized within LAIA—the Common Market of the South (MERCOSUR), made up of Argentina, Brazil, Paraguay, and Uruguay. In that year MERCOSUR signed a framework agreement with the United States with a view to negotiating free trade. The organization sought to expand its membership to other South American States. In 1996 Bolivia signed a complementation agreement and Chile became an associate member, preludes for both states to join as full members. In December 1995 MERCOSUR and the European Union signed a framework agreement for free trade and serious negotiations continued in 1996. MERCOSUR also commenced negotiations for reciprocal trade preferences with a wide range of other countries.

The world outside Latin America and the Caribbean is also differentiated so far as the regional states are concerned. They are essentially divided into relations with (1) the other Americas and (2) global and extrahemispheric actors.

INTER-AMERICAN SYSTEM

The Inter-American System (IAS) refers to formal multipurpose regional (Western Hemisphere-wide) organization among the American states that originated in 1889 and evolved thereafter to the present day. The designation denotes not a centralized institution overseeing subordinate organizations, but an "umbrella" concept covering an uneven yet uninterrupted history and current network of institutional principles, policies, procedures, and organizations. Today the IAS largely consists of the separate but coordinated Organization of American States (OAS) and Inter-American Development Bank (IDB). Other elements include a scattered system for the peaceful settlement of disputes and a once vigorous but now moribund Inter-American Treaty of Reciprocal Assistance (Rio Treaty) regime. In 1991 the OAS achieved universal membership of all 35 sovereign states in the Americas—the 33 Latin American and Caribbean states, the United States, and Canada. (Cuba is technically a member since sanctions imposed in 1962 deny participation, not membership, to the Castro government.) IAS activities evolved over the years to promote economic, social, and cultural cooperation, conflict resolution, nonintervention and sovereign equality, codification of international law, mutual security, and representative democracy and human rights. In recent years the problems of the narcotics traffic and environmental degradation were added.

Latin Americans were increasingly dissatisfied with U. S. efforts to transform the IAS into an anti-communist alliance, especially after the United States intervened militarily in the 1965 Dominican Republic civil war and then insisted on its conversion to an inter-American problem for settlement. The IAS became virtually impotent in the field of mutual security; it continued economic development activities but was not an important arena for addressing the external debt difficulties.

In the latter 1980s the OAS became an important actor in the Central American peace process, at the invitation of the Central American presidents who were leading the efforts. The revitalization continued with the emergence of a more positive Latin American nationalism and the return of the United States to a multilateral orientation, elements of the political changes in Latin America and the end of Cold War. Member states again perceived the IAS as an appropriate problem-solving forum. The promotion of democratic governance and human rights and economic well-being were the main principles that defined the new era, with other issues subsumed under them. The IAS has been highly active in terms of developing these principles, with resolutions, declarations, and OAS charter amendments, and engaging in policy action. The end of the Cold War did not alter the reality of asymmetrical inter-American power relations. Nevertheless, the nature of the issues, with their high domestic content, seemed to mute the consequences of asymmetry inasmuch as they required multilateral resolution.

THE GLOBAL SYSTEM AND EXTRAHEMISPHERIC ACTORS

Latin American and Caribbean governments seek to be active participants in the evolving global system. Latin Americans were instrumental in shaping the United Nations system at its inception. They later took leadership roles in the New International Economic Order (NIEO), a formal Third World association pursued especially in the serial United Nations Conference on Trade and Development (UNCTAD) and in the General Assembly. Beginning in 1961 many of them also joined the Nonaligned Movement. Latin American military regimes reduced their active interest in extra-regional affairs during the 1970s and into the 1980s but the succeeding democratic governments sought to reintegrate.

The end of the Cold War challenged the identity of both the Nonaligned Movement and the NIEO; alignment was no longer an issue in the former instance and the demise of the Soviet Union reduced the leverage of the latter. Latin American interest in both movements consequently declined. The United Nations presence increased in the Americas, however, in the broad and critical arena of conflict resolution for peace and security —matters in which the UN had formerly deferred to the IAS. Beginning in 1987, the two organizations developed a division of labor as highly active participants in the ongoing Central American peace process. The UN continues as the sponsor of the external peacekeeping presence in Haiti.

As a general matter, Latin American and Caribbean leaders seek to maintain and expand their relations with the European Union (EU) and other international associations, Japan and other states, and transnational political parties and nongovernmental organizations. In the critical area of international trade and investment, they were fully aware that hemispheric free trade would link their integration organizations more closely to the U.S. economy. To ensure they would not become a U.S. dominated economic preserve, they acted to expand extrahemispheric connections to parallel hemispheric arrangements. The EU responded positively and a number of significant actions occurred. In 1991 the EU and the Rio Group began to hold regular annual meetings of their foreign ministers. At the Sixth Institutionalized Meeting of Rio Group-European Union Foreign Ministers in April 1996 in Bolivia, initial agreements were signed opening the possibilities of free trade between the EU and Andean Community, Mexico, and Chile. The EU also held meetings with the Central American states. By the time of the Bolivia meeting the array of issues discussed had expanded dramatically. The foreign ministers addressed economic integration, inter-regional trade and investment, and strengthening economic and commercial relations, and sustainable development; democracy and human rights, women's rights, and respect for ethnic diversity and indigenous peoples' cultural heritage; and the international drug traffic. On December 15, 1995 the EU and MERCOSUR signed a wide-ranging Inter-Regional Framework Agreement as a first step toward progressive liberalization of trade (if realized the free trade area would constitute the largest in the world with some 600 million people). In 1996 MERCOSUR began negotiations for reciprocal trade preferences with some developing countries, among them Mexico, Colombia, India, Korea, the Philippines, and Egypt, and scheduled talks with Japan and Russia.

GLOBALIZATION AND TRANSNATIONALIZATION

The ideas of globalization and transnationalization have been increasingly adopted as key concepts for understanding current Latin American and Caribbean international relations. Globalization refers to the expansion of those relations at all systemic levels in the context of the new democratization and agenda of issues. Transnationalization elevates the prominence of non-nation-state actors and intensifies phenomena that evolve in a largely autonomous manner parallel with interstate relations. Thus, in the globalization process, states are joined by multinational corporations, nongovernmental organizations, international political party and labor associations, churches, communications media, immigrants and refugees, artists and entertainers, athletes, educators, and tourists, as well as narcotics traffickers, and others. They engage in transnational activities having immense political, economic, social, and cultural consequences. Goods, money, people, ideas, and images flow across and transcend state boundaries, creating overlapping but distinct political, economic, ethnic, and cultural patterns. Although little prospect exists that the states will cede sovereignty to other actors, globalization and accompanying transnationalization limit their ability to exercise political, economic, and social-cultural authority.

Some phenomena are of particular significance in the American arena. With the rise to prominence of neoliberalism and economic reform in the current international era, and the decline of traditional security concerns and their connection to Latin American and Caribbean stability, the actions and influence of private sector business and commercial influence have increased. They are led by U. S.–based multilateral corporations (MNCs), but Japanese and European MNCs are also of considerable consequence.

At another point on the spectrum, international trafficking in illicit narcotics has created its own culture. The United States provides the major market and many dealers, and people from Latin American and the Caribbean, both at home and in the United States, participate in the production, transporting and marketing of drugs.

More diffuse, less organized social-cultural elements have also had a major transnational impact. The principal phenomena are the proliferation of the U.S. communications and entertainment media, and the millions of Latin Americans resident in the United States with many of them moving back and forth between there and their homelands. This has been particularly true in the Caribbean area, as analysts refer to the consequences of U.S. influence as the "Northamericanization" of the Caribbean and the reciprocal impact as the "Caribbeanization" of the United States. While these transnational linkages have been growing since the 1950s and 1960s, in the early 1980s they began to increase rapidly. The process of North Americanization has resulted in divided Latin American views, and often ambivalence, about the United States. While these phenomena are not a consequence of overt U.S. government policies, those Latin Americans who resent or fear foreign influences see them as continuing cultural imperialism extended in a new international context, objecting to U.S. popular culture, materialism, and secularism. A large number of Latins, many of whom have adopted English as a second language, have welcomed or accepted U.S. ideas, values, products, and life-styles and equate North Americanization with modernization. Others see it as an inevitable consequence of societal proximity, migration, commerce, and cultural contact. In the United States, Caribbeanization has changed the political, social, and popular cultural scenes in several cities, notably New York and Miami. And it has fueled the debate about future immigration policy.

the coca leaf war

A report from Colombia—the front line in Washington's war on drugs.

By Martin Hodgson

IN THE GLARE OF THE MIDDAY SUN, THE banks of the broad Putumayo River in Colombia are an unbroken wall of green. The jungle is so dense that from midstream it's hard to pick out the mouth of a narrow tributary—until three naval patrol boats burst roaring from between the trees.

On the foredeck of the lead vessel, a Colombian marine ratchets the magazine of his heavy machine gun, and as the boats skim past their target, the troops unleash a barrage of automatic fire. They shoot blindly, pounding the undergrowth with .50 caliber rounds—then a sudden calm falls as the speedboats head back to base.

Unnoticed by the marines, a dugout canoe detaches itself from the shelter of the riverbank and noses steadily up river. The patrol boats are almost out of sight as the peasant woman on board paddles silently past the target zone.

Colombia and its allies in the United States are pushing for a massive injection of American cash, which they say will rescue this war-torn country from anarchy. But in their haste for a final victory in the war on drugs, the policymakers seem to have forgotten the Colombian people.

Today's operation on the Putumayo, which at this point separates Colombia and Peru, was just a training exercise, but the marines cannot afford to drop their guard. The jungles of southern Colombia are a lawless region.

On the eastern flanks of the Andes, the remote states of Caqueta and Putumayo are home to thousands of leftist guerrillas who guard illegal coca plantations, secret landing strips, and clandestine laboratories that churn out more than 70 percent of Colombia's cocaine. The naval base in nearby Puerto Leguizamo, on the Peruvian border, has never been attacked, but for as long as anyone can remember, it's been on red alert.

This is the front line in Washington's war on drugs.

"Plan Colombia"

According to army figures, last year the 90th Riverine Battalion destroyed 68 cocaine-processing labs and the marines seized 201 kilograms of cocaine base and 77,700 kilograms of coca leaves. (Although people involved in the drug war are fond of attaching staggering dollar values to such seizures, it would be impossible to put a realistic sum on these seizures if the fully processed cocaine had reached the streets of New York, Chicago, or Los Angeles.)

The 90th was among the first Colombian military units to receive U.S. anti-drug training and equipment. Now the battalion is hoping to benefit once more from the extra $1.7 billion in emergency aid currently under debate in the U.S. Senate.

If approved, the money will go toward an ambitious two-year plan that the Colombian government says will stamp out the country's illegal drug trade, revive its ailing economy, and end 36 years of bloody civil conflict.

Colombia and its allies in the United States are pushing for a massive injection of American cash, which they say will rescue this war-torn country.

Administration officials in Colombia and the United States say the money will bring peace by rooting out the social conditions that breed violence. Cynics argue that what little humanitarian aid is included in the plan is a fig leaf that scarcely conceals the package's real goal: military victory over Latin America's longest-surviving left-wing insurgency.

U.S. aid to Colombia has grown tenfold since 1995, making it the third-ranking recipient of U.S. military aid after Israel and Egypt. Last year alone Colombia received about $300 million in equipment and training, reflecting a growing U.S. concern that this Andean country is heading toward a major crisis.

Nevertheless, despite two decades of aggressive narcotics interdic-

PHOTO BY MARTIN HODGSON

An attack by FARC guerrillas last December destroyed the police station in Curillo.

tion, the drug business is booming. The U.S. government estimates that Colombia produced some 520 metric tons of cocaine and up to eight tons of heroin last year.

Drug money has bred corruption, undermined the country's legal economy, and fueled an increasingly savage internal conflict that pits left-wing guerrillas against government forces and far-right paramilitaries. In the past 15 years nearly 1.9 million Colombians have been forced from their homes by violence—including some 12,000 who fled last year into neighboring Panama, Venezuela, and Ecuador.

Further, warring factions regularly cross the country's borders to carry out kidnappings and secure supply routes, and some U.S. officials warn that the conflict—which already spills over Colombia's frontiers—now threatens to destabilize the entire region.

As Barry McCaffrey, the White House's anti-drug chief, said during a visit to Bogotá last year: "Clearly we have a democratic regime in trouble. The money, corruption, and violence brought by drugs are the heart and soul of its problems."

McCaffrey—an outspoken advocate of the proposed aid package—stresses that "Plan Colombia" is not just a military strategy; it also includes money for judicial reform, human rights protection, and economic development.

The total two-year cost of Plan Colombia is $7.5 billion. According to Colombian officials, the remainder of the cash—destined for social and economic recovery schemes—will be raised from the Colombian government budget and donations from European countries, the International Monetary Fund, and the World Bank.

But the U.S. contribution will be overwhelmingly military, with around $1 billion earmarked for strengthening the Colombian army and police with weapons upgrades, intelligence infrastructure, and training. (Curiously, non-American diplomats say the original draft of Plan Colombia was written in English, not Spanish, and while the military portion was ready in late 1999, the Colombian government has yet to present a coherent social investment program.)

Until the plan is presented, few governments will be willing to climb aboard what is widely perceived as an American project to clean up its backyard. "Nobody wants to be seen at the tag end of a U.S plan," said one European diplomat.

An unfortunate comparison

U.S. personnel are already involved in many of Colombia's anti-narcotics programs, although they are barred by law from joining in military operations against drug traffickers or rebel groups. At any time, between 200 and 300 U.S. soldiers—mostly special forces trainers, intelligence officers, and radar technicians—are stationed in the country.

Last year, U.S. trainers helped prepare a new thousand-person specialized anti-narcotics battalion. Two more elite anti-narcotics units will be trained in 2000. In Puerto Leguizamo, for instance, U.S. Special Forces commandos taught four river combat courses.

"U.S. training is useful here because they gained so much experience on the rivers in Vietnam. They lost a lot of men, but they learned plenty," says Lt. German Arenas, a Colombian marine who was trained by the Green Berets.

That is the sort of comparison that makes U.S. politicians squirm.

America's interest in Colombia is clear: 80 percent of the world's cocaine—and most of the heroin sold in the United States—comes from Colombia. But in Washington, some lawmakers fear that increased military aid may eventually drag the United States into another complex and unwinnable jungle war.

The single most expensive element of the American aid package will be the loan and maintenance of 63 combat helicopters, costing around $400 million.

These helicopters will support the new anti-narcotics troops as they push deeper into southern Colom-

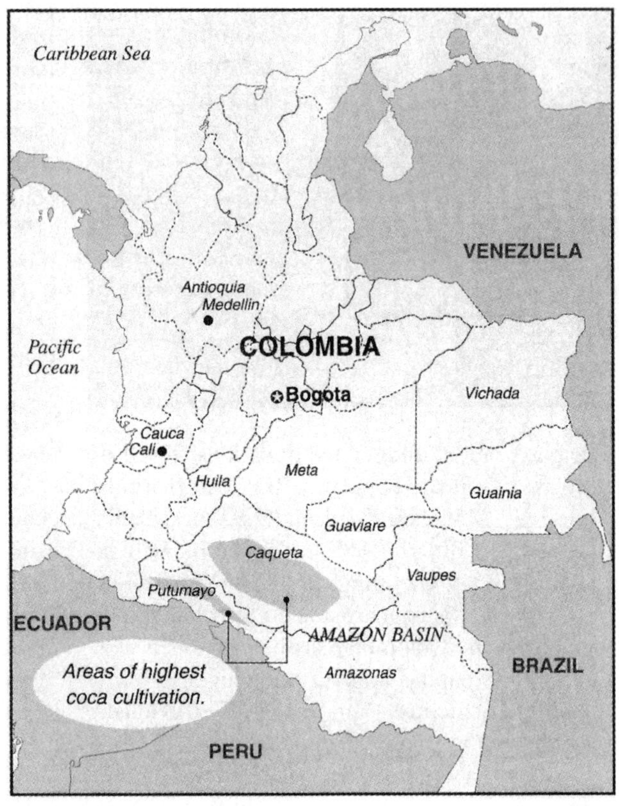

AP/WIDE WORLD

bia's rain forests, clearing the way for crop-duster planes to spray drug plantations with herbicides.

Inevitably, this will bring the military into direct conflict with the guerrillas of las Fuerzas Armadas Revolucionarias de Colombia—the Revolutionary Armed Forces of Colombia, or FARC—who dominate the remote south and rake off millions of dollars in drug kickbacks and protection fees.

Formed in 1964 from an alliance between landless peasants and the Colombian Communist Party, the FARC has grown steadily stronger in recent decades. Although the guerrillas have little support in urban centers, they control about 40 percent of rural Colombia, especially in the grasslands of the Orinoco basin and the jungles of the Amazon south.

Fifteen years ago, the FARC had barely 3,000 persons under arms; now it fields a force of nearly 16,000. Ironically, the money that paid for this quantum leap came from the United States. Like Colombia's construction companies, antique dealers, and luxury car importers—in fact, like most of the country's legitimate economic sectors—the rebels rode the flood tides of the drug bonanza, filling their coffers with "war taxes" on drug operations in their zones of influence.

"At every step of the drug industry, from planting the seeds to extracting cocaine itself, the guerrillas make a profit," says Gen. Ismael Trujillo, head of Colombia's anti-narcotics police.

Of course, the rebels are not alone in profiting from the drug trade. Their right-wing paramilitary enemies participate directly in the trade as well, funding about 6,000 combatants with the proceeds of narcotics deals.

Originally set up by drug dealers and landowners tired of guerrilla extortion, these militias are a growing military force, battling the rebels for control of strategic regions such as Putumayo, where the jungle frontiers of Colombia, Ecuador, and Peru are open corridors for weapons, drugs, and the chemicals needed to process the drugs.

President Andres Pastrana and his military high command have promised to crack down on members of the military linked to the paramilitaries, but human rights monitors say that many officers still tolerate or even collaborate with the militias.

U.S. officials calculate that between them, the rebels and the paramilitaries may earn as much as $600 million a year from drugs. The chaos and anarchy of near–civil war in parts of Colombia provide ideal conditions for the narcotics industry to continue.

Since January 1999, the FARC has participated in slow-moving peace negotiations with President Pastrana. But the rebels say that a cease-fire is out of the question until the talks start to bear fruit—and that could take years. The leaders of FARC say they want much more than favorable terms for a cease-fire:

"Many people think that the peace process just means that the guerrillas give up their weapons, but it means significant changes in all areas of Colombian life," says Maria Teresa Bernal of Redepaz, a Colombian foundation that promotes local peace initiatives.

Last May, the two sides agreed on a 12-point agenda including wide-ranging political and social reforms and an overhaul of Colombia's military. But since then there has been no real progress, and the fighting continues.

Cover operation?

FARC commanders repeatedly accuse the United States of using the war on drugs as a cover for a military campaign aimed at destroying once and for all the hemisphere's oldest rebel army.

"Plan Colombia, as we understand it, is no more than a way for hawks in the United States to become more deeply involved in our internal affairs. It's a declaration of war by the United States," said chief FARC negotiator Raúl Reyes in February.

Other critics of the plan question why the strategy focuses on the south of the country—long a traditional rebel stronghold—rather than on those mainly northern regions where paramilitaries control the drug trade.

Anti-narcotics operations have become increasingly militarized as interdiction missions run up against heavily armed FARC fighters. Rebels often shoot at fumigation planes, which are escorted by helicopter gunships. At least five helicopters and one crop-duster have been shot down in recent years while on fumigation sorties. (Since 1981 more than 3,000 anti-narcotics police have died on anti-drug missions.) The rebels are rumored to have obtained ground-to-air missiles, although intelligence officials say that this has yet to be confirmed with hard evidence.

Military analysts say that greater air power has already boosted the army's operational capacity, helping the troops retake the initiative after a string of guerrilla victories. The 63 additional U.S. helicopters, which would be provided by the aid bill now before the Senate, could be enough to tip the balance in their favor, they add.

Although U.S. officials insist that they have no interest in straying more deeply into Colombia's labyrinthine internal conflict, in the jungles of Putumayo that distinction is hard to maintain.

"We don't differentiate between counterinsurgency and counternarcotics operations—they're the same thing," Lt. Col. Jose Leonidas Muñoz, commander of the 90th Battalion, told me in March.

Despite their record of success, the marines operate under huge handicaps. Without air support, they use an aging fleet of 1950s gunboats and U.S.-made speedboats (known locally as "piranhas") to patrol the more than 3,000 kilometers (1,800 miles) of rivers that lace the jungle.

Longer missions can last several months, with groups of up to a hundred marines traveling upriver on armored tugboats, hitting one drug laboratory after another as they go. Following tips from local informers, the marines slog for hours down rough jungle trails to reach the drug installations.

Typically by the time they arrive, the peasants who run the crude processing units have already fled. Open combat with rebels or paramilitaries is uncommon, but the marines regularly come under fire from unseen snipers.

"Around here we're in constant danger. The enemy is all around, but if they see a strong unit they hide among the trees—or they disguise themselves as peasants," says Lieutenant Arenas.

"But we're totally on the offensive," he adds.

Bodies for bullets

In its *World Report 2000,* Human Rights Watch describes the relationship between the Colombian Army's Medellín-based Fourth Brigade and a paramilitary group headed by Carlos Castaño, the most feared paramilitary leader in Colombia. In a process called *legalización,* Castaño's men turned over civilian corpses to the army in exchange for weapons. The army then dressed the corpses in uniforms and claimed they were guerrillas who had been killed in combat.

As the United States prepares to give more than $1 billion in military aid to Colombia to fight the country's narcotics trade, allegations about the military's involvement in human rights abuses loom large, particularly concerns about such relationthips between the army and paramilitary outfits. The U.S. State Department, in its *1999 Country Reports on Human Rights Practices,* concludes that "security forces actively collaborated with members of paramilitary groups by passing them through roadblocks, sharing intelligence, and providing them with ammunition."

In their efforts to "cleanse" the countryside of guerrillas, paramilitaries have massacred, tortured, and otherwise terrorized anyone suspected of guerrilla sympathies. According to Human Rights Watch, during one week last year, "authorities registered over one hundred killings attributed to paramilitaries, who mutilated some of their victims and dumped their bodies into rivers to destroy evidence."

To win over critics of the U.S. aid package, U.S. and Colombian officials claim that the military has taken steps to stamp out abusive practices. Evidence of this, they say, is a newly revised military penal code, which includes a number of judicial reforms regarding the prosecution of military personnel, and the dismissal of four army generals last year who either ignored or were complicit in violations.

But according to the State Department, little has changed. Its report states, "Government forces continued to commit numerous, serious abuses, including extrajudicial killings, at a level that was roughly similar to that of 1998."

Independent human rights groups say that many of the reforms lack teeth. In particular, they argue that the much-touted military penal code fails to adequately establish how human rights cases involving military officers will be prosecuted. Human Rights Watch alleges that although human rights cases fall under civilian jurisdiction, "the military continued to dispute and often win jurisdiction." As a result, very few soldiers have faced prosecution.

The rights group concludes that the U.S. decision to focus its aid package on the Colombian military "threatens to turn some American officials into apologists for the army's human rights record."

—*Michael Flynn*

Caught in the crossfire

As the newest U.S.-backed offensive gathers momentum, human rights groups fear that once again the civilian population will be caught in the cross-fire.

Some 350 miles northwest of Puerto Leguizamo, locals in the town of Curillo are convinced that more U.S. aid will further fuel the flames of war.

Don't forget to change the oil

The Clinton administration insists that Colombia needs more coca-hunting Bell and Sikorsky helicopters, and U.S. helicopter builders always want new customers. So Colombia will be getting some free helicopters—30 new Sikorsky UH-60 Blackhawks, at a cost of $10 million each and $1,500 an hour to fly, as well as 33 improved Vietnam-era UH-1 Hueys, at $1 million each and $500 an hour to fly.

The last time the United States sent helicopters to Colombia, however, things didn't go so well. When Colombia received 12 "previously owned" U.S. Hueys in 1997, each could be flown less than 10 hours before requiring an overhaul, and only two were flying two months later (*Time*, March 6, 2000).

—*Bret Lortie*

"We're expecting the most atrocious violence. They say this aid package is to bring peace, but it will be the peace of the tomb," says one villager, Emilio Vivero.

Curillo, deep in the southern savanna, is a typical town in the remote backlands now dominated by the FARC. A few miles down the road, rebels in uniform are stationed at a checkpoint. Crowning the hill above the town center is the burnt-out shell of the police station, abandoned after a FARC attack in December.

Three officers died in the assault and eight others were captured. Three months later, nobody dares to remove the painted portrait of the FARC's septuagenarian commander-in-chief, Manuel Marulanda, which the rebels left hanging in front of the mayor's office.

For years the FARC's rule was rarely challenged in Curillo and, according to one U.N. official, the rebels eventually took control of the local drug trade.

The guerrillas' involvement with narcotics has grown steadily since the 1993 death of Medellín kingpin Pablo Escobar and the mid-1990s collapse of the Cali cartel, says Klaus Nyholm, coordinator of the Bogotá office of the U.N. Drug Control Program.

With the disappearance of those vertically integrated cartels, the Colombian drug business fragmented into a network of small and medium-sized drug traffickers. In Curillo a new set of middlemen appeared—and with them came the paramilitaries.

"The FARC didn't like it. Some of these people were allied to the paramilitaries, and others underpaid the campesinos for their coca leafs. So in some areas, the FARC took over the local trade," explains Nyholm.

The rebels impose their own form of justice in the region, punishing thieves and drug addicts, and forcing drug intermediaries to pay the standard fee of 2 million pesos (just over $1,000) per kilo of coca base—plus another 800,000 pesos in "tax."

Sitting on a shady porch above the Caqueta river, Lucas Caquimbo, who heads an association of former coca growers, says bitterly: "The government doesn't care if the guerrillas are here or not—it's got nothing to lose. The only state presence in this town is when they collect taxes or fumigate the crops."

As if on cue, two OV-10 military planes used for fumigation and reconnaissance buzz low across the chocolate-colored waters.

"We've grown used to that sound," says Caquimbo.

A growth industry

Last year government planes sprayed around 42,000 hectares (104,000 acres) with herbicides in the relentless campaign against illegal crops. Despite the spraying, U.S. and Colombian data show that coca production in Colombia has more than doubled since 1995.

Officials claim that without the spraying the figure would be even larger, but the evidence suggests otherwise. "Fumigation kills the coca, but the peasant moves further into the forest—and they plant much more than they need just to be sure that some of it survives," says the U.N.'s Nyholm.

In Caqueta and Putumayo, the two states targeted by Plan Colombia, recent history seems to confirm this analysis. Putumayo—which now produces two-thirds of Colombia's cocaine—saw an explosion of coca cultivation after a major fumigation campaign in 1997 and 1998 wiped out production in eastern Guaviare state, Colombia's previous cocaine capital.

Caqueta also saw an increase in production, but its proximity to antinarcotics bases left it open to a more aggressive fumigation campaign. Local government officials describe the effects of that campaign as catastrophic.

"There has been indiscriminate fumigation of legal and illegal crops. Fumigation causes displacement and damage to the environment," says Hever Gomez, a local state ombudsman.

Aerial eradication is carried out by private U.S contractors and Colombian police pilots who spray drug crops with glyphosate, a water-soluble herbicide produced in the United States by Monsanto and marketed as a garden weed killer.

The U.S. Department of Agriculture describes glyphosate as harmless to humans, but environmental activists say that exposure to the chemical can produce respiratory problems, diarrhea, and eye problems—and that aerial fumigation is impossible to accurately control.

Fifteen minutes upstream from Curillo, farmer Jaime Cabrera surveys a five-hectare swathe of scorched and twisted vegetation, the result of a January fumigation run.

"This was all yucca. I had a good little crop—until the planes came over. All my work has been lost," he

PHOTO BY MARTIN HODGSON

Farmer Cabrera among his yucca plants destroyed by planes spraying herbicides.

The small coca producers in Curillo say they themselves would destroy their illegal crops—if only they had a financially viable alternative.

says, his voice cracking with sadness and anger.

Pointing to the few surviving plants, he shows how their leaves are twisted and deformed. When the edible tubers are pulled from the black soil they are withered and sick-looking.

Cabrera says that with six children in school and $4,000 in debts, he has no choice but to try again.

"The fumigation planes fly over all the time, but I'm planting seeds again. We'll see which runs out first—their poison or my determination."

Colombia's top anti-narcotics cop, General Trujillo, says he's heard it all before. "We know the routine—that we fumigated breadfruit, maize, plantain, or that we damaged the forest, or some animals died or people were hurt or killed by fumigation. It's not true. It can't be true. Fumigation isn't improvised; it's scientific and organized."

According to Trujillo, crops are sprayed only if they have been identified from French- or U.S.-supplied satellite images and aerial photos. But he admits that mistakes can be made:

"In some instances there may be a margin of error—there are no absolutes in anything, but fumigation is controlled by technology."

A living wage

Technology has so far proved ineffective against the many large-scale plantations that operate safely outside the range of the crop-dusters in the far eastern regions of Guainia, Vaupes, and Vichada, say some Colombian drug experts.

Meanwhile, in Curillo, small coca producers say they themselves would destroy their illegal crops—if only they had a financially viable alternative.

Farmer Caquimbo tore up his plot of coca in 1993 after a six-month jail sentence. With the support of a United Nations scheme, he planted sugar cane and maize. "We showed that you could switch to legal crops without fumigation—and without violence. To eradicate you must start with the conscience of the campesino," he says.

But change is not easy: Peasants in the southern reaches of Colombia live hundreds of miles from the nearest markets, and agricultural prices have been deeply undercut by cheap imports. It's nearly impossible for them to survive on legal crops.

Despite the high cost of fertilizers and processing chemicals, those growing coca can make a living wage. "People are tired of coca. People want to change, but they don't want to end up with empty bellies," says ombudsman Gomez.

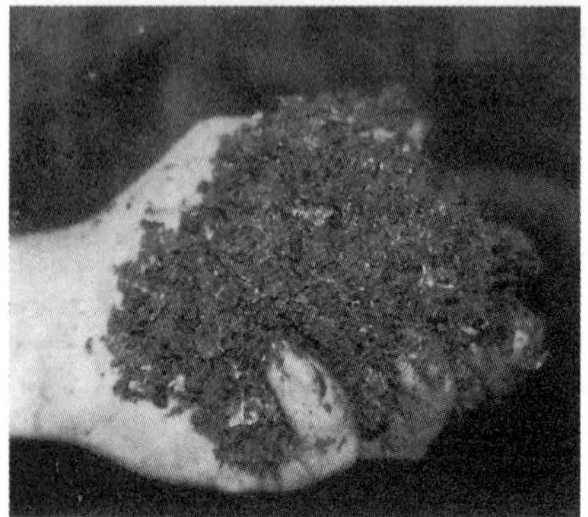

PHOTOS BY MARTIN HODGSON

Coca farmers deliver their crop to a "kitchen," where the leaves are ground, cooked, then mixed with cement, gasoline, and acid. The leaves, stripped of their cocaine alkaloids, are discarded. The remaining liquid is further processed into a dry cocaine base.

Outside a makeshift coca "kitchen" a few miles outside Curillo, Abelardo, a 33-year-old coca farmer, says he has little choice other than to grow coca.

"What's the point of planting yucca if nobody will buy it? At least with coca I make just enough to feed the family," he says, as he unloads bales of coca leaf from the back of a scrawny horse.

Under the rickety tin roof, Abelardo empties the leaves in the corner before shredding them with a lawn trimmer. Later he'll mix the leaves with construction cement which acts as a catalyst when the mixture is left to soak overnight in a drum of gasoline. In the morning

The *Bulletin* blew it again

In another example of the *Bulletin*'s failure to get on the gravy train, the editors of this magazine were as surprised as everyone else when investigator Daniel Forbes reported in *Salon* (March 30) that six magazines have been the beneficiaries of particularly sweet advertising deals cut with the Office of National Drug Control Policy. They are: *U.S. News & World Report* ($652,000), *Family Circle* ($1.425 million), *Seventeen* ($144,000), *Sporting News* ($414,000), *Parade* ($1.85 million), and *USA Weekend* ($418,000).

These magazines signed contracts with the drug policy office in which they agreed to run one free anti-drug ad for every ad the office paid for. There was a way to avoid running those free ads, though—the magazines could publish certain stories that met the guidelines the office had laid down for editorial content.

According to reporter Forbes, the drug policy office sent the magazines formal instructions called "Strategy Platforms," which outlined not only the sorts of articles the magazines were expected to run, but in which months. In the case of a story for *Sporting News,* the office even designated which writer the magazine should hire.

Had we only known . . .

—*Linda Rothstein*

Abelardo drains off the gasoline, now rich with cocaine alkaloid. The brown mulch of leaves is discarded on the foul-smelling heap behind the kitchen—just a few yards from the stream which brings water to a nearby farmhouse.

Next, Abelardo adds sulfuric acid to the gasoline solution and stirs it until an alkaloid-bearing "water" forms. After separating the liquid, he adds caustic soda to neutralize the acid, then filters the "water" through potassium permanganate, before leaving the residue to dry in the sun. It forms a yellowish powder—cocaine base.

Cartel buyers and middlemen travel for hundreds of miles to purchase this crude form of cocaine, which is then refined for export in high-tech "crystallizing" labs.

"If you've worked in a kitchen, you'd never take cocaine. Not after seeing all the things that go into it," jokes Caquimbo.

Although he makes an occasional profit, the gasoline fumes, acid spills, police raids, and fumigation planes mean that Abelardo's job is invariably unpleasant and stressful.

"I would have left this all a long time ago, if there was anyone who'd help me," says Abelardo.

Limited choices

The United Nations and the Colombian government have both explored alternative agricultural products, experimenting with tropical fruits, dairy farming, and fish breeding. But the thin alluvial soils of southern Colombia are ill-suited to large-scale agriculture—and nobody has yet found a crop as profitable as coca leaf. When the market was at its height in Curillo in the mid-1990s, 100 grams of cocaine base fetched the same price as a ton of maize.

As fumigation continues, the rural poor will face fewer and fewer options for survival, says Gabriel Peña, age 27. He counts himself as lucky. When his family's coca plot was eradicated, they had enough money to buy a small grocery store. Other youngsters face a starker choice:

"They join the army, they join the guerrillas, or they join the paramilitaries. In Curillo there are 300 unemployed men, but who'll give them work? At least in the guerrillas they give you food and clothes," Peña said.

The U.S. aid package includes $145 million dollars earmarked for social development projects, and temporary aid for as many as 10,000 people forced from their homes. But in private, some U.S. officials say the plan may displace 10 times that many.

The newly homeless may continue the cycle of displacement and colonization by heading deeper into the virgin jungle. Or they may join the thousands of other war refugees who have fled to the slum neighborhoods that ring Bogotá and other major cities.

They probably won't find much support from Plan Colombia, said Marco Romero, head of political sciences at the National University in Bogotá.

"The military element and the social element of Plan Colombia are not at all coordinated. So far the only certainty is the U.S. military aid, but nobody is willing to invest in social reconstruction," he said.

Carlos Salinas of the human rights organization Amnesty International likens Colombia to a house in flames, and he describes the pending aid package as a gruesome farce. "There's one guy with a bucket of water, three guys with flame-throwers, and then somebody shows up with a packet of seeds for the garden," he says.

"Unfortunately the flame-throwers are going to win the day and the house is going to burn to the ground."

Martin Hodgson is a freelance journalist based in Bogotá.

Is Latin America Doomed to Failure?

by Peter Hakim

In Peru, an autocratic president has curbed the power of the congress and the courts and muffled the press. Voters in Venezuela last year elected the leader of a failed military coup d'état as president and now overwhelmingly support his campaign to radically transform the nation's political institutions. Guerrillas in Colombia have the free run of half the country. Brazil was forced to devalue its currency in January 1999, provoking an open rift with Argentina and threatening the survival of MERCOSUR, Latin America's most successful trade pact. In the region's worst performance in more than a decade, nearly every major Latin American economy has fallen into a deep slump this year.

Repressive military regimes, Cuban-style revolutionaries, and boom-and-bust economies were supposed to be Latin America's past, not its future. Earlier in the decade, sustained economic growth, social progress, decent government, and genuine hemispheric partnerships all seemed within reach—and with good reason.

Consider the remarkable political transition Latin America had undergone. The military juntas and dictators who had ruled in all but a handful of Latin American countries were thrown out, replaced by elected civilian leaders (everywhere except Cuba, of course). Negotiated settlements brought an end to the civil wars that had plagued Central America, and former guerrilla leaders began to compete for power in elections. Between 1978 and 1990, some 15 Latin American countries cast aside dictatorial regimes and began to elect their leaders. Only a few of them had any significant democratic traditions, and some, such as Bolivia, El Salvador, and Nicaragua, had virtually no experience with democracy.

Economic reforms were at least as revolutionary. During the late 1980s and into the 1990s, nearly all of Latin America's governments began to run their economies in accord with the Washington Consensus, the orthodox, free-market economic policies promoted by the International Monetary Fund (IMF) and the World Bank. In Argentina, 51 state-owned firms were sold for $18 billion between 1989 and 1992. The Mexican government auctioned off nearly a thousand companies for $12 billion between 1987 and 1993. Between 1985 and 1992, Costa Rica dropped its average tariff protection from 92 to 16 percent, Brazil from 80 to 21 percent, and Colombia from 83 to 7 percent. With the introduction of disciplined economic management, Latin America's average inflation plummeted from an average of more than 450 percent between 1986 and 1990 to little more than 10 percent today. Almost overnight, Latin America joined the world economy.

Expectations were high everywhere that Latin America would transcend the populist and authoritarian legacy that had so badly hobbled the region for most of its history and that rapid and sustained progress was now possible. Yet, as the decade comes to a close, these expectations are far from fulfilled. Many people are asking whether they ever will be. Across the continent, democracy and markets remain on trial.

Déjà Vu All over Again

The global economic turmoil of the last two years has revealed the vulnerability of Latin America's economies and cast doubt on the assumption that the region can quickly achieve rapid, long-term growth. True, Latin

Many citizens appear willing to give up some measure of democracy and accept authoritarian governments that they believe can solve their problems.

America's dramatic economic restructuring and policy reforms have delivered sharply lower inflation, increased exports, and expanded access to international capital. But bottom-line results remain elusive. For the entire decade, the region's economies will have grown, on average, at a rate of less than 3 percent a year. That is better than the 1.9 percent growth of the 1980s, but it is less than half of Latin America's 6 percent average in the 1960s and 1970s and below the 3.4 percent minimum that the World Bank estimates is necessary to reduce poverty. It is far short of what the region's economic reforms were supposed to deliver. The Asian Tigers were the models for Latin America, but so far only Chile has managed to emulate them.

Of 20 Latin American countries, only three—Argentina, Chile, and Peru—will average 5 percent yearly growth during the 1990s. Three others will come close: the Dominican Republic, El Salvador, and Panama. A disturbing number of countries, including Colombia, Ecuador, Paraguay, and Venezuela, have lost ground. Their per capita income in 2000 will be almost the same as it was 10 years earlier. This decade will be the second in a row in which GDP growth per capita is less than 1.5 percent, leaving most Latin Americans almost as poor in 2000 as they were in 1980.

At the same time, inequalities of income and wealth are worsening almost everywhere. Latin America suffers the worst income disparities of any region in the world (with sub-Saharan Africa running a close second). Today, more than half of Latin America's national income goes to one seventh of the population. Per capita income among the richest 20 percent of Latin Americans is nearly 12 times that of the poorest 20 percent. In East Asia and the Middle East, that ratio is less than seven; in South Asia, it is about four and a half.

This mediocre economic performance over the last 10 years stands in sharp contrast to the hyperbolic predictions of some U.S. and Latin American officials, the heads of several multilateral organizations, and many Wall Street firms and private banks. That inflated rhetoric has given way to harsh realities. It should not be surprising that Latin America's democratic governments are under strain. Their citizens have grown tired of stagnant economies and recurrent financial crises dragging down living standards.

But it is not only economic hardship that is undermining democracy's credibility. Few of Latin America's democratic governments are governing well. In country after country, they have failed to address the problems that most concern their citizens.

A large share of Latin America's population has little or no access even to minimal government services. In many countries, cities are crumbling and health care and education have deteriorated. Traffic and pollution, along with skyrocketing crime and ingrained corruption, degrade the quality of life and welfare of citizens everywhere. Virtually every city in Latin America is far more violent and dangerous today than it was a dozen years ago. The region's homicide rate of 300 murders per 1 million people is twice the world average. Guatemala, Colombia, and El Salvador all have rates exceeding 1,000 per million. In some places—Colombia, Peru, and Panama, for example—the number of murders more than quadrupled between the early 1980s and 1990s.

The region also lags badly in educational standards. Latin American students score worse on international tests than their counterparts from Asia, Eastern Europe, and the Middle East. Only one of three Latin American children attends secondary school, compared with more than four of five in Southeast Asia, and most drop out before graduating. On average, Latin American workers receive two years less schooling than workers in identical jobs in other countries with similar income levels.

Compounding these problems, Latin America's basic democratic institutions—judicial systems, legislatures, political parties, and even the presidency—are weak and discredited in most countries. Sometimes, they barely work at all. By comparison, freedom of the press has been a bright spot, but the media still face sharp restrictions in a number of countries, including Argentina, Chile, Mexico, and Peru.

Fatigued by dubious governing, ordinary citizens are losing faith in democracy. In *Latinobarómetro* surveys taken in South America and Mexico in 1997 and 1998, more than 60 percent of those polled were unsatisfied with democracy. Almost one third favored or were indifferent to authoritarian rule. Not surprisingly, the greatest discontent was found in countries—Peru, Ecuador, Colombia, Paraguay, and Brazil, for example—where respondents had the least favorable view of democracy and felt that their own national progress had stalled.

Many citizens appear willing to give up some measure of democracy and accept authoritarian governments that they believe can solve their problems. That has certainly been the case in Peru, and it may be the course that Venezuela pursues. Nobody can predict how the practice of democracy in Colombia will suffer if the guerrilla conflict there continues to escalate. Recent events in Peru and Central America and earlier experiences in Argentina fail to reassure. In each case, intensifying conflict between guerrillas and the government produced massive human-rights violations and made a mockery of democratic rules.

Looking back over the last decade, it is hard to imagine that many of the region's democratic governments will enjoy quick or painless rebounds in the next one. Most countries will have difficulty generating rapid and sustained growth, building a more vibrant form of democracy, and satisfying the needs of ordinary citizens.

The Unpaved Road Ahead

Debates over whether Latin America's glass is half empty or half full miss the point. The region will neither leapfrog to full-fledged democracy and prosperity overnight, nor will it spiral into anarchy. Certainly the region is in trouble. Some countries will weather the rough ride, and some will even prosper. If they are to do so, however, Latin America's leaders must find ways to build healthier democratic institutions, attack poverty and inequality successfully, and stabilize roller-coaster economies.

Economic reform still has a long way to go. Tax collection, for instance, needs to be increased and made more efficient and fair. Although industrialized countries take in about 24 percent of their gross domestic products in taxes, Latin American receipts are stuck at about 14 percent. State employment needs to be reduced. Public salaries and benefits consume the lion's share of national expenditures in most countries, leaving governments with scarce funds for other costs of delivering services. And some countries have lost control of their pension systems for public employees. This year in Brazil, the shortfall between social security contributions and payments will be nearly $25 billion, equal to about 5 percent of GDP or a third of all federal tax revenues.

Although Latin America's economies will, for some time, remain vulnerable to external economic shocks, the region has no choice but to remain deeply enmeshed in the global economy. Foreign capital from trade, investment, and borrowing is essential for sustained economic expansion. The recent global financial turmoil demonstrated the resilience of the region's restructured economies and their capacity for intelligent responses to crises. A dozen years of policy and institutional reform provided important protection to Latin America, enabling the region to avoid the meltdown that consumed Russia and several Asian countries. Nevertheless, the costs—economic, social, and political—of the crisis remain extremely high.

Realistically, Latin America needs a favorable global economic context to succeed. Even assuming the best, the region will be held back by dismally low savings rates, continued dependence on commodity exports with wildly fluctuating prices, low educational standards, and vast inequalities everywhere in income and wealth.

A political forecast reveals other barriers to progress. Widespread crime and corruption, stifling bureaucracies, and feeble legislatures and judicial systems will complicate the road ahead. Polarizing differences between rich and poor and between ethnic and racial groups may worsen. The limited democratic experience of so many countries and the region's historical propensity to turn to authoritarian or populist alternatives are sobering even to the most committed optimists.

One of the pillars of democracy—political parties—has begun to crack. Once the mainstay of democratic politics in nearly every Latin American country, parties are now declining sharply in many places, fragmenting politics and ensnarling governments. In Brazil, party loyalty hardly exists, with a large number of members of the congress switching parties since last year's elections. In Peru and

Venezuela, traditional parties have been hit hard. In both countries, independent candidates won the two most recent elections for president. In Venezuela, the two parties that had run the country for 40 years failed to elect a single representative to the 131-seat constitutional assembly this year. Even in countries where political parties remain powerful, they are usually the least trusted of all national institutions, ranking behind the police, the judiciary, and the congress.

The Coming Quagmire

Some countries will start to make slow and steady gains in the next decade. All told, four or five countries in Latin America may be poised to expand their economies. A similar number could begin to enjoy robust and productive democratic politics.

Chile has set the standard. In the last 10 years, it has achieved steady growth of about 6 percent a year, slashed poverty (although inequality between economic classes remains), and improved government services. Chile's democratic institutions are growing stronger and more effective despite the burdens of some Pinochet-era restrictions.

Argentina has made impressive economic and political advances since democratic rule was restored in 1983 and is now well-situated—probably better than any other Latin American country—to accelerate its progress on both fronts.

Uruguay and Costa Rica, which along with Chile have the strongest democratic heritage in Latin America, will almost surely sustain the vitality of their democratic institutions and maintain the quality of their public services. The future of their economies is harder to predict. Historically, the economic performance of both countries has been uneven, and both are heavily dependent on their larger neighbors.

Mexico shows good prospects of significant economic success, particularly if the U.S. economy remains strong. The quality of its politics, however, will be hampered by its short experience with democracy; continuing deep political divisions; and extensive drug problems, criminal violence, and corruption.

Among the region's smaller countries, El Salvador, Panama, and the Dominican Republic have demonstrated recent economic vitality.

Brazil, which accounts for nearly one third of Latin America's population and economic activity, will heavily influence the region's overall economic performance in the coming years. It is the wild card. True, Brazil's growth throughout the 1990s has been sluggish and will average less than 2.5 percent a year for the decade. Nevertheless, the country succeeded far beyond anyone's expectations in squeezing inflation out of its economy and quickly recuperating from its recent currency crisis. At this point, there is no telling whether Brazil's economy will turn up or down. The country's fortunes hinge on the political skills and luck of President Fernando Cardoso and his advisers, who need to manage an unruly congress and fickle public opinion to keep reform efforts on track. Brazilian politics—fragmented, weakly institutionalized, and driven by local and regional interests—are a feeble underpinning for a modern economy and society. Yet few Latin American countries can boast richer political debate on key national issues, a more free and vigorous press, or a stronger trade union movement.

As many as one third of all Latin American countries, possibly including Brazil, may enjoy economic expansion and political liberalization in the coming decade. The remaining two thirds, however, will probably manage only modest growth and mediocre government performance. Several countries will do even worse.

A vicious circle has taken hold in Ecuador. Economic failure has drained the government of the authority and support it needs to implement the tough policies required to address the nation's myriad problems. As a result, the economy continues to slow, the government is further crippled and less able to act, and citizens lose confidence in democratic leaders and institutions.

Other Latin American countries may be heading toward this kind of quagmire. One of them is Colombia, where massive criminal and political violence, not economic deterioration, is the central problem. Nowhere in South America are crime and violence more pervasive and deadly or the lack of personal security greater. Some 20,000 guerrillas roam freely over nearly one half the country. Upwards of 3,000 deaths a year result from Colombia's internal warfare, and more than 1.5 million Colombians have been displaced from their homes (more than the 700,000 ethnic Albanians who fled Kosovo). The level of human-rights abuses is ghastly. To make matters worse, Colombia is the world's leading producer of cocaine. These black marks have accumulated, helping debilitate Colombia's once envied economy. No one should be surprised if, at some point, voters in Ecuador and Colombia give up on democracy and conclude that stronger, more authoritarian leadership is needed to solve their problems. Peruvian and Venezuelan voters have already done just that.

No country in South America has drifted further from accepted standards of democracy than Peru. President Alberto Fujimori tightly controls political power; other branches of government serve mostly as rubber stamps. Fujimori was first elected in 1990 when, after 10 years of democratic government, the Peruvian economy was suffering from both depression and hyperinflation, and the terrorist violence of the Shining Path guerrillas was running out of control. Two years later, Peruvian voters applauded his so-called self-coup, which suspended the activities of the congress and the courts. Today, Fujimori retains considerable popular support and may win a constitutionally questionable third term.

Like the Peruvians, Venezuelans turned against the traditional democratic leaders and parties that they believed had run the nation into the ground. On taking office in February 1999, President Hugo Chávez moved quickly to transform Venezuela's politics. The nation's congress and its supreme court were stripped of most of their powers, although the actions were arguably within the letter of the law and were certainly carried out with the support of the people. Soon, the country will have a new constitution. It is still too early to know whether democratic rights and procedures will survive the Chávez presidency and whether his revamped government will satisfy the needs of ordinary citizens. He has already gone a long way toward eliminating the constraints on executive power normally associated with democratic rule, and his extensive involvement of the military in government is troubling [see "Two Hours with Hugo Chávez"].

Peru and Venezuela represent a complex mixture of authoritarian and democratic elements. On one hand, national leaders are selected through competitive elections. There are few restrictions on opposition activity. Institutions such as the congress, the judiciary, the press, political parties, and labor unions, enjoy some measure of autonomy. An harsh repression is not used as an instrument of political or social control. On the other hand, power is concentrated and politics is highly personalized. Through a combination of mass appeal and military support, Presidents Fujimori and Chávez invariably get their way. Presidential authority is limited by few constraints beyond the need for re-election every four or five years. These hybrid systems—not fully democratic and not quite authoritarian—have yet to spread widely in Latin America, but they may represent a growing danger for countries where democratic governments perform badly over extended periods.

A Shaky Consensus

Even though Latin America will fall short of expectations, most of the region will avoid disaster. Neither true military dictatorships nor populist economic strategies are likely to re-emerge, at least not any time soon. Most of the region's political leaders and financial managers are betting on democratic politics and market economics and are struggling to make them work.

Until now, governments across the region have resisted the populist temptations that typically have plunged Latin America's economies into crisis. They are trying to maintain fiscal discipline by controlling spending and collecting more taxes. Nowhere is there any serious discussion of renationalizing privatized enterprises, reinstituting high tariff barriers, or shutting the door on foreign investment. Even President Chávez, who denounced "savage market capitalism" and promised to radically redistribute Venezuela's wealth, has not strayed from market orthodoxy. In Argentina, Chile, and Colombia—all countries facing their worst economic recessions this decade—governments have stuck with the standard market policies promoted by the IMF and multilateral banks even in the face of eroding public support. That was the approach Mexico used to surmount its 1995 currency crisis and the way Brazil responded this year: Both nations recovered faster than expected.

The political costs of implementing market policies in Latin America's newly elected democratic governments were not trivial. Today, market policies are not only considered the best route to economic progress, they also appear to be the best way to achieve political success. With rare exceptions, the winning candidates in Latin America's presidential elections in the last 6 years have been those committed to market reforms. This trend

Two Hours with Hugo Chávez

By Thomás Eloy Martínez

In the teeming river of dictators that runs through Latin American history, never has one so inscrutable surfaced as Venezuela's Hugo Chávez. Defining him through a series of negations is perhaps more appropriate than describing his elusive personality.

Is he a dictator? Perhaps the term depicts what Chávez says better than what he does. Yet even his deeds suggest that he interprets democracy differently than most people. Unlike Juan Perón or Augusto Pinochet, he has not choked off freedom of expression or of the press, but neither has he eliminated the fear that these liberties may end with the first bout of government insecurity. There are no political prisoners as in Cuba, but dozens of judges have been arbitrarily removed for presumed corruption. Emphasizing the "patriotic and voluntary" nature of its exertions, the army builds hospitals, repairs bridges, and purchases food in the countryside to sell at cost in public markets. Who could oppose that? "With Venezuela's terrible social drama," Chávez says, "we cannot afford the luxury of having 100,000 men in the barracks, eating and standing guard while people starve on street corners." He may be right. But he used to be just a cashiered lieutenant colonel, and resentment may lurk among Venezuela's generals. They are, however, very aware of his popularity with the troops, and they know that a general without full control of his troops is somewhat irrelevant.

Neither is Chávez a radical leftist seeking to overturn property laws. Yet in campaign speeches he defended the right of the needy to occupy the weekend homes of modest middle-class families, while his letter to Carlos the Jackal (a Venezuelan terrorist jailed in Paris) and admiring words about Fidel Castro smack of the rhetoric of the old left. And while he preaches friendship with the United States, his foreign affairs minister wastes no opportunity to exhibit his long-held anti-Americanism.

When I sat down for a two-hour conversation with Chávez in the Palacio de Miraflores in Caracas, I expected to confront a terrible despot. But he radiates the opposite image: that of a simple country boy, open to criticism and willing to admit mistakes. His gestures are seductive. He refers to visitors by their first names, occasionally calling them "brother," inviting them to join his travels, his crusades against poverty in Venezuela's interior, his Sunday morning call-in radio show.

When I listened to the tapes of our conversation, however, I learned how deceiving first impressions can be. Behind his affable demeanor, Chávez is wed to a few rigid and recurring ideas. Initially, he seems to agree with the arguments offered him, but later, when the subject reemerges, he reverts to prior formulations, as though he had memorized a single speech from which he was unwilling or unable to depart. Is this insecurity or fanaticism? It's difficult to know. For Chávez there is always a single truth, with no shades of gray. Although his personality has much in common with those of earlier Latin American dictators, Chávez understands that authoritarianism faces stiffer resistance now. Will he be more astute than predecessors such as Perón, Rafael Trujillo, or Venezuela's Marcos Pérez Jiménez, who he personally invited to his presidential inauguration?

Since his adolescence, the president has felt predestined to fulfill the legacy that Simón Bolívar left unfinished 170 years ago. He can recite the Liberator's writings and surrounds himself with portraits and symbols commemorating his hero. But unlike Bolívar, whose political plans were always painstakingly designed, Chávez is not always predictable. His unwillingness to clarify how much he shares of his radical allies' anachronistic economic thinking has scared foreign investors and whatever is left of a once strong business community.

Because of his inexperience and provincial worldview, Chávez appears not to understand that complex interests swirling outside Venezuela could cause his projects to fail. He seems naive and irresponsible. When I asked if he feared dashing the hopes he had planted in so many people and speculated that such disenchantment could lead to chaos, he looked at me as though the idea had never crossed his mind. "God is with us," he said.

During the 1970s and even later, Latin America's authoritarian leaders believed that they were forever altering their countries' political traditions. Pinochet, Jorge Rafael Videla, and Jean-Claude Duvalier did so, at least partially. After their tenures, Chile, Argentina, and Haiti were never the same. Chávez is attempting to shake the foundations of Venezuelan democracy and replace them with new institutions displaying doubtful democratic affinities, though anchored in popular support. Is he creating a new model for authoritarianism that could spread throughout the Americas? Or is he a social avenger who will come to understand that without playing by the new rules of a globalized world—markets and democracy—he is doomed to fail? Although Chávez remains an enigma, it seems likely that, rather than remaking history, he will be remade by it.

TOMÁS ELOY MARTÍNEZ, *director of the Latin American Studies Program at Rutgers University, is the author of many works on Peronism. His latest novel is* Santa Evita *(New York: Alfred A. Knopf, 1996).*

shows no immediate sign of abating, certainly not in the elections scheduled over the next year. Indeed, in most of the contests, all the leading candidates support disciplined, market-oriented economics.

Latin American politics, however shaky, are still mainly democratic. Nowhere in Latin America today is democratic rule threatened by military takeover, as it has been through most of the region's history. Aside from Haiti's President Jean-Bertrand Aristide, no elected executive in Latin America has been removed from power by armed force since 1976, nearly a generation ago. In the last 12 years, military coups were attempted in only three countries and all of them failed. Latin America has changed too much for a return to military dictatorship. Civilians no longer look to the armed forces to resolve their political problems; both civilian and military leaders are aware of the immense costs that financial markets impose on economies plagued by political disruption. Nearly every hemispheric government would repudiate a military coup anywhere in Latin America. The military rulers would be isolated and subject to sanctions. A coup attempt in Paraguay in 1996 was averted by the quick and forceful action of the United States and the country's MERCOSUR partners (Brazil, Argentina, and Uruguay), which threatened, among other things, to expel Paraguay from the trade pact.

Aside from Peru, where controversy over Fujimori's standing for a third term may mar the elections, presidential votes this year and next—in Chile, the Dominican Republic, Guatemala, Uruguay, and Mexico—are all expected to be free and fair. Plus, for the first time ever, Mexico's long-ruling Institutional Revolutionary Party (PRI) selected its candidate in an open primary, and the subsequent general elections are likely to be the most competitive in the country's history. Although Bolivia, El Salvador, and Nicaragua were novices at democracy when they took their first steps away from authoritarianism, all three governments have now survived two or three changes of administration—and during tough times. No doubt, democracy will be on trial in Latin America for the foreseeable future, but Latin Americans are not likely to give up the benefits of the ballot box.

Whatever its future trajectory, Latin America will probably be unable to count on much help from the United States. The withdrawal of the world's only superpower from a positive hemispheric agenda is unmistakable. Despite continuing prosperity at home, North Americans appear to have become less confident in engaging Latin America.

The beginning of the 1990s was accompanied by high expectations for U.S. relations with the region. Presidents Bush and Clinton talked effusively about the Western Hemisphere community and took important first steps in that direction. Nevertheless, the United States promised more than it delivered on an array of important inter-American issues. Trade especially stands out. There is still no fast-track trade-negotiating authority for the U.S. president, no deal with Chile, and no arrangement for the Caribbean Basin countries, all pledged by the United States at the Miami Summit of the Americas in 1994. True, the administration acted promptly when financial crises hit Mexico in 1995 and Brazil in 1998, helping avert economic meltdowns in both countries and wider regional crises. Washington also responded generously and constructively to the Hurricane Mitch disaster in Central America. These were exemplary responses to crisis situations. Yet, these actions provide scant evidence that the United States has the interest or capability to design and conduct the kind of long-term cooperative policy that will help reinforce democracy and economic progress in Latin America. For better or worse, Latin Americans are on their own.

Measured against the high expectations that took hold early in the decade, the 1990s were disappointing for Latin America. Growth was too slow. Economic volatility prevailed. Too little progress was made in fighting either poverty or corruption. The institutions of government and civil society remained wobbly without firm roots in most places.

Is Latin America doomed to failure? Surely not. With few exceptions, most countries in the region need to worry more about stagnation than backsliding. The region will still have its share of success stories, but no giant leaps forward can be expected any time soon.

Want to Know More?

For a review of democracy in Latin America, see Scott Mainwaring's **"The Surprising Resilience of Elected Governments"** (*Journal of Democracy*, July 1999) and Michael Shifter's **"Tensions and TradeOffs in Latin America"** (*Journal of Democracy*, April 1997). Jorge Domínguez discusses the region's political parties and other representative institutions in ***"Latin America's Crisis of Representation"*** (*Foreign Affairs*, January/February 1997).

The "Washington Consensus" was originally set forth in John Williamson, ed., *Latin American Adjustment: How much has happened?* (Washington: Institute for International Economics, 1990). A critical view and prediction of its downfall appears in John Cavanagh and Robin Broad's **"The Death of the Washington Consensus"** (*World Policy Journal*, Fall 1999). ***Beyond the Washington Consensus: Institutions Matter*** (Washington: World Bank, 1998), edited by Shahid Javed Burki and Guillermo Perry, offers a useful look at the failures of Latin America's vital institutions.

Sebastian Edwards' ***Crisis and Reform in Latin America: From Despair to Hope*** (New York: Oxford University Press, 1995) and Perry and Burki's ***The Long March: A Reform Agenda for Latin America and the Caribbean in the Next Decade*** (Washington: World Bank, 1997) provide historical overviews of the economic reform efforts undertaken in the region.

The Inter-American Development Bank's annual report on economic and social progress in Latin America for 1998–99, entitled ***Facing Up to Inequality in Latin America,*** is a rich source of information and analysis on the vast income and wealth disparities in the region.

There have been a large number of publications on Mexico's 1995 currency collapse. Among the best are Edwards and Moisés Naím, eds., ***Mexico 1994: Anatomy of an Emerging-Market Crash*** (Washington: Carnegie Endowment for International Peace, 1997); and Nora Lustig's ***Mexico: The Remaking of an Economy,*** second edition (Washington: Brookings Institution Press, 1998). Useful information on the 1997 Asia crisis and its impact on Latin America can be found on the Web site, **What Caused Asia's Economic and Currency Crisis and Its Global Contagion?,** by Nouriel Roubini.

For a good introduction to the alarming level of criminal violence in Latin America, see the Inter-American Development Bank's recent book, ***Too Close to Home: Domestic Violence in the Americas*** (Washington: Inter-American Development Bank, 1999).

The best cross-country surveys of public opinion in Latin America are presented in the annual publication, ***Latinobarómetro,*** published by PROMPERU.

For a thorough review of the troubled state of education in Latin America and what it will take to improve it, see ***The Future at Stake*** (Washington: Inter-American Dialogue, April 1998).

Some good recent assessments of the politics and economics of individual Latin American countries include Shifter's **"Colombia on the Brink"** (*Foreign Affairs*, July/August 1999); Ken Maxwell's **"The Two Brazils"** (*Wilson Quarterly*, Winter 1999); Amaury da Souza's **"Cardoso and the Struggle for Reform in Brazil"** (*Journal of Democracy*, July 1999); Steven Levitsky's **"Fujimori and Post-Party Politics in Peru"** (*Journal of Democracy*, July 1999); Mark Falcoff's **"Argentina: An Electoral Turning Point"** (*Latin American Outlook*, October 1999); and M. Delal Baer's **"Misreading Mexico"** (FOREIGN POLICY, Fall 1997).

For an early optimistic view of the potential for cooperation in the Western Hemisphere, see the Inter-American Dialogue's 1993 report, ***Convergence and Community.*** Abraham Lowenthal offers a more cautious assessment in **"Latin America: Ready for Partnership?"** (*Foreign Affairs*, 1993).

For links to relevant Web sites, as well as a comprehensive index of related FOREIGN POLICY articles, access **www.foreignpolicy.com.**

PETER HAKIM *is president of the Inter-American Dialogue.*

Unit 6

Unit Selections

Key Points to Consider

- Explain why you agree or disagree with the assessment that 1989 marked a turning point in European history and an end of the balance-of-power politics in Europe.
- What types of changes do you expect to see in Europe during the second post–cold war decade?
- Explain why you do or do not expect to see a separate European defense force in your lifetime? What about a common European foreign policy?
- Will an expanded European Community be able to rival or exceed the performance of the U.S. economy within a few years? Explain.
- Describe what you believe are the most important and most lasting effects of the revolutions of 1989 for three Central or Eastern European countries.
- Explain why you believe Serbia will or will not remain a democracy in future years.

www.dushkin.com/online/

19. **Central Europe Online**
    http://www.centraleurope.com
20. **Europa: European Union**
    http://europa.eu.int
21. **NATO Integrated Data Service**
    http://www.nato.int/structur/nids/nids.htm
22. **Social Science Information Gateway**
    http://sosig.esrc.bris.ac.uk

These sites are annotated on pages 4 and 5.

Europe

Nineteen eighty-nine marked the end of the cold war and a break in European history as the old balance-of-power system in Europe came to an end. The first decade of the new century promises more breathtaking changes throughout the Continent. A new security system and way of thinking about foreign affairs is emerging. As other parts of the world become more disorderly, Europe faces the twin challenge of making its own new model of security work while living with a world operating on the old balance-of-power rules.

The North Atlantic Treaty Organization (NATO) air campaign against Yugoslavia and subsequent deployment of 50,000 peacekeepers to Kosovo revealed the huge military disparity between the United States and other members of NATO. The United States carried 90 percent of the load in the 47-day air campaign in which the weapons, planes, and pilots were all Americans. Many allies found that they lacked the equipment necessary to gather detailed intelligence, to strike targets with precision, and sustain forces during 78 days of high-tempo operations. European countries had to struggle to get some 40,000 troops together to serve in Kosovo. Most analysts believe that Europeans are not investing enough in military capabilities even though Europe spends over 60 percent of what the United States spends on defense.

Since Kosovo, European allies have initiated a spirited defense debate. Most European governments now support the creation of a regional defense structure, the European Security and Defense Identity, that would make it possible for Europeans to operate in situations in which NATO itself is not engaged. The dilemma is that most European governments currently lack the military capability to sustain such a force, which would require European countries to move forces rapidly, to sustain them outside their national territories, and to equip their military with modern technology. In "Their Own Army?" Philip H. Gordon describes how Europe is about to create a unified military force. If done right, the development of a serious EU defense force could be a good thing for the United States and Europe. Done wrong, it could strain transatlantic relations and weaken European defense. How to build an independent European defense capability without weakening the ties of European countries to NATO promises to be a long-term security challenge for European members and the United States.

In December 2000, 15 European Union leaders endorsed a new defense policy that includes creation of a 60,000-member rapid reaction force, but assuaged U.S. concerns by making the new force dependent on NATO for its command structure, planning, and intelligence capabilities. This agreement underscored the fact that establishing a separate European defense identity will not be easy. France is downsizing and shifting to a smaller, more professional military. The French want a European identity instead of a NATO identity while the British and Germans remain Atlanticists. At the same time, large majorities in most Western European countries favor additional defense cuts. The left-of-center German government favors upgrading the role of the 55-nation Organization for Security and Cooperation in Europe (OSCE) while reducing NATO's role. In such an environment, it is hardly surprising that the emerging European security architecture consists of overlapping rather than new institutions. What is surprising is that many of these existing institutions are morphing together and creating unexpected coexisting processes.

In "The Search for a Common Foreign Policy," Reginald Dale describes how the European Union is making progress towards the long-term goal of a common European foreign policy. The European Community is using the principle of "constructive abstention" to assure member governments that their national policies will not be overruled. At the same time, the war in Kosovo, the need to stabilize southeastern Europe, and recent political trends are fueling public support and government efforts to implement long-dormant efforts to develop European military capabilities. Many key issues remain to be resolved as Europe strives to forge a common policy. At stake is how much power each member will be able to exercise within the organization. This issue needs to be resolved if the EU is to meet its schedule of admitting 13 additional members by 2004. The European Commission tried to accelerate this ambitious expansion scheme by declaring that negotiations with top contenders for membership and the admission process will be concluded by the end of 2002. The six top contenders are: Poland, Hungary, the Czech Republic, Slovenia, Cyprus, and Estonia.

Another integration milestone for the European Union (EU) occurred on January 1, 1999, with the introduction of a new single currency, the euro. If all goes as planned, the gradual phase-in of the European Monetary Union (EMU) and use of the euro as a common currency will be completed by 2002 except in Britain, Denmark, Sweden, and Greece, which did not join in 1999. In the long term the euro is expected to transform every level of European business and society as travel and commerce for millions across the continent is eased. Initially, the euro stimulated a spate of mergers within Europe and between European and American companies. The new currency and trade block has a population larger than the United States and a GDP that is 77 percent of the United States'. The general expectation is that the euro will in time create a more efficient economy, increase the volume of trade with major trading partners, provide another currency that may soon rival the dollar, and stimulate further cultural and political integration in Europe.

Sustaining progress toward greater economic integration will not be easy. Germany has paid a disproportionate share of the costs of the European Union. Germany plans to work to achieve a reduction in its net EU annual contribution by cutting the Union's farm-support program, which consumes 70 percent of the EU's budget. Germany is also pushing for other EU countries to accept more political refugees. At present, nearly half of all political refugees settle in Germany.

The European Union continues plans to expand membership to eligible countries in central and eastern Europe. The Czech Republic, Hungary, Poland, and Slovenia remain leading candidates. For many in Eastern Europe, revolutions have meant a return to ethnic tensions and a realization of the high cost of freedom. Despite ethnic conflict, inequality, corruption, and dead hopes, staff reporters for *The Economist* conclude in a survey of post-communist Europe that the region is a lot better off than it was in 1989. Continuing poverty in rural parts of Eastern Europe remains as one of the stiffest challenges facing the European Union.

NATO extension and European integration are more complicated today due to the continued multinational peacekeeping missions in Bosnia and Kosovo. Joshua Hammer and Zoran Cirjakovic describe, in "Free at Last," how a wave of popular discontent forced Europe's last dictator, Slobodan Milosevic, to step down after he was defeated in elections in 2000. Serbia prepares to re-enter the democratic world while Milosevic weighs his next move.

Their Own Army?

Making European Defense Work

Philip H. Gordon

At the end of this year, Europe is scheduled to take its first serious steps toward creating a credible unified military force. The clock began ticking at a December 1999 summit in Helsinki, Finland, where the leaders of the European Union (EU) announced their intention to create a rapid reaction force able to act autonomously, send up to 60,000 troops abroad within two months, and sustain them for at least a year. They also announced plans to create a new Political and Security Committee, a Military Staff able to advise EU leaders, and a Military Committee of defense chiefs modeled on NATO's. Coming after decades of failed attempts to build a meaningful European military capability, the Helsinki declaration was widely heralded as a sign of Europe's new willingness to take more responsibility for its own defense and perhaps even project power independently. The new structures are scheduled to be in place by the end of this year.

Apart from the hoopla surrounding it, this latest initiative seems more serious than its many predecessors, for three reasons. First, the United Kingdom, whose forces are necessary to any credible European military, is engaged wholeheartedly for the first time. Second, the Kosovo conflict brought home to Europeans just how militarily dependent on Washington they are and will remain unless big changes are made. And third, the Helsinki declaration is not a call to revive the eternally moribund Western European Union (WEU)—Europe's ostensible defense arm—but a plan to transfer responsibility for defense and security to the EU, an organization backed by real political will and momentum.

If done right, the development of a serious EU defense force could be a good thing for all concerned—reducing American burdens in Europe, making Europe a better and more capable partner, and providing a way for Europeans to tackle security problems where and when the United States cannot or will not get involved. If done badly, however, the EU project risks irrelevance as an empty institutional distraction—or even worse, a step back toward the situation in the Balkans in the early 1990s, when separate European and American strategies and institutions led to impotence and recrimination. The advantages of an EU better able to act forcefully and independently must therefore be weighed against the danger that the new initiative could exacerbate differences between Europe and America, duplicate costly NATO structures and assets, alienate NATO's non-EU members such as Turkey, Norway, and Poland, and create prematurely the illusion of European military self-reliance.

This is not to say that a case cannot be made for Europeans' taking over full responsibility for their own security sometime in the future. One good reason for the EU initiative is to lay the groundwork for such a contingency should it ever become necessary. As deeply engaged as the United States is today, it cannot guarantee that it will remain so forever. If America ever needs to pull its troops out of Europe to deal with a major crisis elsewhere, it will be glad to have in place a European pillar able to ensure regional stability.

Preparing for such a contingency in the distant future, however, is quite different from precipitating it now or even soon. For all their new enthusiasm about an EU defense role, Europeans are not ready, willing, or able to replace the United States. The Balkan operations conducted in the 1990s stretched Europe's military forces to their limits, even with the United States providing most of the military muscle. Building serious military capabilities will take vast amounts of money and at least a decade of preparation. So even if that is what Europeans want, it makes sense for now to preserve the advantages of a transatlantic security partnership while strengthening Europe's contribution to it.

Most of those involved with the Helsinki initiative understand this basic point. But with European leaders newly determined to carve out a prominent foreign policy and defense role for the EU, with Washington tempted by unilateralism and pursuing a national missile defense program opposed by most Europeans, and with lingering resentments over Bosnia and Kosovo heightening tensions on both sides, the EU defense initiative could easily cause a range of unintended—and unwelcome—consequences. Americans and Europeans need to work closely together to make sure the new project strengthens the transatlantic partnership and does not pull it apart.

WHY NOW?

If the new project manages to live up to the high expectations created in Helsinki, historians will likely locate the origins of its success in a place not normally known for its EU initiatives: London. It was there in 1998—only a year after vetoing a Franco-German proposal to bring defense into the EU—that U.K. Prime Minister Tony Blair underwent a conversion. Publicly castigating Europeans for their glaring defense deficiencies, he suggested that the way to overcome them was for the EU to play a defense role after all. Blair's new line, a sharp break from the anti-European rhetoric and policies of his Conservative predecessors Margaret Thatcher and John Major, was music to the ears of the French, who had long called for the EU to get serious about defense and foreign policy. By December, after several months of close coordination, Britain and France had agreed on a new call for the EU to develop credible, autonomous military forces. They announced the plan with fanfare at a bilateral summit in Saint-Malo, France.

Blair's new thinking stemmed from two main factors. The first, left unstated, was that the prime minister and his Labor government genuinely supported European union and wanted Britain to be a part of it. Because public hostility to monetary integration prevented them from joining the most important European project, however, they had to find another way to signal their support. Defense cooperation was a logical choice, given Britain's strength in this area.

The second factor, stated publicly and often, was the realization that Europeans were not pulling their weight in a NATO alliance dominated by the United States—and that Europe was paying for this with a loss of political influence and military effectiveness. According to senior British officials, the prime minister was appalled when briefed during the spring of 1998 at how little the Europeans could bring to the table should a NATO campaign in Kosovo ever be required. Blair's aides pointed out—using figures that turned out to be remarkably accurate during Operation Allied Force a year later—that Europeans would have to rely on the Americans to fly 80 percent of the combat missions and to provide key logistics, intelligence, and communications. Blair was equally appalled at the briefings he got on how Europe might manage the operation if the United States chose not to get engaged. The endless, complex series of meetings, committees, and untested arrangements that such a scenario would entail made the idea of a solo operation seem fantastic. This, the prime minister concluded, was no way to run a war.

Blair's subsequent initiative was warmly welcomed not only by the French but by other EU partners, for a mix of reasons ranging from the desire for more influence on Washington to the concern that Europe might have to fend for itself if the U.S. Congress took an isolationist turn. Many EU members also supported the initiative simply to promote further integration, which they felt would never be complete without a defense dimension. Then came Kosovo, which illustrated Europe's military deficiencies in ways that could never be conveyed by Blair's speeches alone.

That Kosovo provided such an impetus was surprising, because if anything should have spurred the Europeans forward, it was their experience in Bosnia years earlier: initial U.S. disengagement, followed by unilateral initiatives, and eventually, a dominant American negotiator sidelining the Europeans and dictating the peace. Curiously, however, the Europeans reacted to Bosnia not with an initiative to strengthen the EU as an alternative to NATO, but rather with a renewed commitment to strengthen NATO itself. Even Paris began a rapprochement, which almost culminated in France's rejoining NATO's integrated military command structure in 1996.

So why was the impact of Kosovo different? One reason was the 1997 change of government in London. Another was the realization of just how close the Americans were this time to staying out. And still another was the military strategy employed in Kosovo—to use airpower almost exclusively—dictated by Washington because of its greater military contribution. Europe's feeling of marginalization, indeed humiliation, for its military dependence was far greater in Kosovo than it had been in Bosnia, where its militaries played a more significant role.

For all their complaints about having ceded strategy to Washington during the crisis, it is unclear just what Europeans would have done differently if left in charge. It was less the realistic availability of other, more effective strategies for the war that fueled European discontent—certainly there was little enthusiasm for a ground invasion—than something closer to pique. Just as many Americans concluded that they should never again fight a war by committee, with French leaders vetoing target sets and British generals refusing to implement NATO's orders, many Europeans concluded that they should never again cede authority to American generals and the White House. The result was the agreement at Helsinki to create a rapid-reaction capability and build the institutions to manage it.

SIX STEPS TO SUCCESS

The Helsinki initiative will force the United States to put up or shut up. In the past, Washington's public support for greater European defense efforts has always masked a certain ambivalence. Europeans were welcome to contribute more, it was understood, but only to causes defined by the United States. Moreover, it was always easier for Washington to support Brussels' defense initiatives when they were unlikely to add up to much—as has reliably been the case in the past. Now that Europeans might actually do something, however, the United States needs to consider whether it really wants them to. The question of the day is thus whether a European security policy can be constructed that allows Europeans to contribute more and exercise more influence without dividing NATO and driving the Americans out. The answer is maybe—but only if leaders on both sides of the ocean keep six guiding principles in mind.

First, Europeans need to give far greater priority to modernizing, streamlining—and sometimes using—their military capabilities than to creating new institutional structures. In the Balkans, for example, political will, police forces, firepower, and troops are all in far greater demand than are the committees and institutions to manage them. EU members, however, often seem more interested in building security institutions than in using them. It makes sense to bring defense policy into the European integration process, but the EU must recognize that institution-building is not an end in itself. If all the latest initiative achieves is another layer of bureaucracy—but no greater willingness or ability to act militarily—Europe as a whole will not be better off.

The greatest obstacle to an effective European security policy, in any case, has been not an inability to decide, but rather a lack of means to act. Although highly experienced and adept at peacekeeping, most European forces lack the means to conduct truly demanding, modern military operations: airlift, sealift, satellite intelligence, precision-guided munitions (PGMs), and all-weather and night-strike capabilities. Kosovo demonstrated not only how much Europeans must rely on the United States for these, but also that the Europeans could not maximize the effectiveness of the one resource—manpower—that they actually had in relative abundance. As NATO Secretary-General George Robertson has pointed out, European members of NATO have nearly 2 million men and women in uniform, yet had great difficulty mustering 40,000 troops—just 2 percent of their forces—for Kosovo. Unless and until this capabilities gap with the United

States can be closed, the European defense initiative will remain a largely paper exercise, and the prospect of significant autonomous EU actions a mirage.

The good news here is that Europeans now seem to understand better than before how great the capabilities gap is. The bad news is that neither their publics nor their leaders seem prepared to make the financial sacrifices necessary to procure such capabilities any time soon. U.S. defense spending has fallen significantly since the end of the Cold War but has now leveled off at around $285 billion per year, about 3.2 percent of gross domestic product. Members of the EU, on the other hand, together spend around $165 billion annually—less than 60 percent of the U.S. amount and only 2.1 percent of GDP—and their defense budgets are still falling. Germany, the EU's largest and richest country, now spends less than 1.5 percent of its GDP on defense. With 10 percent unemployment and a widespread recognition of the need for tax cuts, there is little prospect that this amount will rise any time soon. These may well be legitimate choices reflecting different national priorities. But Europe's lack of influence within NATO and its inability to conduct autonomous operations is bound to endure until this situation changes.

Second, Europeans should make clear that NATO remains their first choice when it comes to military force, and that EU military operations are not intended for areas where NATO is already engaged. NATO is the most inclusive military organization in Europe, provides the institutional mechanism for military cooperation with the United States, has elaborate structures and standards already in place, and happens to be the organization deployed in Europe's war zones. Europeans understandably reject any formalization of what they consider to be the subordination of the EU to another organization, but they should recognize their own interest in using NATO where possible.

Third, NATO's assets must be made available for use by the EU. NATO has thousands of military planners and staff (most of whom are European) as well as an extensive network of command posts and headquarters throughout Europe. Duplicating these structures on anything approaching a similar scale would allow the EU to stop relying on NATO, but at considerable cost. Some Europeans will argue that they need separate EU structures because the United States can veto the use of NATO assets. But this concern is exaggerated, and Washington should work to make it even less so. It is highly unlikely that the United States would both decline to participate in a mission and use its veto to prevent Europeans from carrying that mission out. After all, nothing would be so certain to drive the Europeans to create the separate defense structures Americans hope to avoid. The more relevant point is that some of the most essential assets that Europeans lack—such as airlift, cruise missiles, and PGMs—are not "NATO assets" at all, but American ones. The solution to this problem is for Europe to get more military equipment, not the structures and institutions that surround it.

Fourth, links must be created between the EU and NATO. Although they share the city of Brussels, the two institutions have heretofore had no contact other than the occasional meal between the NATO secretary-general and the president of the European Commission. Such an arrangement was fine when the EU was uninvolved in defense matters, but it is unacceptable now. Regular informal contacts between the two bureaucracies—and not just at the top level—should begin right away, even if more formal links have to wait until the EU has finalized its new structures. The creation of separate EU and NATO bureaucracies that do not talk to each other can only contribute to divergent transatlantic perspectives, when the goal should be to harmonize them.

Fifth, transatlantic institutional and military cooperation must be underpinned by increased industrial cooperation. So far, the post-Cold War trend has been consolidation within the U.S. and European defense industries rather than between them. But a continuation of this trend over the long run would be unhealthy. It would deny both sides the opportunity to exploit the most advanced technologies available, limit competition (as overseas firms are excluded from major procurement deals), and contribute to the development of a technology and compatibility gap. American concerns over the transfer of sensitive technology are legitimate but need to be balanced against the equally great danger of a bifurcated alliance.

Finally, the EU must involve non-EU European allies as closely as possible in their new initiative. With NATO's recent enlargement, 8 of the 19 NATO members—Poland, the Czech Republic, Hungary, Norway, Turkey, Iceland, the United States, and Canada—are not in the EU. The non-EU European allies understand that they cannot have a permanent seat at the EU's decision-making table. But there is much the EU can do to include them in its plans—such as regular discussions of matters affecting common security, the opportunity to be involved militarily if the EU decides to undertake an operation, and the creation of structures (modeled on NATO's Partnership for Peace) that allow non-EU members to be involved in decision-making for any mission in which they are taking part.

The Helsinki initiative could wind up in one of three ways. It may help bring about a stronger and more flexible transatlantic alliance. It may amount to nothing, like its predecessors. Or it may create bitterness and dissension among many of the world's leading democratic powers, leaving the Europeans to fend for themselves before they are able to do so. The first outcome is obviously the most desirable but will require a great deal of effort, resources, and goodwill to pull off. If such will is lacking, however, we should hope—for both Europe's and America's sakes—that we end up with the second option, not the third.

PHILIP H. GORDON is Senior Fellow in Foreign Policy Studies and Director of the Center on the United States and France at the Brookings Institution. He served as Director for European Affairs at the U.S. National Security Council from 1998 to 1999.

The Search for a Common Foreign Policy

By Reginald Dale

The Past

As the great enterprise of European integration has struggled forward over the past half century, its grandest ambitions have always attracted skepticism. Sometimes the skeptics have been right, more often they have been wrong, or at least behind the times.

But perhaps no project has engendered more doubts and disbelief than the attempt to create a common foreign policy, in which the member states of the European Union would ultimately speak with a single voice in world affairs.

Those doubts have hardly been alleviated by the EU's plans, first officially formulated in the early 1990s, to include security policy in the search for common positions.

The skeptics ask how fifteen proud nations with such different cultures, histories, and interests could possibly reach common ground on the vital issues of foreign and security policy that lie at the heart of national sovereignty.

Some American commentators have confidently stated that the European Union will never have a common foreign and security policy, still less the single telephone number that former secretary of state Henry Kissinger used to say he wanted for his diplomatic dealings with Europe.

But "never" is a dangerous word to use in politics, and experience suggests it is also unwise to apply it to the tortuous process of European integration. Although the unification process often moves crabwise and sometimes backward, it has consistently reached most of its objectives, though admittedly not always on time. Now, from an unexpected quarter, the war in Kosovo has suddenly injected a new sense of urgency into the efforts to create a common foreign and security policy. European leaders have been shocked by the inadequacy of their disparate armed forces in the crisis and by the extent of their dependence on uncertain US leadership.

That painful awakening led to big steps forward. At their summit meeting in Cologne in early June, the EU's leaders took a series of ambitious decisions intended to bring foreign and security issues into the framework of the EU institutions and approved plans for combined, if limited, EU military operations in future emergencies in Europe.

Underlining their new found readiness to press ahead, they appointed a high-profile international official, Javier Solana of Spain, the NATO secretary general, to the new post of European high representative for foreign and security affairs.

There are good reasons why progress in foreign and security policy should have lagged behind most other fields of cooperation. The integration strategy adopted by the European Union's founding fathers called for economic unification to precede political union.

In the EU's formative years, the importance of that sequence was dramatically demonstrated by some bad experiences in the field of common foreign and defense policy—after which the very words "common foreign policy" remained taboo for almost forty years.

The first unhappy experience came in the early 1950s, even before the establishment of the original six-nation European Economic Community, when the French parliament rejected plans for a European Defense Community.

The plan had been hatched by the six countries that would subsequently go on to found the EEC—France, Germany, Italy, Belgium, the Netherlands, and Luxembourg—in the hope of creating a common European army under the aegis of a European political community with federal institutions.

Against the background of the beginning of the cold war and the Korean War, the aim was to create a framework that would allow German rearmament without rekindling the fires of German militarism. German rearmament, of course, eventually went ahead, but the call for a common European army was far ahead of its time.

The next attempt—the so-called Fouchet Plan launched by France under President Charles de Gaulle in 1961–2—was equally ill-fated, for virtually the opposite reasons. This time France's partners rejected proposals designed to lead to a unified foreign policy and coordinated defense policies.

While the French parliament felt the proposed defense community went too far in a federal direction, France's partners thought the Fouchet Plan did not go far enough. They found the plan too intergovernmental, leaving too much power in the hands of national capitals, especially Paris. They also feared it might threaten defense links with the United States in NATO.

Following those two failures, the next attempts were more modest. In 1970, the six began cooperation on foreign policy, by means of closer links between their diplomatic services, in order to strengthen their solidarity on major international issues. The process was known as European political cooperation (EPC).

But the process yielded few spectacular results in the 1970s. It was not until ten years later that the political and economic (not military) aspects of security were included in EPC, and it was not until the mid-1980s that steps were taken to give EPC a formal structure, including a secretariat.

From 1970 to 1986, European diplomacy was harmonized through informal agreements, with France insisting on keeping the process intergovern-

Reprinted from *Europe,* July/August 1999, pp. 25-29. *Europe,* ©1999 by Magazine of the European Union.

mental, not subject to normal Commmunity disciplines that would have reduced the influence of national capitals.

Foreign policy cooperation finally began to get serious in the mid-1980s, when the Single European Act relaunched economic and political integration after years of near-stagnation. In addition to setting up the EU's single market, the act, which came into force in 1987, formalized the EPC system.

The act provided for meetings of foreign ministers at least four times a year, regular meetings of the political committee (composed of the political directors of the national foreign ministries) and a separate EPC secretariat. A reference to closer cooperation on security questions was included for the first time in an EU treaty.

Foreign policy cooperation remained a matter for national governments, outside the regular EU institutional framework. Nevertheless, both the Commission and the European Parliament were drawn somewhat closer into the process, with provisions for the Commission to be "fully associated with the proceedings," and the Parliament to be kept regularly informed.

The member countries undertook to work toward "the convergence of their positions and the implementation of joint actions." But it was not until the Maastricht Treaty on European Union, which came into force in 1993, that a more solid structure was built on these foundations. That treaty is the basis for most of today's foreign policy and security cooperation.

The Present

The early 1990s, with the Gulf War and the beginning of hostilities in Yugoslavia, gave the EU countries plenty of reasons to believe that common policies were increasingly necessary. The idea that the time was ripe was also fostered by the end of the cold war and German unification, both of which seemed likely to boost the international role of the EU, in Europe if not beyond.

At the same time, the move to a single European market at the beginning of 1993, and the Maastricht commitment to economic and monetary union later in the decade, was giving a new dynamism to political as well as economic integration.

With the cold war over, many Europeans also assumed that the US military presence in Europe would be wound down, making a stronger European defense and foreign policy capability both more necessary and more achievable.

At the start of the troubles in Bosnia, the then Luxembourg foreign minister Jacques Poos gained widespread notoriety by announcing that the "hour of Europe" had arrived. It turned out that it had not—the EU lamentably failed to resolve the Bosnian crisis.

Nevertheless, the EU's efforts to present a common front to the world intensified. The Maastricht Treaty set one of the Union's objectives as "the implementation of a common foreign and security policy, including the eventual framing of a common defense policy."

European political cooperation had been implemented by means of consultations, information exchanges, and the issuing of joint declaration.

Now, following Maastricht, the EU governments are actively pursuing the more demanding aims of agreeing "common positions" and implementing "joint actions." The Amsterdam Treaty, which came into force in May, added a loosely defined concept of "common strategies."

CFSP activities have included moves to encourage the settlement of border disputes among Central and East European countries, monitoring elections in Russia and South Africa, dispatching humanitarian aid to Bosnia, administrating the Bosnian city of Mostar, and supporting the Gaza-Jericho agreement in the Middle East.

Special envoys have been appointed to represent the Union in the Middle East peace process and to help resolve crises in Africa's Great Lakes region and in the countries of former Yugoslavia.

None of these activities has had a huge impact on the course of world events. Even the most ardent supporters of the CFSP would admit that the EU has not proved terribly effective in the major areas in which it has sought to play a role, especially Bosnia and the Middle East.

In Bosnia, the key diplomatic and military players turned out to be the United States, NATO, and the United Nations, not the European Union. In the Middle East, Israel and, to a lesser extent, the US has successfully kept the EU at a safe distance from the heart of the peace process, correctly assuming that the EU is more sympathetic than Washington to the Arab point of view.

The EU's policymaking has suffered from a lack of clear definition of the EU's interests and objectives, as opposed to national interests. Some Europeans fear a pattern is emerging in which the United States makes the main geopolitical decisions and Europe pays for them.

The EU is by far the main provider of humanitarian assistance to the former republics of Yugoslavia and of economic aid to Russia, the countries of Central Europe, and the Palestinians. It is the main source of international development aid and will inevitably have to bear most of the cost of rebuilding Kosovo.

That is at least partly a reflection of the fact that the EU is much more credible as a commercial and economic power on a world stage than as a political player.

The EU's efforts to assume a political role have been handicapped by awkward institutional arrangements, designed to separate the CFSP from the usual EU decision-making process with its greater limits on national sovereignty.

Those arrangements have now been simplified: The general principles of the CFSP are defined by EU leaders meeting in the European Council. Decisions are taken in the Council of Foreign Ministers, who must act unanimously except in the implementation of some joint actions.

However, the aim is still to prevent national governments being overruled on sensitive foreign policy issues—the consequence of which, in the past, has been to give every and any member state a veto over the formulation of a common position.

The Amsterdam Treaty seeks to resolve that problem with the introduction of the concept of "constructive abstention." Henceforth, a member state that does not like a proposal can abstain and not be obliged to apply the resulting decision. But the abstaining government must accept that the decision commits the Union and must refrain from doing anything that would conflict with the EU action.

The Future

The war in Kosovo has injected a sudden note of reality into some of the more abstruse discussions of the common foreign and security policy. Many European leaders are making clear they see the crisis as a decisive test of their ability to purge Europe of its old nationalistic demons and present a common front to the world in the coming century.

Joschka Fischer, the German foreign minister, has gone so far as to describe the hostilities over Kosovo as a "unification war" that will lead to a much more united Europe. The war will oblige Europeans to grasp the need for a common defense, as well as for the expansion of both NATO and the EU to incorporate most or all of Central and Eastern Europe, he says.

Romano Prodi, the president-designate of the European Commission, has even revived calls for a European army.

Work is underway in Brussels on a new pact aimed at stabilizing southeastern Europe by drawing the countries of the Balkans closer to the EU, with the possibility of membership in the distant future acting as an incentive for the hostile ethnic groups to learn to live together.

It is a huge task, involving the creation of civilized market democracies in the region virtually from scratch. It will be a major test for the CFSP, as will the efforts to create a more integrated and more independent European defense capability that many European leaders are now urging. Rudolf Scharping, the German defense minister, says that Europe must acquire its own major military assets, such as satellite reconnaissance and airlift capacity, for which it is currently obliged to turn to the United States. The same proposal has been made by other leading Europeans, although few of them have yet begun to tackle the issue of how such grandiose plans should be paid for—and whether European taxpayers are prepared to foot the bill.

Nevertheless, there is no doubt that Kosovo has given a big boost to proposals for integrating defense policies more closely into the EU structure. Plans are afoot to fold the Western European Union, the long-dormant European defense cooperation forum, into the EU, thus giving the Union a formal defense dimension.

Another consequence of Kosovo is likely to be that cooperation on defense policies will now take over the lead from foreign policy coordination as the driving force of the CFSP.

After a May meeting in Bremen, northern Germany, the WEU's defense and foreign ministers said they were now committed to "the development of an effective European defense and security policy."

Scharping, who chaired the meeting, stressed that the aim was not to replace or compete with NATO but to "strengthen Europe's voice" within the transatlantic alliance.

At their Cologne summit meeting, the EU leaders took these ideas a step further. In addition to appointing Solana as high representative, a post created by the Amsterdam Treaty, the leaders agreed that the EU should have its own military capabilities to tackle regional crises in Europe, backed by adequate intelligence and strategic planning capacities. They agreed on a number of possible ways for bringing defense into the EU's traditional decision-making process, including the participation of defense ministers in meetings of the Council of Foreign Ministers.

Other proposals include the creation of an EU military committee, composed of military personnel, that would make recommendations to a permanent new political and security committee in Brussels.

Until now, such ideas would have been dismissed as fantasy, implying as they do a central control over defense policies, which is unacceptable both to major member states, like France and the United Kingdom, and to the EU's neutral countries.

Prospects for closer defense cooperation had already begun to improve before the bombing in Kosovo started. Last fall, the United Kingdom dropped long-standing opposition to merging the WEU with the EU and agreed to a joint declaration with France at St. Malo calling for a stronger European defense policy.

Germany, shedding lingering inhibitions stemming from World War II, has been showing growing readiness to play an active European security role—an evolution dramatically underlined by the inclusion of German combat troops in the peacemaking forces in Kosovo.

The United Kingdom, anxious not to undermine NATO and US leadership, has traditionally resisted efforts to create an independent European defense capability. But Prime Minister Tony Blair is now keen to find new areas of cooperation with Europe in order to assert his leadership on the international stage.

With the United Kingdom not among the eleven nations that have adopted the single European currency, the euro, defense is the most obvious field for cooperation, and stronger defense links with Europe are surprisingly popular with British public opinion.

Surveys suggest that the British public is more in favor of defense and foreign policy cooperation with the rest of Europe than it is of the trade and economic cooperation that is the bread and butter of EU membership.

The trend long predates Kosovo. Polling by the United States Information Agency shows that the British have long been highly supportive of European defense cooperation, somewhat less supportive of foreign policy cooperation, and much less favorable to the single currency.

A similar pattern exists in Germany, where public opinion favors foreign policy cooperation most of all and prefers defense cooperation to membership in the single currency. In France, there is much more support for the euro but still higher levels of support for defense and foreign policy cooperation.

For all these reasons, optimists believe it will finally be possible to take big steps forward in foreign policy and defense cooperation. However, it remains easy to be skeptical. Cynics might point out that the climate has been propitious before—as it was at the beginning of the 1990s—and the EU failed to take advantage of it.

But it would be wise not to be too cynical. Only a year or two ago, skeptics on both sides of the Atlantic were predicting that European economic and monetary union would never happen and that the euro would be indefinitely delayed. That was to underestimate the forces driving Europe toward closer integration. Those forces have now been reinforced by Kosovo.

"Kosovo could be our military euro," Ulrich Beck, a professor at Munich University, told the *New York Times* in April. The Balkan crisis, he argued, could create "a political and defense identity for the European Union in the same way as the euro is the expression of economic and financial integration."

That may be a little overambitious. But at least, with Javier Solana's appointment as 'Mr. CFSP', the EU now has someone to answer the telephone when Washington calls.

Reginald Dale is a columnist for the International Herald Tribune.

EUROPE AFTER COMMUNISM

Ten years since the wall fell

Despite ethnic mayhem, inequality, corruption and a small cemetery of dead hopes, post-communist Europe is a lot better off than it was in 1989

HOW simple it all once seemed. You drew the line, in Churchill's ringing image, "from Stettin on the Baltic, to Trieste on the Adriatic", peered muzzily eastwards at a vast slab of grey, and wept. As far as the map would unfurl, from Budapest and Warsaw across ten time zones to Vladivostok, the same monolithic monster prevailed, the same brutal but phoney triumphalism, the same glowering statue of Lenin on his pedestal in thousand upon thousand of town squares, the same crushed, resentful expressions of the drab millions unable to leave their vast workers' prison.

To be sure, there were some minor permutations. The Balkans, under their own mini-Stalins, produced small variations on the theme—in Albania, in Yugoslavia, perhaps even in Romania. But the similarities of content were far more compelling: the ubiquitously stultifying central plan and the death of free enterprise; the greyness, tackiness and poverty; the hostility to religion; the tyranny of one ideology, the totalitarian control of a single party in the grip of a privileged few; the murderous terror of the entire Stalin period (shorter but no less intense in Central Europe than in the pioneering Slav heartlands farther east), and then the deadening coercion of the Brezhnevite era; above all, the crushing of free thought, suffocating and perverting just about every soul in communism's thrall, bar a handful of Sakharovs, Havels and Walesas.

What happened in 1989, once a Russian leader had tried to reform the unreformable and lost his grip, was—still is—as dramatic an upheaval as the one in France exactly two centuries before, though a lot less bloody. Now, however acute the trauma of transition during this first post-communist decade, it is at least undeniable that Europe is not just free but once again supremely diverse; and yet, at the same time, a large central chunk of it has returned *en bloc* to its home at the heart of the continent.

No fewer than 27 countries (28 if Montenegro leaves the Serb rump of Yugoslavia, as it soon may; 29 or 30 if Kosovo and Chechnya are counted) have emerged out of the eight that once made up the main communist area: the Soviet Union, another five Warsaw Pact countries in a slab between Poland and Bulgaria, plus Yugoslavia and oddball Albania. Just about all of the new list (even, in its agonised way, Russia) strive to look west. Most want, as they put it, to "rejoin Europe". By any measure, a good half of them are well on the way. Several have already been knitted right back in.

Which Europe? Central Europe? Mitteleuropa? Eastern Europe? Central and Eastern Europe, as the international agencies cumbrously have it? The problem of how to define the continent's new geography testifies to the pluralism of the new order.

History, religion, cultures, people: they all count again. The political geography of freedom is necessarily blurry. It would be misleading to see Europe as two halves neatly put back together again. Nowadays there are various Europes. Imagine a large cartographic quilt, tightly stitched in parts but with ragged and jagged edges, with bright patches and threadbare ones in the middle. Then imagine different pairs of hands trying to sew the quilt together, pulling one bit in one direction, another bit in another. One piece threatens to tear off. Another is stitched on. Borders fray. It is ungainly. But it is more or less—in George Bush's words—"whole and free".

Certainly the line no longer runs neatly from north to south. Bits of the former Soviet Union, such as the

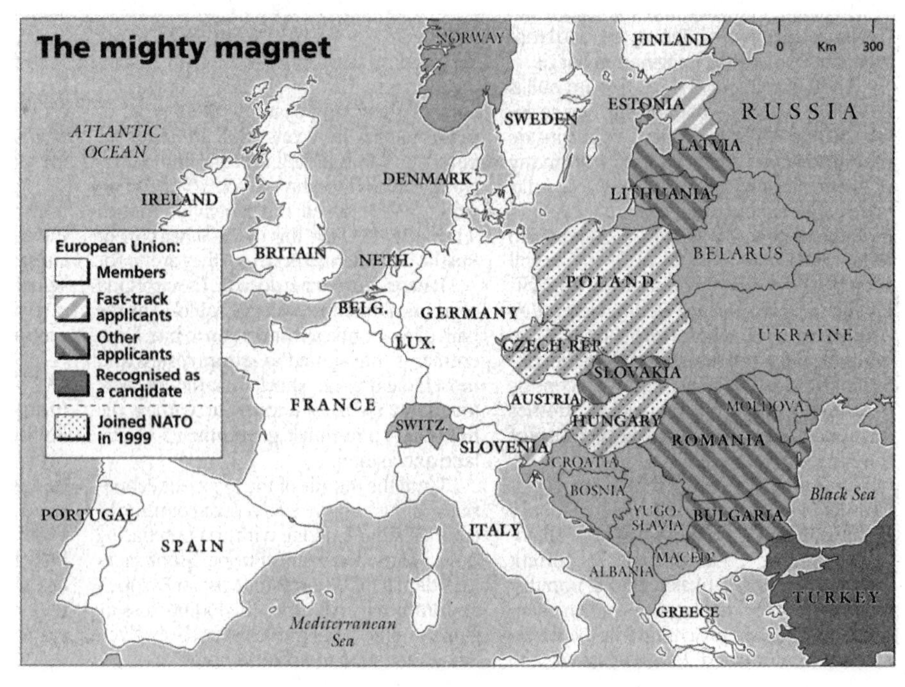

Baltic trio, have hoisted themselves, wholesale, back into the West. Estonia, the northernmost of the three, has become almost Nordic. "We want to be just another boring Nordic country," says its foreign minister (a man brought up in America). Lithuania snuggles up to its historic rival, Poland. Moldova, one day, may rejoin its ethnic kin in Romania. Western Ukraine pulls its country's centre of gravity westward.

Little states can do much to affect the quality of the fabric, for better or for worse. Some hold threads together, others threaten to weaken them. Up north, Latvia is the Balts' weak strand, its capital, Riga, more tightly tied to Russia than those of the other two Baltic countries. In the middle of the quilt, a thuggish populist, Vladimir Meciar, pulled Slovakia eastwards in the mid-1990s, back towards Russia and its authoritarian ways; but now, under a liberal coalition, Slovakia is struggling gamely westwards again.

Bulgaria and Romania are the perennial laggards of the old Warsaw Pact. Romania, once a breadbasket, could with its 23m people be a powerhouse of south-eastern Europe, just as Poland with nearly 40m has emerged incontestably as the new dynamo of east-central Europe between Germany and Belarus-Russia. In the past two years, Bulgaria has looked perkier than Romania. But even the backward Bulgarian-Romanian pair are, very slowly, westernising.

Even in the Balkan peninsula some bits are becoming truly European again. Slovenia has jumped right back into the old Habsburg-Austrian backyard. Croatia has so far failed to do so; but, if it shed its leader, Franjo Tudjman, it soon could. With Kosovo now a western protectorate, Serbia is the only Balkan country that sets its face against the new pattern, preferring friendship with Russia.

The ex-Soviet Caucasus countries, at a crossroads of Europe and Asia, are really a patch apart. But even there Georgia and Azerbaijan want to attach themselves to the fabric of the new Europe. Only the Central Asian quintet of the old Soviet Union, east of the Caspian Sea, can hardly claim to be European—though four of them, astonishingly, have joined NATO's "partnership for peace".

Wherever the central and eastern parts of Europe begin or end, the EU is a mighty magnet, tugging the continent relentlessly west. With Germany rapidly absorbing its old ex-communist part and its Austrian cousin thinking of shedding its cold-war-era neutrality, German-speakers are back at the heart of Europe. The punchily revived Poles, along with Czechs, Hungarians, Estonians and Slovenes, are all poised to join the club. Lithuania and Slovakia are catching up. This year, Poland, Hungary and the Czech Republic joined NATO. Ten years ago that would have made the imagination boggle.

Another element of the westward pull is the movement of people leaving their countries behind. Millions formerly locked inside the old Soviet zone have headed west, many of them illegally. Even the physical links have tightened out of all recognition. Good motorways now tie countries like Slovenia to Milan and Vienna. High-speed trains will soon put Warsaw only hours away from cities such as Hanover via Berlin, Germany's new-old capital, whose move from Bonn dramatically symbolises the shift in the continental centre of gravity. Within the coming decade, it is a fair bet that eight countries once under Russian sway will be members of the European Union.

Only the Slavic core of the old Soviet Union—Russia, Ukraine and Belarus—looks manifestly unable to move fast, if at all, towards "Europe". Belarus, under its current leader, Alexander Lukashenka, a populist tough who once managed a state chicken-farm, may be the only country in the whole of the ex-communist zone consciously to head back east, and even to want to reunite with Russia. Many Ukrainians feel that way too, but if their incumbent president, Leonid Kuchma, wins the second round of a current election Ukraine will probably prefer to stay independent and edge westwards. In Russia itself, a big change has been the growth of regional power. Places like Tatarstan, a legally constituted republic in the middle of Russia, increasingly run their own affairs. This is dangerous (witness Chechnya). But it is also, on balance, good.

Across the continent those on the "wrong side" of these new lines mutter about "new Yaltas", as if they will be frozen out by the kind of treaty that sliced Europe down the middle for half a century. They should not be. The whole point about the new lines is that they are porous, fading, variable. No one is disqualified by geography or history from joining the EU or NATO.

Will westward mean wealthier?

Yet heading west has not brought instant contentment. Far from it. Take a look at the balance sheet, and examine three types of performance: in economics; in terms of peace; and in building up civic and democratic values (morality, if you will). The results are very mixed; but generally—though it is harder to argue this in the Slavic core of Russia, Ukraine and Belarus—they are good.

It has been a rough decade. The euphoria of political freedom wore off quickly as the pain of economic reform began to bite. Governments that started to reform fastest and most radically, the "shock therapy" lot, were invariably the most unpopular: witness the first post-communist governments of Poland and Estonia.

Until the middle of the 1990s, the economies of just about every post-communist country shrank, along with the purchasing power of its inhabitants. Strobe Talbott, now President Bill Clinton's strategist for Europe's ex-communist countries (including Russia), glumly opined that the Poles had been given "too much shock, too little therapy".

Even now, the list of losers is long. Everywhere the chorus goes up: the people who bossed us about before, the communist "nomenklatura", are still on top. It was the clever apparatchik, the tough factory manager, who best made the switch to capitalism, benefiting from insiderish privatisation deals. Corruption is rife throughout the old communist world. Organised crime, with little opposition from policemen, judges and politicians, has swept across the region.

The plight of middle-aged professionals as well as ill-educated people in one-industry towns that have gone bust is wretched. Almost everywhere, the over-60s are miserable, their savings and pensions pathetic. Life for the duller sort of intellectual who once served the old order is pretty grim, too: in the old days, even poets and painters got their monthly stipend and virtually free flat. Unemployment has gone from virtually nil (though vast hordes were employed to do pretty well nothing) to a good 10% across the board. An irony of the immediate post-communist era was that the very workers —shipbuilders and miners, for instance— who had done so much to bring down communism were often the first to lose their jobs in the brave new world.

Although most countries in the old Warsaw Pact zone are growing again, the gap between haves and have-nots is widening. Other gaps have opened up between metropolis and small town, between town and country. The farther east you go, the worse the farming. Reviving village life has been hard everywhere. And in Poland, where a fifth of the people are farm-connected, getting into the EU will probably mean squeezing that fraction to about 5%.

In almost every ex-communist country, standards of health care have plunged. In some, lives have suddenly grown shorter. In Russia, the average male dies at 58, as early as in many parts of Africa; the total population (now about 147m) has been declining by nearly 1m a year. Farther west, though, the lifespan is lengthening again.

The sharpest division is between generations. For the young, the bright, the pushy, the well-educated, the new world is still exciting. The breath of freedom—to choose, to switch jobs, to travel—still intoxicates. You rarely hear people under 35 sighing for the certainties of cradle-to-grave socialism.

Coming good?

In any case, it is hard to measure real growth. But in general there was a huge drop in GDP over the first half-decade after 1989, hitting bottom in the mid-1990s. There followed steady or even rapid growth in the past few years. The direction of trade has been strikingly reversed, so that when Russia crashed last year economies once tied to the Soviet Union proved surprisingly immune to the eastern shock.

Most of Central Europe's economies are looking far better equipped to compete in the real world. Poland, the biggest economic success of recent years, has been expanding at a breakneck pace. Over the past four years, average annual growth has been 6%. Ownership of cars and houses has soared. Several other countries—Hungary, Slovakia and the three Balts—are now growing fast.

The most striking feature is that dispensing harsh medicine early on—selling off the whole of state industry, reducing subsidies fast, letting prices go free and thousands of factories go bust, and at the same time de-dollarising, keeping inflation down and the currency stable—has brought the highest dividends. The men who heroically incurred unpopularity at the time for doing the hard thing, Leszek Balcerowicz of Poland and Mart Laar of Estonia, both hounded from office in the early 1990s, are now back in charge of economies that—thanks to those early reforms—are prospering.

When tax collection is spotty, the tax man bribable and money still sent abroad (especially the farther east and south-east you go), the figures are not always so cheerful. But the dramatic rise in car- and house-ownership across the ex-communist world shows that money is not just going to a gangster-connected handful. Even in Russia and Ukraine, a short drive out of any major city reveals hundreds of smart new chalet-style houses sprouting in old-fashioned villages off the beaten track. A new property-owning middle-class is steadily emerging.

Another encouraging feature is the new free-market consensus. By the mid-1990s, the Czech Republic, Estonia and Latvia were the only ex-communist countries where ex-communists had not recovered power in government or as head of state. Yet in none of them was the course towards privatisation and free enterprise abandoned.

And all this from the most primitive of beginnings. Most companies had virtually no accounts: factory bosses were simply told how many widgets to produce. There were no stockmarkets, no private banking system, no securities and exchange commissions, virtually no mechanism for buying and selling property. People had no credit cards, no mortgages, no land deeds or lease-holdings of their own (except in Poland, where peasants had held on to most of the land). In the Soviet Union there were not even public telephone books or street maps. In 1987, Mikhail Gorbachev daringly gave permission for three hairdressers in Estonia to go private. Now Russia has 900,000 small businesses.

Is it a safe place?

The revolution of 1989 was miraculously peaceful. Except in Romania, where President Ceausescu and his wife were summarily shot, the old regimes were dealt with leniently. Since then it has got fiercer. Most of the Balkans, chunks of ex-Soviet Central Asia and the southern rim of Russia itself, including Chechnya, have blown up. But Central Europe has been remarkably peaceful.

Above all, the cold war has become the faintest of memories. The entire Warsaw Pact, including bits of the ex-Soviet Union, is changing geopolitical sides and Russia, however resentful, is doing nothing about it. After a long argument, Russia has conceded Ukraine's right to the Crimean peninsula, with Russia leasing back part of Sebastopol bay for its navy. Russia's troops have abandoned the lands to their west, except for a slice of Moldova (and the Kaliningrad enclave, still a part of Russia). They sit tight only in pockets of the Caucasus and ex-Soviet Central Asia. And Russia's efforts to build up a military group among the former Soviet republics, known as the Commonwealth of Independent States, have been notably feeble.

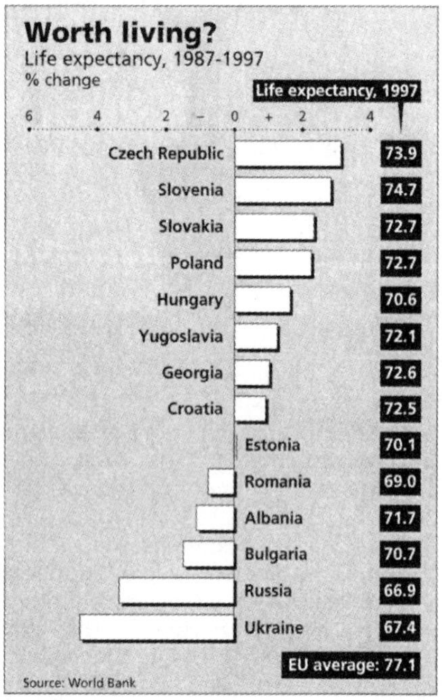

Worth living?
Life expectancy, 1987-1997
% change

Country	Life expectancy, 1997
Czech Republic	73.9
Slovenia	74.7
Slovakia	72.7
Poland	72.7
Hungary	70.6
Yugoslavia	72.1
Georgia	72.6
Croatia	72.5
Estonia	70.1
Romania	69.0
Albania	71.7
Bulgaria	70.7
Russia	66.9
Ukraine	67.4
EU average	77.1

Source: World Bank

The worst violence in the region has been ethnic. Multi-ethnic Russia has had its share of strife, not just in Chechnya. But the worst tragedy of the entire decade has been the bloodiness of Yugoslavia's break-up and the special horror of Bosnia. The massacre at Srebrenica, where 7,000 Muslim men were taken away by Serbs and never seen again, was the worst single act of violence in Europe since the second world war. The ensuing war in Kosovo to protect Kosovars from Serbs was the first time that NATO countries had gone into action in the ex-communist world.

In ex-communist countries outside the Balkans, ethnic tensions have been kept under better control—partly because of the lure of the EU, with its good-behaviour requirements as the price of entry. The Slovaks split off peacefully from the Czechs in 1993. Romania and now, post-Meciar, Slovakia are willing to treat their Hungarian minorities better. The Balts want to assert their own language and culture in place of Russia's, but are being told to be gentle with their Russian minorities. Instructively, it turns out that the best way to make the local Russians happy is to make them rich: as they notice the poverty of their kin on the Russian side of the border, more and more of them are preferring, these days, to settle down and be good Balts.

Democracy the winner

But the biggest change has been the entrenchment of democracy. Governments have come and gone at the voters' wish. And with multi-party alternation of regimes has come a surprising degree of consensus.

In Poland an ex-communist president cohabits fairly comfortably with the anti-communist free-marketeers who run the government. In the Czech Republic the Social Democrats rule the ministerial roost while a Thatcherite ex-prime minister, Vaclav Klaus, helps to set the agenda as parliament's speaker. In Slovakia a disparate four-party coalition has fended off Mr Meciar. In Hungary the free-marketeers attempting another round of economic reform are following pretty much the path charted by their ex-communist-turned-capitalist predecessors. In the Baltic trio reform has for the most part ploughed steadily ahead.

One of Russia's many tragedies is that no free-market party of the centre-left has emerged; the old Communist Party has utterly failed to reinvent itself. Russia's most frightening aspect is the rise of mumbo-jumbo Slavophilia, deeply anti-western and with some dark racialist undertones. And yet, so far, both Russia and Ukraine have continued to plod haltingly towards a more western way of doing things. Flawed as their societies are, the holding of genuine elections, a free press, the right to travel and to set up a business, are achievements that make the old days feel like another century. It was only in 1992, remember, that Russia's new era began, after 75 years of the grossest tyranny, and not much enlightenment before that.

What has yet to happen, however, is the growth of a new public morality, of a sense of civic virtue. The ex-communist world is in some ways a caricature of the vicious capitalism the old communist propagandists warned the masses about. Money, for many, is the new master. The judicial systems, even in Poland, Hungary and the Czech Republic, are grubby. Policemen and customs people are far more bent than they are in the West.

The new middle class is still too small, too frenetic, too worried, too acquisitive to involve itself in charities, in school meetings, in churches, even in politics. "Normality" was the goal of the people who overturned communism. Central and Eastern Europe are not yet normal, because the ugliness of the communist state has yet to be replaced by a sense of civic decency and a genuine belief in the law. But they are getting there, and doing it faster than many people had feared.

Free at Last

Power to the people: A wave of popular discontent finally forces Europe's last dictator to step aside. Serbia prepares to re-enter the democratic world—and Milosevic weighs his next move.

BY JOSHUA HAMMER AND ZORAN CIRJAKOVIC

IN THE END, IT WAS THE ordinary workers who turned the tide. As dawn broke over Serbia last Thursday, a cavalcade of buses, trucks and battered Yugos choked the roads leading into Belgrade. They carried men from towns like Cacak, Kragujevac and Kraljevo: grimy industrial backwaters that had once been the heartland of Serb nationalism, but were now overcrowded with Serb refugees from Kosovo and scarred by last year's NATO bomb attacks. They included farmers, factory workers and miners—men such as Marko Petrovic, 40, a strapping mechanic at the Kolubara coal mines. Until two years ago, Petrovic had idolized Slobodan Milosevic as the father of the Serb nation and scorned the opposition as weaklings and traitors. But sickened by the country's deepening misery and Milosevic's blatant fraud in the Sept. 24 election, he was driving to the capital to demand that Milosevic surrender. "We have to bring him down in Belgrade," Petrovic said. "We have to enter his bedroom. Only then he'll be gone."

Thirty-six hours later, he was. As the world watched in amazement, Serbs by the hundreds of thousands took to the streets in an outpouring of people power that few could have imagined two weeks ago. Milosevic's ouster came 10 days after he lost a presidential election that he had believed would cement his hold on power—and following a series of desperate gambits intended to prolong his rule. He was tossed out of office by the same forces that had kept him in power through 13 years and wars in Bosnia, Croatia and Kosovo: ordinary Serbs. But now they were fed up with his lies and policies of destruction. In the end, the despot's uncanny knack for self-preservation deserted him. Gambling that opposition forces would crumble and that street protests would fizzle out, Milosevic made the latest in a series of miscalculations that have pushed his country to the abyss. The man whom many held primarily responsible for a decade of bloodshed and horror in the Balkans seemed finished.

The end came swiftly—and, miraculously in a country saturated with weapons, with a minimum of violence. A huge opposition rally in Belgrade on Thursday afternoon turned into a popular uprising that echoed the revolutions that swept through Eastern Europe a decade ago. The Parliament building and state television—two symbols of Milosevic's rule—were invaded and torched. Government authority crumbled. Jubilant mobs roamed through the streets of Belgrade, brandishing weapons seized from police stations. Despite the outpouring of rage, only two died and fewer than 100 were injured. Milosevic loyalists abandoned ship. False rumors swirled that Milosevic had fled the country, was holed up in a bunker in eastern Serbia or had committed suicide. In a brief TV address, a subdued Milosevic recognized Vojislav Kostunica, the 56-year-old jurist who had defeated him at the ballot box, as the new president. Milosevic announced his plans to rest and spend time with his family—wishful thinking, perhaps, for the world's most-wanted war criminal. As the armed forces pledged their loyalty, Kostunica officially assumed power on Saturday in an inaugural ceremony at a shopping mall that replaced the torched Parliament. "This is a great moment for our country," he declared. "After all the suffering, this may bring us peace."

In Yugoslavia and across the world, reaction to the despot's fall mixed delight with disbelief. Tens of thousands spilled into the streets of Belgrade on Friday night and the city erupted in a chorus of cheers, shouts, honking horns and gunfire. "I think we are dreaming," exulted Sladjana Milicevic, 27, a housewife, as she wandered the streets in a daze. World leaders expressed support for Kostunica and pledged to normalize relations with the destitute pariah state. British Foreign Secretary Robin Cook promised to "bring down the barriers between Serbia and Europe." In Washington, President Bill Clinton called Milosevic's defeat "a big blow for freedom," and compared it to the fall of the Berlin wall. "The lion's share of the credit belongs to the people," he said. "It's a day for celebration."

It was a celebration that few had believed would come so soon. Blindsided by his defeat at the ballot box, Milosevic had bounced back with his usual ruthless determination. First his handpicked electoral commission falsified the results of the election—tacking on nearly 200,000 votes to Milosevic's total to deprive Kostunica of his majority. Opposition leaders cried foul, vowed to boycott a runoff—and called for a countrywide general strike. Yet for a few tense days Milosevic appeared to be outmaneuvering his foes. Kostunica and other opposition leaders seemed to bicker over the wisdom of the second-round boycott; some argued it would play into Milosevic's hands by allowing him to run unchallenged. The general strike initially achieved mixed results. Piles of garbage accumulated on Belgrade's streets, cafés closed their doors and the public-transit system was paralyzed, but the shutdown had little economic impact—because most Serbs are out of work anyway. The opposition frittered away precious momentum as its strategists debated whether strikes should go on for three hours, five hours or a full day.

The turnaround came at the Kolubara mines near the town of Lazarevac, a former Milosevic stronghold about 40 miles south of Belgrade. On Sept. 29, 7,500 workers walked off their jobs at four enormous open-pit mines that provide coal to the country's main thermoelectric plant. The strike threatened to cut off power to one third of Serbia. Milosevic sent in hundreds of riot police to break up the strike and ordered the arrest of 11 strike leaders and two opposition figures for inciting sabotage. On Wednesday, police surrounded a group of miners at a canteen in an attempt to take control of the mine. Angry people from across Serbia rushed to the scene to show their solidarity with the strikers—commandeering bulldozers and ramming through police barricades. Bewildered and frightened, the police retreated.

The strike in Milosevic's heartland galvanized the lagging opposition. Leaders escalated their demands, calling on Milosevic to recognize Kostunica's victory, drop the arrest orders against the miners and opposition leaders, and fire the top management of state-run television. They set a deadline of Thursday afternoon, and exhorted supporters throughout Serbia to march on Belgrade. On Thursday morning, more than half a million people converged on the city. Jobless men from gritty Serb towns—seething with rage over Serbia's lost wars and impoverished isolation—mingled with the urban intelligentsia. Young mobsters, decked out in the latest Versace fashions, protested alongside them; even they had abandoned Milosevic. The mood seemed to be a combustible mix of anger and anticipation. Alcohol was abundant.

The spark was struck at 3:30 in the afternoon. After a series of desultory speeches by pro-opposition celebrities, an impatient mob broke through metal barricades erected in front of the Yugoslav Federal Parliament building; police officers opened fire with hundreds of canisters of tear gas. Enraged, the protesters attacked the Parliament, forcing the police to flee through rear doors. The mob seized control of the building, trashing offices, setting fires, hurling pictures of the hated despot into the street. Outside, Jovan Nikolic, a hulking factory worker, wiped gas from his eyes, watched smoke billow from the windows and spat in contempt for the dying regime. "Let the Parliament burn," he said. "We'll build a new one." Protesters hauled a captured officer from the Serbian Special Units—an elite police force considered loyal to Milosevic—before the jeering crowd. He addressed them over loudspeakers: "My colleagues fired tear gas at you and beat you with truncheons, but we are not doing this of our own will," he proclaimed. "Good luck."

A block away at Serbian State Television headquarters, a bloodier battle raged. Police fired rubber bullets, then live ammunition, at protesters who surged toward the building. Four were wounded, and a young woman died when a bulldozer commandeered by demonstrators ran over her. After an hour-long battle, the mob set fire to the building, taking the TV station off the air and driving out 2,000 police. Just before being seized, the station reported that "at this moment, terror rules in Belgrade. [Opposition forces] are attacking everyone they see on the streets, and there is chaos." After issuing that statement, the station switched briefly to music videos. Then it went dark.

As daylight faded over the smoke-filled capital, the government appeared to have lost all authority. The entire police force at Belgrade's downtown police station surrendered to the crowds. Opposition supporters stormed the building, seizing bulletproof vests, Kalashnikovs and pistols—and trashing what was left inside. At city hall, opposition leaders unloaded a yellow truck filled with machine guns, supervised by five friendly policemen who wore white ribbons on their left shoulders in a gesture of solidarity. Many celebrants strutted happily past the looted and burned perfume shop belonging to Marko Milosevic, Slobodan's much-reviled son; Marko was reported by the Yugoslav press to have fled with his wife and son on a Yugoslav Airlines flight to Moscow, using passports with false surnames. Three state-owned TV stations, three state radio networks and Politika, a powerful media house run by an ally of Milosevic's wife, Mirjana Markovic, declared their loyalty to Kostunica. Even the management of Serbia's most popular entertainment network, the Pink Channel—which alternated Slobo propaganda with Latin American soap operas and reruns of "The X-Files"—switched to the opposition.

Throughout the night, Milosevic and his wife were monitoring the meltdown from a villa in the luxurious Dedinje neighborhood overlooking Belgrade. Built by the Yugoslav communist leader Tito in the 1950s, the official presidential residence was heavily damaged by NATO bombs last year. It is known to be honeycombed by bunkers and a labyrinth of tunnels that can provide an easy escape in times of civil unrest or invasion; they were also used to store priceless art works during the NATO bombing campaign. But Milosevic and his wife were hardly contemplating a hasty exit, experts believe. Confident of the support of the military and the police, the Milosevices almost certainly believed that they'd survive in power.

The Rise and Fall of Slobodan Milosevic

He started his political career as a communist apparatchik. But he made his bloody mark on the Balkans as a ruthless and opportunistic Serbian nationalist.

1987 After taking over Serbia's ruling League of Communists, Milosevic becomes a hero to Serbs with a nationalist speech in their Kosovo heartland, now mainly Muslim.

1990 Following the collapse of communist rule, he is freely re-elected president of Serbia.

1991 Yugoslavia breaks up as Slovenia and Croatia declare independence. Fighting erupts in Croatia and later in Bosnia.

1992 Serbia and Montenegro form a new Yugoslav federation. The United Nations imposes economic sanctions on Yugoslavia for fomenting war in Croatia and Bosnia, where thousands of atrocities are committed, mostly by Serbs.

1995 After intense negotiations, spearheaded by U.S. diplomat Richard Holbrooke, a peace accord on Bosnia is signed in Dayton, Ohio.

1997 Ineligible to run for another term as Serbian president, Milosevic is elected president of Yugoslavia, a post with less actual power.

1998 Tensions rise in Kosovo amid reports of Serbian atrocities against local Muslims of Albanian extraction. But when NATO threatens airstrikes, Milosevic starts to withdraw some of his security forces from Kosovo.

February 1999 U.S. Secretary of State Madeleine Albright helps to negotiate a Kosovo autonomy plan at meetings in Paris. The Kosovars accept, but Milosevic turns it down.

March 1999 NATO starts its air war against Serbian forces. Milosevic steps up his campaign in Kosovo, driving out hundreds of thousands of ethnic Albanians. In June, he gives up and withdraws his forces from Kosovo, the signal for refugees to return.

September 2000 Running for re-election, Milosevic faces a surprisingly strong challenge from Vojislav Kostunica, who is backed by 18 opposition parties. Kostunica appears to win an outright victory in the first round of balloting. Milosevic stalls, but massive protests finally persuade him to resign.

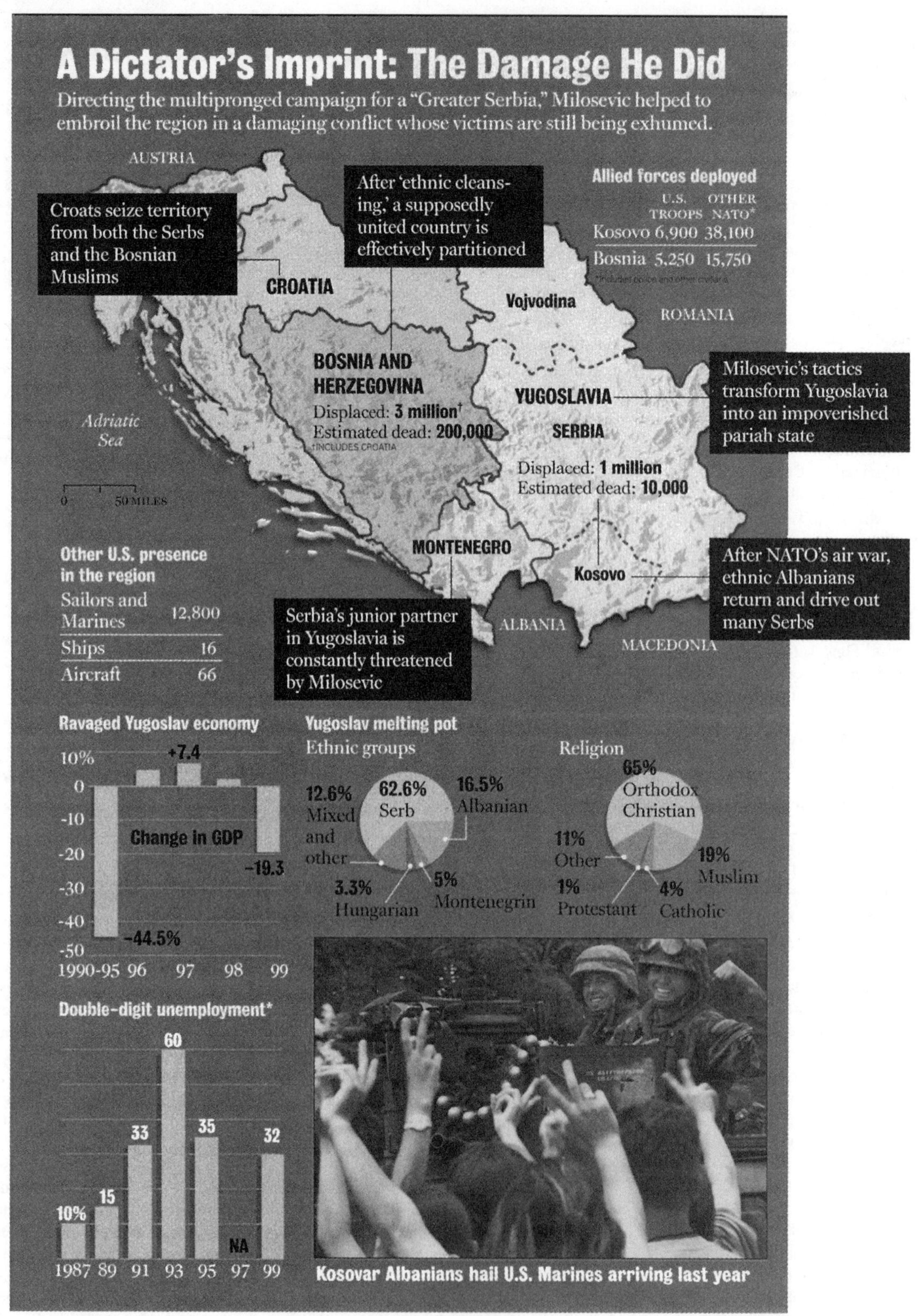

*ESTIMATE SOURCES: THE CIA WORLD FACTBOOK; DEPARTMENT OF DEFENSE; UNHCR; EUROPA WORLD YEARBOOK 2000, WORLD BANK, PRESS REPORTS

But the dictator's time was growing short. On Friday more pillars of support crumbled. Russian Foreign Minister Igor Ivanov met Kostunica at the Federation Palace, the formal seat of the Yugoslav presidency, and told him that the Russian government now recognized him as the country's leader. Ivanov then met Milosevic at his bombed-out villa and urged him to accept defeat. Milosevic, defiant, informed him that he intended to keep playing a role in Serbian politics. Then the Army weighed in: Chief of Staff Nebojsa Pavkovic, who had remained on the fence until late afternoon, visited Kostunica and pledged his support. The two men drove to Dedinje and confronted Milosevic in a small billiard house built by Tito beside the bombed villa. Milosevic and Kostunica shook hands for the first time. Pavkovic reportedly told Milosevic that the battle for the Yugoslav presidency was over. Then he left the two men alone. They talked for an hour, reports say. Milosevic agreed to recognize Kostunica's victory at the polls, but he didn't bother to ask his successor about the possibility that he might be prosecuted by Yugoslav or international courts.

By Saturday it appeared that Milosevic intended to keep fighting. Loyal henchmen, surrounded by muscular bodyguards, took their seats in the Yugoslav Parliament's makeshift headquarters as worried oppositionists watched. "We have nothing. We don't have the police. Our lives are still in danger," said Zarko Korac, an opposition leader and new member of Parliament. "[Milosevic] can order us to be killed any time."

Although he now lacks any official title, Milosevic still commands the loyalty of powerful officials, including the Interior minister, who oversees a police force of 150,000 men. It is still conceivable that he could pull the strings in the Parliament and have a crony elected prime minister. Still, he's lost the media and control over large parts of the country, and most believe the damage to him is beyond repair.

So far he had managed to avoid the fate of Romania's dictator Nicolae Ceausescu, who was captured and executed shortly after his fall and attempted escape in December 1989. But Milosevic is widely hated, and if he keeps fighting for his political life, he risks antagonizing the masses further. He also risks standing trial for war crimes—and a certain life sentence. On Friday night Kostunica repeated his promises that there would be "no revenge" against people from the old regime, and attacked The Hague tribunal as a puppet of the U.S. government. But Kostunica could still yield to Western demands for international justice. As a last resort, Milosevic could take refuge in the former Soviet republic of Belarus, which on Friday offered him a home in exile.

For Kostunica, the real struggle is just beginning. He now must consolidate his position in Serbia and deal with the lingering threat from Milosevic. Only then can he turn to Serbia's crumbling economy, which is dominated by criminal gangs and fueled by smuggling. More than 30 percent of the work force is unemployed, and the infrastructure, battered by NATO bombs and neglected after eight years of sanctions, is in tatters. If he manages to take real power, he should finally bring some stability to one of the most dangerous corners of the planet. Kostunica has already expressed his readiness to talk with independence-minded leaders in Montenegro; he'll be tougher on the Kosovars. But it's probably premature to speculate on geopolitics as long as Milosevic is in a position to make mischief. If the old dictator won't go quietly, the masses may be forced into the streets one more time.

Unit 7

Unit Selections

Key Points to Consider

❖ What do you think Vladimir Putin's main foreign policy priorities are likely to be over the next few years?

❖ Why do you agree/disagree with the thesis that the Russian Federation is likely to unravel as ethnic groups struggle to achieve their independence from Moscow?

❖ What faction among the competing elites do you think will be the most important in determining the future direction of Russian foreign policy?

❖ Explain why you do or do not agree that conflicts in the Caucasus and Central Asian region indicate that a more political brand of Islam, rather than Islamic militancy, is now a major factor in understanding politics in this region.

Links **www.dushkin.com/online/**

23. **Russia Today**
http://www.russiatoday.com
24. **Russian and East European Network Information Center, University of Texas at Austin**
http://reenic.utexas.edu/reenic.html

These sites are annotated on pages 4 and 5.

The former USSR is a region composed of 15 independent nation-states, with each state trying to define separate national interests as it experiences extreme economic problems. Today many ex-Soviet citizens share a sense of disorientation and "pocketbook shock" as their standard of living is lower today than it was under communism. About half of these states are experiencing political instability and growing discontent. Ukraine was the only state to peacefully transfer power from one elected president to another during the early post-USSR era, but its economy remains highly interdependent with the Russian economy. Consequently, it and most other former Soviet states suffered with the devaluation of the ruble.

Uncertainty is the principal characteristic of the current Russian political system. The Russian government was disintegrating after having failed in attempts to impose austerity measures and collect taxes when the IMF approved a $22.6 billion IMF-led rescue loan for Moscow in July 1998. Shortly afterwards the Russian government devalued the ruble, defaulted on domestic bonds, and placed a moratorium on paying overseas creditors. The actions triggered the worst economic crisis in Russia since the collapse of communism and increased fears worldwide that the IMF was powerless to prevent "contagion" effects from spreading worldwide.

Most observers hailed Russia's parliamentary election at the end of 1999 as a step toward democracy. These optimistic assessments were made despite the fact that these elections were characterized by widespread mudslinging, dirty tricks at the polls, and corruption. While the Communist Party remains a powerful force in the State Duma, the lower house of parliament, two pro-government parties won surprisingly large percentages of the vote. The widespread support for these recently formed parties that lack political platforms was interpreted as a strong nationalistic desire to support the current government's military offensive in the breakaway province of Chechnya. The vote was also viewed as an endorsement of then–prime minister Vladimir Putin, the sixth prime minister to be appointed to Yeltsin's government during a two-year period. At the same time, the International Monetary Fund (IMF) delayed releasing an installment loan to Moscow. This action was at least in part a reaction to the military offensive directed at civilian areas by the Russian military as they fought to retake Grozny in Chechnya.

Boris Yeltsin, who abruptly stepped down as president in January 2000, named Prime Minister Vladimir Putin as his successor. One of Putin's first acts was to grant Yeltsin blanket amnesty from any future investigation of his family finances. After winning the 2000 presidential elections, Putin displayed a willingness to use military force in Chechnya, to rely more on nuclear weapons, and to plan reductions in the size of conventional armed forces. Unlike Boris Yeltsin, Putin has built bridges to rival politicians and undertaken measures designed to reign in the power of the country's economic oligarchs. After the bungled rescue attempt of the Kursk submarine that cost 118 sailors their lives and became a national scandal, Putin formulated a plan to transform Russia's internal balance of power in his favor by reorganizing the country into seven "super-regions" with Kremlin loyalists in charge. Putin argued that only with a strong state can Russia establish the rule of law and the foundations of a civil society on which democracy rests. Provincial elections at the end of 2000 suggested that Putin's approach has wide support with Russian voters. The overwhelming majority of Russians in recent public opinion polls indicated a willingness to trade away some democratic freedoms if it is necessary to achieve order. Most Russians for now seem willing to support Putin's efforts to make the country governable.

During the Yeltsin years, it was fashionable in the West to cite Russia's weak state as the source of Russia's ills. Michael McFaul in "Putin in Power" notes that Vladimir Putin's ascension to power has demonstrated that the Russian federal state still has tremendous power—if the man in control of a state is vigorous, ambitious, and popular. Ten years after the Soviet Union's collapse, the whims of one man at the top still can profoundly influence the fate of the whole Russian regime. Russia's protracted transition from Communist rule is not over, and the end point of this transformation remains uncertain.

Putin, like other recent Russian presidents, is critical of Russia's reliance on foreign capital and Western advice. Few Russians benefited from privatization or other free-market reforms. Instead, the country turned toward oligarchic capitalism, dominated by a few wealthy tycoons and giant conglomerates that enjoy special privileges and a cozy relationship with the state. This "tycoon model" is also found in regions outside Moscow where local governors and magnates mirror the Moscow tycoons. Thus, 10 years into reform in Russia, many considered U.S.–backed economic reforms as being wealth confiscation rather than wealth creation measures.

The magnitude of the economic crisis is so great that the Russian state is shrinking. Nowhere is this more apparent than in the Russian military-security complex where a breakdown of cohesion and morale in the Russian military reflects a general loss of stability in Russian society.

It is not possible yet to know the domestic and international consequences of the current period of instability on Russia's future leaders or how Russia will define its national interests. Alvin Z. Rubinstein, in "Russia Adrift: Strategic Anchors for Russia's Foreign Policy," explains how Russia since 1991 has been trying to fashion a national-security policy to fit its changed status in a new era. Today, Russian strategists are deeply concerned by the failure to secure Russia's links to CIS states and by the paucity of promising options. The Primakov Doctrine sought to delineate Russia's national interests, but most Russian foreign policy elite consider themselves *derzhavniki*—believers in strong central government and Russia as a nuclear superpower and great power in Eurasia and East Asia. Whether this elite can accept the tenets of a more modest Russian foreign policy remains uncertain.

Some analysts interpret recent fighting in the Caucasus as further evidence of a "clash of civilizations" between the Islamic world and other geopolitical blocks. In "Chaos in the Caucasus," writers for *The Economist* reject this view. Instead, they view conflicts in the Caucasus and Central Asia as underscoring the fact that Islam exists in many different forms. They suggest that as Islamic militancy recedes in the Middle East, political Islam is spreading to the periphery.

A thorough understanding of the cultural trends is important because the Central Asian states bordering the Caspian Sea are poised to undergo dramatic changes as their oil and gas reserves, estimated to be worth between $2.5 and $3 trillion dollars, are developed. These untapped resources have stimulated a growing web of recent deals in Central Asia and increasingly make the area appear to be a new kind of post–cold war battleground pitting the interests of three former military rivals—China, Russia, and the United States—and a variety of multinational corporations against each other.

Putin in Power

"During the Yeltsin years, it became fashionable in the West to cite Russia's weak state as the source of Russia's ills. Putin has demonstrated after only a few months in office that the Russian federal state still has tremendous power—perhaps too much power—if the man in control of that state is vigorous, ambitious, and popular."

MICHAEL MCFAUL

When Yeltsin appointed Vladimir Putin prime minister in August 1999, few were impressed. An obscure bureaucrat recently recruited from St. Petersburg, with no electoral experience and few political allies, most analysts reasoned that Putin was a caretaker head of government who would not last much longer than the previous three prime ministers.

Almost everyone underestimated Putin. In one year he catapulted from the head of the Federal Security Service or FSB (the domestic successor to the KGB) to prime minister, to acting president, to an elected president who won the March 2000 presidential election on the first ballot.[1] As prime minister and acting president, Putin aggressively pursued a single policy: the prosecution of the second Chechen war. Since becoming the elected president of Russia, however, Putin has demonstrated a similar degree of vigor in virtually every policy area.

In the realm of foreign policy, Putin already has achieved some goals, floated several intriguing new ideas, and maintained a busy travel schedule. He pushed through the Russian parliament ratification of the Comprehensive Test Ban Treaty and the second Strategic Arms Reduction Treaty (START II), which had languished in the Duma for seven years. As for new ideas, Putin has articulated a clear desire for Russia to become a fully integrated member of Europe and the Group of Eight Western industrial democracies (in which Russia is a political but not financial member). His new foreign policy doctrine, unveiled over the summer, states that he and his government plan to follow a rational and realistic foreign policy that will serve Russian economic and political interests. Such a strategy includes active engagement with the West. His foreign policy doctrine further stresses that "Russia shall actively work to attract foreign investments," and will strive "to ensure favorable external conditions for forming a market-oriented economy in our country." He has emphasized that he sees Russia as a European country that shares many interests with other European nations.

At the same time, Putin has made clear that Russia will not allow the West to dictate the terms of this engagement. His counterproposals regarding missile defenses have won praise in Europe and China and put the United States on the defensive. His controversial but intriguing visits to North Korea and Libya—where Putin perhaps hopes to serve as a mediator between these "rogue states" and the Western world—as well as successful trips to England, Spain, Germany, Japan, and China—signal that Putin wants to reassert Russia's role as a major international player.

Putin's economic actions also have been bold. He selected a known face from the Yeltsin era, Mikhail Kasyanov, to head his first government. A former finance minister who was responsible for negotiating a major debt-restructuring agreement with the West, Kasyanov came to the job with promarket credentials. Other Putin appointees on the economic team—including the new first deputy prime minister and finance minister, Aleksei Kudrin; the new minister for economic development and trade, German Gref; and the president's personal adviser on economic affairs, Andrei Illarionov—are considered radical promarket reformers. This new team came to power with a comprehensive reform program that included major new proposals for tax reform, land privatization, deregulation, social policy restructuring, and new bankruptcy procedures. In the first three months of work with the Duma, Putin already achieved victory on one of the most important pillars of this reform agenda, a new tax code that decreases the income tax on individuals and corporations to a flat 13 percent.

Putin's multitude of initiatives regarding foreign policy and economic reform notwithstanding, his boldest changes have been in the political arena. During his short tenure in office, Putin has attempted to weaken every major source of independent political power in the Russian political system originally erected by Yeltsin. For the most part, he has succeeded; the balance of power within this regime has changed radically in his favor. In the Yeltsin era, the Duma, the Federation Council (the upper house of parliament), the media, the oligarchs, and the regional leaders all acted as checks on presidential power. Today, every one of these independent sources of power is weaker than it was a year ago. Yeltsin's military campaign against Chechnya in 1994–1996 exposed the weakness of the Russian military and threatened to undermine Russia's territorial integrity in the Caucasus; Putin managed to reverse, at least temporarily, this challenge to the Kremlin's power. Throughout this period, Putin has maintained a solid popular majority. In August of this year, 70 percent of the Russian population gave Putin a positive job-approval rating, a level of support not enjoyed by Yeltsin since the fall of 1991 (Yeltsin's approval rating in the last years of his presidency hovered in the low teens and single digits). Soviet and Russian leaders customarily devoted their initial time in office to consolidating political power; Putin must rank with Stalin and Gorbachev as one of the century's most successful and speediest consolidators of power.

How did Putin achieve so much so fast? What do these changes mean for the future of Russian democracy? Although it is still too early to assess the real consequences of these political changes or the intent of Putin's actions, the comprehensive nature of political change and the manner in which it has been pursued offer some clues to the future of Russian politics. In the long run, the commitment of the Russian people to become a European country integrated into the community of democratic and market-oriented states will compel Russia's leaders to adhere to some basic principles of democracy. The path to this long-run outcome, however, may include some authoritarian detours, including the road that Putin has hinted that he intends to follow.

MUSCLE BUILDING IN CHECHNYA

Putin has consistently promoted the necessity of reconstituting a stronger Russian state, a policy objective that he values above all others. Consequently, in response to an invasion by rebels from the Russian republic of Chechnya into the neighboring republic of Dagestan in the summer of 1999 and terrorist attacks in Moscow and elsewhere in Russia that killed hundreds of civilians last fall, Prime Minister Putin deployed massive military force against the Chechen fighters in Chechnya.[2] At the time, President Yeltsin was still the commander in chief, but Prime Minister Putin assumed primary responsibility for the new military campaign. Emboldened by some early battlefield successes, Yeltsin and Putin expanded the initial objectives of this second invasion to include complete military subjugation of the breakaway Chechen republic. Putin abandoned the old strategy of negotiation with Chechen leaders and indifference to developments within Chechen territory.

To the surprise of many, Putin's new strategy for dealing with Chechnya won popular and elite support and eventually propelled Putin to the presidency the following year. At the beginning [of] the campaign, no one believed that a quick little war with the Chechens would be the formula for delivering electoral success in the presidential campaign. On the contrary, when Yeltsin ordered the Russian military to respond to the Chechen incursion in August 1999, most electoral analysts in Russia thought that the counteroffensive would result in another unpopular military debacle similar to the first Chechen war. The circumstances of this new military campaign, however, were different.

First and foremost, Russian citizens understood the new war to be a defensive action taken against an invading military force. Chechen military commander Shamil Basayev stated explicitly that his armed forces had entered Dagestan to liberate it from Russian imperialism. This was a direct threat to Russian national security and the first time since 1941 that a "foreign" army had invaded Russia. The terrorist attacks on apartment buildings in Moscow and elsewhere shortly after the invasion left the nation feeling besieged. The Russian people demanded a response from their leaders, and Putin responded.

Second, the military action appeared to be a success. In the first Chechen war, the Russian forces seemed to be losing the war from the outset—both because they performed so miserably, and because the rationale for the war was not embraced by either the Russian army or the population as a whole. Independent media, led by the national television network NTV, reported on military setbacks and questioned Russia's war aims.

In the second Chechen war, the Russian army used different tactics, relying on air power much more than in the first war (a change in tactics that resulted in the complete demolition of the Chechen capital of Grozny). Media coverage of the second war also changed, with most reporting much more supportive of the Russian armed forces. The Russian state also exercised a greater degree of control over media coverage of this war, including imposing strict limits on media access to areas of the conflict; it has learned the value of conducting its own propaganda war on the airwaves to help sustain the military offensive on the ground.

Thus, the second Chechen war has enjoyed considerable popularity in Russia. During the 2000 presidential campaign, public support for the war remained steady at roughly 60 percent. This support, in turn, translated into positive approval ratings for Putin. Opinion polls conducted in the fall of 1999 demonstrated that people were grateful to Putin for accepting responsibility for the security of the Russian people. He looked like a leader who had taken charge during an uncertain insecure time and had delivered on his promise to provide stability and security. By the end of 1999, he enjoyed an astonishing 72 percent approval rating, which he maintained throughout the presidential campaign. Without question, Putin's execution of the war in Chechnya was a crucial ingredient (though not the only one) to his electoral success this March.

In the long term, the war may also help strengthen the power and prestige of the Russian state. The Russian Federation's dissolution, while always a remote possibility, now seems even less likely and potential defectors have become less vocal in their criticism of Russian central authorities. If the Russian military eventually prevails—Russian armed forces occupy most of the territory, but they are still engaged in a guerrilla war—the military's prestige also might be restored, a development that in turn might serve to strengthen the Russian state. Yet, the benefits to Putin personally and to the Russian state potentially have come at a high cost to Russian democracy. Russia has a right and Putin an obligation to defend Russia's territorial integrity. However, the means deployed have grossly violated the human rights of Chechnya's people, who after all are Russian citizens. Testimony gathered by Russian and international human rights groups points to systematic and indiscriminate use of force against both civilians and those who care for the wounded. Evidence suggests that Russia may even be in violation of the Geneva Convention and the Universal Declaration of Human Rights. This record reveals the low priority Putin has assigned to human rights.

No one in Russia or the West who fought to destroy Soviet communism can celebrate the election of a former KGB agent to the presidency.

SUBDUING THE DUMA

If demonstrating Moscow's resolve against Chechnya was Putin's first act of enhancing the Kremlin's power and breaking with past political practices of the Yeltsin era, Putin's second target was the lower house of parliament, the State Duma. In seeking to weaken this center of opposition to the Kremlin, Putin's tactics, although more democratic, still jeopardize long-term democratic consolidation.

Since the first postcommunist Duma election in December 1993, political groups that opposed Yeltsin and the Kremlin have dominated this legislative body. The 1995 parliamentary election especially, which gave the Communist Party of the Russian Federation control of the legislature, positioned the Duma to act as a check on executive power. Yet constitutionally, the Duma is a weak institution, with only limited authority to block presidential activity. Toward the end of the last decade, however, the Communist-dominated Duma exercised these powers to their fullest extent. The Communists achieved their greatest victory in the wake of the August 1998 financial crisis, forcing President Yeltsin to accept their candidate, Yevgeny Primakov, for prime minister.

In the fall of 1999, Putin and his allies wanted to change the dynamics of the relationship between the president and the Duma by making the parliament more loyal to the Kremlin. They pursued this objective through the electoral process. In the runup to the December 1999 parliamentary elections, the Kremlin created a new party, Unity, that was completely dependent on the Kremlin for financial resources, access to television exposure, organizational muscle, and campaign expertise. In an amazing reinvention, Unity became the new "party of power" by disassociating and even criticizing the old party of power. Unity accomplished this transformation by selecting a new, young, popular, and apolitical party leader, Emergencies Minister Sergei Shoigu, who then firmly identified himself and his party with Putin and Putin's one distinctive policy, the war in Chechnya.

This strategy helped attract to Unity the nonideological and nonpartisan voter, who in earlier elections had not identified firmly with a specific political party. A hard-hitting negative television assault conducted by the two national television stations controlled by the Kremlin (ORT and RTR) against the Fatherland–All Russia coalition—Unity's chief competitor for the nonideological voter—further assisted Unity's electoral prospects. Unity's electoral performance was impressive; a party

Putin may not openly aspire to become a dictator, yet he has displayed no passion for defending democracy.

that did not exist just weeks before the election won an amazing 23 percent of the popular vote on the party list vote, capturing just one percentage point less than the Communist Party of the Russian Federation.

The Kremlin's Unity bloc soundly defeated Fatherland–All Russia, the electoral bloc headed by former Prime Minister Yevgeny Primakov—who had been dismissed by Yeltsin in May 1999—and Moscow Mayor Yuri Luzhkov. Instead, Fatherland–All Russia won only 12 percent of the popular vote, which led Primakov to withdraw from the presidential race.

In addition to Unity's rise and Fatherland's demise, Putin benefited from the surprising performance of the liberal bloc, the Union of Right Forces (SPS). Late in the campaign, Putin endorsed this coalition of small, liberal, right-wing parties headed by former Prime Minister Sergei Kiriyenko. Although most electoral experts predicted that SPS would fail to cross the 5 percent threshold necessary to obtain seats through the party list vote, the coalition won almost 9 percent of the popular vote and soundly defeated the other main liberal party and chief Kremlin critic on the ballot, Yabloko. Since the election, the SPS faction in the Duma has given only lukewarm support for several of Putin's political initiatives, but has nonetheless endorsed unequivocally his legislative initiatives concerning economic policy.

When the distribution of seats from single-mandated races are added into the equation (these constitute half the seats in the 450-member parliament), the balance of power within the Duma has moved in a decisively pro-Putin direction. The Communist Party still controls a solid minority of seats, but cannot construct opposition majorities to Kremlin initiatives. Putin has further weakened the Communist opposition by courting individual leaders in an attempt to divide the party. The current speaker of the Duma, Communist Party member Gennady Seleznyov, is more loyal to Putin than to his party's leader, Gennady Zyuganov (when Seleznyov ran for governor for Moscow Oblast in December 1999, Putin endorsed his candidacy in the second round when he faced an opponent from Fatherland–All Russia. Seleznyov, however, lost this election). Tension between Seleznyov and Zyuganov grew so considerable in the spring and summer of this year that Seleznyov took the initial steps—with the Kremlin's backing—of forming a new left-of-center organization called Rossiya.

The combination of a loyal Unity, a divided and weakened Communist Party, a sometimes supportive SPS, and strong backing from independents and other smaller factions has produced a parliament supportive of Putin on major issues. This parliament approved Mikhail Kasyanov, Putin's candidate for prime minister, without a fight, has ratified all his major economic reform bills, and has supported in overwhelming majorities his reform initiatives regarding relations between Moscow and the regions. Yet Putin and his advisers did not stop there. This fall, Putin plans to announce a major set of reforms for the reorganization of the Duma. A central component of this reform package is a proposal to amend the Duma electoral law.

Putin's objective of rendering the Duma more supportive of his presidency is one any executive in any democracy would desire. That this redistribution of power took place through the ballot box rather than through armed conflict also must be commended. At the same time, the means deployed to achieve this end could be damaging to the democratic consolidation over the long run. The Kremlin helped produce the new balance of power within the Duma by deploying the massive resources of the Russian federal state to support its parties and undermine its enemies. Unity, moreover, was more of a virtual party than an organization with established policy positions, regional organizations, or a well-defined electorate. The state, not the people, created this electoral bloc: Unity boasted no history, no platform, and no membership, yet captured almost a quarter of the popular vote. The sudden success of an organization like Unity undermines the formation of a real multiparty system in Russia. Putin's recent proposals for amending the Duma electoral law to decrease the number of seats allocated according to proportional representation and increase the minimal threshold needed to win seats on the party list will further weaken independent political parties. Instead of a multiparty system, Russia could be gravitating toward a one-and-a-half party system: one loyal to the Kremlin that always wins, and the other—a remade Communist Party—in slight opposition to the Kremlin that always loses.

WEAKENING THE FEDERATION COUNCIL

Putin's ability to assemble supermajorities in the Duma—that is, majorities capable of overriding vetoes of Federation Council bills—gave him the ability to alter the very organization of the national system of government. And reorganize he did. To the surprise of everyone, Putin made reform of the Federation Council one of his top political goals in his first months in office. The Russian constitution states that two deputies from each region of the Russian Federation shall be members of the Federation Council: one from the representatives and one from the executive bodies of state authority. The constitution does not specify how these representatives should be selected.

In the first term of the Federation Council (1993–1995), council members were directly elected. After the 1993 elections, however, regional leaders succeeded in changing the law governing the formation of the Federal Council. Rather than direct elections to the Federation Council, regional executives (presidents in republics and governors in the administrative units called oblasts and krais) and heads of regional legislative parliaments pushed for direct elections for their regional offices, followed by automatic appointment to this national body. This gave governors increased local legitimacy and greater autonomy from Yeltsin and Moscow since elected governors would be harder to dismiss than appointed ones. It also gave governors a direct voice in the national legislative affairs, blurring the divisions both between executive and legislative power and between the national and subnational units of the federal system. Under this configuration, the Federation Council rarely opposed Yeltsin directly but did emerge as a powerful lobby for regional interests.

Soon after coming to office, Putin proposed a third formula on Federation Council appointments. Instead of direct elections or personal representation of regions by governors and legislative heads, Putin's plan called for the appointment of two representatives from each region to the Council.[3] Federation Council members resisted this reform, knowing that they would lose their Moscow apartments and offices, their immunity as members of the national parliament, and their influence in the corridors of power of the Russian government. After a fierce battle in which the Duma threatened to override a Federation Council veto and Kremlin officials allegedly threatened governors with criminal investigations if they did not support Putin's plan, the Federation Council ratified the new formulation at the end of July 2000.

This change, scheduled to go into effect in 2002, weakens another institutional check on the president's power. Because the new members of the council will not be elected, they will not have the same political authority or public standing as current council members. The new formula also will make it more difficult for regional leaders to coordinate their actions with the federal government. Moreover, some have speculated that this new formation of the council is an interim step toward Putin's ultimate goal of abolishing the upper house altogether (as a concession to Russia's most powerful regional leaders, Putin has vowed to create a so-called State Council, on which leading figures from all of Russia's political institutions would serve).

It is too early to tell how this reform will influence democratic consolidation in Russia. Respected proponents of liberal democracy in Russia, including former Duma deputy and constitutional expert Viktor Sheinis, have long argued that the Federation Council must be reorganized; governors' service in the national legislature violates both the principle of separation of power between executives and legislators, and separation between federal and regional power. In addition, the old formulation is highly inefficient—regional leaders have major local responsibilities and therefore can devote only small amounts of time for travel to Moscow to attend to legislative matters. The new members of the Federation Council will be permanent legislators, who could organize themselves to be a more professional and engaged body. Still, this new formulation gives considerable powers—including some powers such as the ratification of several federal appointments on which only the Federation Council votes—to nonelected officials. Over time, this lack of legitimacy could undermine the council's ability to make independent decisions.

EXPANDING MOSCOW'S REACH

Putin's assault against regional executives has not been confined to reconfiguring the Federation Council; he also has introduced other reforms and laws designed to rein in the power of the regional barons in their own territories. In one of his first acts as president, Putin created seven new supraregional districts, each to be administered by a supragovernor personally appointed by the president. Though only in its early phases of development, the creation of new federal representatives outside Moscow will establish a more authoritative federal presence throughout Russia, which in turn may assist in the enforcement of federal laws in all regions. These new supraregional authorities also will have direct authority over all federal employees working in the regions, including tax inspectors, treasury employees, and regional divisions of prosecutor general's office, the FSB, and the Ministry of the Interior. During the Yeltsin years, these federal employees became increasingly dependent on local governors. Putin hopes to recapture their allegiance to the federal government through the creation of these new plenipotentiaries. If they work in unison, these federal branches will constitute a powerful set of levers for enforcing Moscow's will on regional government officials. Strikingly, five of seven new supraregional representatives have professional experience in the FSB, the military, or the police; only two are civilians.

Even before these new territorial authorities opened for business, federal officials had already initiated criminal investigations against allegedly corrupt officials working within regional executive branches. Another new reform, proposed by Putin and passed into law in July 2000, now gives the president the power to remove from office elected governors accused of wrongdoing by the prosecutor general's office. Formally, the president can only remove these governors temporarily until criminal charges have been resolved. Given that criminal proceedings could drag out indefinitely (especially if the president recommended that they be dragged out indefinitely), this new law informally gives the president the ability to remove elected officials from office at will. He also can dismiss regional legislatures if they pass legislation that violates federal laws or the constitution. Another law passed in July gives the president the power to remove mayors in cities of 50,000 or more inhabitants.

On paper, these reforms—which also include the transfer of a greater percentage of regional tax revenues to Moscow—constitute a radical redistribution of power in favor of the Kremlin. Some previously dissident regions have already responded to the new regime: Bashkortostan, a republic that had stopped paying taxes to the federal government, began to make transfers to Moscow anew—which is exactly the kind of response Putin wants. Whether the package of changes will produce a more rational and predictable relationship between the center and the regions remains to be seen. While most agree that the center has been too weak over the last several years, the resurrection of a unitary centralized state has the potential to reverse the positive elements of decentralization and to prevent further development of Russia's young federalism.

THREATS TO THE PRESS AND CIVIL SOCIETY

Taking on both houses of parliament as well as Russia's powerful regional barons simultaneously represented an amazingly ambitious agenda for President Putin's first three months in office. Yet throughout the spring he also moved aggressively against another source of independent power: the free press. In several respects, an independent, critical, and pluralistic press was one of the greatest democratic achievements of the Yeltsin years. In the early years of the last decade, several independent newspapers, such as *Nezavisimaya Gazeta, Kommersant,* and *Segodnya,* sprouted, putting pressure on traditional print publications to become more critical as well. While the government still has a controlling stake in two of the largest national television channels, ORT and RTR (the state holds a majority share in ORT and still owns 100 percent of RTR), the first private national television network, NTV, formed and thrived under Yeltsin. Started by Vladimir Gusinsky, NTV provided a truly independent source of information that reached beyond Moscow and was not afraid to criticize Yeltsin and his government.

But the independent media has become less independent. Russia's oligarchs have captured control of most major media sources, while the state continues to be the largest owner of all. Competition among Russian national television networks effectively ended during the 1996 presidential election when NTV joined forces with ORT and RTR to back Yeltsin. But when NTV attempted to criticize the state again during the second Chechen war and the 1999 parliamentary elections, the network came under vigorous attack from the Kremlin. The harassment continued this year, when NTV offices were raided and Gusinsky was arrested allegedly for a corrupt privatization deal he orchestrated several years ago. Gusinsky was later released and even allowed to leave the country, but many speculate the price he paid for his freedom may be the surrender of his media empire, Media-Most (which also includes a daily newspaper, a national radio station, and a weekly magazine), to the gas company Gazprom. A major stockholder in NTV already, Gazprom is still closely tied to the state; the federal government remains the majority owner. The Kremlin also has launched a major campaign to wrestle control of ORT away from Boris Berezovsky, a minority shareholder in the television station who has nonetheless dominated its programming for years.

The real question is to what purpose Putin will deploy his newly consolidated political power.

Individual journalists, academic researchers, and civic leaders critical of the state also have felt the Putin regime's wrath. Commentators and columnists critical of Putin report that many newspapers are unwilling now to carry their articles. Self-censorship has returned to Russia. At a minimum, many in Russia argue that it is harder to be a social or political activist today than at any time in the post-Soviet period. Many in the Russian NGO community believe that Putin is hostile to criticism and competition. The Russian government has gone on record claiming that the protection of human rights is the business of the state and not independent groups. Accordingly, the state has refused to register many human rights groups, leaving them legally vulnerable to being shut down. Environmental NGOs also have come under increased harrassment from the FSB following an interview in a Russian newspaper with Putin in July 1999 in which he claimed, but provided no evidence, that these groups were in the employ of foreign intelligence agencies.

If Putin's plans with respect to the parliament and center-regional relations might produce eventually some redeeming reforms— perhaps even democratic reforms—these threats to the press and civil society more generally cannot be considered in any way positive for democratic consolidation in Russia. Putin remarked in his state of the union address on July 8, 2000 that "free speech has been and will remain an inviolable value of Russian democracy. This is a position of principle for us." The actions of his government have not, however, been in keeping with this "position of principle."

SCARING THE OLIGARCHS

With relatively cost-free victories already recorded against the parliament, the regional barons, and the press, Putin began to assault another source of independent power—the oligarchs—in the summer of 2000. Gusinsky's arrest was seen as a direct attack against independent media. When Putin's government opened charges and threatened criminal investigations against several other tycoons, the aims were more ambiguous. Putin's government has threatened to arrest Interros holding company head (the owner of the giant Norilsk Nickel plant) Vladimir Potanin, and has announced the opening of criminal investigations against LUKoil, Russia's largest oil company, and AvtoVAS, Russia's largest car producer, while others were put on notice that they would be investigated next. Most unexpectedly, these attacks prompted business tycoon Boris Berezovsky to break ranks with Putin—the same Berezovsky who was one of the original forces behind Putin's rise to power. Putin eventually convened a summit between the Kremlin and the oligarchs in late July as a gesture to diffuse the confrontation. Still, few believe that the meeting signaled a permanent reconciliation or an end to the attacks on the oligarchs.

In principle, these state actions against some of Russia's richest businessmen might be interpreted as progress. Oligarchic capitalism in Russia needs to end; the rule of law needs to begin. But the discriminate process regarding who is and is not prosecuted has undermined the integrity of these acts. Gusinsky's media outlets have criticized Putin and supported his opponents. Gusinsky was arrested. Roman Abramovich—one of Russia's most notorious oligarchs, not likely more law abiding than Russia's other business leaders—has supported Putin, and has avoided arrest or investigation. In fact, many of the investigations launched have been against Abramovich rivals, prompting some to conclude that the antioligarch campaign is designed to redistribute privilege and wealth again, and not to establish the rule of law equally applicable to all.[4]

THE FUTURE OF RUSSIAN DEMOCRACY

Putin has accomplished more in three months as president than most world leaders could hope to achieve during their entire tenure in office. In making bold changes in the organization of the Russian political system, Putin has made real progress toward consolidating his own political power in Russia. In the process, he also may have taken steps toward strengthening executive power and state power more generally. During the Yeltsin years, it became fashionable in the West to cite Russia's weak state as the source of Russia's ills. Putin has demonstrated after only a few months in office that the Russian federal state still has tremendous power—perhaps too much power—if the man in control of that state is vigorous, ambitious, and popular.

At the same time, Putin's political reforms have illuminated how weak societal checks on state power remain in Russia. Russia today has no effective political opposition. Political parties are weak, economic elites appear seemingly unwilling to challenge the power of the president, and regional leaders are on the defensive. Yet the people still firmly support Putin and his reforms. Alternative sources of power may reorganize, especially if an economic crisis or an expansion of the war in the Caucasus erodes Putin's popularity, but these events are unlikely in the near future.

The real question is to what purpose Putin will deploy his newly consolidated political power. Will he build a strong democratic state that will create the necessary conditions for economic growth? Or does Putin hope to use a strong authoritarian state to implement market reforms but at the expense of democracy? Or will he use his power to simply resurrect a police state in Russia whose main aim will be keep Putin in office?

A year after his rise to power, compelling evidence can be found to support all these claims about Putin's strategy. While many already have proclaimed Putin to be a dictator, the evidence to support this remains circumstantial. Yet Putin also has proved indifferent to democracy. No one in Russia or the West who fought to destroy Soviet communism can celebrate the election of a former KGB agent to the presidency. Putin has matched his reputation as a strong man with some highly antidemocratic deeds. No excuse can be made for the harassment of the press or civic leaders. Putin may not openly aspire to become a dictator, yet he has displayed no passion for defending democracy. Instead, Putin has demonstrated that he is willing to use the power of the state and ignore the democratic rights of society in the pursuit of "more important" objectives, such as state building and economic reform.

To date, the pursuit of these allegedly more important objectives has only slightly collided with Russia's fragile democratic institutions. While his government has harassed journalists and weakened important democratic institutions, Putin has not suspended the constitution, postponed elections, or implemented emergency rule. And he was, it should be remembered, elected by the Russian people in a relatively free and fair election. He will continue to allow an independent press, elections, and individual liberties as long as they do not conflict with his agenda of securing Russia's borders, strengthening the Russian state, and promoting market reform.

Tragically, 10 years after the Soviet Union's collapse, the whims of one man at the top still can profoundly influence the fate of the whole Russian regime. Russia's protracted transition from Communist rule is not over; and the endpoint of this transformation remains uncertain.

NOTES

1. Russia has a two-ballot system for the office of the president. If no candidate wins a majority in the first round, then the top two vote winners compete in a second round. Putin avoided a second round by capturing 52.9 percent of the popular vote in the first round. By contrast, Yeltsin won only 35.3 percent in the first round of the 1996 presidential election and therefore needed a second-round win for a majority.
2. Who was responsible for these bombings still remains unclear. Likewise, the executors of another terrorist attack that killed several people and wounded many others in downtown Moscow this August have not been determined.
3. The formula for selecting these representatives is complex. One Federation Council representative is selected by the regional speaker of the regional assembly and confirmed by the assembly as a whole. The regional executive selects the second Federation Council representative. The regional assembly can veto the governor's nominee with a two-thirds majority. Representatives serve at the pleasure of those who select them.
4. Few believed that Putin would alter fundamentally the political system erected by Yeltsin over the last decade, a system dominated by financial oligarchs, regional barons, and Kremlin insiders close to the president often called the "Family." Yeltsin, in fact, selected Putin because he believed him to be a defender of the status quo. In pardoning Yeltsin in his first move as acting president, Putin cast himself as a loyal servant who would not rock the boat. Not surprisingly, most of the oligarchs, regional barons, and Family members supported Putin enthusiastically during the spring presidential campaign.

MICHAEL MCFAUL *is a senior associate at the Carnegie Endowment for International Peace and an assistant professor of political science and Hoover fellow at Stanford University. His latest book,* Russia's Troubled Transition from Communism to Democracy, *will be published in the summer of 2001.*

Chaos in the Caucasus

No, the fighting in the Caucasus is not evidence of a "clash of civilisations" between the Islamic world and other geopolitical blocks

AT LEAST until recently, the main enemy of Islamic terrorism seemed to be the United States. However diverse and quarrelsome its practitioners, they knew what they hated most: the global policeman whom they accused of propping up Israel, starving the Iraqis and undermining the Muslim way of life with an insidiously attractive culture.

Anti-Americanism, after all, has been a common thread in a series of spectacular acts of violence over the past decade. They include the bombing of the World Trade Centre in New York in February 1993; the explosion that killed 19 American soldiers at a base in Saudi Arabia in June 1996; and the deadly blasts at the American embassies in Kenya and Tanzania in August 1998.

In many of the more recent attacks it has suffered, the United States has discerned the hand of Osama bin Laden, the Saudi-born co-ordinator of an international network of militant Muslims. In February last year, he and his sympathisers in Egypt, Pakistan and Bangladesh issued a statement declaring that "to kill the Americans and their allies—civilian and military—is an individual duty for every Muslim who can do it." Such blood-curdling talk was inevitably seized on by believers in the "clash of civilisations" described by Samuel Huntington, a Harvard professor who said in 1993 that cultural or religious fault-lines were the most likely source of conflict in the post–cold-war world.

Now, it might appear, Russia's turn has come to do battle on a new front in this many-sided conflict. The Russian government has blamed terrorists from the country's Muslim south for a series of bomb blasts in Moscow and other cities which have claimed over 300 lives. And it has launched a broadening land and air attack against the mainly Muslim republic of Chechnya, where the terrorists are alleged to originate.

In their more strident moments, officials and newspaper columnists in Moscow say that Russia is in the forefront of a fight between "civilisation and barbarism" and is therefore entitled to western understanding. "We face a common enemy, international terrorism," Russia's prime minister, Vladimir Putin, told President Bill Clinton last month. As evidence that anti-Russian and anti-American guerrillas have at least one common source, officials in Moscow have pointed to the alleged involvement of Mr bin Laden and his fighters, both in the Caucasus and in the urban bombing campaign.

In most of their comments, President Boris Yeltsin and his lieutenants have been careful to distinguish between their current adversaries and Muslims in general. "Terrorists are an enemy with no faith or nationality," Mr Yeltsin has said. Russian diplomats are stressing the support they have received from many Muslim governments—particularly Iran's, which is seen in Moscow as an important strategic partner and counterweight to western influence in the Caspian.

Whereas western countries have chided Russia (mildly) for its military operation against Chechnya, Iran has been much more supportive. Kamal Kharrazi, Iran's foreign minister, has promised "effective collaboration" with the Kremlin against what he has described as terrorists bent on destabilising Russia. Russia, for its part, has thanked Iran for using its chairmanship of the Organisation of the Islamic Conference to present the Russian case.

Perhaps because of Russia's friendship with certain parts of the Muslim world, Mr Putin has firmly rejected the view that the "bandits" Russia is now fighting could properly be described as Islamic. "They are international terrorists, most of them mercenaries, who cover themselves in religious slogans," he insists.

But ordinary Muslims in the Moscow street—whether they are of Caucasian origin, or from the Tatar or Bashkir nations based in central Russia—fear a general backlash. "Politicians and the mass media are equating us, the Muslim faithful, with armed groups," complains Ravil Gainutdin, Russia's senior mufti. Patriarch Alexy II, the head of the Russian Orthodox church, has been urging his flock not to blame their 18m Muslim compatriots for the recent violence. "Russian Christians and Muslims traditionally live in peace," he has reminded them. His senior bishops—probably with a nod of encouragement from Russian officialdom—are engaged in a set-piece theological dialogue with Iran's spiritual leaders.

Clash, or conspiracy?

But even if Russia's southern war is not yet a "clash of civilisations", might it soon become one? And if so, would that bring Russia closer to the West, or push it farther away?

Islam is certainly one element in the crisis looming on Russia's southern rim, but it is by no means the only one. The latest flare-up began in August in the wild border country between Chechnya—which has been virtually independent since Russian troops were forced out, after two years of brutal war, in 1996—and Dagestan, a ramshackle, multiethnic republic where a pro-Russian government has been steadily losing control.

Two factors came together to set the scene for conflict. One was the long-running feud between Aslan Maskhadov, Chechnya's elected president, and Shamil Basaev, a younger and more militant figure with a history of

Action replay in Chechnya?

MOSCOW

SO FAR, the Russians have had the easiest part of their new war against Chechnya. Since the ground offensive started on October 1st, the Kremlin's forces, some 30,000 strong, have moved from the neighbouring republics of Dagestan and Ingushetia, and from Russia's Stavropol region, to seize the most accessible and least-defended part of Chechnya, its northern third. The Russians have also shown their ability to bomb civilian and economic targets (such as oil refineries) in the capital Grozny at will. These achievements are not surprising, given Russia's huge superiority in men, armour and aircraft.

The big question is what happens next. Russia's first claim to be establishing just a buffer zone, seems not to be the full story. By mid-week, Russian forces had taken up positions along the Terek river, and some were within artillery range of Grozny. But a Russian attempt to stop the war by declaring victory now would not work. It would give the Chechens a chance to regroup and harry the occupying soldiers. That in effect would repeat the history of the 1994–96 war, when Russian soldiers bloodily conquered Chechnya, only to see guerrillas stealthily retake the country once victory had been declared.

Pushing the offensive further—which Russian officials do not exclude—looks unattractive too. The Chechens are already celebrating the shooting down of at least two Russian aircraft, and claim to have destroyed half a dozen armoured vehicles and captured several Russian soldiers. Russia says only two of its men have been killed, and 22 wounded. Even if true—and the Chechens claim to have killed dozens of Russians—that total would rise sharply should the fighting become hand-to-hand in Chechnya's towns, let alone mountain warfare. In that sort of conflict, the gritty Chechens excel. The riskiest part of Russia's immediate plan will be to establish control over Chechnya's border with Georgia. This has yet to begin.

Both sides seem to think time is on their side. Russia is backing up its military offensive with economic warfare—for example, by cutting back gas and electricity supplies. It has also indicated that it will resettle refugees in the Russian-controlled sector of Chechnya, whether or not they came from there originally. This zone will presumably be well supplied with energy and utilities, to make the point that life under Russia is better.

On the Chechen side, internal squabbles have been set aside. Shamil Basaev, the best-known Chechen warlord, has sarcastically said he is "very grateful" to Russia for creating a new sense of unity among his people. His erstwhile rival, President Aslan Maskhadov, has called on Chechnya's religious leaders to rally the nation to holy war, "to defend the [country's] sovereignty and integrity in the name of Allah the benevolent and merciful." Martial law has been declared in Grozny, although it is not clear who will enforce it.

Over the next few months, it is likely that the combination of winter and Russia's endemic military disorganisation will hurt the invading forces more than the defenders, although the greatest misery is now borne by the 120,000 refugees.

So far there is no sign of a political compromise between Russia and Chechnya's leadership. Russia has dusted down the collaborationist Chechen parliament which it used in the previous war, and partly withdrawn its grudging recognition of the Chechen government and president. The Russian side has so far provided no evidence of the terrorist training camps that the war is meant to destroy.

The most worrying thought is that the war may be a prelude to a wider conflict. Russia has denied Azerbaijani claims that its air force bombed a village in Azerbaijan on October 1st, although it has admitted bombing villages in Georgia last month, and has increased the number of soldiers based there. Russia has warned Azerbaijan not to allow aid to Chechnya to cross its territory. In Shia Muslim (but not very devout) Azerbaijan, and in Orthodox Christian Georgia, people are united in hoping against hope that their hard-won modicum of stability, and independence from Russia, are not about to be forfeited.

involvement in spectacular acts of violence. The other factor was the emergence, in the morass of lawlessness and poverty that has engulfed both republics, of a new and more zealous form of Islam, mainly imported from Saudi Arabia.

A few weeks ago, Mr Basaev and his militant Dagestani friends (who, at least so far, have been a small, unpopular minority among their compatriots) proclaimed a sort of mini-state inside Dagestan. They spoke of creating a Russia-free zone stretching at least from Chechnya to the Caspian Sea. In its biggest show of force for three years, the Russian high command blasted the rebels with fighter-bombers and artillery. By early September, it claimed to have forced them to retreat from Dagestan into Chechnya.

The story took an entirely new turn with a series of bomb attacks in Russian cities in September. The worst, on September 13th, claimed 119 lives. The authorities were quick to blame the explosions on Chechen terrorists, though they did not provide evidence, and Chechen leaders denied involvement.

Many people in Russia did not need any evidence; the government's allegations simply confirmed the anti-Chechen, and generally anti-Caucasian, prejudice they already harboured. Other Russians take a more cynical view. They believe the bomb attacks are somehow related to the power struggle raging in Moscow as the "courtiers" of President Yeltsin try to cling to their power and privilege in the face of looming electoral defeat.

Even those who believe that Chechens, and only Chechens, are responsible for the bombs have had their faith tested at times. In the town of Ryazan, the security services were caught virtually red-handed after placing a quantity of explosives in an apartment building. They claimed it was part of an exercise to "test the readiness" of the population.

Such incidents are grist to the mill of Moscow's conspiracy theorists. Some believe that the bombs were indeed the work of Chechen extremists, but insist that the fighting in the south is mainly the result of Russian provocation; some say it is the other way round. Whatever the truth, the crisis has certainly played into the hands of the most hardline elements in Russia's leadership. But there are also signs that people from outside Russia have been stirring the pot.

Mark Galeotti, a British lecturer on Russia's armed forces, says there is evidence that Mr bin Laden, while not the instigator of the urban bombing campaign, has offered financial help to its perpetrators. And fighters under the influence of Mr bin Laden have certainly been active in Chechnya and Dagestan—though their presence is probably not the main reason why war is raging now.

With or without some mischief-making by dark forces in Moscow, Russia would have a problem in the northern Caucasus. Hostility between Russians and Chechens goes back to the north Caucasian wars of the 19th century, when the tsar's forces took more than 50 years to bring the Chechens under control. As well as strong family loyalties, part of the glue that held the Chechens and other north Caucasian people together was Sufism, the mystical strand of Islam.

Although Sufism is often associated with contemplation, among the proud mountain clans of Chechnya and Dagestan it acquired a strongly anti-Russian flavour. The Sufi sheikhs, or holy men, preached that a true Muslim could not tolerate the rule of foreign infidels. There were two acceptable forms of *jihad*, or holy war. A Muslim could serve Allah as a fighter or as a scholar. The Chechens became famous for their warrior prowess, the Dagestanis for their Koranic learning.

The Bolshevik revolution of 1917 promised to liberate all the subject peoples of the tsarist empire. As civil war loomed, Lenin and Stalin made a cynical bid for Muslim support by promising the creation of semi-independent Islamic states in Russia and Central Asia, saying: "All you whose mosques and houses of prayer have been destroyed, whose beliefs and customs have been flouted by the tsars and the oppressors of Russia—from now on your beliefs and customs, your national and cultural institutions are free and inviolable."

The reality of Soviet rule was, of course, very different. Periods of repression alternated with periods of relative toleration, but repression was the norm. In 1944, the Chechens (along with seven other ethnic groups) were deported en masse to Kazakhstan as part of Stalin's policy of punishing "untrustworthy" ethnic groups. But Chechen culture, in particular, proved remarkably hard to destroy.

By the 1980s, there were estimated to be 50m Soviet citizens of Muslim ancestry. For most of them, Soviet rule had had a powerful secularising effect. Out of cultural habit, many still circumcised their baby boys and buried their dead according to Muslim custom. But the closure of all but a handful of mosques, and the virtual end of religious education, meant that knowledge of Islam had nearly evaporated.

Among the few places in the Soviet Union where Islam remained fairly strong was the northern Caucasus. The Sufi tradition was well able to survive in semi-clandestine conditions. Even without mosques, the Chechens were able to go on venerating the memory of their local sheikhs and performing traditional dances and chants. Anna Zelkina, a Russian expert on Islam, says the KGB knew a lot about the Sufi brotherhoods, but found Sufism too deeply rooted to be eradicated.

Enter the Wahhabis

Since the collapse of the Soviet Union in 1991, the Sufi tradition has faced a challenge of a very different type. Emissaries from the Arab world, especially Saudi Arabia, have flooded into the Caucasus and Central Asia, seeing an opportunity in the spiritual and economic wasteland left by Marxist ideology.

Financed by Saudi petrodollars, these preachers have begun propagating a new form of Islam, which has become known (through a slight over-simplification) as Wahhabism: in other words, the austere form of Islam dominant in Saudi Arabia. The new version of Islam strives to be as close as possible to the faith's 1,400-year-old roots. It opposes the secularism of Russian life. Its universalising message aims to transcend ethnic and linguistic barriers, and it has no place for the local cults of Sufism.

Many Chechens and Dagestanis find the new form of Islam alien and uncomfortable, and some actively oppose it. It has caused division, and even violence, within families. But by building mosques and establishing scholarships, the Wahhabis have won a following, especially among the young—often impatient with what they see as a corrupt official religious establishment left over from Soviet times. Moreover, in the confusion of post–Soviet Russia, the new creed offers disillusioned and unemployed young men money and weapons and a sense of purpose which they cannot find anywhere else.

"For the disenchanted," writes Nabi Abdullaev, a journalist based in Makhachkala, the Dagestani capital, "Wahhabism has become a spiritual refuge." At first, the Wahhabis acted peacefully. They took over a few villages in Dagestan and established new communities where their strict interpretation of Islam was followed. But they gradually began to arm themselves and set up semi-autonomous enclaves where they enforced the *sharia* (Islamic law).

They claimed they needed weapons for self-defence because of harassment by the police and the local authorities. But local officials became convinced they were dangerous foreign-backed fanatics. In 1997, the Dagestani authorities outlawed "Wahhabism" and a number of the movement's leaders were arrested. Some escaped, with or without their followers, into neighbouring Chechnya. With its long tradition of warrior prowess, Chechnya became the military base of the "new Islam", and Mr Basaev its military leader.

A daredevil hijacker and hostage-taker, Mr Basaev took part in the Russian-backed war against Georgia in 1992–93, and then fought ruthlessly against Russia in the Chechen war of 1994–96. Trained in the Soviet army, he now says his life's mission is to wage holy war against Russia and avenge its crimes against his people. He is not himself a Wahhabi, but he seems to have decided that the new Muslims would make useful recruits for his *jihad*, even though he does not share their extreme puritanism.

Mr Basaev is both a Muslim and a Chechen patriot; the two qualities are inseparable. But despite his bushy beard and talk of holy wars, he does not quite correspond to the image of a single-minded fundamentalist. His heroes, after all, include Garibaldi and Abraham Lincoln. There is, however, another member of the Basaev camp who comes closer to fitting the bill: a young Arab fighter known as Khattab, whose trademark is a mane of long black hair.

Educated in Saudi Arabia, Khattab fought the Russians in Afghanistan before settling in Chechnya. In other words, he is one of the "Afghanis"—the 15,000 or so volunteers from all over the Middle East (particularly Saudi Arabia, Yemen, Egypt and Algeria) who did battle, with strong American support, against the Soviet occupiers of Afghanistan. Since the war ended, these fighters have returned to their homelands, or moved to other countries, in search of new Islamist causes to fight.

It is the existence of the Afghanis (of whom the most notorious is Mr bin Laden himself) which helps to explain why Russia regards its own Islamic adversaries as Frankensteinian monsters created by western governments and their friends in Saudi Arabia and Pakistan. The Afghani connection also helps to explain why Russia and Iran see eye-to-eye on the question of Islamist violence. As well as loathing the West and all its works, some of the Afghanis—as zealous practitioners of Sunni Islam—are sworn enemies of the Shia Muslim faith, of which Iran is the main bastion.

Ramzi Youzef, the Afghani (and protégé of Mr bin Laden) who was convicted of bombing the World Trade Centre, has also been linked with the June 1994 bombing of a Shia holy place in Iran. From Iran's point of view, both the Afghanis and the Taliban movement that now controls most of Afghanistan are manifestations of the Sunni fundamentalism that has been called into existence by the United States and its friends.

Iran has always been resentful of America's connections with Saudi Arabia and Pakistan, even though its own relations with those two countries have been improving. Russia sympathises, to put it mildly, with that resentment. America, for its part, is highly suspicious of Russia's friendship with Iran.

The many faces of Islam

If there is a geopolitical stand-off involving Russia, America and the Islamic world, it is not a simple triangle. If anything, Russia and America have each identified different bits of the Islamic world as friends, and each is suspicious of the other's partnerships.

Although Russian diplomacy has been quite adept at manipulating the geopolitical divisions within the Muslim world, there is a real possibility that its own clumsiness and brutality could create a Muslim enemy within its borders, as well as alienating Muslims farther afield. Already, the Kremlin's heavy-handedness has galvanised the Chechens to mobilise for a new war against Russia. The neighbouring Ingush people, related to the Chechens but hitherto willing to accept Russian authority, may now be drawn into the conflict—along with at least four or five other north Caucasian peoples who have until now been content to let Russia run their affairs.

If Russia found itself at war with half a dozen Muslim peoples in the Caucasus, the effects would certainly be felt in places farther north, such as Tatarstan. Tatarstan's leader, Mintimer Shaimiev, has trodden a careful line between co-operation with the Kremlin and indulging the anti-Slavic feelings of local Tatar nationalists and Muslims. In recent days, he has insisted that no conscripts from his republic will fight Russia's war in the Caucasus.

But if some sort of common Muslim front ever emerges in Russia, resentment of Moscow will be the only factor that holds it together. In the Caucasus and elsewhere, Muslims are fragmented; there is not even a united or coherent Wahhabi movement.

Nor is there any natural unity between Chechnya and Dagestan. Chechnya (a bit smaller than Wales) is ethnically homogeneous. Dagestan (the size of Scotland) is a mosaic of 34 distinct ethnic groups. The two also differ over their relations with Russia. The Chechens still feel the scars of their last war with the Russians, and so the secessionist impulse is much stronger than in Dagestan, which has little sense of a common national identity and is economically heavily dependent on Russia.

Nor is it inevitable that Islamic militancy in the northern Caucasus and in other parts of the Muslim world will reinforce one another. Rather than being proof that political Islam is spreading, the fighting in the Caucasus is a reminder that Islam exists in many different forms. In the heartland of the Muslim world, the Middle East, the wave of Islamic militancy appears to be receding. In the early 1980s, the years immediately after the Iranian revolution, the Arab countries and Turkey felt themselves most vulnerable to political Islam.

Those expectations are now subsiding. Egypt, Tunisia, Saudi Arabia—all countries that experienced serious Islamic opposition—have survived, bruised but intact. Even Algeria, where Islamism took the most violent form and was suppressed with particular harshness, seems to have entered a more hopeful phase.

Olivier Roy, a French expert on Islamic movements, believes that the phenomenon has moved from the centre to the periphery—from the Middle East to the fringes of the Muslim world. In the Middle East, the main promoter of political Islam (the Iranian revolution) came in 1979, so the movements which imitated the Iranian experience have had two decades to play themselves out.

In the Caucasus and Central Asia, as in former Yugoslavia, the moment of opportunity for political Islam came a decade or so later, with the collapse of communism, and so the new Islamic movements are younger and still developing. They are a powerful and potentially destabilising force, but they are no more destined to win power than their equivalents elsewhere.

There is, however, a form of "peripheral" Islam which ought to be giving Russian policymakers food for thought: the impressive strength of the Muslim faith, sometimes accompanied by political radicalism, in western cities that lie thousands of miles from the heartlands of Islam. From Detroit to Lyons, young Muslims have been rediscovering their beliefs and identity—often as a reaction against the poverty, racism and (as they would see it) sterile secularism of the societies around them. This phenomenon owes nothing to geopolitical calculation, or to the policies of any government, either western or Middle Eastern; nor can it be restrained by government action. If radical forms of Islam can flourish in places like Glasgow and Frankfurt, there is no reason why they cannot do so in Moscow and Murmansk—particularly if the Russian government seems to be fighting a brutal, pointless war at the other end of the country.

Russia Adrift

Strategic Anchors for Russia's Foreign Policy

ALVIN Z. RUBINSTEIN

Ever since Christmas Day 1991, when Russia was thrust precipitately onto the international stage as a nation-state, it has been trying to fashion a national security policy for its changed status in a new era. The other 14 union-republics of the former Soviet Union welcomed independence; Russia did not. Where other republics embraced the uncertain future and quickly learned to play the game of regional and world politics—some better than others, but all with a mixture of shrewdness and accommodation geared to preserving their unexpectedly bequeathed sovereignty and status—Russia's leaders were divided, fractious, and unable to forge consensus or cooperation.

The Romantic Interregnum

Initially, the foreign-policy orientation of Russian President Boris Yeltsin was unmistakably pro-West. Secretary of State James A. Baker III found him reassuring, forthcoming, and informed, noting that Yeltsin looked forward to developing a "strategic partnership" with the United States and that he agreed to work with the other former Soviet republics to control nuclear weapons, curb nuclear proliferation, and push quickly for ratification of the Strategic Arms Reduction Treaty (START) and the Conventional Forces in Europe treaty (CFE). Yeltsin's foreign minister, Andrei Kozyrev, was in the Westernizing tradition of Russian foreign policy. Keen on collaboration with the West, he was confident that economic concessions and assistance would be forthcoming and prepared for an evolving political-strategic partnership that recognized Russia's role as a great power and charter member of the post-Soviet European Concert of Powers.

But the possibility of a Russian-American strategic relationship was never really explored. Yeltsin expected too much. His hopes that the United States would use its "peace dividend" to help finance Russia's democratic transformation and political integration into the West were disappointed in 1992 and dashed in 1993. Early on, Russia's reformers fell victim to Yeltsin's indecisiveness, to internecine turf struggles in the Kremlin, to the resistance of government bureaucracies, and to the rampant corruption spawned by crony capitalism. By 1994, Yeltsin's priorities were more accurately characterized as holding the line and the reins of power than as pushing basic reforms. The economy continued to show negative growth: from 1992 to 1999 there was not a single year in which Russia's GDP increased.

With the reformers discredited and the ultra-nationalists gaining in strength, in part because of NATO's preparations for enlargement, Yeltsin reversed course. Stung by his political opponents and seeking to strengthen his position for the presidential election in June 1996, Yeltsin sacked Kozyrev in January 1996 and superseded his pro-Western orientation with an eclectic "balance-of-interests" approach favored by Kozyrev's successor, Yevgeny Primakov. Perhaps Kozyrev's only success in collaborating with the United States was in persuading Belarus, Kazakhstan, and Ukraine to relinquish their nuclear-weapons capabilities and join the Nuclear Nonproliferation Treaty (NPT) as non-nuclear powers, thus making Russia the sole successor to the Soviet Union's status as a nuclear superpower and a logical partner with the United States in managing the complex nuclear issue.

The Return of Geopolitics

Though slow to crystallize, an ongoing and far-ranging debate did emerge among Russia's elites on what Russia's foreign and defense policy should be in a world of new realities starkly defined by the disintegration of the former Soviet Union and Russia's new borders. These debates invariably assumed that Russia would remain a world power and that its economy would soon recover. Furthermore, they expected that a coherent policy would be crafted for ensuring a strong military, coping with separatist movements, and keeping abreast of the growth and technological advances of other leading industrial nations. As the 20th century drew to an end, such assumptions were more self-indulgent romanticism than reality.

The most difficult problem was psychological: How would an elite whose historical memory and political experience was steeped in an imperial tradition respond to a drastically different set of circumstances? Geopolitically, the Russian Federation represented a spatial reversal of more than 400 years of imperial history. Shorn of 24 percent of the territory of the former Soviet Union and about 40 percent of its population, Russia found itself squeezed out of Europe, with its European perimeter moved significantly eastward both territorially and strategically. Its position in Transcaucasia is a throwback to the 17th century, when Russia vied with the Persian and Ottoman Empires for dominance. The loss of Central Asia opened vulnerabilities in its soft underbelly not known since the Middle Ages. In brief, in the past decade Russia lost the commanding control of non-Russian surrogate-states and space that made for a strong national security.

A renewed Russian interest in geopolitics accompanied this stunning historical upheaval. "Geopolitics," which deals with the interrelationships between political actors and their spatial environment, was regarded during the Soviet era as a synonym for aggressive "bourgeois" expansion and associ-

From *Harvard International Review,* Winter/Spring 2000, pp. 14-19.

ated with Nazism and the ideas of the German strategist Karl Haushofer. Its prominence in Russian political and military thinking may be inferred from the establishment of a Committee on Geopolitical Issues by the Russian Duma. For Russians, the strategic, political, and economic implications of their changed environment has become tied to the debate on what the national interest should be and how Russia should adapt to its new environment. A changed geography mandates new strategies for defense, economic development, and diplomacy. Repeated attempts by Yeltsin's National Security Council to devise a suitable national security strategy document have failed. The most recent formulation, "Russian Federation National Security Blueprint," dated December 17, 1997, is a hodge-podge intended to mollify competing factions and constituencies, not to guide policy or establish priorities.

A power in decline, Russia knows it must adapt to an evolving international system unlike any heretofore known. Not only are empires and imperial expansion out of fashion, but so too are traditional alliances.

Atlanticism vs. Eurasianism

Russia's first foreign-policy debate pitted Atlanticism (or Westernism) against Eurasianism. The Atlanticists, epitomized by Andrei Kozyrev and his adherents in the Ministry of Foreign Affairs, maintained that Russia's democratization, socioeconomic transformation, and integration into Western civilization and international institutions depended on the West's goodwill and support. In keeping with Mikhail Gorbachev's advocacy of a "common European home," which would have included full partnership for the Soviet Union, they urged reforms to shift the country's command economy to a market-oriented economy and heavy reliance on the United States and the major West European powers. Their optimism, buoyed by the dramatic way the Cold War ended—supposedly with no winners and no losers—led them to expect that the West would be generous and welcoming and that Russia's re-entry into Europe would secure the peace, making Russia's democratization irreversible.

In the countervailing camp were the adherents of Eurasianism. Neither a new phenomenon nor a unitary concept, Eurasianism initially appeared on Russia's political and philosophical stage in the latter half of the 19th century as a reaction to the narrowness of Panslavism. The 1990s variant was introduced by Sergei Stankevich who, like Kozyrev, was a member of Yeltsin's early foreign-policy circle. He acknowledged the Atlanticist approach to be "rational, pragmatic, and natural: that's where the credits are, that's where the aid is, and that's where the advanced technology is," but warned that a policy of pragmatism unleavened "by a healthy idealism will most likely degenerate into cynicism." While not rejecting Atlanticism, he and other moderate Eurasianists argued that given its geographical and geopolitical boundaries as well as its imperial patrimony and distinctive civilization, Russia should strike a balance of Western and Eastern orientations. Accordingly, they favored differentiating Russia's partners in the Commonwealth of Independent States (CIS), distinguishing between those who intended to go their own way and those for whom the Commonwealth—and close ties to Russia—was a fundamental choice and preference. They also supported a strong policy of defending the rights of Russians in the near abroad (a term referring to the space of the former Soviet union-republics) as well as close ties to countries such as Turkey, India, and China. At its core, the Eurasianist position considered Russia uniquely situated to serve as a land bridge between Europe and Asia, culturally more effective in interacting organically with peoples of Eurasia.

Established on the eve of the USSR's dissolution, the CIS was quickly enlarged, with only the Baltic states—Estonia, Latvia, and Lithuania—electing to go their own way. The chief priority of Russian diplomacy was said to be the transformation of the USSR into a community of sovereign and equal states desiring to promote political stability on the territory of the former Soviet Union, prevent and settle ethnic conflicts, foster economic cooperation, and build a system of security by forestalling the rise of hostile coalitions. Moscow sought to institutionalize Russia's leadership role through a "carrot-and-stick" approach. The "carrots" were security under Russia's nuclear umbrella, domestic stability, territorial integrity guaranteed by Russian-dominated CIS peacekeeping contingents, and economic largesse. The "sticks" were veiled threats of economic sanctions against those who refused to participate and tacit (as well as covert) support for oppositionist and secessionist forces within particular republics.

By late 1995, with Atlanticism increasingly discredited in elite circles, Yeltsin veered to the right, responding to increased antagonism toward NATO's plans for eastward expansion, the West's demonization of Serbia in the Yugoslav wars of succession, and the inadequacy of Western financial and investment flows to make much of a difference in Russia's internal situation. Other factors also contributed to the growing chill in Russian-American relations—tensions over nuclear issues, relations with Iran and India, rivalry in Transcaucasia, and arms sales to China. Indeed, in September, four months before his replacement of Kozyrev officially signalled the end of "romanticism" in Russia's relationship with the West, Yeltsin had issued a wide-ranging decree ("The Establishment of the Strategic Course of the Russian Federation with Member States of the CIS") which called for the creation of "an economically and politically integrated alliance of states" with Russia taking the lead in forging "a new system of inter-state political and economic relations over the territory of the post-Soviet expanse." Although Foreign Minister Yevgeny Primakov later solemnly declared that the sovereignty of all CIS states "is irreversible," he also said that this did not rule out economic reintegration. Eurasianism seemed ascendant.

Is the CIS Finished?

For a time, a cooperative strategy served Russia's interests as well as those of most CIS states. Decline at home, however, precluded Russia from providing the resources and expertise desired by CIS members lying to its south. Competing political factions in Moscow stifled policy initiatives and reinforced the influence of hidebound bureaucracies intent on staking out Soviet-style fiefdoms: indeed, bureaucratization may have become an even worse problem underYeltsin than it was under Gorbachev. A persisting, ugly animosity between Yeltsin and the Duma made for stalemate and stagnation, both of which heightened dissatisfaction in Transcaucasia and Central Asia. In addition, Russia's embarrassing military setback in Chechnya in 1995 left Yeltsin with little time and few resources with which to pursue an ambitious Eurasian strategy of integration.

In the non-Slavic sector of the CIS, Russia sought a mix of imperial influence, confederational integration, strategic denial, and security arrangements. But its faltering economy, inept efforts to create an effective customs union, weak currency, and growing emphasis on security threats have led individual countries to look elsewhere for development, trade, and even security. Kazakhstan, Turkmenistan, and Azerbaijan want to attract Western investors and commitments to participate in bringing their natural gas and oil to Western markets; Kyrgyzstan sees China as a potential market for its abundant hydroelectric power; and Georgia, Ukraine, Azerbaijan, and Moldova—together known as GUAM—formed an informal association to enlist Western help in developing the energy resources of Transcaspia.

At the CIS meeting in October 1997, Yeltsin admitted that too little had been done to foster economic integration. His proposals failed to rectify the damage. In the spring of 1999, Uzbekistan decided not to renew the CIS mutual-defense treaty; Georgia, Turkmenistan, and Kazakhstan followed suit, invoking clauses designed to curtail Russia's military presence and alerting Moscow to their interest in exploring options to their heretofore reliance on the Russian security connection. Along with Uzbekistan, there is a shared suspicion of Moscow's growing military presence and intrusiveness. The CIS seems destined for the dustbin of history. If so, it would signify a sharp setback to Moscow's hope to safeguard its exposed and weak southern flank by establishing a Russian variant of the American "Monroe Doctrine" in Trancaucasia and Central Asia.

An "Orthodox Axis"?

Russian strategists are deeply concerned by the failure to secure Russia's links to CIS states and by the paucity of promising options. Upset by signs of assertiveness in regions of Russia's historical preeminence and already uneasy over NATO's expansion to the East, they see further challenges in Western efforts to acquire a significant stake in Transcaspia's energy resources and pipelines and in NATO's attempts to develop military bridgeheads in Eurasia through a combination of joint exercises, arms sales, and defense-cooperation agreements. Innocuous individually, together these ventures may mislead regional actors into thinking that they are obtaining more from the Western powers than is the case; they may exacerbate Russian concerns unnecessarily, precipitating needless confrontations and reinforcing existing suspicions. It would be unfortunate if Russia believed that the United States was inclined to pursue a"Great Game" for influence in Eurasia.

At present, Russia feels isolated. With the exception of Belarus, it has no ally or close friend along its 12,500 miles of land borders. As it casts about for congenial partners, Russia can take little solace from its experience with policy oriented along religious or cultural lines. Panslavism, which was discussed but seldom influential in the late 19th century, was not a homogeneous force: some of its adherents stressed religion, others ethnicity, and still others the strengthening of the Russian state. Panslavism championed the liberation of Slavs ruled by the Austrian and Ottoman Empires. Though useful to Russia's rulers as a manipulative instrument, it rarely determined actual policy, and was never adopted as official policy or strategy.

In his widely-discussed *Foreign Affairs* essay, "The Clash of Civilizations?" Samuel Huntington postulates a future aggregation of major political coalitions and conflicts in international politics along civilizational lines. Broadly defined, culture is viewed as a primary determinant, reinforced by such catalysts of identity as language, ethnicity, religion, and historical memory. In Europe, for example, the divide of civilizations is between Western Christianity and Eastern Orthodox Christianity, in which Russia is the dominant power. Thus, Huntington notes that in Bosnia, Russia sided with Eastern Orthodox Serbia (Yugoslavia), while the West backed Roman Catholic Croatia.

However, reality is more complex than the most imaginative efforts made to conceptualize it. There is little likelihood that Russia will put much stock in the prospect of an alliance or alignment of partners based on shared cultural traditions. It understood that the West's strong military intervention in Bosnia on behalf of Muslims and against Serbs in late summer of 1995 was a reaction to the massacre of Muslims at Srebrenica. In Kosovo in the spring of 1999, the West's intervention against Serbia was again undertaken to help Muslims (Albanians). Moscow wanted to help fellow Orthodox Serbia, but it lacked the military capability to do so; diplomatically it was thwarted by the refusal of kinship countries—Greece, Bulgaria, and Macedonia—to grant permission for flights over their territory. Indeed, these Orthodox countries, looking to their own national interest, aligned themselves with NATO against Serbia. Even though they have reason to fear the emergence of a Greater Albania, they were reluctant to jeopardize NATO's goodwill and support. In the final analysis, the need to avoid a great power's enmity was worth more than any cultural-religious affinity for a beleaguered neighbor. None of this theorizing can succor a Russia intent on finding a counterweight to US power and intrusiveness in Europe and Eurasia. Just as there was no "Orthodox axis" in the 19th century, there is no substance or geostrategic coherence for one in the 21st century.

A power in decline, Russia knows it must adapt to an evolving international system unlike any heretofore known. Not only are empires and imperial expansion out of fashion, but so too are traditional alliances—patchwork coalitions of states seeking to contain the hegemony or ambitions of a rising power. At the dawn of a new century, nuclear weapons give otherwise weaker powers the ability to keep stronger powers at bay. It is of course true that globalization contributes to shaping the sea change underway in how governments relate to one another in the international system. But a tectonic shift in great power relationships is also in motion, taking us from a bipolar world to an acentric world.

Unlike the familiar multipolar world, each center in the emerging acentric world is characterized by possession of a credible nuclear deterrent. Such a deterrent obviates the need for alliances and rests on a strategy of nuclear deterrence. In June 1999, after its helplessness in the face of NATO's air war against Serbia, Moscow announced that it was predicating any future defense on a "first-use" policy—a readiness to use nuclear weapons against any invading force or force threatening its security.

Virtually all of Russia's foreign-policy elite, broadly conceived, would consider themselves *derzhavniki*—believers in Russia's great-power status—as well as *gosudarstvenniki*—believers in strong central government. They believe that as a nuclear superpower, Russia's interests in Europe, Inner Eurasia, Transcaucasia, and East Asia deserve recognition and respect. The perception of being marginalized by the United States has spawned a growing bitterness. But with the balance of power shifting against Russia and the domestic "time of troubles" showing few signs of abating, Moscow has a weak hand to play.

The Primakov "Doctrine"

Yevgeny Primakov, experienced academic, analyst, intelligence agent, diplomat, and respected politician, has as highly developed a sense of Russia's national interests as anyone in Russian politics today. As foreign minister in May 1998, he spoke at a ceremony commemorating the 200th anniversary of the birth of Prince Alexander M. Gorchakov, Russia's foreign minister during the reign of Alexander II.

Drawing on the Gorchakov legacy, Primakov used the occasion to compare the two epochs—the challenges Russia faced and the lessons to be learned. Gorchakov became foreign minister in 1856, the year after Russia's defeat in the Crimean War when "many thought they were present at a funeral for the Russian Empire or at any rate witnessing its transformation into a second-rate power." Primakov spoke with respect of his predecessor's skillful maneuvering and adept use of a variety of often contradictory tactics to safeguard and advance Russian foreign-policy interests. Having Russia's present situation clearly in mind, he contended that some of Gorchakov's views were as applicable now, and he singled out the following from Gorchakov's "arsenal of foreign policy tactics."

First, a weak Russia must not withdraw from the international arena, but on the contrary, pursue an active foreign policy. Even as Russia strives to implement necessary economic and military reforms (thus far, unsuccessfully), it must vigorously defend its position as a great power and as one of the principal players in the international arena.

Second, Russia should follow a multifaceted policy and avoid a unidimensional approach. In relations with the United States, Germany, France, Great Britain, Japan, China, and India congenial adroitness is important; but relations with secondary powers such as Turkey, Iran, Indonesia, Syria, and Greece must also be pursued. Without diversification of its foreign connections, Russia will not be able to overcome its difficulties or regain its great-power status.

Third, Primakov left no doubt that Russia had important chips to play. He stressed its "accumulation of political influence, special geopolitical position, early membership in the world's nuclear club, status as a permanent member of the UN Security Council, growing economic possibilities, and military production, which establishes the condition for military-technological cooperation with numerous foreign partners." Used cleverly, this assortment of diplomatic instruments can frustrate American policies and advance or safeguard Russia's interests.

Fourth, Primakov observed that many countries resent and fear a US dominated-world, and that their uneasiness could be mobilized to Russia's advantage.

Finally, like Gorchakov, Primakov believes that "there are no constant enemies, but there are constant national interests." Ruefully, he acknowledged the commission of serious mistakes during the Soviet period, when "we often deviated from this vitally important truth, and as a result in the circumstances of the time the national interests of our government were sacrificed in the struggle with 'permanent adversaries' and on behalf of 'permanent allies.' " Today, he said, we need to pursue a "rational pragmatism" devoid of romanticism and unaffordable sentimentality, and Russia needs to look much farther afield for "constructive partnerships," especially to China, India, and Japan, as well as Iran, Libya, Iraq, and others.

How and when—and indeed if—Russia's leaders can turn the tenets of Gorchakov and Primakov into practice is one of the important questions whose answer lies in the decades ahead.

ALVIN Z. RUBINSTEIN is Professor of Political Science at the University ofPennsylvania and Senior Fellow of the Foreign Policy Research Institute. His work include Red Star on the Nile *(1977) and* Moscow's Third World Strategy *(1988).*

Unit 8

Unit Selections

Key Points to Consider

- Pick an Asian country, describe recent economic and political trends, and explain why you believe this country is or is not likely to continue recovering from the economic crisis within the next few years.
- What foreign policy is Taiwan likely to pursue in future years? Is it in the United States' interest to promote economic reforms in China? Why, or why not?
- What types of political changes do you expect to see in Southeast Asian countries over the next decade?

Links **www.dushkin.com/online/**

25. **ASEAN Web**
    http://www.asean.or.id
26. **Inside China Today**
    http://www.insidechina.com
27. **Japan Ministry of Foreign Affairs**
    http://www.mofa.go.jp

These sites are annotated on pages 4 and 5.

Conventional wisdom about economic development was shaken by the economic instability experienced by the Asian "tigers" and by a prolonged recession in Japan. Analysts now worry about the political fallout from the economic downturn on domestic political stability. Many analysts remain concerned that the financial crisis will continue to have a lingering impact on several countries in the region. The economic slowdown crisis occurred at the same time as a relatively unstable Pacific Basin security environment experienced a series of shocks. Indian and Pakistani nuclear tests and North Korea's continued development of missiles raised new security concerns.

The slowdown started during 1997 in Thailand's supercharged economy, when a run on the local currency burst the speculative bubble. Thailand was the first of several Asian tigers to devalue its currency and to accept harsh austerity measures as a condition for an IMF bailout package. The Thai crisis triggered a wider regional slowdown. By early 1998 local stock markets had lost two-thirds of their value, unemployment was rising, prices skyrocketing, living standards were falling, and recession spread throughout the region.

Some analysts now view the Southeast Asian currency crises of 1997 as part of a pattern of financial instability that often accompanies rapid economic growth. These analysts predict that Asian economies will continue to grow and account for over half the world's income by 2025. Economists and financial analysts continue to debate whether recent economic recovery is a meaningful upswing fueled by consumer demand in the United States or a temporary recovery. Most analysts agree that sustained economic recovery will require growth in the economies of both Japan and China.

Although its economy has also slowed, to date China has managed to avoid a currency devaluation. The downturn of Hong Kong's stock market was another blow. Although the transition from control by Great Britain to China went smoothly, Hong Kong experienced a dramatic drop-off in tourism and a sell-off of property stocks after the island reverted to Chinese control.

China is struggling with the dislocations caused by government efforts to reform its "iron rice bowl" economy based on socialistic principles. Economic reforms are eliminating many of the subsidies for food, housing, and jobs that had been promised to all citizens under socialism. China is also eliminating nonperforming state entities and halving the number of state workers. The result is massive unemployment, growing resentment over increased disparities, and a fundamental change in the relationship between the state, the Communist Party, and workers.

Since 1998, China has been implementing a series of reforms in a cautious, piecemeal fashion. Inefficient state enterprises must close. State banks must eliminate bad loans from their books and only make loans on commercial terms. The government is supporting a housing and investment boom in the hope that private business will be able to employ millions who are being released from state enterprises and the military. As the military shifts to a volunteer force, millions of demobilized former soldiers are joining the ranks of the unemployed. The government is also trying to reform and dismantle the huge complex of over 1,500 businesses currently run by the military.

The Chinese government celebrated the fiftieth anniversary of Communist rule with a massive military parade in 1999. The celebrations followed a widespread crackdown on the now-banned sect Falun Gong. The government views this growing spiritual movement as a potential threat to Communist rule and has detained hundreds of followers.

Despite continued repression at home, China's foreign policies increasingly resemble those of a status quo power. China works closely with the United States, Japan, and other major powers to cope with regional problems. Most analysts predict that China will continue to cooperate with the United States and other major powers as long as it believes it is regaining its rightful place in the world after a century of "humiliation." In "Does China Matter?" Gerald Segal goes further than much of the conventional wisdom in discounting the importance of China as an emerging power. Segal outlines the reasons why China is overrated as a market, a military or political power, and a source of ideas in international relations.

The most important foreign policy issue for the Chinese government is the status of Taiwan. China considers the island a renegade province that split from China after the 1949 civil war. There has been increasing continuous concern since the late 1990s about whether China will follow through on threats to use military force against Taiwan if Taiwan moves toward independence. Initially, the Chinese government was reacting to statements made by former president Lee Teng-Hui that Taiwan is a separate sovereign state. Concerns mounted again after Taiwan's 2000 election ended 50 years of Nationalist rule. The victory of Chen Shui-bian, the candidate of a formerly pro-independence party, was a clear rebuff to China's Communist government. After his presidential victory, Chen Shui-bian offered an olive branch across the Taiwan Strait by permitting a few ships to sail legally between Taiwan and China at the beginning of 2001. Many observers hope that these links are the start of direct transit and trade between China and Taiwan, an island separated by the 100-mile-wide Taiwan Strait and 50 years of conflict.

Policymakers worldwide focus on the instability of the North Korean government because there is continuing uncertainty about what foreign policies the leader of this isolationist nation-state is likely to pursue. The ongoing humanitarian emergency and the needs of the North Korean economy provide opportunities to transform the security stalemate on the Korean peninsula. "Kimaraderie, At Last" describes how the leaders of the two Koreas met for the first time in nearly half a century in 2000. While the meeting was warm, it will take time for many South Koreans to reconcile the conflicting images of North Korea's leader, Kim Jong Il. This meeting was the first step on a long journey.

Spreading economic problems throughout Southeast Asia threaten three decades of political stability. The economic crisis in Asia wiped out the gains of a large proportion of middle class citizens. The economic upheaval that has occurred to date is fueling major political changes in Thailand, Malaysia, Singapore, Vietnam, Indonesia, and the Philippines. Many analysts believe that major political change has only just begun. The reaction of a government-backed militia to an independence vote in East Timor in 1999 seemed to confirm these predictions.

Economic slowdown in Asia may also have had the unintended consequence of speeding up efforts to reduce the influence of international financial institutions dominated by the major industrialized countries in the region. In "Towards a Tripartite World," Fred Bergsten describes new regional arrangements that are being fashioned in East Asia by Japan, China, South Korea, and the 10 members of the Association of South-East Asian Nations (ASEAN). The ASEAN+3 group illustrates how a growing number of states in different regions are turning to subregional preferential trade pacts and cooperative financial arrangements.

Does China Matter?

Gerald Segal

MIDDLE KINGDOM, MIDDLE POWER

DOES CHINA matter? No, it is not a silly question—merely one that is not asked often enough. Odd as it may seem, the country that is home to a fifth of humankind is overrated as a market, a power, and a source of ideas. At best, China is a second-rank middle power that has mastered the art of diplomatic theater: it has us willingly suspending our disbelief in its strength. In fact, China is better understood as a theoretical power—a country that has promised to deliver for much of the last 150 years but has consistently disappointed. After 50 years of Mao's revolution and 20 years of reform, it is time to leave the theater and see China for what it is. Only when we finally understand how little China matters will we be able to craft a sensible policy toward it.

DOES CHINA MATTER ECONOMICALLY?

CHINA, UNLIKE Russia or the Soviet Union before it, is supposed to matter because it is already an economic powerhouse. Or is it that China is on the verge of becoming an economic powerhouse, and you must be in the engine room helping the Chinese to enjoy the benefits to come? Whatever the spin, you know the argument: China is a huge market, and you cannot afford to miss it (although few say the same about India). The recently voiced "Kodak version" of this argument is that if only each Chinese will buy one full roll

Reprinted by permission of *Foreign Affairs,* September/October 1999, pp. 24-36.

of film instead of the average half-roll that each currently buys, the West will be rich. Of course, nineteenth-century Manchester mill owners said much the same about their cotton, and in the early 1980s Japanese multinationals said much the same about their television sets. The Kodak version is just as hollow. In truth, China is a small market that matters relatively little to the world, especially outside Asia.

If this judgment seems harsh, let us begin with some harsh realities about the size and growth of the Chinese economy. In 1800 China accounted for 33 percent of world manufacturing output; by way of comparison, Europe as a whole was 28 percent, and the United States was 0.8 percent. By 1900 China was down to 6.2 percent (Europe was 62 percent, and the United States was 23.6 percent). In 1997 China accounted for 3.5 percent of world GNP (in 1997 constant dollars, the United States was 25.6 percent). China ranked seventh in the world, ahead of Brazil and behind Italy. Its per capita GDP ranking was 81st, just ahead of Georgia and behind Papua New Guinea. Taking the most favorable of the now-dubious purchasing-power-parity calculations; in 1997 China accounted for 11.8 percent of world GNP, and its per capita ranking was 65th, ahead of Jamaica and behind Latvia. Using the U.N. Human Development Index, China is 107th, bracketed by Albania and Namibia—not an impressive story.

Yes, you may say, but China has had a hard 200 years and is now rising swiftly. China has undoubtedly done better in the past generation than it did in the previous ten, but let's still keep matters in perspective—especially about Chinese growth rates. China claimed that its average annual industrial growth between 1951 and 1980 was 12.5 percent. Japan's comparable figure was 11.5 percent. One can reach one's own judgment about whose figures turned out to be more accurate.

Few economists trust modern Chinese economic data; even Chinese Prime Minister Zhu Rongji distrusts it. The Asian Development Bank routinely deducts some two percent from China's official GDP figures, including national current GDP growth rates of eight percent. Some two or three percent of what might be a more accurate GDP growth rate of six percent is useless goods produced to rust in warehouses. About one percent of China's growth in 1998 was due to massive government spending on infrastructure. Some three percent of GDP is accounted for by the one-time gain that occurs when one takes peasants off the land and brings them to cities, where productivity is higher. Taking all these qualifications into account, China's economy is effectively in recession. Even Zhu calls the situation grim.

China's ability to recover is hampered by problems that the current leadership understands well but finds just too scary to tackle seriously—at least so long as East Asia's economy is weak. By conservative estimates, at least a quarter of Chinese loans are nonperforming—a rate that Southeast Asians would have found frightening before the crash. Some 45 percent of state industries are losing money, but bank lending was up 25 percent in 1998—in part, to bail out the living dead. China has a high savings rate (40 percent of GDP), but ordinary Chinese would be alarmed to learn that their money is clearly being wasted.

Some put their hope in economic decentralization, but this has already gone so far that the center cannot reform increasingly wasteful and corrupt practices in the regions and in specific institutions. Central investment—20 percent of total investment in China—is falling. Inter-provincial trade as a percentage of total provincial trade is also down, having dropped a staggering 18 percent between 1985 and 1992. Despite some positive changes during the past 20 years of reform, China's economy has clearly run into huge structural impediments. Even if double-digit growth rates ever really existed, they are hard to imagine in the near future.

In terms of international trade and investment, the story is much the same: Beijing is a seriously overrated power. China made up a mere 3 percent of total world trade in 1997, about the same as South Korea and less than the Netherlands. China now accounts for only 11 percent of total Asian trade. Despite the hype about the importance of the China market, exports to China are tiny. Only 1.8 percent of U.S. exports go to China (this could, generously, be perhaps 2.4 percent if re-exports through Hong Kong were counted)—about the same level as U.S. exports to Australia or Belgium and about a third less than U.S. exports to Taiwan. The same is true of major European traders. China accounts for 0.5 percent of U.K. exports, about the same level as exports to Sri Lanka and less than those to Malaysia. China takes 1.1 percent of French and German exports, which is the highest in Asia apart from Japan but about par with exports to Portugal.

China matters a bit more to other Asian countries. Some 3.2 percent of Singapore's exports go to China, less than to Taiwan but on par with South Korea. China accounts for 4.6 percent of Australian exports, about the same as to Singapore. Japan sends only 5.1 percent of its exports to China, about a quarter less than to Taiwan. Only South Korea sends China an impressive share of its exports—some 9.9 percent, nudging ahead of exports to Japan.

Foreign direct investment (FDI) is even harder to measure than trade but sheds more light on long-term trends. China's massive FDI boom, especially in the past decade, is often trumpeted as evidence of how much China does and will matter for the global economy. But the reality is far less clear. Even in 1997, China's peak year for FDI, some 80 percent of the $45 billion inflow came from ethnic Chinese, mostly in East Asia. This was also a year of record capital flight from China—by some reckonings, an outflow of $35 billion. Much so-called investment from East Asia makes a round-trip from China via some place like Hong Kong and then comes back in as FDI to attract tax concessions.

Even a more trusting view of official FDI figures suggests that China does not much matter. FDI into China is about 10 percent of global FDI, with 60 percent of all FDI transfers taking place among developed countries. Given that less than 20 percent of FDI into China comes from non-ethnic Chinese, it is no surprise that U.S. or European Union investment in China averages out to something less than their investment in a major Latin American country such as Brazil. China has never accounted for more than 10 percent of U.S. FDI outflows—usually much less. In recent years China has taken around 5 percent of major EU countries' FDI outflow—and these are the glory years for FDI in China. The Chinese economy is clearly contracting, and FDI into China is dropping with it. In 1998 the United Nations reported that FDI into China maybe cut in half, and figures for 1998–99 suggest that this was not too gloomy a guess. Japanese FDI into China has been halved from its peak in 1995. Ericsson, a multinational telecommunications firm, says that China accounts for 13 percent of its global sales but will not claim that it is making any profits there. Similar experiences by Japanese technology firms a decade ago led to today's rapid disinvestment from China. Some insist that FDI flows demonstrate just how much China matters and will matter for the global economy, but the true picture is far more modest. China remains a classic case of hope over experience, reminiscent of de Gaulle's famous comment about Brazil: It has great potential, and always will.

It does not take a statistical genius to see the sharp reality: China is at best a minor (as opposed to inconsequential) part of the global economy. It has merely managed to project and sustain an image of far greater importance. This theatrical power was displayed with great brio during Asia's recent economic crisis. China received lavish praise from the West, especially the United States, for not devaluing its currency as it did in 1995. Japan, by contrast, was held responsible for the crisis. Of course, Tokyo's failure to reform since 1990 helped cause the meltdown, but this is testimony to how much Tokyo matters and how little Beijing does. China's total financial aid to the crisis-stricken economies was less than 10 percent of Japan's contribution.

The Asian crisis and the exaggerated fears that it would bring the economies of the Atlantic world to their knees help explain the overblown view of China's importance. In fact, the debacle demonstrated just how little impact Asia, except for Japan, has on the global economy. China—a small part of a much less important part of the global system than is widely believed—was never going to matter terribly much to the developed world. Exaggerating China is part of exaggerating Asia. As a result of the crisis, the West has learned the lesson for the region as a whole, but it has not yet learned it about China.

DOES CHINA MATTER MILITARILY?

CHINA IS a second-rate military power—not first-rate, because it is far from capable of taking on America, but not as third-rate as most of its Asian neighbors. China accounts for only 4.5 percent of global defense spending (the United States makes up 33.9 percent) and 25.8 percent of defense spending in East Asia and Australasia. China poses a formidable threat to the likes of the Philippines and can take islands such as Mischief Reef in the South China Sea at will. But sell the Philippines a couple of cruise missiles and the much-discussed Chinese threat will be easily erased. China is in no military shape to take the disputed Senkaku Islands from Japan, which is decently armed. Beijing clearly is a serious menace to Taiwan, but even Taiwanese defense planners do not believe China can successfully invade. The Chinese missile threat to Taiwan is much exaggerated, especially considering the very limited success of the far more massive and modern NATO missile strikes on Serbia. If the Taiwanese have as much will to resist as did the Serbs, China will not be able to easily cow Taiwan.

Thus China matters militarily to a certain extent simply because it is not a status quo power, but it does not matter so much that it cannot be constrained. Much the same pattern is evident in the challenge China poses to U.S. security. It certainly matters that China is the only country whose nuclear weapons target the United States. It matters, as the recent Cox report on Chinese espionage plainly shows, that China steals U.S. secrets about missile guidance and modern nuclear warheads. It also matters that Chinese military exercises simulate attacks on U.S. troops in South Korea and Japan. But the fact that a country can directly threaten the United States is not normally taken as a reason to be anything except robust in defending U.S. interests. It is certainly not a reason to pretend that China is a strategic partner of the United States.

The extent to which China matters militarily is evident in the discussions about deploying U.S. theater missile defenses (TMD) in the western Pacific and creating a U.S. national missile defense shield (NMD). Theoretically, the adversary is North Korea. In practice, the Pentagon fears that the U.S. ability to defend South Korea, Japan, and even Taiwan depends in the long term on the ability to defend the United States' home territory and U.S. troops abroad from Chinese missiles. Given the $10 billion price tag for NMD and the so-far unknowable costs of TMD, defense planners clearly think that China matters.

But before strategic paranoia sets in, the West should note that the Chinese challenge is nothing like the Soviet one. China is less like the Soviet Union in the 1950s than like Iraq in the 1990s: a regional threat to Western interests, not a global ideological rival. Such regional threats can be constrained. China, like Iraq, does not matter so much that the United States needs to suspend its normal strategies for dealing with unfriendly powers. Threats can be deterred, and unwanted action can be constrained by a country that claims to be the sole superpower and to dominate the revolution in military affairs.

A similarly moderated sense of how much China matters can be applied to the question of Chinese arms transfers. China accounted for 2.2 percent of arms deliveries in 1997, ahead of Germany but behind Israel (the United States had 45 percent of the market, and the United Kingdom had 18 percent). The $1 billion or so worth of arms that Beijing exports annually is not buying vast influence, though in certain markets Beijing does have real heft. Pakistan is easily the most important recipient of Chinese arms, helping precipitate a nuclear arms race with India. Major deals with Sudan, Sri Lanka, and Burma have had far less strategic impact. On the other hand, arms transfers to Iran have been worrying; as with Pakistan, U.S. threats of sanctions give China rather good leverage. China's ability to make mischief therefore matters somewhat—primarily because it reveals that Chinese influence is fundamentally based on its ability to oppose or thwart Western interests. France and Britain each sell far more arms than China, but they are by and large not creating strategic problems for the West.

Hence, it is ludicrous to claim, as Western and especially American officials constantly do, that China matters because the West needs it as a strategic partner. The discourse of "strategic partnership" really means that China is an adversary that could become a serious nuisance. Still, many in the Clinton administration and elsewhere do not want to call a spade a spade and admit that China is a strategic foe. Perhaps they think that stressing the potential for partnership may eventually, in best Disney style, help make dreams come true.

On no single significant strategic issue are China and the West on the same side. In most cases, including Kosovo, China's opposition does not matter. True, the U.N. Security Council could not be used to build a powerful coalition against Serbia, but as in most cases, the real obstacle was Russia, not China. Beijing almost always plays second fiddle to Moscow or even Paris in obstructing Western interests in the Security Council. (The exceptions to this rule always concern cases where countries such as Haiti or Macedonia have developed relations with Taiwan.) After all, the Russian prime minister turned his plane to the United States around when he heard of the imminent NATO attack on Serbia, but the Chinese premier turned up in Washington as scheduled two weeks later.

NATO's accidental May bombing of the Chinese embassy elicited a clear demonstration of China's theatrical power. Beijing threatened to block any peace efforts in the United Nations (not that any were pending), but all it wanted was to shame the West into concessions on World Trade Organization membership, human rights, or arms control. China grandiosely threatened to rewrite the Security Council resolution that eventually gave NATO an indefinite mandate to keep the peace in Kosovo, but in the end it meekly abstained. So much for China taking a global perspective as one of the five permanent members of the Security Council. Beijing's temper tantrum merely highlighted the fact that, unlike the other veto-bearing Security Council members, it was not a power in Europe.

In the field of arms control, the pattern is the same. China does not block major arms control accords, but it makes sure to be among the last to sign on and tries to milk every diplomatic advantage from having to be dragged to the finish line. China's reluctance to sign the Nuclear Nonproliferation Treaty (NPT), for instance, was outdone in its theatricality only by the palaver in getting China to join the Comprehensive Test Ban Treaty. China's participation in the Association of Southeast Asian Nations Regional Forum—Asia's premier, albeit limited, security structure—is less a commitment to surrender some sovereignty to an international arrangement than a way to ensure that nothing is done to limit China's ability to pursue its own national security objectives. China matters in arms control mainly because it effectively blocks accords until doing so ends up damaging China's international reputation.

Only on the Korean Peninsula do China's capacities seriously affect U.S. policy. One often hears that

China matters because it is so helpful in dealing with North Korea. This is flatly wrong. Only once this decade did Beijing join with Washington and pressure Pyongyang—in bringing the rogue into compliance with its NPT obligations in the early phases of the 1994 North Korean crisis. On every other occasion, China has either done nothing to help America or actively helped North Korea resist U.S. pressure—most notoriously later in the 1994 crisis, when the United States was seeking support for sanctions and other coercive action against North Korea. Thus the pattern is the same. China matters in the same way any middle-power adversary matters: it is a problem to be circumvented or moved. But China does not matter because it is a potential strategic partner for the West. In that sense, China is more like Russia than either cares to admit.

DOES CHINA MATTER POLITICALLY?

THE EASIEST category to assess—although the one with the fewest statistics—is how much China matters in international political terms. To be fair to the Chinese, their recent struggle to define who they are and what they stand for is merely the latest stage of at least 150 years of soul-searching. Ever since the coming of Western power demonstrated that China's ancient civilization was not up to the challenges of modernity, China has struggled to understand its place in the wider world. The past century in particular has been riddled with deep Chinese resistance to the essential logic of international interdependence. It has also been marked by failed attempts to produce a China strong enough to resist the Western-dominated international system—consider the Boxer movement, the Kuomintang, or the Chinese Communist Party (CCP). Fifty years after the Chinese communist revolution, the party that gave the Chinese people the Great Leap Forward (and 30 million dead of famine) and the Cultural Revolution (and perhaps another million dead as well as a generation destroyed) is devoid of ideological power and authority. In the absence of any other political ideals, religions and cults such as the Falun Gong (target of a government crackdown this summer) will continue to flourish.

China's latest attempt to strengthen itself has been the past 20 years of economic reforms, stimulated by other East Asians' success in transforming their place in the world. But the discourse on prosperity that elicited praise for the order-sustaining "Asian values" or Confucian fundamentals was burned in the bonfire of certainties that was the Asian economic crisis. China was left in another phase of shock and self-doubt; hence, economic reforms stalled.

Under these circumstances, China is in no position to matter much as a source of international political power. Bizarre as old-style Maoism was, at least it was a beacon for many in the developing world. China now is a beacon to no one—and, indeed, an ally to no one. No other supposedly great power is as bereft of friends. This is not just because China, once prominent on the map of aid suppliers, has become the largest recipient of international aid. Rather, China is alone because it abhors the very notion of genuine international interdependence. No country relishes having to surrender sovereignty and power to the Western-dominated global system, but China is particularly wedded to the belief that it is big enough to merely learn what it must from the outside world and still retain control of its destiny. So China's neighbors understand the need to get on with China but have no illusions that China feels the same way.

China does not even matter in terms of global culture. Compare the cultural (not economic) role that India plays for ethnic Indians around the world to the pull exerted by China on ethnic Chinese, and one sees just how closed China remains. Of course, India's cultural ties with the Atlantic world have always been greater than China's, and India's wildly heterogeneous society has always been more accessible to the West. But measured in terms of films, literature, or the arts in general, Taiwan, Hong Kong, and even Singapore are more important global influences than a China still under the authoritarian grip of a ruling Leninist party. Chinese cities fighting over who should get the next Asian Disneyland, Chinese cultural commissars squabbling over how many American films can be shown in Chinese cinemas, and CCP bosses setting wildly fluctuating Internet-access policies are all evidence of just how mightily China is struggling to manage the power of Western culture.

In fact, the human-rights question best illustrates the extent to which China is a political pariah. Chinese authorities correctly note that life for the average citizen has become much more free in the past generation. But as Zhu admitted on his recent trip to the United States, China's treatment of dissenters remains inhuman and indecent.

Still, China deserves credit for having stepped back on some issues. That China did not demand the right to intervene to help Indonesia's ethnic Chinese during the 1998–99 unrest was correctly applauded as a sign of maturity. But it was also a sign of how little international leadership China could claim. With a human-rights record that made Indonesia seem a paragon of virtue, China was in no position to seize the moral high ground.

Measuring global political power is difficult, but China's influence and authority are clearly puny—not merely compared to the dominant West, but also compared to Japan before the economic crisis. Among the reasons for China's weakness is its continuing ambiguity about how to manage the consequences of modernity and interdependence. China's great past and the resultant hubris make up much of the problem. A China that believes the world naturally owes it recognition as a great power—even when it so patently is not—is not really ready to achieve greatness.

DOES IT MATTER IF CHINA DOESN'T MATTER?

THE MIDDLE KINGDOM, then, is merely a middle power. It is not that China does not matter at all, but that it matters far less than it and most of the West think. China matters about as much as Brazil for the global economy. It is a medium-rank military power, and it exerts no political pull at all. China matters most for the West because it can make mischief, either by threatening its neighbors or assisting anti-Western forces further afield. Although these are problems, they will be more manageable if the West retains some sense of proportion about China's importance. If you believe that China is a major player in the global economy and a near-peer competitor of America's, you might be reluctant to constrain its undesired activities. You might also indulge in the "pander complex"—the tendency to bend over backward to accommodate every Chinese definition of what insults the Chinese people's feelings. But if you believe that China is not much different from any middle power, you will be more willing to treat it normally.

This notion of approaching China as a normal, medium power is one way to avoid the sterile debates about the virtues of engaging or containing China. Of course, one must engage a middle power, but one should also not be shy about constraining its unwanted actions. Such a strategy of "constrainment" would lead to a new and very different Western approach to China. One would expect robust deterrence of threats to Taiwan, but not pusillanimous efforts to ease Chinese concerns about TMD. One would expect a tough negotiating stand on the terms of China's WTO entry, but not Western concessions merely because China made limited progress toward international transparency standards or made us feel guilty about bombing its embassy in Belgrade. One would expect Western leaders to tell Chinese leaders that their authoritarianism puts them on the wrong side of history, but one would not expect Western countries to stop trying to censure human rights abuses in the United Nations or to fall over themselves to compete for the right to lose money in the China market.

To some extent, we are stuck with a degree of exaggeration of China's influence. It has a permanent U.N. Security Council seat even though it matters about as much as the United Kingdom and France, who hold their seats only because of their pre–World War II power. Unlike London and Paris, however, Beijing contributes little to international society via peacekeeping or funding for international bodies. China still has a hold on the imagination of CEOs, as it has for 150 years—all the more remarkable after the past 20 years, in which Western companies were bamboozled into believing that staying for the long haul meant eventually making money in China. Pentagon planners, a pessimistic breed if ever there was one, might be forgiven for believing that China could eventually become a peer competitor of the United States, even though the military gap, especially in high-technology arms, is, if anything, actually growing wider.

Nevertheless, until China is cut down to size in Western imaginations and treated more like a Brazil or an India, the West stands little chance of sustaining a coherent and long-term policy toward it. Until we stop suspending our disbelief and recognize the theatrical power of China, we will continue to constrain ourselves from pursuing our own interests and fail to constrain China's excesses. And perhaps most important, until we treat China as a normal middle power, we will make it harder for the Chinese people to understand their own failings and limitations and get on with the serious reforms that need to come.

GERALD SEGAL is Director of Studies at the International Institute for Strategic Studies in London and co-author, with Barry Buzan, of *Anticipating the Future*.

ASIA

Kimaraderie, at last

A surprisingly warm welcome awaited the president of South Korea when he ventured north this week, but the bill has yet to be presented

SEOUL

WHEN they met at last on June 13th, it looked more like a family reunion than a summit between the leaders of two countries that have technically been at war for nearly half a century. Kim Jong Il, the rarely seen leader of North Korea, surprised everyone by turning up at the airport to greet Kim Dae Jung, the South's president. When they shook hands, many South Koreans watching the live broadcast on television suddenly started to applaud. Some shed tears. It was as if the last frontier of the cold war was suddenly about to melt away.

Although the two Kims signed a wide-ranging communiqué during the three-day visit, there remains a long way to go. They agreed in principle to find ways to promote economic co-operation, to achieve reconciliation and eventually to reunify their two countries without "interference" from others. The details are supposed to be fleshed out by officials in forthcoming meetings. In August, some of the families that have been separated since the Korean war ended in an armed truce in 1953 are to be allowed to meet. How many will be involved and where their meetings will be held have yet to be decided. Kim Jong Il has also accepted an invitation to visit South Korea, although the date of his visit is likewise yet to be arranged.

The two Kims clearly got off to a good start, holding hands in the back of a Lincoln Continental for the 50-minute journey from the airport to the state guest house in the North's capital, Pyongyang. It was exactly the sort of face-to-face and away-from-the-notetakers sort of meeting that officials in Beijing are believed to have urged upon the northern Mr Kim when he suddenly scuttled off to China only days before the summit. The two could have talked about anything; it probably did not matter so long as the ice was broken.

The encounter between the leader of the world's most reclusive country and the head of the capitalist and democratic South was quite a show. Some 600,000 North Koreans were mobilised along the route from the airport, many dressed in national costume and waving pink plastic flowers. However carefully orchestrated, the welcome left many South Koreans in a state of shock. Their knowledge of North Korea has been limited by its regime's secretiveness and their own past governments' reluctance to encourage fraternisation with communists. Until now they have mostly regarded North Korea as a bizarre, if not mad, totalitarian state, unable to feed its 21m people but still determined to invade the South.

It was a theme which the North's Mr Kim played to. Him a hermit? Never. The western media had got it all wrong, he said. He was no recluse. Indeed, he let it be known that he had made unofficial trips to several countries, including Indonesia. He also revealed that he had a habit of watching South Korean television, a pleasure he allows few others in North Korea to enjoy.

Mr Nice Guy

So, what is Kim Jong Il up to? He is clearly determined to improve relations with the outside world. Having normalised diplomatic links with Italy and Australia earlier this year, he seems anxious to get closer to the South and to do so while Kim Dae

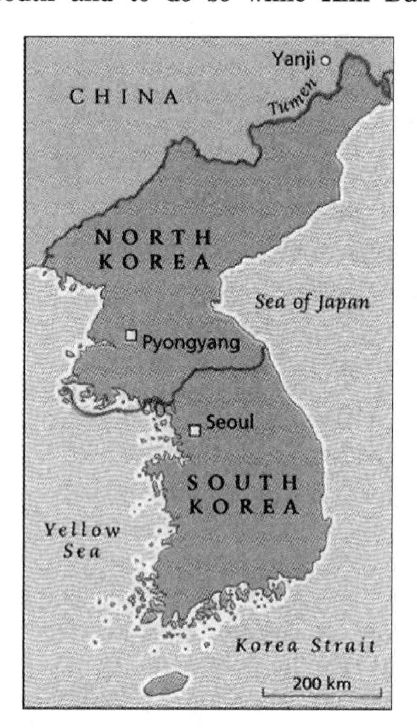

Jung is in power. Unlike his predecessors, the southern Mr Kim has been warm to the North ever since he took office in February 1998. He has consistently pursued what he calls his "sunshine policy" of engaging the North in economic co-operation in the hope of unfreezing political contacts. Improving relations with the South may also give North Korea more bargaining power with Japan and America.

China will not be displeased either. Officials in Beijing do not want their former ally in the Korean war to continue as a dangerous rogue nation, giving America and Japan the excuse to beef up their military forces in the region. Nor do Chinese officials want North Korea to collapse, sending waves

The other side of North Korea

YANJI

Having accepted an invitation to visit South Korea's capital, Seoul, North Korea's leader, Kim Jong Il, who is said to be wary of flying, will probably travel by road. That means he will pass through the heavily-fortified "demilitarised" zone that separates the two Koreas. Although refugees once swarmed along this route to escape the Communists and their Chinese allies, few people have made the journey since the Korean war ended in 1953. Since then, the only way out of North Korea has been to cross the Tumen river, which marks the border with China.

About 100,000 northerners are believed to have crossed into north-eastern China, where some 2m ethnic Koreans have lived alongside the Chinese since the mid-1800s. Recently, the numbers crossing the river have slowed down, partly, it is thought, because the famine in North Korea has eased. But the North Korean guards have also doubled the bribe they demand from those they let pass.

Some people return home after scavenging for food, but many remain, hoping to better their lives or to escape persecution. They face a perilous existence, in constant fear of being caught and deported. It is from these refugees that a picture of the grim existence of North Koreans emerges. They also give a glimpse of the extent of the opposition to Kim Jong Il's rule.

That opposition is feeble. Some of it comes from Christian groups, especially those established by South Korean missionaries who look after some of the refugees. A mission in Yanji, for instance, helps to care for 100 or so North Korean children and 50 adults. Missionaries say they convert about one in five to Christianity and some are then sent back to North Korea to spread the word.

There are said to be about 50 underground churches in North Korea, usually houses where people go to pray and read the Bible in secret. Although there is little sign of it yet, some people think that the Christians could one day openly stand up for their rights, as the Falun Gong movement has in China.

Other refugees seem more determined to overthrow rather than challenge the North's leaders. A group of armed North Korean soldiers sneaked into China in May to join a resistance group hiding in the mountains, according to one missionary. This, he claims, has made China strengthen its frontier controls.

A North Korean academic, who came to China two years ago to carry out a survey of the refugees, says he decided not to return home: after experiencing life in China and learning about South Korea, he felt betrayed by the North's regime. Now he says he is determined to help overthrow it.

Some people talk of attempted coups. One is supposed to have been staged by the 6th Army Corps in the north-east of the country in January 1996, but was quickly put down. Officers were executed and the unit has since been dissolved, recalls a former lieutenant in a North Korean special-forces unit who crossed the Tumen river with his wife and son three years ago.

A woman who fled a year ago says one of the North's big problems is a lack of food-processing skills. Only when she came to china did she realise that canned fish could be sold for more money than raw fish. She plans to use this valuable piece of capitalist knowledge if warmer relations ever allow her to go home.

---

of refugees across the northern border into China, to follow all those who have already escaped thither (see box). Worst of all would be the arrival of interfering western aid agencies to help sort out the mess. China supplies North Korea with much of its grain and oil. During his recent visit to Beijing, Kim Jong Il is thought to have tried to secure more economic aid in return for being nice to the southerners. He was, it is said, also deeply interested in learning how China had opened up, questioning in particular how it could be done without damaging the future of socialism. That is something China's leaders have been giving some though to lately.

Kim Jong Il appears to have consolidated his power after taking over from his father, Kim Il Sung, who died of a heart attack in 1994. Yet his power base may not be solid. This may be one reason why he wanted to keep his trip to China a secret until his train was safely back in North Korea.

In the past he has tried, with some success, to be paid to be less nasty. By threatening to withdraw from the Nuclear Non-Proliferation Treaty in 1994, he secured two western-designed nuclear power plants. By test-firing a new rocket over Japan in 1998, he caught outside attention again. He has suspended further test launches while talks take place with America. He has demanded lots of cash to end his missile sales to countries like Iran and Pakistan. Meanwhile, America is about to ease some economic sanctions. Japan may normalise relations, although for that North Korea will claim up to $10 billion in reparations for the long Japanese occupation of the peninsula. So, being nice to South Korea will also carry a price.

This week, though, the South Koreans were not adding up what the bill is likely to be. The seemingly courteous and jocular Kim Jong Il, who appeared on television as he briefly opened the door of his mysterious kingdom, was a surprise. Was this really the face behind the bombing in Yangon in 1983 that killed 17 South Koreans, including several cabinet ministers? Four years later, North Korean agents were believed to have blown up a South Korean airliner.

It will take some time for many South Koreans to reconcile the conflicting images of Kim Jong Il, let alone to decide what to make of their northern cousins. If anything, this week's summit may have shown people in the South how much more deeply Koreans are divided than the two Germanies were. Because of that, the cost of reconciliation, both financial and emotional, is bound to be far higher. For now though, like the South Korean students who hung out North Korean flags in defiance of their country's strict laws, it is enough simply to celebrate the first step on a long journey.

EAST ASIAN REGIONALISM

Towards a tripartite world

This week, the leaders of the big industrialised countries are preparing to meet in Okinawa. But a challenge to their dominance of the world's financial and trading systems is stirring right under their feet, argues Fred Bergsten

WASHINGTON, DC

WHEN it comes to international finance, two bodies like to think they are in charge of the architecture: the G7 group of industrialised countries (G8, when Russia is included), and the International Monetary Fund. Not quite so. In the medium term, at least, the most important changes to the world's financial architecture are likely to come from the new regional arrangements being fashioned in East Asia by Japan, China, South Korea and the ten members of the Association of South-East Asian Nations (ASEAN).

In trade, the same is true. The most striking changes in the world trading system, especially in the short run, are not likely to flow from the World Trade Organisation or the proposed "mega-regional" arrangements, such as a Free-Trade Area of the Americas or an expanded European Union. Instead, they will probably come from the host of sub-regional trade agreements now being busily negotiated by Japan, South Korea, Singapore and other countries in East Asia.

Virtually unnoticed by the rest of the world, East Asian countries are getting together to make their own economic arrangements. As a result, for the first time in history, the world is becoming a three-block configuration. Not only global economic relationships, but political ones too, will turn on the direction these new agreements take—and on how the United States, and others outside the region, decide to respond to them.

The early steps

It was Mahathir Mohamad, the prime minister of Malaysia, who first proposed an East Asian Economic Group (EAEG) a decade ago. Nothing happened, partly because Dr Mahathir was under suspicion as a protectionist, but largely because the United States feared "drawing a line down the middle of the Pacific". America pushed instead, successfully, for relying on the Asia-Pacific Economic Co-operation forum (APEC). With very little fanfare, however, Asia has now created the "ASEAN+3" with precisely the same membership (ASEAN, China, Japan and South Korea) envisaged by Dr Mahathir. The group has held its own summits for three years in a row, has set up a "vision group" to guide its work, and holds regular meetings of its finance ministers.

Structurally, at least, the ASEAN+3 is starting to look like the G7. It has become the most active regional grouping outside Europe, and already has more sophisticated machinery than the North American Free-Trade Agreement (NAFTA). But it is still at an early stage and, for reasons that will be discussed later, it does not yet have the substance or integration of these other partnerships.

The new Asian regionalism is proceeding more rapidly on financial issues than on trade. This looks unusual: in the European Union and other big precursors, the sequence was the other way round. But trade arrangements (as witness the vexed world trade rounds) are politically difficult and slow to organise. Monetary agreements can proceed without discrimination against outsiders, unlike most trade deals. Besides, financial problems lay at the heart of the East Asian implosion of a few years ago.

The ASEAN+3 have announced a region-wide system of currency swaps to help them deal with future Asian crises. This is similar to the network installed by the Group of Ten industrial nations in the early 1960s, when they faced the first global monetary hiccups of the post-war period. Sub-regional financial structures are developing as well: ASEAN has created a surveillance mechanism to try to anticipate and head off future crises, using sophisticated early-warning indicators, and the North-East Asian countries are jointly keeping an eye on short-term capital movements in the vicinity. There is much talk of common currency baskets and joint intervention arrangements, to replace both the discredited dollar pegs of the past and the costly free floats imposed by the crisis.

An Asian Monetary Fund (AMF) is thus beginning to evolve, only three years after the idea was rejected out of hand. China, which condemned the original Japanese proposal, supports the present initiatives. Hong Kong and the Philippines have proposed an Asian currency unit on the euro model: an idea that would obviously take years to come to pass, but would not even have been considered a little while ago.

Nor have the East Asians been idle on trade issues. There is no discernible movement towards the East Asian Free-Trade Area proposed by the Philippines. But a growing number of bilateral and plurilateral agreements are being negotiated, notably by Japan, the second-largest national economy in the world and by far the largest in the region. Japan had relied completely on the multilateral system, but it is now actively pursuing preferential arrangements with South Korea, Singapore, Mexico and Canada. South Korea, the third-largest economy in the region—and also opposed to preferential deals in the past—is negotiating with New Zealand and Chile as well as Japan.

Similarly, the South-East Asians are negotiating the linkage of their ASEAN Free-Trade Area (AFTA) with the existing FTA of Australia and New Zealand. A North-East Asia Free-Trade Area of China, Japan and South Korea is being studied in all three countries, and might merge with AFTA into a grouping that covers the whole of East Asia.

Frustration, inspiration

Why have Dr Mahathir's EAEG, Japan's AMF and the long-dormant Asian trading-group idea sprung back to life at the outset of the 21st century? There are four basic reasons: the East Asian financial crisis; the failures of the WTO and of APEC to make headway on trade liberalisation; the positive inspiration provided by European integration (especially the euro); and a broad disquiet with the behaviour of both the United States and the European Union.

The single greatest catalyst for the new East Asian regionalism, and the reason it is moving most rapidly on the monetary side, is the financial crisis of 1997–98. Most East Asians feel that they were both let down and put upon by the West. In their view, western banks and other lenders created much of the crisis by pulling out. The leading financial powers then either declined to take part in the rescue operations, as the United States did in Thailand, or built the much-ballyhooed "second lines of defence" so deviously that they could never be used.

At the same time, the IMF and the United States dictated much of the Asian response to the crisis. Fealty to the "Washington consensus" was seen as necessary to qualify for official help and to restore access to private capital markets. The visual symbol of all this, captured in a photograph sent round the world, was the managing director of the IMF looming over the president of Indonesia like some imperial tyrant from ages past. The widespread view that the IMF programmes made things worse, at least for a while—a view proclaimed by some economists in the West itself—makes Asians still more resentful. And Malaysia's recovery without the IMF implies that acceptance of the global norms may not have been so crucial after all.

This Asian perception of the events of 1997–99 is highly selective. Japanese banks were probably the biggest culprits in triggering the currency runs. Since most of the crisis countries are now recovering rapidly, the IMF programmes were basically successful. The United States kept its economy booming and its market open, accepting a huge further increase in its trade deficit. By contrast, Japan fell into recession and the yen plummeted. Japan's record trade surplus therefore rose even higher, and made the Asians' problems worse. However, inept American diplomacy failed to capitalise on these stark contrasts; and Japan recovered, at least in part, by pouring in government money to meet Asians' most urgent needs.

Whatever the right and wrongs of its opinions, East Asia has decided that it does not want to be in thrall to Washington or the West when trouble hits in future. It is not rejecting the multilateral institutions, let alone opting out of the international capital markets or the globalisation of trade—which it knows would weaken rather than strengthen its prospects. It seems to want to work with, and within the framework of, existing bodies.

But East Asia also clearly feels that multilateral institutions, on which it was previously willing to rely, are no longer infallible. It notes that its aggregate economy and external trade are about as large as those of the United States and the EU, and that its monetary reserves are much larger (see table). Hence it wants its own institutions, and a central say in its own fate. As East Asia regains its strength, it is determined never to be totally dependent again.

A bombshell from Seattle

Added impetus for this feeling comes from the failures of the global trading system. Unfortunately, all the East Asians, including China and Japan, continue to depend heavily on export expansion for their economic growth. The crisis countries have become even more dependent on exports as they struggle to recover.

In consequence, all these countries want better access to foreign markets. Moreover, they realise that there is a constant risk of a relapse towards protectionism if the system does not continue to liberalise. They know that the threat is particularly acute in the United States, their largest market, where domestic support for new liberalisation has been bogged down for five years despite a buoyant economy,

Three-way balance

1997, $bn

	Output			
	market exchange rates	purchasing-power parity	Trade with rest of world	Official monetary Reserves
East Asia*	6,382	9,431	1,380	668
EU	8,093	7,559	1,640	380
United States	7,834	7,665	1,586	71†

*ASEAN 10 plus China, Japan and South Korea
†With gold at official value of $42.42 per ounce; total would be about $140bn with gold valued at market price
Source: F. Bergsten

and where the trade deficit is heading towards $500 billion. They see the EU, too, as distinctly unenthusiastic about further liberalisation.

Not only Seattle failed. Trade talks through APEC have stalled for similar reasons, including American domestic drag and sharp differences between the United States and Japan. East Asians cannot envisage a revival of American leadership, or even active American participation, without the imposition of new conditions they strongly oppose, including serious agricultural reforms (resisted by Japan, South Korea and China) and trade-related labour and environmental standards (rejected by virtually all developing countries in the region). They note that the United States failed to follow up its own "P5" initiative (with Australia, Chile, New Zealand and Singapore) at last year's APEC summit, though those countries were hand-picked to minimise grumbling at home.

For all these reasons, a growing number of Asians are turning to sub-regional trade pacts to get the liberalisation, and the insurance policies, they need. As yet, none of these pacts poses a particular threat to American or European trade interests. For that reason, they have not attracted much attention. But continued paralysis in the WTO and APEC could lead to a broadening of the new East Asian trade framework and a comprehensive East Asian FTA; or, at the least, a hook-up between China, Japan and South Korea in North-East Asia. Either of these would alter the structure of world trade.

This East Asian evolution is not happening in isolation. It is part of a broader pattern of preferential trade negotiations: for example, transatlantic ones between the EU and Mexico and the EU and Mercosur, and trans-pacific pairs such as Chile and South Korea and Canada and Singapore. These pacts are being negotiated around the United States, since America is unable, for the moment, to take part in new liberalising itself. Any new outbreak of American (or European) protectionism would of course give East Asia's efforts an extra push.

Wasn't Monnet a painter?

Yet those efforts are also meeting obstacles. The region contains vast differences in cultures, political systems and levels of economic development. There are at least as many designs and strategies for an East Asian partnership as there are countries in the region. And the atmosphere is charged with political distrust and even hostility, notably between China and Japan.

Moreover, most of the countries, even those in South-East Asia that have been linked institutionally through ASEAN for three decades, continue to see each other as competitors rather than partners. Protectionists in East Asia are no keener to liberalise with neighbours than on a broader scale. No leaders, individual or collective, have emerged to guide the process. Asians themselves joke that most of their compatriots think Monnet was a painter and Schuman a composer.

But not many observers, only a few years ago, would have predicted even the present modest degree of co-operation. And many Asian leaders are serious about going much farther. The European model is now widely admired, rather than disparaged for its bureaucracy. The rest of the world should realise what this evolution means, if it continues: eventual regional alignments which, even if they fall far short of Europe's integration, will be sufficiently advanced to create the tripartite world that has been expected, or feared, for some time.

An East Asian economic grouping could have many implications for the global system. At one extreme, it could reproduce much of the European experience. China and Japan, which have warred as viciously as France and Germany, could obliterate the possibility of future military rivalry and assure stability in what is, potentially, the world's most volatile area. Asian economic integration would create a formidable competitor, but also a huge stimulus to global growth, trade and investment. A uniting East Asia would be more likely to do its bit to ensure international peace than individual Asian countries acting alone, and could become an effective trilateral partner with the United States and Europe in managing the world economy.

At the other extreme, a unifying East Asia could become a highly disruptive force. With huge national savings and over $800 billion in monetary reserves by now, it could develop its own capital markets and increasingly ignore the advice, let alone the dictates, of the global financial institutions (as Europe has been able to do). East Asia is easily large enough to pursue regional development strategies and discriminate against outsiders (as Europe has also been able to do); and some of its trade deals will probably violate WTO rules by excluding agriculture and other sensitive sectors. The other big powers could decide to respond in kind, perhaps by reviving the idea of a Transatlantic Free-Trade Area that would discriminate against Asia. Any sign that East Asia is rejecting transpacific co-operation could strengthen isolationists in the United States and trigger an American retreat, from security arrangements as well as economic ones.

So Asian regionalism, like regionalism elsewhere, could go either way. The outcome will be determined by policy, both in East Asia and in other countries as they work out a response. The most likely result is an intermediate, quasi-European one: an East Asia with sufficient autonomy to allow independent action at times of crisis, but still co-operating with the rest of the world, in both economic and security terms, in normal times. It would probably side with the United States against Europe on some issues and with Europe against the United States on others, inducing each of the three to seek a permanent alliance with one of the other two. This, of course, exposes the inherent instability of a three-part configuration.

A first requirement for achieving cooperative evolution is for East Asians and outsiders to consult actively and candidly, perhaps with the United States in APEC and with Europe in ASEM (the Asia-Europe Meetings). Even Asians and non-Asians of an internationalist outlook are extremely wary of each others' intentions at this early stage. East Asians need to tell the world clearly what they think they are doing, and how they believe it fits in with the global and mega-regional (APEC) systems. Outsiders need to listen carefully and prod them, if possible, in an outward-looking direction.

The other obvious course is to energise and modify the existing global institutions in ways that would answer the complaints of East Asians and make them less eager to go off on their own. Reform of the international financial architecture needs to go deeper, and the multilateral trading system needs to be cranked into forward motion again. In addition, East Asia deserves a much larger presence in the IMF and the World Bank, where Europeans are ridiculously over-represented. The appointment of the deputy prime minister of Thailand as the next director-general of the WTO is a good sign, and Asians need to be increasingly considered for top posts in all the key institutions.

East Asian regional pacts and the global system could nonetheless work well together. Early warning and early action to prevent crises may be easier at the regional level; near neighbours tend to know the situation better, and may have more legitimacy when they ask their colleagues to take preventive measures. Contagion is largely a regional phenomenon, and standby financial facilities, used in conjunction with IMF lending, would avoid the need to cobble together ad hoc rescue packages. A properly structured Asian Monetary Fund could do much for the international financial system, just as the Asian Development Bank (and other regional development banks) have done for global development finance for over 30 years.

Sub-regional, and even East Asia-wide, trade agreements could catalyse the global trading system in the same way. Successive milestones in European integration, from the creation of the common market to the coming of the single market, did much to stimulate the three big post-war multilateral trade negotiations (the Kennedy, Tokyo and Uruguay Rounds). The creation of NAFTA and APEC helped persuade Europe to conclude the Uruguay Round. Positive responses by the United States and Europe to the new Asian trade pacts could both limit their discriminatory effects and embed them in revitalised global and Asia-Pacific regimes.

East Asia may be on the brink of an historic evolution, as Europe was half a century ago. Of course, Asians themselves must steer their efforts in directions that promote international stability. But it would be tragic if these initiatives were rejected rather than respected. The rest of the world must accept a global role for East Asia, and modify its own institutions with East Asia in mind. The success or failure of this process will do much to shape the world for the next 50 years.

Fred Bergsten is director of the Institute for International Economics in Washington, DC. From 1993 to 1995 he chaired the Eminent Persons Group of APEC, which developed APEC's strategy of "free and open trade and investment in the region by 2010–20".

Unit 9

Unit Selections

Key Points to Consider

❖ What can the United States and other Western countries do to facilitate the resumption of the peace process in the Middle East?

❖ What can the United States and other Western countries do to limit the appeal of Islamic fundamentalists such as Usama bin Laden who call for more terrorist acts against the United States?

❖ Explain why you do or do not favor lifting U.S.-backed economic sanctions on Iraq. Be sure to explain whether your position is guided more by humanitarian, pragmatic, national security, or other criteria.

❖ What can be done to promote peace and stability in the African conflicts such as those in the Great Lakes region of Africa?

❖ What can the United States and other Western countries do to promote democracy in Nigeria? In Zimbabwe?

❖ What are the shared characteristics of successful HIV/AIDS programs in African countries? Are there other measures that the United States, Western countries, or the international community can take to help stem the spread of the HIV virus in Africa?

Links

www.dushkin.com/online/

28. **Africa News Online**
    http://www.africanews.org
29. **ArabNet**
    http://www.arab.net
30. **Israel Information Service**
    http://www.accessv.com/~yehuda/

These sites are annotated on pages 4 and 5.

The fallout across the Middle East from the violent collapse of the Israeli-Palestinian peace negotiations in 2000 shows how much America's standing and leverage in the region has come to depend on its ability to deliver on this core issue. Rosemary Hollis, in "Frightening Fall-Out," notes that the United States had to turn to other players, from the UN Secretary General to the Russians and the European Union, to cope with this multifaceted crisis. Hollis warns that down the line, the price to be paid for this help may be acceptance of a more inclusive, multilateral approach to the pursuit of regional peace and security. But the crucial task of calming Israeli fears and balancing pragmatism and principle will remain primarily an American responsibility. In the meantime, the "Al Aqsa intifada" is creating new antagonisms between Israelis and Palestinians that will make a lasting peace agreement more difficult to achieve. Recent events have inflamed the whole Arab world. There are now very different views of the reasons for the failed peace process and few analysts predict an early return to negotiations.

The resumption of fighting between Israel and the Palestinians overshadowed important recent changes in several Arab states. The son of Syria's long-time dictator, Hafez Assad, assumed power after his father died in 2000. In Syria, much like in Morocco, Jordan, and Bahrain, young rulers recently took over from fathers with autocratic instincts. While all three are edging slowly towards freer societies, all face dilemmas about how to satisfy conflicting demands for economic and political change. The choices facing these new leaders are not simple. Throughout the region they face increased numbers of citizens who are disenchanted with the current political status quo. Many youths and some of their elders are embracing the ideology of radical Islamacists.

The terrorist bombing of the USS *Cole* in Aden harbor in October 2000 and the bombing of U.S. embassies in Kenya and Tanzania during the summer of 1998 are both alleged to be the work of supporters of the radical Islamacist, Usama bin Ladin. In "License to Kill: Usama bin Ladin's Declaration of Jihad," Bernard Lewis emphasizes the importance of Americans' understanding what drives Islamic extremists. Lewis describes how the main Islamacists' grievance—the infidel U.S. troops in Arabia—was published in a little-noticed declaration of *jihad* by Usama bin Ladin in an Arabic newspaper prior to the bombings. Most Muslims reject this declaration as a gross distortion of America's role in the region and also for advocating the use of terrorism. However, the few who accept the extreme interpretation will continue to use terrorism in the future to rid the region of infidels.

Recurring U.S.-Iraqi confrontations since the Persian Gulf War peaked in mid-December 1998 when the United States and Great Britain launched military strikes against Iraq in response to Iraq's lack of cooperation with UN weapons inspectors. Subsequent efforts to reach a new set of terms to permit UN weapons inspectors to re-enter Iraq failed. While the United States and Great Britain continue to maintain the no-fly zones over southern and northern Iraq, pressures were building throughout the international community in 1999 to lift more of the sanctions on Iraq for humanitarian reasons. Iraq now sells some oil abroad under the terms of a UN-sponsored oil-for-food program.

Especially before the implementation of the oil-for-food program, UN sanctions on Iraq placed a moral crisis before the international community as continued international sanctions hit the young and weak in Iraq especially hard. A fundamental paradox of this conflict is that a decade of bombing and sanctions strengthened, rather than weakened, Saddam, who uses a permanent state of war to strengthen his power base. In "The Trap That Suits Saddam—and the U.S.," two *Washington Post* reporters, who recently visited 15 of Iraq's 18 provinces, describe how the status quo standoff between Baghdad and Washington suits all parties concerned, except for the vast majority of Iraq's 23 million people. These reporters warn that the long-term costs for all sides are great and growing. Sanctions have decimated the middle class as well as the children, and for now, the peoples' anger is directed at Washington. Sanctions have also eroded respect for the powers of the UN and the United States while not necessarily preventing Saddam Hussein from reconstituting covert weapons of mass destruction capabilities. Western intelligence sources warn that Hussein has rebuilt a covert chemical and biological weapons operation. Reports that Hussein offered to launch weapons of mass destruction against Israel if a neighboring state would permit him to place missiles on their territory after the resumption of fighting between Israel and the Palestinians add credence to these recent intelligence warnings.

Generalizations about political and economic trends in sub-Saharan Africa are difficult to make because conditions vary widely among countries and between sectors in the same country. Many countries in sub-Saharan Africa are neither on the verge of widespread anarchy nor at the dawn of democratic and economic renewal. Economic growth in Africa is stronger today than in the disastrous 1980s but most countries have been adversely affected by the downturn in many commodity prices during the late 1990s. Clinton's talk of "a new African renaissance" during his historic visit in March of 1998 seemed premature. Most African economies remain highly fragile and dependent on world commodity prices and other forces beyond the control of their national policy makers.

In several ongoing conflicts in African states, restoration of political stability is likely to require a substantial modification of the territorial and political status quo as well as extensive involvement by UN peacekeepers. Eritrea and Ethiopia finally reached agreement on the terms of a lasting peace settlement in 2000 but both countries must now cope with the consequences of massive deaths incurred during their border war.

Concerns that UN peacekeepers might be unable to stop rebels from regaining control of the capital of Sierra Leone after an internationally sponsored peace agreement broke down led the British to send troops during the summer of 2000. The UN continues to struggle to find nation-states willing to send troops to Sierra Leone to boost the size of the peacekeeping force of 13,000 to over 20,000. At the same time UN efforts to stop the sale of diamonds from Liberia failed to stem a conflict that had spread to neighboring Guinea by the end of 2000.

Neither the United Nations nor the major regional organization in southern Africa, the Southern African Development Organization (SADO), has been able to obtain the withdrawal of foreign troops or help broker a lasting cease-fire among combatants in the Democratic Republic of the Congo. A series of interrelated clashes throughout the Great Lakes region since the mid-1990s have led many observers to label the situation as the first continental conflict in modern Africa. The difficulties encountered by the UN in their efforts to send peacekeepers to monitor the cease-fire along the Eritrea-Ethiopian border, to maintain order in Sierra Leone, or to enforce a multilateral cease-fire in the Congo raises serious questions about who will play the role of peacekeeper in Africa in the future.

In "Africa's Security Issues Through 2010" a senior United States Defense Intelligence Officer for Africa, William Thom, reviews emerging security trends in sub-Saharan Africa and predicts that interstate warfare will increase even though disparities in military power on the African continent will continue to increase. William Thom also predicts that transnational criminality and war will become virtually indistinguishable because both are fueled by economic insurgents, warlords for profit, lawless zones harboring criminals, and armies of child soldiers whose political socialization consists of learning how to brutalize and murder civilians. While Thom believes that policing these messy situations will become an international priority, he predicts that some places will remain beyond the reach of Western moral consciousness and continue to experience low intensity conflict indefinitely.

Despite these gloomy forecasts, relatively peaceful and dramatic political changes in several African countries have occurred as a result of grassroots demands for democracy in recent years. However, in other recent elections civilian and military leaders of the ruling elite have managed to retain power in manipulated multiparty elections. General Robert Guei, a military coup leader who won the presidential election by manipulating the election process in Côte d'Ivoire, was forced to flee the country by popular protests that were remarkably similar to the popular outcry that broke out after the rigged elections a few weeks before in Serbia during 2000. After 40 years of Socialist Party rule, the opposition party leader, Abdoulaye Wade of the Senegalese Democratic Party, won a victory with over 60 percent of the vote in a peaceful run-off election in 2000.

These recent elections are only two of several peaceful regime changes that have occurred since the two political giants of Africa, Nigeria and South Africa, experienced relatively peaceful national elections in 1999. Thabo Mbeki won the presidential election in South Africa and replaced Nelson Mandela. Democratically elected civilian rule also returned to Nigeria in 1999. However, peaceful political change is proving to be a difficult process in both political systems. Parliamentary and local elections in South Africa during 2000 indicated that coloured and white voters are supporting the opposition Democratic Alliance in larger numbers while most black South Africans continue to support the ruling African National Congress Party. Support for the ruling ANC Party across the ethnic spectrum is less today than during the heady days of transition in the mid-1990s, as reports of corrupt government officials and the inability of the ANC government to deliver jobs and decent housing for the majority of South Africans persist. A similar disenchantment with the new democratic regime is evident in Nigeria. As Minabere Ibelema describes in "Nigeria: The Politics of Marginalization," optimism associated with the election of a civilian president, Olusegun Obsanjo, after 14 years of military rule in Nigeria was quickly replaced by ethnic agitation and conflict as virtually all regions and nationalities claim to be marginalized. Ibelema concludes that Nigeria's future well-being will require accommodations and perceptions of adequate representation by all Nigeria's ethnic groups.

Many analysts have observed that another Southern African country, Zimbabwe, has been ripe for revolution in recent years. The current president, Robert Mugabe, faced growing political opposition at the polls, in parliament, and from political demonstrators during 2000. Clashes between Mugabe's supporters and those of the opposition Movement for Democratic Change continue to increase. The comparatively well-run, well-off country that Robert Mugabe inherited is now a corruption-riddled, autocratic mess sent into economic free-fall by its kleptomaniacal president's whims—including tampering with elections, sending troops to the Democratic Republic of the Congo, and hiring thugs to invade and take over white-owned farms.

The diversity of responses to recent demands for democratic reforms suggest that countries of sub-Saharan Africa will sometimes resolve demands for democracy in peaceful ways that approximate democratic practices in Western states, and sometimes resolve political conflicts in ways that will not be acceptable to the international community. What, if anything, the international community should do in these latter cases remains in dispute.

The tragedy in many African states today is that the government must cope simultaneously with fragile economies, demands for democratic reforms, and ethnic tensions at the same time that they are being forced to confront a spreading HIV/AIDS epidemic. In parts of east and southern Africa, the HIV epidemic is reducing life expectancy, raising mortality, lowering fertility, and leaving millions of orphans in its wake. There are many unknowns in the effects of the HIV epidemic on the demographic equation but one thing is certain: it is not being given the priority it deserves by either the countries most affected or within the international community. This is unacceptable because many of the remedies are now obvious. The authors of "A Turning-Point for AIDS?" note that the 13th AIDS conference in Durban, South Africa, in July 2000 illustrated that AIDS is also a political disease. The goal of this conference was to "break the silence" about a disease that, like war, kills those in the prime of life. Today, 25 million of the 34 million infected people in the world live in Africa. While the result of AIDS in Africa is extreme social dislocation, the situation is not hopeless. The contrasting experiences of Uganda and Senegal regarding anti-AIDS programs suggest that it is never too late to act. Good science and sensible public policy can defeat this modern pandemic.

Frightening fall-out

The violent collapse of Israeli-Palestinian peace negotiations revealed how exclusive and narrowly focused the US-brokered process had become. The fall-out across the Middle East shows how much America's standing and leverage in the region has come to depend on its ability to deliver on this core issue. In short, the whole multi-faceted crisis provides food for thought on the extent and limits of US influence in the region.

Rosemary Hollis

ARAB SUPPORT FOR THE US-led coalition that expelled Iraq from Kuwait in 1991 with UN blessing was based on an understanding that the international community in general and the United States in particular would turn to comprehensive peace-making on the Arab-Israeli front. This task was indeed embraced, beginning with the Madrid conference of November 1991. It was convened on the basis of the relevant UN resolutions, and under the joint patronage of Washington and Moscow, with the Europeans in attendance.

The following eighteen months saw tortuous negotiations conducted simultaneously between Israel, its Arab neighbours and the Palestinians. Meanwhile, multilateral talks allowed broad regional and international involvement.

FEW AT THE TABLE

This multi-track approach was clearly complex and unwieldy, so when separate and secret talks between Israel and the Palestine Liberation Organisation (PLO) produced a breakthrough in Oslo in 1993, Washington greeted the news with alacrity and adopted the so-called Oslo process as the lynchpin of the broader quest for peace. Syria, Lebanon and Jordan were less thrilled that PLO Chairman Yasser Arafat had circumvented the Madrid formula, and so they pursued their own interests unilaterally.

Thus it was that the Middle East Peace Process was progressively narrowed down until, by the time President Bill Clinton convened the Camp David summit in July this year, he, the Israeli Prime Minister, Ehud Barak, and Palestinian leader, Yasser Arafat, together with their aides, were the only ones at the table.

Thanks to the Oslo accords, Arafat was elected president of the Palestinians in the West Bank and Gaza Strip. It also brought him full autonomy in nearly twenty percent of these areas, including the main Palestinian cities, plus shared control, with Israeli security forces, of just over another twenty percent. Yet his leverage as a peace-maker depends on his capacity to deliver Palestinian acceptance of a final status agreement. His standing in the community in turn depends on what the process produces and his popularity ratings have been tempered by resentment of his security apparatus and corruption in his administration.

MAKING DEALS

At Camp David the relevant UN resolutions were the backdrop to the discussions only in so far as the deal envisaged would involve an exchange of land for peace. The 'right of return' for Palestinian refugees enshrined in UN Resolution 194 of 1948 was expected to be traded for Palestinian statehood, while UN resolutions referring to Jerusalem were treated as marginal in the formulae mooted for sharing parts of the eastern side of the city.

This is not to say that any deal must adhere to UN resolutions in order to be workable. Indeed, throughout the years of negotiations since Madrid the United States has maintained that the key to arriving at a solution is to find and cement areas of agreement between the core parties to the conflict and build forward to peaceful coexistence. What counts is the agreement of the protagonists today not the views of UN members in times past. However, it may be worth looking at how a deal which departs from expectations and norms embodied in international law would be received in the region and beyond.

Had Camp David produced an agreement which challenged accumulated international conventions and precedent, that would have implications for conflicts and rights issues elsewhere, particularly in relation to refugees. Specifically in the Middle East it could undermine efforts to enforce UN resolutions dealing with other problems, for example with regard to Iraq.

Clearly the United States sought to find a balance between upholding principles and managing practicalities. In

From *The World Today,* November 2000, pp. 7-8.

fact, the kind of agreement suggested by Ehud Barak at Camp David marked a departure from stated Israeli positions, especially on Jerusalem. This could have run aground in the referendum to which Barak had committed on any final status agreement.

The Israeli Prime Minister went out on a limb and he, like President Clinton, was duly exasperated when Arafat turned him down. Seemingly, the Palestinian leader was afraid that he would be pilloried if not killed if he failed to deliver on Arab and Muslim aspirations, especially, but not only, on the holy sites in Jerusalem.

ATTENTION AND SYMPATHY

There has been much speculation about Arafat's desire to preserve his image as champion of the Palestinian cause, even at the expense of passing up the most generous proposals he could hope for from the Israelis. Yet Arafat was reportedly reluctant to go to Camp David at all in July, fearing that the ground was not sufficiently prepared for a conclusive agreement. In any case, he is now charged with wanting a new Palestinian uprising to strengthen his bargaining position, even though the visit of hardline Likud leader Ariel Sharon to the Muslim Haram al-Sharif, on the same site as the Jewish Temple Mount, provided genuine provocation.

The sight of stone throwing civilians and rifle-toting Fatah youth pitted against Israeli tanks and helicopter gunships, has undoubtedly won the Palestinians international sympathy and attention. However, if the bloodletting was deliberately invited, the tactic has not narrowed the divide between the protagonists. The subsequent conflagration has hardened attitudes on both sides and all but demolished the Israeli peace camp. The more plausible explanation for Arafat's strategy is that his authority among the Palestinians depends on his capacity to read the public mood and act accordingly. He can orchestrate but not assuage Palestinian anger single-handedly.

Arafat himself chose Oslo over Madrid and thereby ended up dependent on what the United States could help him secure from the Israelis. He may now rue the day. Under US stewardship the Oslo process has brought together a small circle of elite strategists, but not their populations. Now both sides have regrouped and reintegrated on their respective fronts. Meanwhile, the Palestinians have received new expressions of solidarity from across the Arab and wider Muslim world.

RESENTMENT

The anti-American character of pro-Palestinian demonstrations in the Middle East is about more than US custodianship of the Oslo process and the sense that this has served Israeli interests better than Palestinian aspirations. There are other causes for resentment against the United States.

Since the liberation of Kuwait in 1991 US forces have maintained a presence in the Gulf region. They have pre-positioned military supplies in Arab Gulf states and conducted joint exercises with these countries as well as Egypt and Jordan. The justification for this arrangement has been containment of Iraq and Iran. US as well as British forces still patrol the so-called 'no-fly' zones over Iraq and periodically bomb Iraqi targets in retaliation for anti-aircraft fire. The United States is also committed to maintaining UN-imposed sanctions on Iraq so long as the government of Saddam Hussein endures.

PRAGMATISM AND PRINCIPLE

The fall-out from this has been two-fold. On the one hand there is popular sympathy in the Arab countries for the continued suffering of the Iraqi people, coupled with resentment that Iraq is being punished in the name of upholding UN resolutions. On the other the perception has taken hold that the US presence is to protect American interests and autocratic Arab regimes at the expense of broader Arab and Muslim sensitivities and aspirations.

Meanwhile, high population growth rates in Arab countries have not been matched by increased job opportunities, while accusations of corruption in high places and inequitable wealth distribution are commonplace. Seemingly fearful of what frustrations greater political freedoms could unleash in their countries, Arab governments have fought shy of expanding participation in decision-making.

The one issue on which popular demonstrations are generally permitted is the Arab-Israeli conflict. Along with expressions of hatred toward the Israelis comes anger at the US role in the affairs of the region. It is no surprise, therefore, that the United States has bowed to the renewed involvement of other players, from the UN Secretary General to the Russians and European Union in calming the crisis on the Israeli-Palestinian front.

Down the line, the price to be paid by Washington for this help in extremity may well be acceptance of a more inclusive, multilateral approach to the pursuit of regional peace and security. But if so, the crucial task of calming Israeli fears will still fall to the Americans and the fundamental dilemma of balancing pragmatism and principle will re-emerge.

Dr. Rosemary Hollis is Head of the Middle East Programme at Chatham House.

License To Kill

Usama bin Ladin's Declaration of Jihad

Bernard Lewis

On February 23, 1998, *Al-Quds al-Arabi,* an Arabic newspaper published in London, printed the full text of a "Declaration of the World Islamic Front for Jihad against the Jews and the Crusaders." According to the paper, the statement was faxed to them under the signatures of Usama bin Ladin, the Saudi financier blamed by the United States for masterminding the August bombings of its embassies in East Africa, and the leaders of militant Islamist groups in Egypt, Pakistan, and Bangladesh. The statement—a magnificent piece of eloquent, at times even poetic Arabic prose—reveals a version of history that most Westerners will find unfamiliar. Bin Ladin's grievances are not quite what many would expect.

The declaration begins with an exordium quoting the more militant passages in the Quran and the sayings of the Prophet Muhammad, then continues:

> Since God laid down the Arabian peninsula, created its desert, and surrounded it with its seas, no calamity has ever befallen it like these Crusader hosts that have spread in it like locusts, crowding its soil, eating its fruits, and destroying its verdure; and this at a time when the nations contend against the Muslims like diners jostling around a bowl of food.

The statement goes on to talk of the need to understand the situation and act to rectify it. The facts, it says, are known to everyone and fall under three main headings:

> First—For more than seven years the United States is occupying the lands of Islam in the holiest of its territories, Arabia, plundering its riches, overwhelming its rulers, humiliating its people, threatening its neighbors, and using its bases in the peninsula as a spearhead to fight against the neighboring Islamic peoples.
>
> Though some in the past have disputed the true nature of this occupation, the people of Arabia in their entirety have now recognized it.
>
> There is no better proof of this than the continuing American aggression against the Iraqi people, launched from Arabia despite its rulers, who all oppose the use of their territories for this purpose but are subjugated.
>
> Second—Despite the immense destruction inflicted on the Iraqi people at the hands of the Crusader-Jewish alliance and in spite of the appalling number of dead, exceeding a million, the Americans nevertheless, in spite of all this, are trying once more to repeat this dreadful slaughter. It seems that the long blockade following after a fierce war, the dismemberment and the destruction are not enough for them. So they come again today to destroy what remains of this people and to humiliate their Muslim neighbors.
>
> Third—While the purposes of the Americans in these wars are religious and economic, they also serve the petty state of the Jews, to divert attention from their occupation of Jerusalem and their killing of Muslims in it.

Reprinted by permission of *Foreign Affairs,* November/December 1998, pp. 14-19.

> There is no better proof of all this than their eagerness to destroy Iraq, the strongest of the neighboring Arab states, and their attempt to dismember all the states of the region, such as Iraq and Saudi Arabia and Egypt and Sudan, into petty states, whose division and weakness would ensure the survival of Israel and the continuation of the calamitous Crusader occupation of the lands of Arabia.

These crimes, the statement declares, amount to "a clear declaration of war by the Americans against God, his Prophet, and the Muslims." In such a situation, the declaration says, the *ulema*—authorities on theology and Islamic law, or *sharia*—throughout the centuries unanimously ruled that when enemies attack the Muslim lands, jihad becomes every Muslim's personal duty.

In the technical language of the *ulema,* religious duties may be collective, to be discharged by the community as a whole, or personal, incumbent on every individual Muslim. In an offensive war, the religious duty of jihad is collective and may be discharged by volunteers and professionals. When the Muslim community is defending itself, however, jihad becomes an individual obligation.

After quoting various Muslim authorities, the signatories then proceed to the final and most important part of their declaration, the *fatwa,* or ruling. It holds that

> To kill Americans and their allies, both civil and military, is an individual duty of every Muslim who is able, in any country where this is possible, until the Aqsa Mosque [in Jerusalem] and the Haram Mosque [in Mecca] are freed from their grip and until their armies, shattered and broken-winged, depart from all the lands of Islam, incapable of threatening any Muslim.

After citing some further relevant Quranic verses, the document continues:

> By God's leave, we call on every Muslim who believes in God and hopes for reward to obey God's command to kill the Americans and plunder their possessions wherever he finds them and whenever he can. Likewise we call on the Muslim *ulema* and leaders and youth and soldiers to launch attacks against the armies of the American devils and against those who are allied with them from among the helpers of Satan.

The declaration and *fatwa* conclude with a series of further quotations from Muslim scripture.

INFIDELS

Bin Ladin's view of the Gulf War as American aggression against Iraq may seem a little odd, but it is widely—though by no means universally—accepted in the Islamic world. For holy warriors of any faith, the faithful are always right and the infidels always wrong, whoever the protagonists and whatever the circumstances of their encounter.

The three areas of grievance listed in the declaration—Arabia, Iraq, and Jerusalem—will be familiar to observers of the Middle Eastern scene. What may be less familiar is the sequence and emphasis. For Muslims, as we in the West sometimes tend to forget but those familiar with Islamic history and literature know, the holy land par excellence is Arabia—Mecca, where the Prophet was born; Medina, where he established the first Muslim state; and the Hijaz, whose people were the first to rally to the new faith and become its standard-bearers. Muhammad lived and died in Arabia, as did the Rashidun caliphs, his immediate successors at the head of the Islamic community. Thereafter, except for a brief interlude in Syria, the center of the Islamic world and the scene of its major achievements was Iraq, the seat of the caliphate for half a millennium. For Muslims, no piece of land once added to the realm of Islam can ever be finally renounced, but none compares in significance with Arabia and Iraq.

Of these two, Arabia is by far the more important. The classical Arabic historians tell us that in the year 20 after the *hijra* (Muhammad's move from Mecca to Medina), corresponding to 641 of the Christian calendar, the Caliph Umar decreed that Jews and Christians should be removed from Arabia to fulfill an injunction the Prophet uttered on his deathbed: "Let there not be two religions in Arabia." The people in question were the Jews of the oasis of Khaybar in the north and the Christians of Najran in the south. Both were ancient and deep-rooted communities, Arab in their speech, culture, and way of life, differing from their neighbors only in their faith.

The saying attributed to the Prophet was impugned by some earlier Islamic authorities. But it was generally accepted as authentic, and Umar put it into effect. The expulsion of religious minorities is extremely rare in Islamic history—unlike medieval Christendom, where evictions of Jews and (after the reconquest of Spain) Muslims were normal and frequent. Compared with European expulsions, Umar's decree was both limited and compassionate. It did not include southern and southeastern Arabia, which were not seen as part of Islam's holy land. And unlike the Jews and Muslims driven out of Spain and other European countries to find what refuge they could elsewhere, the Jews and Christians of Arabia were resettled on lands assigned to them—the Jews in Syria, the Christians in Iraq. The process was also gradual rather than sudden, and there are reports of Jews and Christians remaining in Khaybar and Najran for some time after Umar's edict.

But the decree was final and irreversible, and from then until now the holy land of the Hijaz has been forbidden territory for non-Muslims. According to the Hanbali school of Islamic jurisprudence, accepted by both the Saudis and the declaration's signatories, for a non-Muslim even to set foot on the sacred soil is a major offense. In the rest of the kingdom, non-Muslims, while admitted as temporary visitors, were not permitted to establish residence or practice their religion.

The history of the Crusades provides a vivid example of the relative importance of Arabia and other places in Islamic perceptions. The Crusaders' capture of Jerusalem in 1099 was a triumph for Christendom and a disaster for the city's Jews. But to judge by the Arabic historiography of the period, it aroused scant interest in the region. Appeals for help by local Muslims to Damascus and Baghdad went unanswered, and the newly established Crusader principalities from Antioch to Jerusalem soon fitted into the game of Levantine politics, with cross-religious alliances forming a pattern of rivalries between and among Muslim and Christian princes.

The great counter-Crusade that ultimately drove the Crusaders into the sea did not begin until almost a century later. Its immediate cause was the activities of a freebooting Crusader leader, Reynald of Châtillon, who held the fortress of Kerak, in southern Jordan, between 1176 and 1187 and used it to launch a series of raids against Muslim caravans and commerce in the adjoining regions, including the Hijaz. Historians of the Crusades are probably right in saying that Reynald's motive was primarily economic—the desire for loot. But Muslims saw his campaigns as a provocation, a challenge directed against Islam's holy places. In 1182, violating an agreement between the Crusader king of Jerusalem and the Muslim leader Saladin, Reynald attacked and looted Muslim caravans, including one of pilgrims bound for Mecca. Even more heinous, from a Muslim point of view, was his threat to Arabia and a memorable buccaneering expedition in the Red Sea, featuring attacks on Muslim shipping and the Hijaz ports that served Mecca and Medina. Outraged, Saladin proclaimed a jihad against the Crusaders.

Even in Christian Europe, Saladin was justly celebrated and admired for his chivalrous and generous treatment of his defeated enemies. His magnanimity did not extend to Reynald of Châtillon. The great Arab historian Ibn al-Athir wrote, "Twice, [Saladin said,] I had made a vow to kill him if I had him in my hands; once when he tried to march on Mecca and Medina, and again when he treacherously captured the caravan." After Saladin's triumph, when many of the Crusader princes and chieftains were taken captive, he separated Reynald of Châtillon from the rest and beheaded him with his own hands.

After the success of the jihad and the recapture of Jerusalem, Saladin and his successors seem to have lost interest in the city. In 1229, one of them even ceded Jerusalem to the Emperor Frederick II as part of a general compromise agreement between the Muslim ruler and the Crusaders. Jerusalem was retaken in 1244 after the Crusaders tried to make it a purely Christian city, then eventually became a minor provincial town. Widespread interest in Jerusalem was reawakened only in the nineteenth century, first by the European powers' quarrels over custody of the Christian holy places and then by new waves of Jewish immigration after 1882.

In Arabia, however, the next perceived infidel threat came in the eighteenth century with the consolidation of European power in South Asia and the reappearance of Christian ships off the shores of Arabia. The resulting sense of outrage was at least one of the elements in the religious revival inspired in Arabia by the puritanical Wahhabi movement and led by the House of Saud, the founders of the modern Saudi state. During the period of Anglo-French domination of the Middle East, the imperial powers ruled Iraq, Syria, Palestine, Egypt, and Sudan. They nibbled at the fringes of Arabia, in Aden and the trucial sheikhdoms of the Gulf, but were wise enough to have no military and minimal political involvement in the affairs of the peninsula.

Oil made that level of involvement totally inadequate, and a growing Western presence, predominantly American, began to transform every aspect of Arabian life. The Red Sea port of Jiddah had long served as a kind of religious quarantine area in which foreign diplomatic, consular, and commercial representatives were allowed to live. The discovery and exploitation of oil—and the consequent growth of the Saudi capital, Riyadh, from small oasis town to major metropolis—brought a considerable influx of foreigners. Their presence, still seen by many as a desecration, planted the seeds for a growing mood of resentment.

As long as this foreign involvement was exclusively economic, and as long as the rewards were more than adequate to soothe every grievance, the alien presence could be borne. But in recent years both have changed. With the fall in oil prices and the rise in population and expenditure, the rewards are no longer adequate and the grievances have become more numerous and more vocal. Nor is the involvement limited to economic activities. The revolution in Iran and the wars of Saddam Hussein have added political and military dimensions to the foreign involvement and have lent some plausibility to the increasingly heard cries of "imperialism." Where their holy land is involved, many Muslims tend to define the struggle—and sometimes also the enemy—in religious terms, seeing the American troops sent to free Kuwait and save Saudi Arabia from Saddam Hussein as infidel invaders and occupiers. This perception is heightened by America's unquestioned primacy among the powers of the infidel world.

TRAVESTIES

To most Americans, the declaration is a travesty, a gross distortion of the nature and purpose of the American presence in Arabia. They should also know that for many—perhaps most—Muslims, the declaration is an equally grotesque travesty of the nature of Islam and even of its doctrine of jihad. The Quran speaks of peace as well as of war. The hundreds of thousands of traditions and sayings attributed with varying reliability to the Prophet, interpreted in various ways by the *ulema,* offer a wide range of guidance. The militant and violent interpretation is one among many. The standard juristic treatises on *sharia* normally contain a chapter on jihad, understood in the military sense as regular warfare against infidels and apostates. But these treatises prescribe correct behavior and respect for the rules of war in such matters as the opening and termination of hostilities and the treatment of noncombatants and prisoners, not to speak of diplomatic envoys. The jurists also discuss—and sometimes differ on—the actual conduct of war. Some permit, some restrict, and some disapprove of the use of mangonels, poisoned arrows, and the poisoning of enemy water supplies—the missile and chemical warfare of the Middle Ages—out of concern for the indiscriminate casualties that these weapons inflict. At no point do the basic texts of Islam enjoin terrorism and murder. At no point do they even consider the random slaughter of uninvolved bystanders.

Nevertheless, some Muslims are ready to approve, and a few of them to apply, the declaration's extreme interpretation of their religion. Terrorism requires only a few. Obviously, the West must defend itself by whatever means will be effective. But in devising strategies to fight the terrorists, it would surely be useful to understand the forces that drive them.

BERNARD LEWIS is Cleveland E. Dodge Professor Emeritus of Near Eastern Studies at Princeton University. His books include *The Arabs in History, The Emergence of Modern Turkey,* and, most recently, *The Middle East: A Brief History of the Last 2,000 Years.*

The Trap That Suits Saddam—and the U.S.

By Warren P. Strobel *and* Kevin Whitelaw

In the northern Iraqi city of Irbil, greengrocer Muhammad Hadi offers political analysis along with the bananas, grapes and cucumbers that cascade from his sidewalk cart. Leaders in far-off Washington "want Saddam Hussein to remain in power," he says matter-of-factly. "This is good for their interests." It's a conspiracy theory that's common in Iraq's souks, which makes it tempting to dismiss. Yet there is a germ of truth in what Hadi says.

On a trip to Iraq, during which we had unusual access from the Kurdish enclave in the north to the Persian Gulf coast in the south, we became convinced of a dirty little secret about U.S. policy toward Iraq: The status quo suits all parties concerned, thank you very much. All parties, that is, except the vast majority of Iraq's 23 million people. But unfortunately for the United States, hewing to the status quo could have disastrous unintended consequences as well.

Both inside the Clinton administration and in Baghdad, there is a lot of *Sturm and Drang* about the possibility of an election-year confrontation. (It was four years ago this fall that Saddam Hussein struck against the Kurds, demolishing a CIA-funded opposition effort and prompting an ineffective missile strike from Washington.) Earlier this month, Hussein's usual bluster was punctuated with incursions by Iraqi jets into Saudi Arabia, and his charges that Kuwait is stealing Iraq's oil are eerily reminiscent of 1990. Washington has mobilized a Patriot missile defense unit for quick dispatch to Israel and issued the now-standard warnings to the Mustachioed One.

A new crisis is always possible. Hussein's craving for the limelight is second only to his survival instinct. But behind the headlines, an odd balance has settled over the standoff between Baghdad and Washington—a sort of codependency now entering its second decade. Secretary of State Madeleine K. Albright underscored this when she announced 10 days ago that the Clinton administration would not use force to compel Hussein to accept the return of U.N. weapons inspectors. We can almost see Hadi nodding his head.

From the viewpoint of all the major players, at least in the short term, there is much to like about the current stalemate.

Consider the Iraqi leader. It's not news that the 10-year-old U.N. sanctions on Iraq, which have done such damage to Iraqi society, no longer seem to threaten his grip on power. But we were surprised to discover just how much the sanctions are helping Hussein. He would be happy to see an end to the embargo. But in the meantime, with oil prices at their highest in a decade, he and his supporters have come to rely on oil smuggling for their skyrocketing wealth.

On a driving tour of the Iraqi capital, we were amazed at the Beverly Hills–style mansions rising in the fashionable Mansour district. (No pictures, please; too many VIPs, our ever-present "minders" from the Ministry of Information warned us.) Walking past sparkling new stores with cosmetics, jet skis and high-tech televisions piled high, we saw how comfortable life has become for Hussein and his sycophants. "You can get anything you want here if you can afford it," says George Sommerwill, the U.N. spokesman in Baghdad.

For the perpetually neglected Kurdish minority, times are also good. The same sanctions regime, along with the four-year-old U.N. program that allows Iraq to sell oil to purchase food and medicines, has, ironically, made the Kurdish areas in the north more stable and prosperous than in decades. That's because Hadi and 3.5 million other Kurds get a 13-percent cut of oil-for-food revenues. They also have come to rely on a brisk oil smuggling business across the Turkish border. Tanker trucks line up by the hundreds to enter Iraq and fill up with the illegal export. "It's our share!" our local guide insisted when asked whether the oil is legal under U.N. sanctions. The Kurds also "tax" the goods that illegally enter Iraq from Turkey. With aid workers building schools and hospitals, and American jets patrolling the skies above northern Iraq, the Kurds are not about to be on the leading edge of another risky effort to overthrow Hussein.

And for the Clinton administration? Oil-for-food has muted some of the international condemnation of the United States for the sanctions. More importantly for the White House, it can claim to have kept Hussein "in his box." This neutralizes what could otherwise be an election-year hazard for Vice President Gore. Despite occasional criticism that the administration's Iraq policy is on autopilot, Clinton and his top aides are relieved to be beyond the cycle of crises over weapons inspections that led to the Operation Desert Fox bombing campaign in December 1998. This explains Albright's having ruled out the use of force. With the Iraqi military weakened by the sanctions and Hussein at least appearing to be contained, senior U.S. policymakers can more comfortably ignore Iraq and focus on other crises.

Prolonging the current policy of sanctions also helps appease a Congress that in 1998 funded Iraqi opposition groups attempting to overthrow Hussein. But despite isolated outbreaks of revolt over the last two years, the Iraqi internal security services are thriving and the re-

Reprinted from the *Washington Post,* September 24, 2000, pp. B1-B2.

gime's confidence is high. It seems every police car is a brand-new Hyundai, and Hussein's soldiers sport crisp, new uniforms. As American journalists, we feared the authorities would sequester us in Baghdad, but within two days of our arrival we each received permission to travel all around Iraq for a week before returning to Baghdad. (Of course, we were always accompanied by our minders. Sometimes, it seemed, even the minders had minders.)

After interviews with several government officials, we quickly began to understand just how confident and self-satisfied Hussein is these days. A.K. Hashimi is a veteran regime figure, given to bombast, and often trotted out to feed the government line to visiting journalists. "Our situation is much better than it was a year ago," he told us. "We are breathing better." Perhaps realizing he had gone too far (in official Iraqi propaganda, after all, the sanctions are supposed to be devastating), he clammed up and refused to elaborate. Iraq's deputy oil minister even bragged about how sanctions have been good for the oil industry in certain ways, having forced Iraqis to develop a domestic capability rather than rely on foreign oil firms.

The status quo might be the policy path of least resistance for Washington, but the long-term costs for all sides are great—and growing. Because Iraq has become so isolated, most of these are invisible to Americans. Sanctions have decimated the middle class—usually the source of leaders who might challenge the government. Iraqi schools are crumbling—UNICEF says up to half are unfit for learning. Iraqis have just suffered through their hottest and driest summer in recent memory—temperatures regularly topped 120 degrees—with daily power cuts in most of the country. (We did notice, however, that certain privileged parts of Baghdad, and Hussein's palaces, never seemed to go dark.) While food is more plentiful these days, child mortality remains dangerously high. Many people have sold their household belongings just to get by. We met a man wearing 17-year-old trousers and children clad in shredded shirts.

Life is toughest on the young, who are often obliged to drop out of school to help their families. "There are no dreams anymore," said Jassan Abdul-Hassan, 23, a shop clerk playing soccer on a pebble-strewn dirt field in the seething slum of Saddam City on the outskirts of Baghdad. A desperately poor enclave of 2 million, this was the only place our minders grew visibly nervous the longer we stayed. Journalists, they told us, have been pelted with rotten fruit in the past. But we wondered whether our minders' true concern was that we might find in Saddam City the roots of real anti-government sentiment.

For now, the peoples' anger is directed at Washington. But current U.S. policy risks producing an entire generation of Iraqis who hate not just the government but the American people. "America is sowing the seeds of hatred and one day it will harvest them," Sa'ad Jassim, a resident of the southern city of Basra, said while playing a game of backgammon.

U.S. officials argue that Hussein is to blame for most of the hardship. He is spending money to build palaces, government buildings and one of the largest mosques in the Middle East, while failing to construct schools or hospitals. True, but it is the sanctions, which the United States spearheaded, that permit such manipulation. They give Iraq's leader the perfect excuse to neglect his people. In effect, Washington has made itself the scapegoat for all of Iraq's problems. And while many Iraqis listen to non-state media like the Voice of America, they still blame the United States. Even away from our minders' prying ears, the most Iraqis would admit is that Hussein shares blame with the United States. "It takes two to tango," one retired civil servant told us privately.

Another frightening consequence of the status quo is a steady erosion in respect for the sanctions internationally, and with it the persuasive powers of the U.N. and the United States. Visits to Baghdad like that of Venezuelan President Hugo Chavez show how tattered is the effort to isolate Hussein. We competed for rooms at our gloomy Baghdad hotel with Yugoslav and Pakistani businessmen. Iraqi entrepreneurs are traveling abroad to sign deals to import and distribute foreign goods, and even Gulf oil sheikdoms have reopened embassies to facilitate trade.

If the United States really wanted to make life difficult for Hussein, it would take one simple, if politically risky, step: Lift the sanctions on all but military items. This would restore morality to U.S. policy. More importantly, Iraqis would suddenly have only Hussein to blame for the country's decrepit hospitals, schools and infrastructure. He would claim victory in the short-term, but would quickly find it difficult to deliver on all the promises of a better life once sanctions are lifted. (Remember, according to Iraqi propaganda, the sanctions are to blame for every ill, from the drought to the national soccer team's recent listless performance.) Iraqis remember a much better, more prosperous life and will expect real improvements immediately.

Hussein also would have a serious problem satisfying the financial demands of the military, the government bureaucracy, his cronies and the religious community he has come to depend upon for support. The resulting competition would put new strains on the regime, which could quickly be beset by serious infighting. Such internal conflict could finally produce enough of a split to spawn some credible high-level opposition inside Iraq.

Despite its campaign to end sanctions, the Iraqi government is ill-prepared for change. Power stations cannot supply both homes and factories. At the main port south of Basra, only 5 percent of the floodlights work and fewer than one in five loading cranes is operational. The University of Basra's medical school is turning out half the doctors it did before the Persian Gulf War. The state's financial system is in a shambles. While the exchange rate is about 2,000 dinars to the dollar, the largest bill is a 250-dinar note. That means that an inch-thick stack of bills is worth less than $25, hardly a sound basis for healthy trade.

To check out of our hotel before the overland trip back to Jordan took two shopping bags full of local currency. Each of the roughly 8,000 purplish notes bore Saddam's image, an inescapable part of Iraq's landscape. Unless Clinton or his successor reexamines the status quo of sanctions, Hussein's image may be on the currency for a long time to come.

Warren Strobel and Kevin Whitelaw cover international affairs for U.S. News & World Report. They recently returned from a two-week reporting trip to 15 of Iraq's 18 provinces.

Africa's Security Issues Through 2010

by William Thom

Prospects for Africa over the next 10 years hinge on the continent's severe security problems. Peace is the foundation for Africa's future because all goals for development, plans for good governance and alleviation of human suffering depend on a secure and stable environment. South of the Sahara, Africa suffers from a vicious cycle of poverty, which contributes to criminal and political violence that inhibits investment and discourages economic development. One in three sub-Saharan states is currently experiencing some form of military conflict.

Abject poverty is at the root of many African conflicts, and the number of risk takers willing to take up arms to claim their piece of the meager economic pie is growing. The global communications revolution fuels rising expectations, and as Africans realize the depths of their poverty for the first time, they are losing patience with ineffective political leaders and traditional rulers—opportunities for economic advancement are painfully beyond their grasp. Poorly governed states with weak or uncontrollable armies face collapse.

Concern for basic safety is another factor. When a state can no longer protect its citizens, its primary reason to exist ceases; individuals will seek protection elsewhere. Insecurity fans ethnic, religious and regional animosities, even where differences have long been beneath the surface. When all else fails, individuals fall back on their tribal unit, encouraging the rise of warlords, often based on ethnic affiliations.

Another major change in Africa's security calculus has occurred in the aftermath of the Cold War: African countries are now setting their own security agendas. After more than 100 years of colonial domination and Cold War distortion, Africans are taking charge of events around the continent. Africans sense a waning security commitment from traditional external powers—their former colonial rulers and Cold War partners.

France's more constrained role recently as the self-styled "gendarme of Africa" is instructive. Paris's unilateral intervention in Rwanda in 1994 brought accusations that France had sided with the Hutu against the Tutsi. Two years later, when longtime French ally Zairian President Mobutu Sese Seko faced a serious rebellion supported by an alliance of regional states, Paris demurred. The inaction sent a message that there were new, more restrictive limits to French intervention in Africa.

Today's African leaders see a new freedom to act militarily. On the positive side, African states are more inclined to take responsibility for solving African security problems. In the post-Cold War era, some 20 countries have participated in peacekeeping and peacemaking operations on the continent, mostly on their own. On the negative side, this new freedom has also fostered military adventures that have complicated regional security problems.

Sub-Saharan Africa's position in the post-Cold War global security constellation is emerging. The continent has unfinished business from the Cold War and even the colonial period. In this land of mostly small internal wars, a limited military investment can potentially yield immense profits. Among the numerous weak states with poor armies and fragile institutions, even a small war can generate great destruction, as in Somalia and Sierra Leone. In 10 years Africa will likely still be at war with itself, continuing the process of nation-building, as relatively strong, stable states survive, and weak, hopelessly fractured ones do not. What follows are some key military themes that will help shape African realities over the next 10 years.

Warfare in the Era of Independence

Since the end of World War II, there have been three identifiable periods of warfare in sub-Saharan Africa. They span the spectrum of combat from guerrilla wars to coalition warfare, but with insurgency as a constant. During this period, an estimated 3.5 million soldiers and civilians have perished in African conflicts. The first period involved wars of liberation against the colonial powers, which extended well into the 1970s. These armed insurgencies against the remaining colonial powers were essentially low-budget, small-scale conflicts backed by communist powers. But, other revolts against colonialism did not align with the communist cause and—at least initially—did not receive significant support from Moscow. Examples from the 1950s and 60s include the Mau Mau revolt in Kenya, the early uprising in Angola and the Eritrean independence struggle. In Southern Africa there were wars of national liberation to end white-dominated settler regimes.

The second period involved the appearance of a few interstate wars and large-scale civil wars that were militarily significant, mostly conventional and politically galvanizing. By the 1970s a number of African states had developed armies capable of projecting power across their borders. The two best examples of African interstate conflict during this period were the Ogaden War between Ethiopia and Somalia (1977–78), and the Tanzania-Uganda War (1978–79). White-ruled South Africa pursued a forward-defense strategy during the 1970s and 1980s, which resulted in episodic combat with black-ruled states to the north. In Angola, however, Pretoria's apartheid government deployed conventional forces in strength to fight Angolan and Cuban forces. Two pivotal states where communist regimes had come to power in the 1970s—Ethiopia and Angola—faced large-scale civil wars in the 1980s. Communist powers poured in troops, advisors and billions of dollars of conventional weaponry in a vain attempt to preserve their perceived strategic gains in these two anchor countries. To balance the ledger, the West provided military assistance to professed anticommunist "freedom fighters" in Angola, and such anti-Marxist bulwarks as Zairian President Mobutu.

By the post-Cold War 1990s, however, a third period had emerged, one that points toward the next decade. The significant wars have once again become mainly internal contests fought at the unconventional or semiconventional level, leading to state collapse and wars of intervention. Easy to finance and difficult to defend against, guerrilla warfare—long the bane of Africa—remains its most prevalent form of conflict. Today's vicious insurgencies differ from yesterday's armed liberation movements in motivation: current struggles are based on power and economics, not a political cause or ideology. In weak states with unprofessional, underpaid armies, armed bandits become armed insurgents as they fill the power vacuum.

War in the 1990s became more destructive as internecine conflicts destroyed already fragile infrastructures. Today's African insurgents tend to be better armed and out number their 1960s predecessors. As the distinctions between guerrilla warfare and organized banditry blur, the targets often become the people themselves. Prolonged internal wars can destroy the fabric of the state and the society. On a continent where the majority of the population is no more than 15 years old, the communications revolution has highlighted the enormous gap between rich and poor. Youth without hope in dysfunctional nation states provide a ready manpower pool for local warlords; elsewhere, children are kidnapped out of villages by roving insurgent bands. The result can be young combatants socialized by an intensely violent right of passage, who begin to see banditry, murder and pillaging as normal behavior.

For African states the present is a time of experimentation with the uses and limits of applying military force. The next 10 to 20 years will bring polarized military power on the subcontinent and a small but growing number of strong states increasingly willing to use military force. Conventional wars will be fought over resources such as oil, other minerals, water and arable land, and to determine regional dominance. Armed insurgency will prevail in many of the weaker states, much as it does now, with regional powers or power blocs selectively intervening to protect their vital interests, often merely the capital and valuable resources in the interior. Eventually, power blocs will give way to dominant subregional military powers willing to engage in conflict, which will frequently take the form of peace enforcement and counterinsurgency.

An Uneven Balance

Nearly all postcolonial African armies began as colonial adjuncts to European armies and served primarily as tripwire forces in the colonies. As such, they were lightly armed and dependent on their colonial power for training, logistics and leadership. For example, the Kenyan African Rifles descended from the King's African Rifles. Over the past 40 years these armies grew to resemble, on a smaller scale, the forces of their colonial rulers or Cold War patrons.

Throughout this period, there have been great inequities in the military capabilities of African states. Until the mid-1990s, power imbalances have been held in check by the threat of intervention by powers external to Africa. During the Cold War in particular, these external powers intervened militarily to reverse adverse security trends or at least level the playing field. Soviets and Cubans intervened in Angola to balance South African intervention in 1975, and France worked to form a posse of African states to save the Mobutu regime in Zaire in 1977 and 1978.

By Western standards, today's African armies are still lightly armed, poorly equipped and trained, and dependent on external military aid. Nevertheless, a growing number of states, notably Nigeria, Angola, South Africa, Uganda, Rwanda, Ethiopia and Zimbabwe, are capable of using military force to pursue their own interests on the continent because of the gross inequities in raw military power. In a conventional scenario a country with a few operational jet fighters or attack helicopters and 30 armored vehicles backed by artillery has an immense advantage over a country that can oppose it with only light infantry units. Without an external or effective regional brake on their activities, emergent local powers can and will take the military option when they believe their vital interests are at stake.

Angola, for example, used its experienced army to intervene once in Congo-Brazzaville and twice in Congo-Kinshasa in the late 1990s to effect outcomes that it perceived as beneficial relative to its struggle with the insurgent Union for the Total Independence of Angola (UNITA). Nigeria managed to field a force up to division size in Liberia and then in Sierra Leone to pursue regional peace enforcement and its own hegemony in West Africa. Zimbabwe also deployed a division-sized force into the Democratic Republic of Congo (DRC), and South Africa (along with Botswana) sent troops into Lesotho to quell disturbances there. Uganda's army fought in three neighboring states in the 1990s—Rwanda, Sudan and the DRC. Rwanda has launched its forces into the DRC twice in recent years, and Ethiopia mobilized a force of 250,000 for its border war with Eritrea and continues to pursue hostile elements into the former Somalia.

The next few years promise little change in this military inequity. In 10 to 20 years the gap between the few dominant military powers and the rest of the countries will likely grow exponentially. Among the stronger states, large infantry forces will give way to smaller, more mobile forces with greater reach and firepower. The most capable states will maintain a variety of forces tailored for specific missions such as power projection, peacekeeping, peace enforcement and counterinsurgency. While the best sub-Saharan armies will grow more impressive, they will remain several generations behind the global leaders.

Regional Powers and Power Blocs

The original continental organization—the Organization of African Unity (OAU)—organized around the principle of decolonizing Africa. But it did not have a mandate to intervene as a regional military organization or adjudicate military disputes. Thus, in the post-Cold War period continental power blocs have begun to develop and act in conjunction with the OAU. They stem mostly from economic unions, the best example being the Economic Community of West African States and its military arm, the Economic Community of West African States Cease Fire Monitoring Group (ECOMOG). Dominated by regional power Nigeria, ECOMOG has served in Liberia, Sierra Leone and Guinea-Bissau, earning both respect and ridicule. Elsewhere, the Southern Africa Development Community, bolstered by South Africa, has assumed a regional security role, but its unity has been strained by sharp disagreement over Zimbabwe and Namibia's involvement in the DRC. On the Horn of Africa, the Inter-Governmental Authority on Development has engaged in diplomatic conflict resolution in Sudan but lacks any military cooperation among it members. The East African Cooperation—composed of Kenya, Tanzania and Uganda—has conducted joint military exercises. Some groupings appear to be ad hoc and temporary, such as the "Frontline States of East Africa" (Uganda, Ethiopia and Eritrea) which foundered when the Ethiopia-Eritrea border war erupted in 1998. The "Great Lakes Powers" of Uganda, Rwanda and Burundi have acted as an informal bloc in the DRC war, although tensions between Kigali and Kampala resulted in a shout-out at Kisangani in 1999.

Other groupings will likely emerge and some extant groupings rearrange themselves to accommodate changing national interests among members. Power blocs attempt to deal with collective regional security concerns as Africans see themselves increasingly on their own. They see viral forms of economic insurgency and highly destructive internal wars that disregard borders and appear out of control. Responsible leaders band together fearing that these conflicts, left unchecked, could destroy states and create pockets of complete lawlessness. The OAU, by its inaction, encourages the development of such subregional groupings. The OAU has only a token military mechanism, and prefers to endorse military interventions by others rather than take the lead itself. Recently, however, the OAU has shown signs of becoming more active by playing a prominent role in helping negotiate an end to the Ethiopia-Eritrea dispute and by sponsoring a joint military commission in the DRC.

Regional power blocs are only as solvent and effective as the powers that lead them. In sub-Saharan Africa few states are powerful enough to lead now. South Africa and Nigeria are the two best-known military leaders in the sub-Saharan region. Both face severe internal challenges but should maintain their roles as regional powers, and in the long run they have the potential to become continentwide powers. Such a development could lead to recolonization by African powers although the context would be different from the

European experience. Pretoria and Abuja, for example, could develop hegemonic tendencies; one could argue that Nigeria already has. Beyond these two countries, predicting other major developing powers is difficult. Among those that could emerge over the next decade or so are Kenya, Angola, Zimbabwe, Ethiopia and perhaps Senegal. Even small countries such as Rwanda and Eritrea have already shown an ability to project force and influence the local military balance.

A proving ground for budding regional powers will be peace enforcement missions and other military interventions in failed states. Peacekeeping may become a lost art in Africa in this century. Namibia and Mozambique have been relative UN successes, but Sierra Leone, Angola, Somalia and Liberia have shown limited returns for expensive peacekeeping ventures. Military interventions in collapsed states will continue, but they are apt to be police actions to ward off insurgents or multinational struggles for resources. The DRC case applies here. The imbalance in military capabilities will not be redressed over the next decade and will likely become more pronounced.

Arms Trade Trends

Arms acquisition is occurring on three levels—light arms, heavy stock-in-trade items and more sophisticated weapon systems. The extremely active trade in small arms and other light infantry weapons has captured international attention since the Cold War because they help fuel local wars around the continent. These light weapons include small arms, machineguns, rocket propelled grenade launchers and small-caliber mortars—all man-portable.

These weapons have three principal origins. During the Cold War millions of assault rifles and other firearms were pumped into Africa, mostly by communist powers equipping "allies," notably Angola, Ethiopia, Mozambique, Somalia and Sudan. Rifles such as the AK-47 have become so numerous that they are regarded as a form of currency in some places. Second, in the post-Cold War era a brisk trade has developed, through middlemen, to acquire light arms from the former Soviet Union and other East European countries where such weapons are now cheap and plentiful. Third, a half-dozen or so sub-Saharan states manufacture light arms, and their production far exceeds their own needs.

Small arms are difficult to track, yet one commercial airliner can carry enough of them and their ammunition to start a guerrilla war. That is precisely why the trade in light weapons is so dangerous. The current glut of small arms in Africa should gradually contract over the next 10 to 20 years as the millions of small arms delivered in the 1970s and 80s age, become unserviceable and are not replaced in such quantities. Nevertheless, light arms will remain relatively easy to acquire and a major concern.

The trade in heavy weapons and large pieces of military equipment increased in the late 1990s with the growing number of conflicts on the continent and the unprecedented number of countries participating in military operations. Throughout 1998 and 1999 African armies deployed to other African nations 19 times, while 17 countries experienced significant combat on their territory. These deployments included armored vehicles, artillery, surface-to-air missiles, and combat and transport aircraft. These weapon systems, although not new to the sub-Saharan scene, are now frequently upgraded versions of old classics. The T-55 tank, for example, is now available with reactive armor, night vision equipment and the ability to fire antitank missiles from its main gun. MiG-21 and MiG-23 fighter-bombers are now frequently upgraded with better avionics, power plants, weapon suites and other performance enhancements. Other popular items of equipment in the 1990s include infantry fighting vehicles, hand-held surface-to-air missiles, multiple rocket launchers, and combat and transport helicopters—most of Soviet design. The next decade will likely see modest growth in the delivery of heavy weapons to sub-Saharan Africa. Although some observers consider armor and combat aircraft inappropriate for African wars, countries that have recently acquired them are shopping for more. For example, the T-55 is now a prime player in wars from the Horn to Angola, from Rwanda to Guinea. Mi-24 HIND attack helicopters are popular as a counterinsurgency and close-air-support platform, and are used by a dozen African countries.

In the late 1990s a new generation of military equipment began to appear in the sub-Saharan region—much of it aviation. The Ethiopia-Eritrea border war has brought Su-27 and MiG-29 fighters, a first for the region. At least a few other countries, such as Angola and Nigeria, will probably acquire these and other new-generation aircraft over next the two to three years. Ethiopia has also received the 2S19 152mm self-propelled artillery system, a quantum leap in sophistication over the post-World War II designed artillery commonly found in Africa. With no Cold War restraints, African countries can successfully seek the next level of sophisticated weaponry.

How can African states afford these arms? The Cold War's military equipment grant aid and easy credit terms are over. The few large or wealthy African countries are understandably in the market for major equipment acquisition. But smaller, poorer countries, driven by perceived threats or the fact that they are already embroiled in a conflict, are also in the arms market. Imaginative financing, such as barter agreements and concessions, makes predictions about who can afford future arms highly speculative.

Black and gray market arms dealers further complicate the scenario as they increasingly replace the classic state-to-state arms deals. Most big-ticket purchases still happen through government agencies, and the dollar costs still overwhelmingly favor state-to-state transactions, but the business going to arms peddlers is increasing. This is a troubling development because the independent dealers are motivated strictly by profit, will sell to anyone—insurgents or governments—and care little about the consequences.

The Question of Privatization

The longstanding reliance on mercenaries will likely continue as African state and substate actors contract out military services to dramatically improve their capabilities. The privatization of state security functions provides African countries with a force multiplier—a cheaper, quicker, albeit controversial, solution for a flagging military. Contractors can be more responsive than states in helping a government. The South African firm Executive Outcomes (EO) was employed effectively in the mid-1990s in both Angola and Sierra Leone and is generally credited with helping to reverse the poor military postures of both governments. EO strayed into operations, however, bringing charges that it was merely a thinly disguised mercenary outfit. The difference between legitimate security contractor and illegal mercenary has blurred. In Africa, mercenaries are a loaded issue, yet many states see contractors as alternatives to Cold War security assistance programs.

State security functions are generally out-sourced in the areas of training, advisory assistance and logistics (maintenance is key deficiency in African militaries). Air transportation has become an especially critical area for privatization. Without contract air transport, many of the recent African engagements would not have been possible. In the current DRC war, air transport is considered the most costly expense for each side.

Security contractors cross the line and become mercenaries when they act as operators and fighters and not just as maintainers and teachers. They cross another line when they begin dealing with substate actors and not recognized governments. Security entrepreneurs may be increasingly willing to sell their services to insurgent movements, tribal militias, local warlords and even nongovernment organizations. While better-known security firms—such as MPRI and Sandline International—strive to foster a legitimate business image, other lesser-known, spin-off or free-lance groups are concerned only with the bottom line and will deal with just about anyone. It seems likely that private security activities will expand both above board and below. Security vendors selling to substate actors will further destabilize the region.

The new wave of interest in contracting and mercenary services stemmed primarily from arms dealers. When items are sold, package deals include trainers, technicians and advisors. From there it is a short leap to providing people to fight. While mercenary combat troops continue to show up occasionally in Africa, the next decade would seem to prize "technomercenaries," technicians who can keep equipment running and train the locals on how to use it, without actually pulling the trigger.

Prospects for Intrastate Wars

African military conflicts since the Cold War have again become almost exclusively internal affairs far more damaging to economic and social underpinnings than traditional interstate wars. The most prevalent forms of conflict in Africa are armed insurgency and civil war, with the latter often growing out of the former. Such unrest seems all but certain to persist over the next 10 years. The conditions that foster the development of economic insurgencies (extreme poverty, large pool of disenfranchised and disaffected youth, ethnic tensions and easy availability of arms) are likely to persist and may intensify. Dissident groups evolve from simple banditry to insurgent warfare as they become larger and more successful. Credos and manifestos are quickly manufactured to provide a fig leaf of political legitimacy. Eventually, insurgencies may become recognized as civil wars as the rebel chiefs acquire respectability as legitimate political leaders.

Almost all internal wars in Africa attract, or in some cases are created by, the meddling of outside powers. Every insurgency depends at some level on outside assistance, so internal struggles can be viewed as proxy wars disguised as internal conflicts. Weak states are vulnerable to collapse, and internal wars hasten the process. State collapse as defined here is not merely the failure of the machinery of government to work, as in Zaire under Mobutu; it is the complete breakdown of national government authority, as in Somalia under a gaggle of feuding warlords. National control disappears when the rot from within erodes the military to the point that it can no longer serve as the guardian of the state. Ironically, either unwise military downsizing, or worse, unwise rapid military mobilization, can exacerbate internal security problems. Armed groups opposing the government, or merely oriented toward self defense, fill the void left by receding state power and create ethnic, regional or social networks. In this regard, the expanding number of paramilitaries (armed militias, political factions and ethnic self-defense forces) contributes to instability by increasing the number of armed substate actors with their own agendas. Further, these groups are susceptible to foreign manipulation. This dangerous form of internal warfare, characteristic of the 1990s, will likely be a major problem in Africa throughout the next decade.

It also seems that solvent, functioning African states will selectively intervene militarily to control insurgencies that either threaten neighboring countries or harbor dangerous elements, such as terrorist groups and radical fundamentalist movements. Strong African states and the subregional bodies they dominate will increasingly recognize danger signs such as the subdivision of insurgent forces into warlord gangs, the manipulation of rebel groups by outside interests seeking to capitalize on conflict and the emergence of a criminal empire in a lawless environment. Over the next decade Western powers will recognize that Africa's internal wars which destabilize some states and cause others to collapse, ultimately threaten their strategic interests as well. This lesson is not likely to be driven home, however, until some environmental or criminal disaster strikes that directly threatens Western interests.

Prospects for Interstate Wars

Wars between sovereign states in sub-Saharan Africa have taken place throughout the era of independence, but they have rarely been more than a regional concern. The Ogaden war between Ethiopia and Somalia gained notice because of the involvement of Cuban troops and Soviet advisors, but most interstate conflicts, like the five-day 1985 Christmas war between Mali and Burkina Faso, have been mere footnotes to modern African history. That may well change over the next 10 to 20 years as the militarily strong states attempt to stake out their areas of interest unintimidated by external powers.

A legitimate question is whether African states can afford to participate in interstate military contests. Countries in the Great Lakes region and on the Horn of Africa have shown a surprising and sobering ability to finance current military campaigns. Even in areas where oil, diamonds or other high-priced natural resources are not evident, countries find ways to pay for heavy, modern weapons. Financing African conflicts, especially conventional interstate wars, remains problematic, but the lack of resources is no reason to rule out future interstate wars.

In the sub-Saharan environment, a growing number of states have the raw military capability to engage in interstate wars, even when they do not involve an adjacent country. Contract air transport has revolutionized warfare in Africa by giving countries strategic reach. Further, many of Africa's new dynamic leaders, such as Ugandan president Yoweri Museveni and Rwandan president Paul Kagame, who came to power by force of arms, tend to view military power as a legitimate—even preferred—tool of statecraft. Additionally, some old-line rulers, such as Angolan president Jos Eduardo dos Santos and Zimbabwe's president Robert Mugabe, also see flexing military muscle as an acceptable way to do business.

As regional powers become more active in the next decade, and their strategic interests become well defined, occasional interstate wars loom. While intrastate conflicts will remain the principal form of warfare, interstate warfare will be more likely than in the past 40 years.

Current Conflicts

The DROC Civil War 1998-?

Status: Peace agreement signed, being violated by most signatories.
Type: Coalition civil war with extensive participation by foreign powers and substate actors.
Number of combatants: 120–140,000.
Displaced persons: 290,000
Significant formations: Battalion, company.
Casualties: 20–27,000 (mostly civilian).
Tactics: Semiconventional (a mix).
Foreign involvement: Zimbabwe, Angola, Namibia, Chad and Sudan for the government; Rwanda, Uganda and Burundi for the rebels.

Angolan Civil War 1998-?

Status: Lusaka Protocol violated by both sides, ongoing conflict.
Type: latest phase of long running civil war.
Number of combatants: 150–180,000.
Displaced persons: over 1.4 million.
Significant formations: Brigade, regiment and battalion.
Casualties: Unknown (mostly civilian).
Tactics: Primarily conventional.
Foreign involvement: Private contract military assistance (both sides).

Sierra Leone Civil War 1991-?

Status: Lusaka Protocol violated by both sides, ongoing conflict.
Type: Coalition civil war with extensive participation by foreign powers and substate actors.
Number of combatants: 30–40,000.
Displaced persons: 600,000+.
Significant formations: Battalion and company.
Casualties: over 10,000 (mostly civilian).
Tactics: Semiconventional (a mix).
Foreign involvement: West African force (headed by Nigeria) transitioning to a UN peacekeeping force for the government; Liberia and private contractors for rebels.

Ethiopia-Eritrea War 1998-?

Status: OAU/UN peace negotiations stalled, temporary lull in fighting.
Type: large scale border war.
Number of combatants: 400,000.
Displaced persons: over 400,000.
Significant formations: Division, brigade and battalion.
Casualties: 30–45,000 killed (military).
Tactics: Conventional.
Foreign involvement: Contract personnel on both sides but primarily in Ethiopia.

Some conflict may take the form of coalition warfare, such as that now underway in the DRC. Others will be more traditional one-on-one contests such as the Ethiopia-Eritrea war. The battle of wills and principles driving that dispute serve as a reminder that many wars are fought for symbolic and moral purposes. More future interstate wars in Africa are, however, likely to be fought over scarce or vanishing resources—and not just high-value commodities such as oil and diamonds. Water, fisheries, arable land and ethnic solidarity will be among the root causes of interstate wars. Borders established by the colonials will continue to become less relevant and more easily altered by Africa's emerging power structure.

Wars in Africa will stem from acute poverty and a sense of hopelessness among its burgeoning population, especially alienated young men. Fed by rising expectations stemming from increased media exposure, these wars will be primarily internal and unconventional. They will exact a high price on the people, the fragile infrastructures and the foundering states themselves. More states will collapse, be propped up by external powers from within Africa or be patrolled by international peacekeepers.

The disparities in military power on the African continent will become even greater. Emergent local powers and power blocs will be the significant military actors on the continent. As great powers limit their involvement, these emerging powers will pursue their own agendas that by 2010 will change Africa's political map.

The current scope of African military conflict is unprecedented. In the late 1990s sub-Saharan Africa may have entered into a "Thirty Years War," a metamorphic process that will profoundly change the continent. In some corners of Africa, the fires of war will remain difficult to extinguish for another reason: they have gone on for so long that they have attained a sense of normalcy. Entire generations in places such as Angola, Eritrea, Liberia and Somalia have grown up knowing nothing other than war.

In Africa, as elsewhere, transnational criminality and war will become virtually indistinguishable. Economic insurgents, warlords for profit, lawless zones harboring criminals, armies of child soldiers and brutalized civilians will all offend the moral senses of Western nations and seemingly demand a response. Policing these messy situations will become an international priority. Nevertheless, some places will remain beyond the reach of Western moral consciousness and continue to experience low intensity conflict indefinitely.

The next two to three years do not portend much change in African security, but by 2010 Africa's political relief map will likely show stark differences. Islands of stability may be built around relatively strong and prosperous states such as South Africa, Kenya and perhaps Nigeria. In countries riven by insurgency and facing collapse, international forces protecting the capital may in effect create city-states. Elsewhere, local powers will demonstrate hegemonic interests, and geographic boundaries will reflect the continent's new political order.

William G. Thom is the Defense Intelligence Officer for Africa, Defense Information Agency, Washington DC. He received a B.S. from the State University of New York at New Paltz and an M.A. from American University. He is a graduate of the US Army War College and the National Security Leadership Course. He has held a variety of positions in the DIA, including chief, Africa Military Capabilities Branch; senior analyst, Directorate for Estimates; and Africa analyst, J2. He has also served as senior analyst for Africa, J2, Headquarters, US European Command, Vaihingen, Germany.

Nigeria: The Politics of Marginalization

"Jostling for power by Nigeria's myriad ethnic groups has, for better and for worse, driven the country's political development since before independence from Britain in 1960. What is new is a rhetoric of the impossible: the marginalization of everyone."

MINABERE IBELEMA

MINABERE IBELEMA *is an assistant professor in the department of communication studies at the University of Alabama at Birmingham.*

After nearly 14 years of virtually uninterrupted military rule, Nigeria returned to electoral democracy in 1999. The restoration of democratic rule—made possible by the sudden death the previous year of the head of state, General Sani Abacha—engendered an optimism comparable only to the euphoria felt at the end of the civil war in January 1970. Yet it was short lived; the new government of President Olusegun Obasanjo was immediately beset by ethnic agitation and conflict. Grievances that had festered under military rule and had been suppressed with draconian measures suddenly found open expression with the democratic dispensation.

The recent institution or planned introduction of shariah (the Islamic penal code) by several Muslim-populated states in northern Nigeria has aggravated the already complex political atmosphere. Since October 1999, at least 5 northern states have passed laws in favor of implementing the code, and one—Zamfara—has signed it into law. Tension over imposing shariah climaxed in February in a bloody clash in the northern city of Kaduna between northern Muslims and southern Christians residing in the north. As many as 400 people were killed, most of them southerners. Reprisal killings of resident northerners soon followed in the southeastern city of Aba. The ensuing insecurity precipitated an exodus of southerners—especially members of the Igbo ethnic group, who are mainly Christian—from northern cities, and of northern Hausa-Fulani—who are mainly Muslim—from the south.

Following a February 29 meeting of the Council of States—attended by state governors and former heads of state—the federal government ordered the suspension of shariah as a criminal code. Its longstanding application to civil cases, which is acknowledged in the constitution, was allowed to continue. The responses of the affected states have been mixed. A few, such as Jigawa and Zamfara, seem intent on defying the federal government; Zamfara demonstrated its resolve in late March by amputating a convicted thief's right hand, as required under shariah. Other states, such as Niger and Yobe, have formally shelved the code, and Kwara has declared it will never implement it. Several states, including Kaduna and Plateau, appear ambivalent about their intent.

These ethnoreligious tensions are reminiscent of the events in 1966 and 1967 that precipitated Nigeria's civil war in which more than 1 million Nigerians died when the Igbos created the secessionist state of Biafra. Emeka Odumegwu Ojukwu, who led the 30-month secession, has been blamed by some northern leaders for fermenting this year's Kaduna crisis. Ojukwu has responded by calling the accusation a hallucination and by suggesting psychiatric examination for the accusers. But he has also said of the Igbos that "we have to get prepared, be on our toes and wait." Leaders used similar language directly preceding the declaration of secession in 1967.

That 36 smaller states rather than four powerful regions now constitute federal Nigeria would seem to militate against secession (Nigeria in 1966 was composed of the North, the East, the West, and the Midwest regions). Regional coordination among states has, however, created powerful alliances. Since the shariah crisis, political and religious leaders from northern, western, eastern, and southern minority states have met as discrete blocs to formulate unified positions or to discuss Nigeria's political future. Youths from the middle-belt states have also called for a separate leadership meeting of their states. Still, differences among the states within each bloc makes regional cohesion and secession unlikely.

As in 1967, claims have been made that some military personnel have supplied weapons to and otherwise aided civilians in the communal attacks. Unlike in 1967, however, the military is officially uninvolved, except in assisting the police when requested. In an address to his officers in the wake of the Kaduna riots, the chief of defense staff, Rear Admiral Ibrahim Ogohi, admonished them to eschew partisanship and to remain loyal to federal civilian authority. He pledged to defend Nigeria's nascent democracy.

Similar statements of commitment to a united and democratic Nigeria have been made by political and religious leaders on all sides. Yet these statements have been countered by others advocating confederation, dissolution, or even secession. Thus, the danger remains that Nigeria could splinter violently. Although the present crisis is veiled in religious differences, it is at root political. The causes of tension and instability in Nigeria remain the same as in the civil war: the fear of domination.

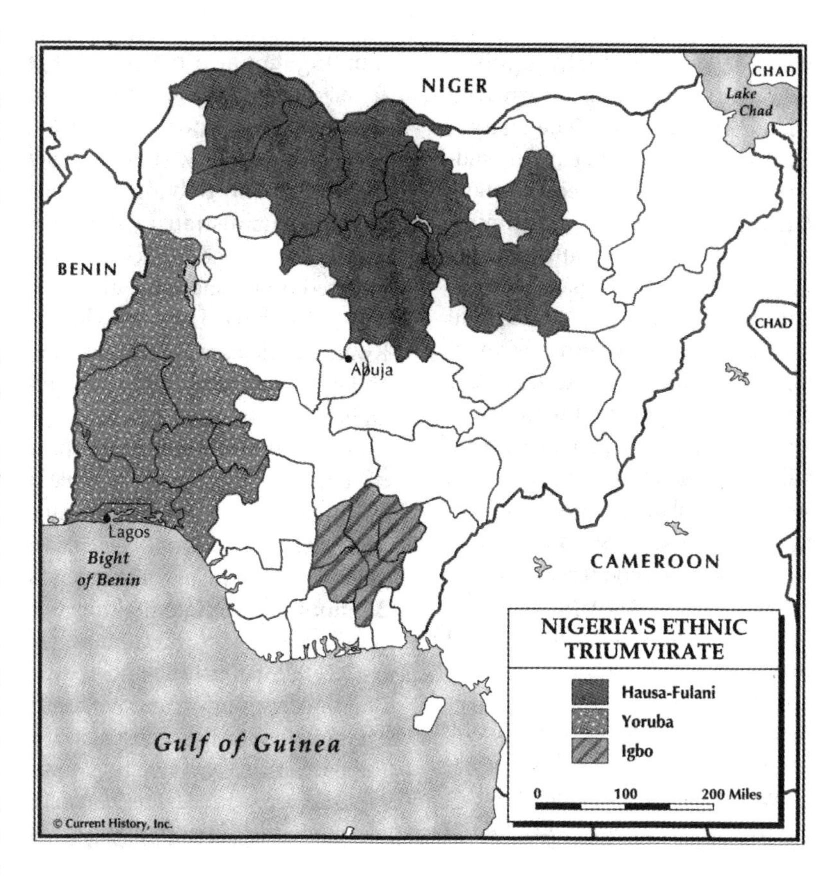

THE RHETORIC OF THE IMPOSSIBLE

Jostling for power by Nigeria's myriad ethnic groups has, for better and for worse, driven the country's political development since before independence from Britain in 1960. What is new is a rhetoric of the impossible: the marginalization of everyone. A perusal of Nigerian newspapers and magazines indicates that virtually all regions and nationalities in the country claim to be marginalized.

Ordinarily, marginalization entails the subordination of peripheral groups' interests by dominant groups in the formulation or execution of national policies. Accordingly, Nigerian minorities in all regions have historically complained of marginalization and domination. Usually, the complaint is directed at one or all of the numerically dominant groups that constitute the ethnic triumvirate of Nigerian politics: the Hausa-Fulanis in the north, the Yorubas in the west, and the Igbos in the east. But today these three groups claim, along with the minorities, to be marginalized.

Faced with this political Gordian knot, Nigeria would seem to have its Alexander the Great in Olusegun Obasanjo, the new president. At crucial moments in Nigeria's history, Obasanjo has emerged to play pivotal but often uncelebrated roles. As an army commander during the civil war, he helped create a unified front from the initially wary northern and western regions that eventually defeated the Biafran secession. In 1976 he became head of the country's military government and shepherded Nigeria's return to civilian rule in 1979. When the military once again stepped into power in 1984, he became an outspoken critic of the series of military leaders who were unwilling to follow Obasanjo's example and return Nigeria to democratic rule—an outspokenness that led to his imprisonment in 1995.

As president, Obasanjo has sought to reduce ethnic tension through meetings and exhortations, but with only moderate success. But for the most part, Obasanjo has been unable to abate Nigeria's myriad ethnic conflicts. His approach to the country's problems appears two-pronged: to grow the economy and alleviate hardship, and to make all groups feel included in the government. Ironically, the latter policy has had the effect of expanding the number of groups claiming to be marginalized.

Claims of marginalization center on four main issues: control of or participation in government, political appointments, leadership of government-owned and -affiliated industries, and budgetary allocations. At some point in Nigeria's recent history, each member of the country's ethnic triumvirate has enjoyed a disproportionate advantage in one or more of these areas. The loss of advantage has created an illusory or exaggerated sense of marginalization.

A major component in the claims is the apparent inequity in revenue sharing. This inequity, however, is inherent in a strong federal system in which a relatively small region of the country (the Niger Delta) accounts for a large proportion of the country's revenue (crude oil exports). The realities of lost privilege and inherent inequity are compounded by the country's economic decline in the past decade, a problem worsened by government graft. The resulting hardship has engendered finger-pointing and scapegoating among Nigeria's ethnic groups.

LOST PRIVILEGES . . .

In the case of the Igbos, the lasting impact of the civil war, along with the effects of the deteriorating economy, has been the main cause of their plight. The war saw an exodus of Igbos from the non-Igbo regions of Nigeria and from political and business positions that they have been unable to regain. With the creation of states in 1967, the Igbos also suffered diminished political and administrative clout in the Niger Delta and other minority areas in the east. Igbo frustration, which had been muted, is becoming increasingly shrill. Ojukwu probably spoke for many Igbos with his recent remark that the "problem is that we are in Nigeria and we are finding it extremely difficult to find accommodation in Nigeria."

The claim of marginalization by ethnic groups in what Nigerians call the core north, led by the Hausa-Fulanis, is an anomaly in the country's politics. Although the north has historically lagged in educational and industrial development, the Hausa-Fulanis have exercised political leadership through much of Nigeria's postcolonial history. The election of Obasanjo, a Yoruba, was itself a concession by the Hausa-Fulanis to southern pressure for a change from northern leadership. The concession reflects an apparent realization by the Hausa-Fulani leadership that Nigerian politics would continue to be haunted by the nullification of the 1993 presidential election if it were not redressed. (The results of the election, which appeared to make Yoruba businessman Moshood Abiola the winner, were canceled by the Hausa-Fulani–led military government, provoking a protracted political crisis.)

The People's Democratic Party (PDP), which nominated Obasanjo for the presidency, was sponsored or backed by several former northern leaders, both civilian and military. The party won substantial votes in the north as well as in the east. Ironically, the only region in which Obasanjo and the PDP lost was in the west, among the Yorubas. In effect, Obasanjo became the first Nigerian to be elected to the presidency without the support of his own ethnic group.

Having given its support to Obasanjo, the core north apparently expected a quid pro quo. But Obasanjo has pursued policies that emphasize inclusiveness and equity rather than patronage.

Of particular significance was Obasanjo's decision, soon after his inauguration in May 1999, to retire hundreds of senior officers in an attempt to rid the military of personnel who had become accustomed to the perquisites of political power. The Hausa-Fulanis believe that they were disproportionately affected because of the preponderance of Hausa-Fulanis in top military positions who were forcibly retired. This complaint was repeated after the Kaduna riots in a pro-shariah pamphlet distributed there by a group that identified itself as "Concerned Muslims."

The shariah crisis has made explicit the extent of some northerners' resentment of Obasanjo's policies. The grievances in the pamphlet are one indication; even more ominous are the utterances of former Nigerian heads of state Shehu Shagari and General Muhammadu Buhari. That the two former leaders, who are both northerners, took public positions against federal suspension of shariah suggests the political tenor of the crisis.

... AND UNREALIZED PRIVILEGES

The Yorubas have benefited enormously because they are the ethnic group native to the southwestern city of Lagos, which until recently was Nigeria's political capital and continues to be the hub of national industry and commerce. Their enviable representation in Nigeria's professional and managerial class is testimony to that privilege. They also gained more than any other ethnic group from the short-lived secession of Igbos in 1967. As the only ethnic group large enough to be a counterweight to the Hausa-Fulanis, the Yorubas rose in political stature during the war. And with their relatively high levels of education, they took advantage of positions abandoned by Igbos and other easterners.

But the failure of a Yoruba to reach the pinnacle of Nigerian politics—the prime ministership or the presidency—left many Yorubas feeling cheated. The election of Obasanjo, a Yoruba, should have rectified this. But a majority of Yoruba voters stunned Obasanjo's candidacy and party, still remembering Obasanjo's ambivalence toward the military's nullification of the 1993 election that would have made Moshood Abiola Nigeria's first Yoruba president. Yoruba fears that Obasanjo's politics would be ultimately dictated from the north have also continued to color their relationship with the government and the rest of the Nigerian polity.[1] Thus, most Yorubas are still unsure of him. On the one hand, he is one of them; on the other, he is not.

Like the Yoruba, Nigeria's marginalized minority groups also believe they have been deprived of full participation in Nigeria's civil order. Although the problem of minority marginalization seemed solved in 1967 when Yakuba Gowon's administration created states out of the country's four regions, separating minorities from their dominant ethnic neighbors, it left unsolved the issue of revenue sharing among the country's minority groups.

An appropriate formula for revenue allocation is especially important for the minority peoples of the Niger Delta, the site of much of Nigeria's crude oil production. What proportion of the country's revenue should be allocated by the criteria of population and how much based on the amount of revenues derived from each region? Successive governments have failed to address this issue satisfactorily.

Because Nigeria's three major ethnic groups would be threatened by any derivation-weighted formula—with those in the north being particularly vulnerable—the criteria remained a minor part of the revenue-sharing equation. Yet if derivation had been applied, a small percentage of the oil revenue would have sufficed for the development of oil-producing communities such as those of the Ijaws, Ogonis, and Ibibios in the Niger Delta. Successive governments failed to do this, though, and the resulting years of frustration have bred radicalization and communal strife among the groups bearing the brunt of oil production, including land and river pollution from spillage. The resulting militancy led to the murder of four Ogoni chiefs in 1994 by youths who believed they had become too close to the Abacha government. This was followed by the execution in 1995 of the Ogoni activist Ken Saro-Wiwa and nine colleagues, whom the government held responsible for the murders.

The Obasanjo administration has thus inherited radicalized minority groups, some of whom have made unrealistic demands. The Movement for the Survival of Ogoni People, for example, once demanded up to 13 percent of Nigeria's oil revenue and $10 billion in royalties and compensation. Given that oil sales accounted for about 80 percent of government revenue, the Ogonis were in effect asking for 10.4 percent of government revenues. For a group numbering about half a million in a country of more than 100 million people, that was

[1]Radical members of the Yoruba group Oodua People's Congress have, for example, attacked non-Yorubas in Lagos at the slightest pretext. In November 1999, a Yoruba and Hausa merchant skirmish over control of a food market spiraled into a conflict that killed nearly 100 people.

improbable. (Of course, the government should clean up the Ogonis' polluted land and water, but that is a different matter from the issue of regular budgetary allocation.)

If oil-producing communities were compensated according to their contribution to government revenues, Nigeria would become a patchwork of Kuwaits and Haitis. An allocation formula that accounts for population, derivation, and needs would instead be the logical solution. Yet a formula that pleases most—let alone all—of the people has proved elusive.

The grievances of the country's ethnic communities would have been muted or mitigated if the country's resources had been managed competently and conscientiously. But Nigeria's governments—both military and civilian—have looted or failed to prevent the looting of the country's treasury, reducing the pool of funds for distribution. This attitude may have changed, however. Since Abacha's death in 1998, the government has uncovered billions of dollars of looted funds Abacha and his aides had stashed in foreign banks.

PROSPECTS

Nigeria's political well-being lies in finding accommodation among its diverse peoples. The most pressing challenge is in dealing with the claims of marginalization, whether real or illusory. A de-escalation of the rhetoric that has accompanied these claims would be a strong start.

The realities and perception of marginalization cannot be redressed or assuaged overnight. Although Obasanjo has taken steps to improve inclusiveness, not all of Nigeria's more than 250 ethnic groups will ever feel adequately represented at the national level. It is improbable that any administration or policy can end the perception of marginalization. But equitable policies—especially with regard to revenue allocation—and realistic expectations hold out the best potential. Ultimately, the specter of another military coup and even civil war should work in favor of amicable solutions and accommodation.

SCIENCE AND TECHNOLOGY

A turning-point for AIDS?

The impact of the global AIDS epidemic has been catastrophic, but many of the remedies are obvious. It is now a question of actually doing something

DURBAN

WHEN Thabo Mbeki, South Africa's president, opened the world AIDS conference in Durban on July 9th, he was widely expected to admit that he had made a mistake. Mr Mbeki has been flirting with the ideas of a small but vociferous group of scientists who, flying in the face of all the evidence, maintain that AIDS is not caused by the human immunodeficiency virus (HIV). His speech at the opening ceremony would have been the ideal opportunity for a graceful climbdown. Instead, he blustered and prevaricated, pretending that there was a real division of opinion among scientists about the matter, and arguing that the commission that he has appointed to look into this non-existent division would resolve it.

AIDS is the most political disease around. People talk a lot about AIDS "exceptionalism", and in many ways it is exceptional. For a start, it is difficult to think of another disease that would have brought the host country's head of state out of his office to open a conference, confused though his ideas may be. It is also exceptional, in modern times, in the attitudes of the healthy towards the infected. Illness usually provokes sympathy. But in many parts of the world those who have HIV are treated rather as lepers were in biblical days. Indeed, Gugu Dlamini, a community activist in KwaZulu Natal, the South African province in which Durban lies, was stoned to death by her neighbours when she revealed that she had the virus. In many parts of the world, as Kevin De Cock, of America's Centres for Disease Control (CDC), pointed out to the conference, attitudes to AIDS can be summed up in four words: silence, stigma, discrimination and denial. Mr Mbeki himself is at least guilty of denial.

Nevertheless, the fact that this, the 13th such AIDS conference, was held in Africa shows that some progress is being made. The previous conference, in Geneva in 1998, claimed to be "bridging the gap" between the treatment of the disease in the rich and poor worlds. It did no such thing. This one set as its goal to "break the silence". It may have succeeded. What needed to be shouted from the rooftops was that, contrary to some popular views, AIDS is not primarily a disease of gay western men or of intravenous drug injectors. It is a disease of ordinary people leading ordinary lives, except that most of them happen to live in a continent, Africa, that the rich countries of the world find it easy to ignore.

In some places the problem is so bad that it is hard to know where to begin. According to United Nations estimates, 25m of the 34m infected people in the world live in Africa. In absolute terms, South Africa has the most cases (4m, or about 20% of the adult population), but several of its neighbours have even worse ratios. In Botswana, for example, 36% of the adult population is now infected with HIV. Barring some currently unimaginable treatment—unimaginable in both efficacy and cost—almost all of these people will die as a result.

The hydra-headed monster

And mere numbers are not the only issue. People talk, rhetorically, of waging war on diseases. In the case of AIDS, the rhetoric could be inverted, for the effects of the illness on human populations are similar to those of war. Most infectious diseases tend to kill infants and the old. AIDS, like war, kills those in the prime of life. Indeed, in one way it is worse than war. When armies fight, it is predominantly young men who are killed. AIDS kills young women, too.

The result is social dislocation on a grand scale. As the diagram on the next page shows, the age-distribution of Botswana's population will change from the "pyramid" that is typical of countries with rapidly growing populations, to a "chimney-shaped" graph from which the young have been lopped out. Ten years from now, according to figures released at the conference by USAID, the American government's agency for international development, the life expectancy of somebody born in Botswana will have fallen to 29. In 20 years' time, the old will outnumber the middle-aged. Nor are things much better in other countries in southern Africa. In Zimbabwe and Namibia, two of Botswana's neighbours, life expectancy in 2010 will be 33. In South Africa it will be 35.

The destruction of young adults means that AIDS is creating orphans on an unprecedented scale. There are 11.2m of them, of whom 10.7m live in Africa. On top of that, vast numbers of children are infected as they are born. These are the exception to the usual rule that infants do not get the disease. Children are rarely infected in the womb, but they may acquire the virus from their mothers' vaginal fluids when they are born, or from breast milk. More than 5m children are reckoned to have been infected in this way. Almost 4m of them are already dead.

It sounds hopeless. And yet it isn't. Two African countries, Uganda and Senegal, seem to have worked out how to cope with the disease. Their contrasting experiences serve both as a warning and as a lesson to other countries in the world, particularly those in Asia that now have low infection rates and may be feeling complacently smug about them. The warning: act early, or you will be sorry. The lesson: it is, even so, never too late to act. Senegal began its anti-AIDS programme in 1986, before the virus had got a proper grip. It has managed to keep its infection rate below 2%. Uganda began its programme in the early 1990s, when 14% of the adult population was already infected. Now that figure is down to 8% and falling. In these two countries, the epidemic seems to have been stopped in its tracks.

As Roy Anderson, a noted epidemiologist from Oxford University, pointed out to the conference, stopping an epidemic requires one thing: that the average number of people infected by somebody who already has the disease be less than one. For a sexually transmitted disease, this average has three components: the "transmissibility" of the disease, the average rate that an infected person acquires new and uninfected partners, and the average length of time for which somebody is infectious.

Cutting off the hydra's heads

The easiest of these to tackle has been transmissibility. Surprisingly, perhaps, AIDS is not all that easily transmissible compared with other diseases. But there are three ways—one certain, one as yet a pious hope, and one the subject of some controversy—to reduce the rate of transmission between adults still further. The first is to use condoms. The second is to develop a microbicide that will kill the virus in the vagina. And the third is to treat other sexually transmitted diseases.

Both Senegal and Uganda have been strong on the use of condoms. In Senegal, for example, the annual number of condoms used rose from 800,000 in 1988 to 9m in 1997. Nevertheless, it still takes a lot of encouragement to persuade people to use them. Partly, this is a question of discounting the future. For decades African lives have been shorter, on average, than those in the rest of the world. With AIDS, they are getting shorter still. A Botswanan who faces the prospect of death before his 30th birthday is likely to be more reckless than an American who can look forward to well over twice that lifespan; a short life might as well be a merry one.

There is also the question of who wears the condom. Until recently, there was no choice. Only male condoms were available. And women in many parts of Africa are in a weak negotiating position when it comes to in-

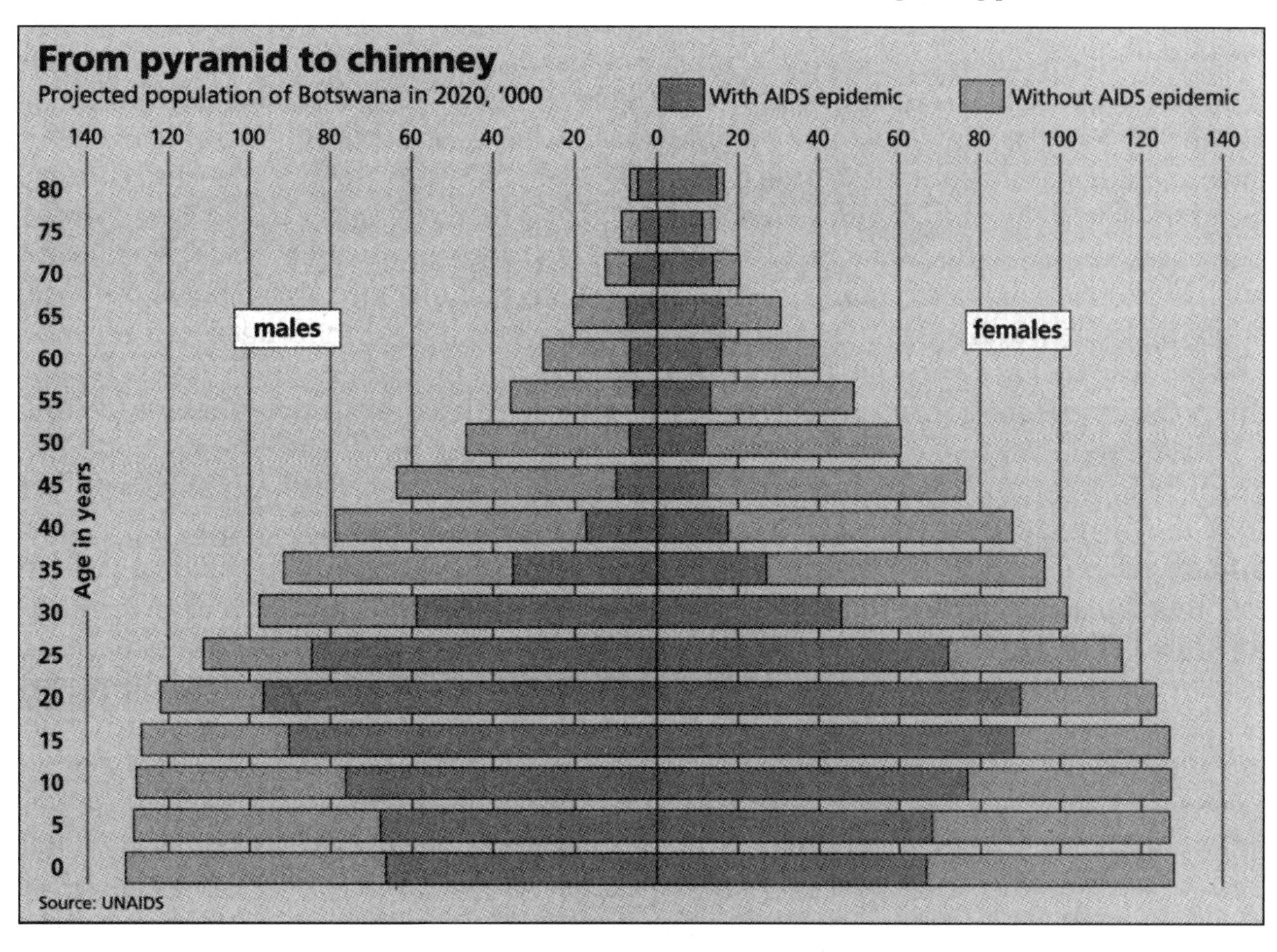

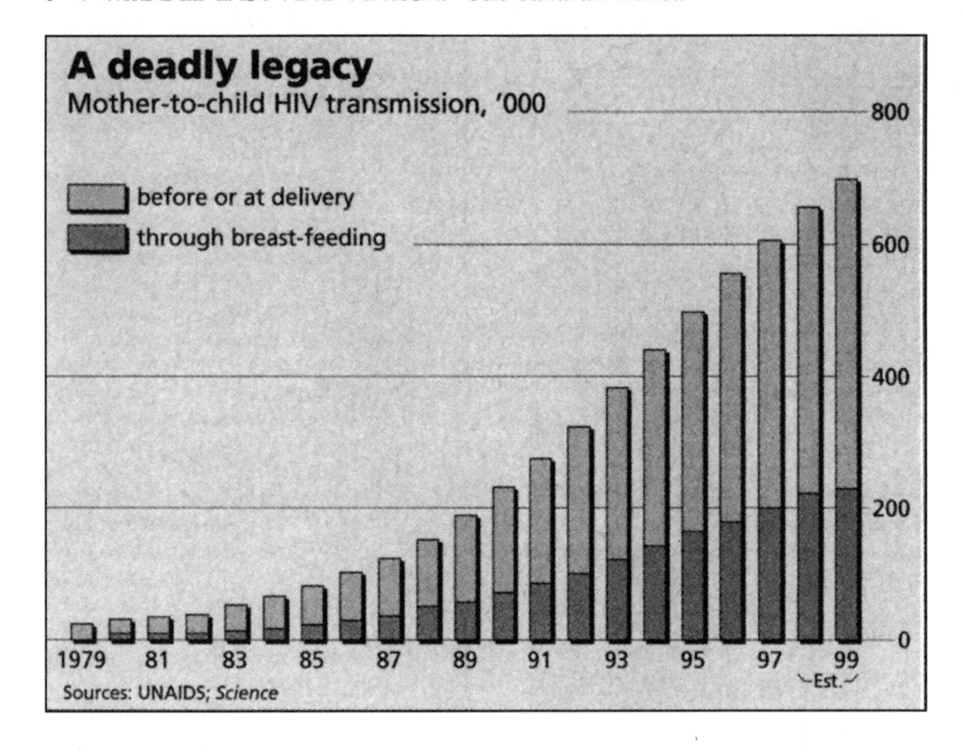

sisting that a man put one on. The best way out of this is to alter the balance of power. That, in general, means more and better education, particularly for girls. This, too, has been an important component of the Senegalese and Ugandan anti-AIDS programmes. A stop-gap, though, is the female condom, a larger version of the device that fits inside the vagina, which is proving surprisingly popular among groups such as Nairobi prostitutes. But an even less intrusive—and to a man invisible—form of protection would be a vaginal microbicide that kills the virus before it can cross the vaginal wall.

Here, however, the news is bad. Much hope had been pinned on a substance called nonoxynol-9 (the spermicide used to coat condoms that are intended to prevent pregnancy rather than disease). Unfortunately, the results of a major United Nations trial announced at the conference have confirmed the suspicion that nonoxynol-9 does not work against HIV. So researchers have gone back to the drawing-board and are searching for suitable (and suitably cheap) substances among the cast-offs from antiviral drugs used to treat AIDS in rich countries.

More equivocal is the value of treating other sexually transmitted diseases as a way of preventing the transmission of HIV. Clearly, such treatment is a good thing in its own right. But a study carried out a few years ago at Mwanza, Tanzania, suggested that it also stymies HIV. That would not be surprising, since the vaginal lesions that other venereal diseases produce should make excellent entry points for the virus. Yet a more recent study at Rakai, Uganda, suggests that other venereal diseases make no difference; the matter is now a subject of much debate.

Sex is not the only way that HIV is transmitted. Infected mothers can give it to their children. But here, too, transmissibility can be reduced dramatically.

A first way of doing this is to test pregnant women to see if they have the virus. If they do, they are unlikely to pass it on to the fetus in the womb, but they are quite likely to do so in the act of giving birth. According to figures presented to the conference by Ruth Nduati, of the University of Nairobi, up to 40% of children born to untreated infected women catch AIDS this way. But that number can be reduced drastically—to around 20%—by giving infected pregnant women a short course of an antiviral drug just before they give birth.

Until recently, the preferred drug was AZT. Many African governments balked at using this because, although it is cheap by western standards, it can stretch African health budgets to breaking point. However, recent studies carried out in Kenya and South Africa have shown that an even cheaper drug called nevirapine will do just as well. A course of this costs $4, still a fair whack for an impoverished country, but worth it both for the life of a child and for the cost-saving of not having to treat that child's subsequent illness.

Once safely born, the child of an infected mother is still not out of the woods. This is because it can be infected via its mother's milk. Oddly, this is a more intractable problem than transmission at birth. Nobody knows (because nobody has tried to find out) if carrying on with AZT or nevirapine would keep a mother's milk virus-free. But the cost would be prohibitive anyway. The only alternative is not to breast-feed.

That may sound easy, but it is not. First, the formula milk that could substitute for breast milk costs money. Second, unless clean water is available to mix with it, the result is likely to be a diarrhoeal disease that may kill the child anyway. And third, by failing to breast-feed, a mother in many parts of Africa is in effect announcing that she has the virus, and thus exposing herself to both stigma and discrimination. Not breast-feeding is, nevertheless, an effective addition to pre-natal antiviral drugs. According to Dr Nduati, combining both methods can bring the infection rate below 8%.

The second of Dr Anderson's criteria, the rate of acquisition of new and uninfected partners, is critical to the speed with which AIDS spreads, but is also far harder to tackle. The reasons why AIDS has spread faster in some places than in others are extremely complicated. But one important factor is so-called disassortative mating.

As far as is known, all AIDS epidemics start with the spread of the disease in one or more small, high-risk groups. These groups include prostitutes and their clients, male homosexuals and injecting drug users. The rate at which an epidemic spreads to lower-risk groups depends a great deal on whether different groups mate mainly among themselves (assortative mating) or whether they mate a lot with other people (disassortative mating). The more disassortative mating there is, the faster the virus will spread.

Sub-Saharan Africa and the Caribbean (the second-worst affected part of the world) have particularly high levels of disassortative mating between young girls and older men. And in an area where AIDS is already highly prevalent, older men are a high-risk group; they are far more likely to have picked up the virus than younger ones. This helps to explain why the rate of infection is higher in young African women than it is in young African men.

Inter-generational churning may thus, according to Dr Anderson's models, go a long way towards explaining why Africa and the Caribbean have the highest levels of HIV infection in the world. And it suggests that, as with condom use, a critical part of any anti-AIDS campaign should be to give women more power. In many cases, young women are coerced or bribed into relationships with older men. This would diminish if girls were better educated—not least because they would then find it easier to earn a living.

The partial explanation for Africa's plight that disassortative mating provides should not, however, bring false comfort in other areas. Dr Anderson's models suggest that lower levels of disassortative mating cannot stop an epidemic, they merely postpone it. Those countries, such as Ukraine, where HIV is spreading rapidly through a high-risk group (in Ukraine's case, injecting drug users), need to act now, even if the necessary action, such as handing out clean needles, is politically distasteful. Countries such as India, where lower-risk groups are starting to show up in the statistics, and where the prevalence rates in some states are already above 2%, needed to act yesterday, and to aim their message more widely. The example of Senegal (and, indeed, the strongly worded, morally neutral advertising campaigns conducted in many western countries in the 1980s), shows the value of early action as surely as do Dr Anderson's models.

To tackle the third element of those models—the length of time that somebody is infectious—really requires a vaccine. Drugs can reduce it to some extent, by bringing people's viral load down to the point where they will not pass on the disease. But effective therapies are currently expensive and, despite the widespread demands at the conference for special arrangements that would lower their price in poor countries, are unlikely to become cheap enough for routine use there for some time. On top of that, if drugs are used carelessly, resistant strains of the virus can emerge, rendering the therapies useless. A study by the CDC, published to coincide with the conference, showed resistant strains in the blood of three-quarters of the participants in a United Nations AIDS drug-access programme in Uganda.

The search for a vaccine

Vaccines are not immune to the emergence of resistant strains. But they are one-shot treatments and so are not subject to the whims of patient compliance with complex drug regimes. Non-compliance is the main cause of the emergence of resistant strains, since the erratic consumption of a particular drug allows populations of resistant viruses to evolve and build up.

In total, 21 clinical trials of vaccines are happening around the world, but only five are taking place in poor countries, and only two are so-called phase 3 trials that show whether a vaccine will work effectively in the real world. Preliminary results from these two trials, which are being conducted by an American company called VaxGen, are expected next year. They are eagerly awaited, for even a partially effective vaccine could have a significant impact on the virus's spread. A calculation by America's National Institutes of Health shows that, over the course of a decade, a 60%-effective vaccine introduced now would stop nearly twice as many infections as a 90%-effective one introduced five years hence.

Even then, there is the question of cost. This is being addressed by the International AIDS Vaccine Initiative (IAVI), a New York-based charity. IAVI, according to its boss Seth Berkley, acts like a venture-capital firm. At the moment, that capital amounts to about $100m, gathered from various governments and foundations. IAVI provides small firms with seed money to develop new products, but instead of demanding a share of the equity in return, it requires that the eventual product, if any, should be sold at a low profit margin—about 10%. If a sponsored firm breaks this arrangement, IAVI can give the relevant patents to anybody it chooses. At the moment, IAVI has four such partnerships, and it chose the conference to announce that one—a collaboration with the Universities of Oxford and Nairobi—has just received regulatory approval and will start trials in September.

None of these things alone will be enough to stop the epidemic in its tracks, but in combination they may succeed. And one last lesson from Dr Anderson's equations is not to give up just because a policy does not seem to be working. Those equations predict that applying a lot of effort to an established epidemic will have little initial effect. Then, suddenly, infection rates will drop fast. The message is: "hang in there". AIDS may be exceptional, but it is not that exceptional. Good science and sensible public policy can defeat it. There is at least a glimmer of hope.

Unit 10

Unit Selections

Key Points to Consider

- Do you support current efforts to increase the role of UN peacekeeping forces, or should UN activities be limited to preventive diplomacy and more modest peace maintenance operations such as monitoring elections and referendums? Explain.

- Should NATO countries be withdrawn from internal conflicts in the Balkans and leave peacekeeping duties in such varied places as Kosovo, East Timor, Haiti, and Sierra Leone to the UN and regional organizations? Who should pay and supply the troops for these peacekeeping operations?

- Can the international community do more to regulate the activities of modern mercenaries? If so, how?

- What is the most effective way to prevent the use of child soldiers? Should the international community do more to help integrate former child soldiers into society after peace settlements are negotiated?

- Explain why you do or do not agree with Paul Brown's conclusion that several future global environmental disasters can be averted if citizens in rich countries make modest adjustments to their lifestyles and apply existing scientific knowledge to minimize pollution.

www.dushkin.com/online/

31. **Commission on Global Governance**
    http://www.cgg.ch
32. **InterAction**
    http://www.interaction.org
33. **Nonprofit Organizations on the Internet**
    http://www.ai.mit.edu/people/ellens/Non/non-old.html
34. **The North-South Institute**
    http://www.nsi-ins.ca/ensi/index.html
35. **United Nations Home Page**
    http://www.un.org

These sites are annotated on pages 4 and 5.

The most visible international institution since World War II has been the United Nations. Membership grew from the original 50 in 1945 to 185 in 1995. The UN, across a variety of fronts, achieved noteworthy results—eradication of disease, immunization, provision of food and shelter to refugees and victims of natural disasters, and help to dozens of countries that have moved from colonial status to self-rule.

After the Persian Gulf War, the UN guided enforcement of economic sanctions against Iraq, sent peacekeeping forces to former Yugoslavia and to Somalia, monitored an unprecedented number of elections and cease-fire agreements, and played an active peacekeeping role in almost every region of the world. However, the withdrawal of the UN mission in Somalia, the near-collapse of the UN peacekeeping mission in Bosnia prior to the intervention of NATO-sponsored troops, and the delayed response of the UN in sending troops to monitor cease-fire agreements in East Timor and Sierra Leone in 1999 raised doubts about the ability of the organization to continue to be involved in peacekeeping worldwide. Some observers now call for the United Nations to scale back its current level of peacekeeping in order to focus more effectively on global problems that nobody else can or will tackle.

In recent years, the United Nations has not heeded this advice. As the authors of "Peacekeeping: The UN's Missions Impossible" note, the United Nations is again in action, called upon to end wars and even run disabled countries after years of experimenting with "coalitions of the willing" among regional groups. The UN runs all Kosovo's civilian affairs in parallel with NATO and is the only authority in East Timor. The world's newest country has become the UN's pet project: an experiment in "nation-building." The UN Transitional Administration for East Timor (UNTAET) is not just helping the new country's government—it *is* that government. But the UN is finding that governing is harder than separating warring parties—especially when the country has been razed to the ground. Creating a democracy from scratch will be even more difficult.

Pressures to reduce UN peacekeeping efforts are also being fueled by the realities of scarce resources created largely by the refusal of many member states, including the United States, to pay back dues. The United States withheld payments of back dues for several years as part of a campaign led by conservative members of the U.S. Congress. These congressmen have demanded that the UN undertake extensive internal reforms and reduce the amount of the United States' contribution before the United States pays its back dues. The United States narrowly averted losing the right to vote in the General Assembly by agreeing at the end of 1999 to pay a portion of its $1.02 billion debt over a 3-year period. At the end of 2000, UN and U.S. negotiators reached agreement on a deal that will probably win approval by the U.S. Congress as it includes a dramatic reduction in the dues that the United States will have to pay. In exchange, the United States will have to accept a slight reduction in the dominant role it has played in dictating administrative changes in the world organization. This compromise may help to mute growing criticism of the United States, especially since the unexpected budget surplus in the United States continues to grow.

Tensions among member states over dues allocation and the proper role of the United Nations reflects more fundamental disagreements over the meaning of international security. The tension between individual human security and state security, as interpreted by the powers that be, is an old and familiar theme in history. Despite the innovation of peacekeeping, the UN has not lived up to expectations in securing a disarmed and peaceful world. This situation is due in part to the fact that the concept of security has been broadened during the post–cold war era to include human security.

In the absence of involvement by the United Nations or major world powers, a variety of nonstate actors play influential roles in communal conflicts. One of the more important actors in many recent conflicts are modern mercenaries. David Shearer in "Outsourcing War" describes the role of mercenaries in a number of conflicts. In several areas of instability, private security businesses are booming, as governments, corporations, NGOs, and the media increasingly contract for their services. While mercenaries have been involved in international conflicts for hundreds of years, the average soldier of fortune today wears a suit and works out of a corporate office in Great Britain or South Africa. David Shearer examines this new type of international actor to determine whether mercenaries are murderous profiteers or the future of international peacekeeping.

Many of the most intractable communal conflicts around the world continue because combatants enlist children to serve as their foot soldiers. In "Children Under Arms: Kalashnikov Kids," writers for *The Economist* describe how children are being used to fight wars, at great cost to themselves and their societies. Today, an estimated 300,000 children in over 60 countries are soldiers. The use of child soldiers in armed conflicts also aggravates peace settlement efforts as the resources necessary for demobilization and reintegration of child soldiers are usually lacking in developing countries, where children constitute nearly half the population.

The UN Convention on the Rights of the Child (CRC), signed in 1989 and ratified by more than 160 nations, was one effort designed to address this abuse by establishing 15 years as the minimum recruitment age for child soldiers. However, several influential nation-states, including the United States, have not yet ratified this treaty. Until the use of child soldiers is ended, post-conflict reconstruction efforts will be seriously hampered.

A number of thorny issues related to the question of "who should fight for whom" are likely to remain controversial in future decades. Many societies must also deal with extreme social dislocations due to continued poverty and an unprecedented death rate caused by the AIDS epidemic among adults. These trends may do more to reshape our collective future than more familiar security problems and threats. In the future, the world may also increasingly have to confront a host of environmental problems that span national borders. In "The Dilemma That Confronts the World," Paul Brown describes the findings of a recently released UN publication, *Global Environment Outlook 2000*. This report warns that water shortages, global warming, and nitrogen pollution threaten the planet's future unless politicians act now. The executive director of the United Nations Environment Programme warns that it is still possible to reverse the process, but conspicuous overconsumption by the world's rich countries has to be cut by 90 percent to do so. According to Brown, these changes do not have to lead to a lowering of living standards if the application of existing science, such as recycling, is widely used.

PEACEKEEPING

The UN's missions impossible

After a year or two in retreat, the United Nations is again in action, called upon to end wars and run disabled countries. It should not take on what it cannot do

NEW YORK

THE use of the United Nations as an international police force has, in the space of the past decade, ballooned, shrivelled again when things went wrong, and now, with Kosovo, East Timor and Sierra Leone, once again grown fat. Increasingly, the liberal world's fitful conscience does not want to live with barbarity, and demands that it be checked. Usually, the UN is the only available instrument. But the one constant, throughout those ten troubled years, is that the Security Council, the world's flawed policy-maker, continues to instruct its policemen to do what needs to be done without providing them with the means to do it.

A great fuss is made of signing a council resolution. But once that is done, the further business of implementing it is passed lightly over, a matter for the UN bureaucracy rather than for member-governments. A report on peacekeeping, to be published this month by a panel chaired by an experienced UN old-timer, Lakhdar Brahimi, takes a sharp look at this and other UN shortcomings, both in the council and in the secretariat. One of its most important messages to the UN's secretary-general, Kofi Annan, is that, if told to do the impossible, he should just say no.

For the UN's first 40 years, peacekeeping usually meant waiting until armies had fought to a standstill, and then interposing monitors between the ex-combatants. An up-to-date version of this sort of peacekeeping is about to occur in Ethiopia and Eritrea, where the UN has agreed to send up to 100 military observers to monitor a ceasefire.

But at the end of the 1980s, the Security Council, over-excited by its release from the cold-war lock, reinvented humanitarian intervention. The council's concerns were extended to

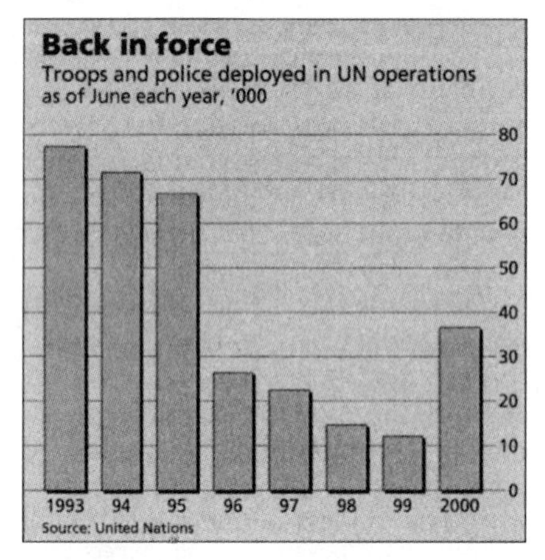

"human security": it would rescue people from the savagery of civil and ethnic conflict. But then came Somalia, whose warlords showed none of the respect for international authority of regular armies, and where the Americans were shocked to discover that peacekeeping could be dangerous. This was followed by Bosnia, where expectations of "safe havens" were raised only to crash in tragedy. Its credibility in shreds, the UN dithered unforgivably through Rwanda's genocide.

It would be better, people began to argue, to enlist regional groups—the "coalitions of the willing"—to take on peace-making or peace-building; let the UN stick to uncontroversial peacekeeping. The NATO alliance, after decades of inactivity, swung into action in the Balkans. The Nigerians led a West African force into Sierra Leone.

Regional peace-making sounds good. But few regions, Europe apart, have either the men or the money to mount such an operation. For a start, the costs fall directly on the participating countries, who have to pay for everything. When democracy returned to Nigeria last year, taxpayers wondered, justifiably enough, why they should be paying both in money and men to stop the Sierra Leoneans from slaughtering one another. The costs of UN missions are paid by all UN members, who are assessed on a scale adjusted to their wealth. Or that is the theory: in practice, when big payers such as the United States fall behind with their dues, it takes a while to repay the countries, often among the world's poorest, who have supplied the troops.

There are other reasons why regional intervention cannot always be the answer. Look, for instance, at Congo, where the neighbours are already fighting over the country like hyenas round a corpse. Australia led a successful coalition into East Timor. But it is rare for a threatened third-world country to have a first-world godfather of that sort, with the political will to lead a charge and the capability to succeed.

So the pendulum is swinging back. The UN has taken on Sierra Leone, and may eventually have to take on Congo too. In both countries, its theoretical job is the traditional one of supporting a peace treaty. But both treaties were horribly flawed. In Sierra Leone, the UN is floundering, its original mandate in tatters, its forces not strong enough to succeed in a more ambitious task. Revealing a modicum of common sense,

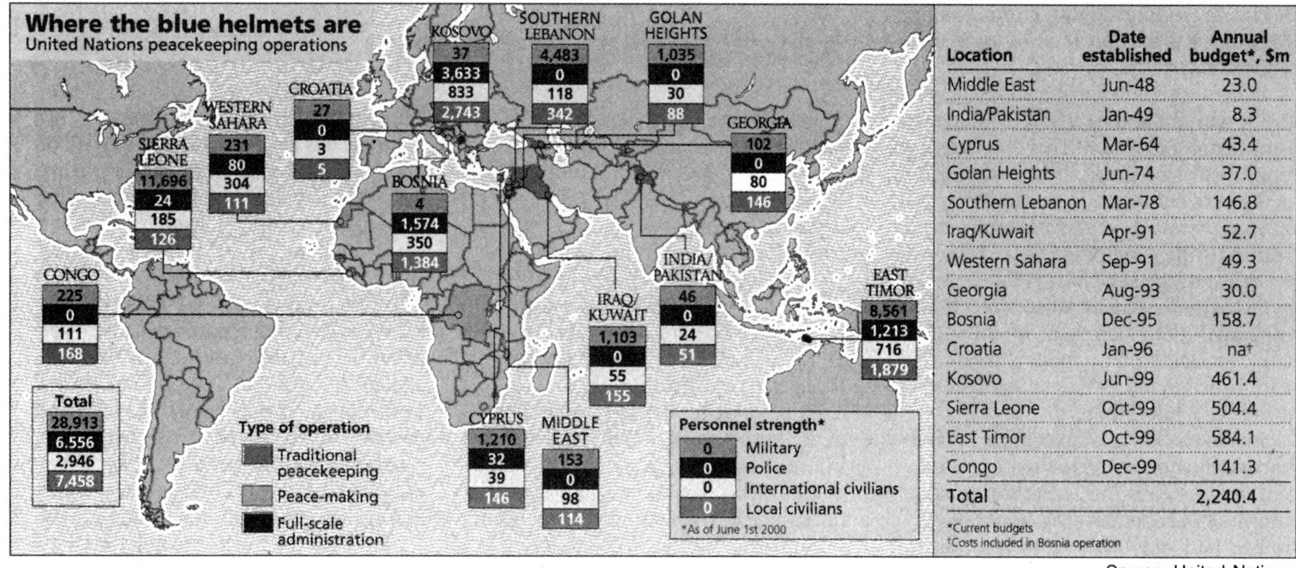

Location	Date established	Annual budget*, $m
Middle East	Jun-48	23.0
India/Pakistan	Jan-49	8.3
Cyprus	Mar-64	43.4
Golan Heights	Jun-74	37.0
Southern Lebanon	Mar-78	146.8
Iraq/Kuwait	Apr-91	52.7
Western Sahara	Sep-91	49.3
Georgia	Aug-93	30.0
Bosnia	Dec-95	158.7
Croatia	Jan-96	na†
Kosovo	Jun-99	461.4
Sierra Leone	Oct-99	504.4
East Timor	Oct-99	584.1
Congo	Dec-99	141.3
Total		**2,240.4**

*Current budgets
†Costs included in Bosnia operation

Source: United Nations

the Security Council has so far held back from ordering Mr Annan to conjure up the 5,000 troops who are supposed to bring order to the vast mayhem in Congo, and protect the handful of UN observers already there.

Congo is an extreme case. But getting peacekeepers together is a constant nightmare for the UN. With the end of the cold war, the governments that traditionally, and generously, supplied well-trained troops—the Nordic countries, Canada, the Netherlands and others—cut their defence budgets and have fewer men available. America, Britain, France, Russia and China, the five permanent members of the Security Council, still have sizeable armed forces but are seldom willing to commit them. Third-world countries tend to have rather large armies, and are usually happy for the UN to employ them. But their soldiers are often ill-trained, and their equipment usually has to be supplied by someone richer.

However desperate the need, the UN is not even allowed to start collecting a peacekeeping force until the council provides its mandate. Supposedly, several countries have troops on stand-by for such emergencies. But when called on, they are almost always unavailable. Supposedly, too, spare UN weapons are stored in Brindisi. But the few arms left in this dump are mostly obsolete.

The UN, in other words, has to fly by the seat of its pants. The result can be seen in the Kafkaesque confusion of Sierra Leone. The Indian general in command was told to support a peace treaty; that treaty was not worth the paper it was written on. Instead he found himself, without new orders, let alone reinforcements, from the council, at war with a bunch of murderous rebels, backed by an almost equally unscrupulous outside power. To help him carry out this operation, he has a motley army including Guineans, who meekly handed their weapons over to the rebels at the first spot of trouble; Zambians, who arrived without even the most basic equipment; and Nigerians, sulky because they are not in command.

No national army would take on such a mission, let alone under such conditions. The Sierra Leonean operation has, so far, been saved from catastrophe by the professionalism of some of its peacekeepers: the Gurkha troops, for instance, and the British battalion that was flown out in a hurry to secure the capital, Freetown. The UN is rightly grateful to the British. But why, ask the less grateful, did the battalion have to come, and go, on Britain's terms, not the UN's?

If it is hard for Mr Annan to assemble troops, it is infinitely harder for him to get the judges, policemen, customs officials and other civilian professionals who are needed for the two huge, unprecedented jobs that have recently been landed on the UN: running Kosovo and East Timor. Most countries, even if they do not admit it, have a bit of fat in their armed forces. But few countries have too many policemen, let alone policemen trained to use arms. The British shook their heads sadly, until they remembered the Royal Ulster Constabulary and spared a few.

The UN runs all Kosovo's civilian affairs (see "Kouchnerism in Kosovo") in parallel with NATO, which handles military matters. In East Timor, a country without any government at all, the UN is in complete control. Although it had a big supervisory role in Cambodia, the UN has never done anything remotely like this before. It is not only training locals to do the job; it is doing the job itself.

Moreover, it is doing it on a wing and a prayer, without any new administrative or institutional provision. The Peacekeeping Department is in charge, though administering a whole country is not something that comes to it naturally, and its resources are stretched to breaking-point. The old vision of the UN as a relaxed and bloated bureaucracy has melted with years of American-enforced zero growth. Although there are still useless people around (and no money to get rid of them, until they retire), the capable are working full-out, under strain.

Should the trusteeship council, presumably under a new name less worrying to the third world, be resurrected to run disabled countries? The counter-argument is that the UN has had only two running-a-country jobs in the past half-century—Kosovo and East Timor—and may not be landed with any more. Perhaps, with its limited resources, it should concentrate on bread-and-butter stuff. It is a hard choice, which the UN may face in its usual way by ignoring it.

To intervene, or not?

The larger question is when, or even whether, the UN should intervene in a country's sovereign affairs for humanitarian reasons. Last year, when Mr Annan urged the case for humanitarian intervention, the General Assembly reacted unhappily, subsequently resolving that the UN should intervene only when invited to do so by the government

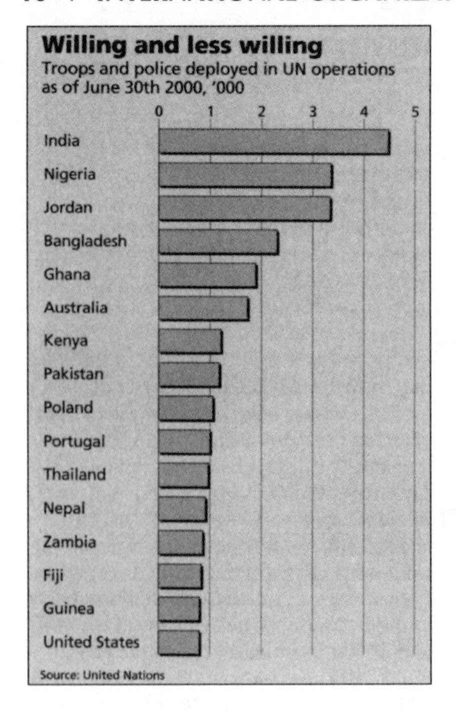

in power. Third-world countries twitch at the notion that it is the first world (plus Russia and China), personified by the Security Council's permanent five, which decides when and how to intervene. Is it, they ask, the right of the powerful to push in, often for their own narrow national interests, or the right of victims to be rescued?

Paradoxes abound. Governments that, in principle, are shrill in defence of national sovereignty, may be the first to call for intervention in individual cases; governments that defend the principle of intervention may be the last to agree to finance or join individual missions. The UN, the sum of its members, is supposed to be impartial, but some now argue that it should openly take sides in a dispute. Others worry that action taken to save lives may result in more being lost as opposing armies use a UN-provided pause to take breath and re-arm.

Third-world anxiety about a first-world-driven UN has a direct effect on peacekeeping. One instance of this was the disappearance of the so-called gratis personnel. In the mid-1990s, the UN, stung by sneers at its military amateurishness, began borrowing pukka military types from willing lenders. The corridors were suddenly abuzz with captains and colonels commanding and controlling as if the secretariat had been transformed into NATO. Unfortunately, that was roughly the way non-NATO countries saw things. Because the officers all came from countries rich enough to lend them, and to continue paying their salaries, the rest of the world scented a conspiracy. The experiment was short-lived.

It was followed by the notion of keeping 12–15 professional officers under permanent UN employment. In an emergency, the officers would be deployed to set up a temporary headquarters. It was a good idea, but Americans thought it smacked of world government. That, too, was abandoned.

Given these limitations, what can the UN do to become a more efficient peacekeeper? For a start, it could improve its intelligence, spotting crises before they arise. There is no excuse these days for being ill-informed; but the UN lacks people to digest and analyse this intelligence, and then to relay it to those who make decisions and policy.

Above all, the secretary-general should be prepared to say no when members of the Security Council ask him to do the impossible. The brutal honesty of the UN's own reports on the Srebrenica and Rwandan tragedies should signal a turning-point. The UN should indeed be prepared to intervene where there is gross cruelty. But when taking on an operation, it must prepare for the worst outcome, not the best. The secretary-general is not in the business of keeping council members happy. Rather, he should tell them as precisely as he can what is needed if a mission is to have any chance of success. And he should refuse to raise their, and the world's, expectations of what the under-equipped UN can do.

Kouchnerism in Kosovo

BARELY five years ago, the whole idea of UN peacekeeping nearly came to an ignominious end in the killing-fields of Bosnia. When a post-war regime for the country was devised, the UN was pointedly left out—until, as an afterthought, it was told to assemble a police force.

In post-war Kosovo, by contrast, the UN's man—Bernard Kouchner, an astute French pioneer of humanitarianism—has received a huge mandate. In the words of a UN handout, his job is to "begin building peace, democracy, stability and self-government." Among other things, this includes establishing a judiciary, coordinating humanitarian relief, collecting tax and preparing for local elections. In a mission that has tested his optimism about human nature, Mr Kouchner has tried to draw Kosovo's ethnic-Albanian majority and its small Serb minority into joint institutions. The Serbs have been told by Belgrade not to co-operate, but have done so intermittently; some Albanians walk out if too many concessions are made to the Serbs.

At the same time, Mr Kouchner is under pressure from western governments to preserve some semblance of multiethnicity in Kosovo. Confusingly, his mandate insists that Kosovo is part of Yugoslavia, whereas the locals hope that he is there to help its evolution into an independent country. As in other places, the UN is filling the gap left by the ambiguity of international policy.

If the UN has acquired a new lease of life in Kosovo, that is partly because it has had to delegate. Military security has been allotted to NATO; the two bodies get on well enough, as they signally failed to in Bosnia. The EU has been entrusted with economic management, and the Organisation for Security and Co-operation in Europe with rebuilding institutions.

But the UN's peacekeeping department remains powerful. For example, it can amend the "laws" by which Mr Kouchner is attempting to bring some semblance of order to the province's wildly unregulated economy. Unfortunately, the expertise needed to bring order to a Hobbesian free-for-all—where property rights are highly fluid and a corrupt form of communism is the only kind of government anyone can remember— is difficult to find, on New York's East River or anywhere else.

Outsourcing War

by David Shearer

For nearly three centuries, the accepted international norm has been that only nation-states should be permitted to fight wars. Not surprisingly, the rise of private military companies in the 1990s—and the possibility that they may view conflict as a legitimate business activity—has provoked outrage and prompted calls for them to be outlawed. The popular press has labeled these companies "mercenaries" and "dogs of war," conjuring up images of freebooting and rampaging Rambos overthrowing weak—usually African—governments. At a press conference convened in June 1997 to discuss the ongoing civil war in Sierra Leone, Secretary General Kofi Annan bristled at the suggestion that the United Nations would ever consider working with "respectable" mercenary organizations, arguing that there is no "distinction between respectable mercenaries and non-respectable mercenaries."

But is this depiction fair? Certainly these soldiers might meet the three most widely accepted criteria defining a mercenary: They are foreign to a conflict; they are motivated chiefly by financial gain; and, in some cases, they have participated directly in combat. They differ significantly, however, from infamous characters such as Irishman "Mad" Mike Hoare and Frenchman Bob Denard, who fought in the Congo and elsewhere in the 1960s. What most sets today's military companies apart is their approach. They have a distinct corporate character, have openly defended their usefulness and professionalism, have used internationally accepted legal and financial instruments to secure their deals, and so far have supported only recognized governments and avoided regimes unpalatable to the international community. As Enrique Bernales Ballesteros, the UN's special rapporteur on the use of mercenaries, has noted, personnel working for these companies, "even when they have a military background and are highly paid" cannot be considered as "coming within the legal scope of mercenary status."

Dismissing private-sector military personnel as little more than modern-day soldiers of fortune would not only be simplistic but would obscure the broader issues that these military companies raise. Why have they emerged in the 1990s? What role might they play in the future? Can they be regulated? Practitioners and academics who specialize in conflict resolution typically argue that private military companies hinder efforts to end wars and broker peace. Yet, the evidence suggests that coercion is often essential to breaking deadlocks and bringing opposing parties to the negotiating table. In this context, military companies can be seen not as part of the problem but as part of the solution—especially for struggling but legitimate governments that lack the resources to field effective fighting forces. As the political and economic costs of peacekeeping continue to escalate, it may increasingly make sense for multilateral organizations and Western governments to consider outsourcing some aspects of these interventions to the private sector.

These Guns for Hire

Private military forces are as old as warfare itself. The ancient Chinese, Greek, and Roman armies employed large numbers of mercenaries, and mercenaries comprised about half of William the Conqueror's army in the eleventh century. During the fourteenth century, Italian city-states contracted private military forces, known as *condottieri,* to protect themselves—an early acknowledgement that hiring mercenaries can often prove more cost-effective than maintaining standing armies. Private forces have also served states' immediate strategic interests. The United Kingdom, for example, hired 30,000 Hessian soldiers to fight in the American War of Independence to avoid conscripting its own citizens. In the late eighteenth century, foreigners comprised half of the armed forces of Prussia and a third of the armies of France and the United Kingdom. Mercantile companies were licensed by the state to wage war to serve their countries' economic interests. In 1815, the East India Company, which colonized India on behalf of the British government, boasted an army of 150,000 soldiers.

But with the rise of nationalism in the nineteenth century, the idea of fighting for one's country rather than for commercial interests gained currency. Governments came to command a monopoly over violence and became increasingly keen on limiting the risks to their neutrality that arose when their citizens fought other peoples' wars. Conscripted armies under the control of the state became the norm—apart from the activities of a few individuals that capitalized on the upheavals caused by African independence throughout the 1960s and 1970s.

In the past decade, however, the increasing inability of weak governments

Reprinted with permission from *Foreign Policy,* Fall 1998, pp. 68-81. © 1998 by the Carnegie Endowment for International Peace.

to counter internal violence has created a ready market for private military forces. This demand has also been fueled by a shift in Western priorities. The strategic interests of major powers in countries such as Mozambique, Rwanda, and Sierra Leone have declined with the end of the Cold War. As a result, Western countries are more reluctant to intervene militarily in weak states, and their politicians are disinclined to explain casualties to their electorates. Furthermore, Western armies, designed primarily to fight the sophisticated international conflicts envisaged by Cold War strategists, are ill equipped to tackle low-intensity civil wars, with their complicated ethnic agendas, blurred boundaries between combatants and civilians, and loose military hierarchies. The failed U.S.–led involvement in Somalia in 1993 reinforced American resolve never to enter a conflict unless vital domestic interests were at stake.

Meanwhile, UN peacekeeping efforts have fallen victim to Western governments' fears of sustaining casualties, becoming entangled in expanding conflicts, and incurring escalating costs. The number of personnel in UN operations has fallen from a peak of 76,000 in 1994 to around 15,000 today. Multilateral interventions appear increasingly likely to be limited to situations where the UN gains the consent of the warring parties rather than—as allowed under Chapter VII of the UN Charter—to be designed to enforce a peace on reluctant belligerents. Bilateral, as well as multilateral, commitments have also been trimmed. France's long-standing deployment of troops in its former African colonies, for example, has declined: French troops will be cut by 40 percent to about 5,000 by 2000. Paris has stated that it will no longer engage in unilateral military interventions in Africa, effectively creating a strategic vacuum.

The increasing inability of weak governments to counter internal violence has created a ready market for private military forces.

Into this gap have stepped today's private military companies. Most such enterprises hail from South Africa, the United Kingdom, the United States, and occasionally France and Israel. They all share essentially the same goals: to improve their client's military capability, there by allowing that client to function better in war or deter conflict more effectively. This process might involve military assessments, training, or occasionally weapons procurement. Direct involvement in combat is less common, although two companies, Executive Outcomes (EO) of South Africa and Sandline International of Great Britain, advertise their skills in this area. EO has provided training and strategic advice to the armed forces of Angola and Sierra Leone; its apartheid-era soldiers have fought in both countries.

Other companies, such as Military Professional Resources Incorporated (MPRI), a Virginia-based firm headed by retired U.S. army generals, has limited its services to training and has hired former U.S. military personnel to develop the military forces of Bosnia-Herzegovina and Croatia. Some organizations engage in more passive activities, such

Portrait of a Private Army

In its promotional literature, Executive Outcomes (EO) describes itself as a company with a "solid history of success," thanks to the efforts of its "highly effective work force." This work force is essentially a demobilized army for hire. Based in South Africa, the company was established in 1989 by Eeben Barlow and is staffed almost exclusively by veterans from the former South African Defence Force. EO claims to be able to draw on over 2,000 personnel and forces, all of whom are assembled on a contract-by-contract basis and recruited chiefly by word-of-mouth. This policy has not only ensured quality control but a preexisting military hierarchy of highly experienced troops. EO personnel have distinguished themselves from other companies by entering into combat, claiming that accompanying the client's troops increases their effectiveness and confidence.

EO's first major contract was in Angola in May 1993 to rescue the Soyo oil fields in the north from the rebel National Union for the Total Independence of Angola (UNITA). The Angolan government then hired over 500 personnel from September 1993 to January 1996 for an estimated $40 million a year (including weaponry) to train nearly 5,000 soldiers. EO's arrival, coinciding with the lifting of the arms embargo on Angola, helped reverse the course of the war, and UNITA suffered significant defeats. EO's second contract, this time with the Sierra Leonean government in May 1995, lasted 22 months and cost $35 million—about one-third of the country's defense budget. EO, working with local civilian militias, battered the Revolutionary United Front into submission. In February 1997, EO was subcontracted to the British military company, Sandline International, to train and plan military operations against the Bougainville Resistance Army in Papua New Guinea.

EO's military effectiveness testifies to its expertise in low-intensity conflict. It has planned its operations closely with government officials and uses government equipment, although it has arranged the purchase of weaponry. Its hallmark has been its highly mobile operations using MI-17 helicopter troop carriers, on occasion supported by MI-24 helicopter gunships and Soviet-made ground attack aircraft. But EO's biggest strength has been its use of intelligence capabilities, particularly through the cultivation of local populations, augmented with night-sighting and radio intercept devices. Casualties have remained relatively light: EO acknowledges that 11 of its personnel died in Angola, with seven still missing, and four killed in Sierra Leone. Two others died from accident and sickness.

—D.S.

as protecting premises and people. The British company Defence Systems Limited, for example, guards embassies and protects the interests of corporations working in unstable areas. Other outfits provide businesses with risk analyses, and several have developed specialist expertise in resolving the kidnapping incidents that plague firms operating in Latin America.

Military companies are unfettered by political constraints. They view conflict as a business opportunity and have taken advantage of the pervasive influence of economic liberalism in the late twentieth century. They have also been quick to adapt to the complex agendas of civil wars. Their ability to operate has been enhanced by an expanded pool of military expertise made available by reductions in Western forces. Many recruits come from highly disciplined military units, such ass the British Special Air Service and the South African and American special forces. Likewise, cheap and accessible Soviet-made weaponry has helped strengthen the companies' capabilities.

When help from other quarters was unavailable, Sir Julius Chan, prime minister of Papua New Guinea, claimed in 1997 that he was forced to "go to the private sector" to counter Bougainville Revolutionary Army (BRA) insurgents. After negotiations with the BRA collapsed, Chan signed a $36 million contract with Sandline International to train his national forces and plan an offensive against the separatists. The government was particularly anxious to reopen Bougainville's Panguna Copper Mine, once the source of 30 percent of the country's export earnings.

Western mining corporations also stand to benefit when a private military company restores order, thereby raising questions as to whether these business entities share any formal ties. In April 1997, the London *Independent* reported that Anthony Buckingham, a director of Heritage Oil and Gas and Branch Energy, introduced EO to the governments of Angola and Sierra Leone. But Buckingham has emphatically stated that "there is no corporate link between Executive Outcomes and the Branch Heritage group." EO officials likewise strongly deny any financial or operational/business links with mining companies. While critics decry even this nebulous relationship as neocolonialist behavior in the worst tradition of Cecil Rhodes, Buckingham observes that "If there is no stability there is no investment and no one benefits."

Outright victories, rather than negotiated peace settlements, have ended the greater part of the twentieth century's internal conflicts.

The lure of rich resources and the risks of exploiting them in unstable areas are powerful incentives for companies to maintain stability in weak states. This motivation can also chime with a government's own wishes. A mining company depends on security to protect its investments; a beleaguered government buys increased security to shore up its rule, while the prospect of mining revenues can supplement its coffers. Furthermore, a military company, while strengthening its client government's military performance, protects a mining company's operations because revenues from these sources guarantee its payment. In the developing world, minerals and hardwoods may soon emerge as the currency of stability. The source of payment is a crucial difference between the intervention of a military company and that of the UN, which is funded by donors, not by the state in question. Coupling multinational companies with an external security force potentially gives foreigners powerful leverage over a government and its affairs—a risk that some governments appear willing to take.

Another trend, reminiscent of the privateers of earlier centuries, is the willingness of private military companies to act as proxies for Western governments. MPRI has specialized exclusively in military services, originally for the privatization-minded U.S. Department of Defense. MPRI's first two major international contracts were with the Croation government in 1994 to update its Warsaw Pact–oriented military. When the sophisticated Croatian offensive, Operation Storm, took the Serb-held Krajina enclave in August 1995, there was inevitable suspicion that MPRI was involved. The operation played an important role in reversing the tide of war against the Serbs and—consistent with American policy—in bringing both sides to the negotiating table. MPRI, although denying that it had played a role, has benefited from these rumors. In 1995, the company was contracted, in the aftermath of the Dayton accord, to strengthen the Muslim-Croat Federation's army in order to deter Bosnian Serb aggression. Since it is funded by the contracting government, MPRI has delivered a cheaper service and done so at less political risk than would have been possible had U.S. troops been used. The scenario serves as an example of how the private military sector can allow policymakers to achieve their foreign-policy goals free from the need to secure public approval and safe in the knowledge that should the situation deteriorate, official participation can be fudged.

Other American companies have also worked to further administration policy. Corporate giants such as Science Applications International Corporation and Braddock, Dunn & McDonald, Inc. and its subsidiary Vinnell Corporation are primarily high-technology suppliers to the military-industrial market but have also diversified into military training. They are contracted by the Saudi government to upgrade and train its armed forces in the use of mainly U.S. weaponry. Some British companies have also supported government interests: The London-based Saladin Security, for example, trains Omani government forces working alongside British Army officers who are seconded there. But on the whole, British companies are smaller and less diversified than their U.S. counterparts and have tended to focus on protecting commercial interests. Nonetheless, they maintain close contacts with Britain's Ministry of Defence and are an important source of intelligence.

The Future of Peacekeeping?

Some private military companies, such as EO, possess sufficient coercive capability to break a stalemate in a conflict. Unlike multinational forces, they do not act impartially but are hired to win a conflict (or deter it) on the client's terms. EO and Sandline International have argued that military force has an underutilized potential to bring conflicts to a close. However, bludgeoning the other side into accepting a peace agreement runs in diametric opposition to most academic studies of conflict resolution. These studies center on consent: bringing warring sides together with the implicit assumption that each wants to negotiate an end to the war. To a large degree, the international community has responded to civil wars in this manner, especially those of limited strategic interest. Ceasefires act as holding positions; mediation seeks to bring combatants to an agreement. Peacekeepers, acting under mandates to be evenhanded and to use minimal force, are deployed to support this process.

The flaw in this approach is that according to recent empirical studies, outright victories, rather than negotiated peace settlements, have ended the greater part of the twentieth century's internal conflicts. Combatants in Angola, Bosnia, and Sierra Leone consistently resisted a negotiated, consent-based settlement. There appeared to be little chance of a breakthrough until more coercive measures were applied. So why has the international community continued to persist with negotiated settlements and even-handedness in cases where one side was clearly at fault? The reason, for the most part, is self-interest. Such an approach avoids direct intervention and the subsequent political risks.

Yet when it suits them, Western states have also been proponents of "battlefield diplomacy" to resolve conflicts. This approach was favored throughout the Cold War when the object was to limit Soviet expansionism. More recently, the United States tacitly supported the aims of Laurent Kabila's military campaign to oust President Mobutu Sese Seku in the former Zaire. France allegedly backed former military ruler Denis Sassou Nguesso's overthrow of Congolese president Pascal Lissouba in September 1997. And by condoning the Croatian capture of Serb-held Krajina, Washington was implicitly recognizing the value of resolution through force.

However, the likelihood that a military solution can bring durable peace to a country depends on the nature of the peace agreement, as well as on how effectively follow-up measures such as demobilization, cantonment of fighters, and rehabilitation are implemented. Despite EO's involvement in Angola, for example, peace is still not finally secure. Nevertheless, its military involvement was instrumental in turning the tables of war in favor of the government's side, a development that coerced the National Union for the Total Independence of Angola (UNITA) to negotiate and eventually sign the 1994 Lusaka Accords. Similarly, in Sierra Leone, EO battered the Revolutionary United Front (RUF) faction into submission, creating sufficient stability to hold the first elections in 27 years. Later military offensives compelled the RUF to return to the negotiating table and sign a peace accord in November 1997. But just three months after EO left, the government was overthrown by disgruntled members of the armed forces, highlighting the importance of implementing postconflict measures.

There is little to stop military companies from working for rebel movements in the future.

These shortcomings are often seized upon as proof that the efforts of military companies have failed. But EO has always acknowledged its limitations. The UN did not engage members of EO in Sierra Leone, possibly because it chose to label them as mercenaries and therefore as untouchable. The entire episode illustrates that it is better to acknowledge the existence of military companies and engage them politically than to ignore them and hope that somehow a peace agreement will stay intact.

Regulating the Market

Since the demand for military force is unlikely to end anytime soon, military companies, in their various guises, appear here to stay. Should there be some attempt to regulate them, or is it the right of sovereign states—as with the purchase of weaponry—to employ who they wish as long as they ensure that their employees behave within acceptable bounds? There is widespread discomfort with a laissez-faire approach, most of it caused by military companies' lack of accountability. Although most military companies have only worked for legitimate governments, there is little to stop them from working for rebel movements in the future.

To make matters even more complicated, deciding which is the "legitimate" side in a civil conflict is not always straightforward. Many modern governments were once classified as "insurgents" or "terrorists" while in opposition, among them South Africa's African National Congress and Ugandan president Yoweri Museveni's National Resistance Army. The governments that grew out of these movements are now internationally recognized.

Military companies are motivated first and foremost by profit and are responsible primarily to their shareholders. Consequently, financial losses, in spite of any strategic or political considerations, may prompt a company to pull out. There are also few checks on their adherence to human-rights conventions. The problem is not a lack of human-rights law. During times of war, the employees of military companies fall under the auspices of Common Article 3 of the Geneva Conventions, which is binding on all combatants. They are also bound by a state's obligations to UN human-rights conventions as "agents" of the government that employs them. What is absent is adequate independent observation of their activities—a feature common to all parties in a conflict but especially characteristic of military companies that have no permanent attachments to national governments.

Efforts at controlling mercenaries through international law in the 1960s and 1970s were led by African states that faced a skeptical reception from the United States and major European powers. The most accepted definition of a mercenary, found in Article 47 of the 1977 Additional Protocols to the Geneva Conventions, is so riddled with loopholes that few international-law scholars believe it could withstand the rigors of the courtroom. International apathy is palpable. France and the United States have not signed the Additional Protocols, and the UN's 1989 International Convention against the Recruitment, Uses, Financing, and Training of Mercenaries has attracted only 12 signatories. Three of these signatories, Angola, the former Yugoslavia, and the former Zaire, have gone on to employ mercenaries. Most states have domestic laws that ban mercenaries but few, if any, have acted on them. Britain's Foreign Enlistment Act, for example, was introduced in 1870, and there has yet to be a prosecution.

The drive to regulate military companies has been most passionate when home governments—not those who contract them—are affected. The British government is currently investigating regulation after Sandline International, claiming it had clearance from the Foreign and Commonwealth Office, appeared to violate UN sanctions by supplying arms and military expertise to the ousted Sierra Leonean government. Sandline executives, portrayed in the media as "mercenaries," embarrassed Britain's new Labour Party government, which had entered office touting its platform of an "ethical" foreign policy.

South Africa too has come under both domestic and international pressure to control the increasing number of companies based there. Its parliament passed the Regulation of Foreign Military Assistance Bill in May 1998. Privately, however, most commentators in South Africa believe that while the legislation provides a framework for government policy and satisfies its critics, its real impact will be limited. Military companies are mostly registered offshore and can easily relocate to other countries, making it difficult to pin them down under specific jurisdictions. A growing trend is for international companies to form joint ventures with local companies, avoiding the effects of the legislation in any one country. Angola, for example, has over 80 security firms, many of them in joint ownership. Companies can also easily disguise their activities by purporting to be security companies performing protection services while actually engaging in more coercive military operations.

The principal obstacle to regulating private military companies has been the tendency to brand them as "mercenaries" of the kind witnessed in Africa 30 years ago, rather than to recognize them as multinational entrepreneurs eager to solidify their legitimacy. Consequently, regulation can be best achieved through constructive engagement. This process would likely expose governments and international institutions to accusations of sanctioning the use of "soldiers of fortune" to shore up the international system. Yet, this tack offers the international community greater leverage to influence the activities of companies that believe legitimacy is the key to their future growth and prosperity. In an effort to broaden their appeal, for instance, military companies have offered greater transparency. Sandline International maintains that it is prepared to place itself under the scrutiny of international monitors and accept an international regulatory framework. This pledge is a necessary step; a careful audit would establish corporate links that might affect the company's operations.

Engagement could well begin with dialogue between key multilateral institutions and the private military sector. Liaison at senior levels of the UN, for example, is needed, and the Department of Peacekeeping is an obvious starting point. UN field personnel should be permitted to contact military companies and plan strategies for conflict resolution where appropriate. Had there been a structured transition between EO's departure and the planned deployment of UN observers, the military coup in Sierra Leone might have been averted. EO could have maintained a threat of enforcement that would have bought time for the UN to fully implement postconflict programs, allowing RUF combatants to become confident enough about their future that they might demobilize. Direct engagement could also provide an opportunity to lay out a code of conduct that might incorporate more specific operational issues rising from the work of military companies. Observation of companies such as EO to ensure that they adhere to basic principles of warfare is needed, something in which the International Committee of the Red Cross could take a lead.

The prospect that private military companies might gain some degree of legitimacy within the international community begs the question as to whether these firms could take on UN peacekeeping functions and improve on UN efforts. Military companies see this as an area of potential growth and are quick to point out the advantages they offer. There is no denying that they are cheaper than UN operations. EO cost Sierra Leone's government $35 million for the 22 months it was there, versus a planned UN operation budgeted at $47 million for eight months. Likewise, its annual cost in Angola was a fraction of that of the UN's operation—for example, in 1996–97, UNAVEM III cost $135 million. Admittedly, EO and other such firms provide military support, not peacekeeping, but there is no doubt that they can mobilize more quickly and appear less sensitive to casualties. However, accepting a UN mandate or conditions may also undermine a company's effectiveness. As any soldier who has served in a UN operation will attest, a peacekeeping mission is only as effective as the operation's mandate.

Give War a Chance

Policymakers and multilateral organizations have paid little attention to private-sector involvement in wars. Yet low-intensity conflicts—the type that military companies have specialized in up to now—will be the wars that prevail in the first part of the twenty-first century. Their virulence and random nature could undermine the viability of many nation-states. These wars defy orthodox means of resolution, thus creating the circumstances that have contributed to the expansion of military companies into this area.

Conflict resolution theory needs to look more closely at the impact of coercion, not dismiss it. Military companies may in fact offer new possibilities for building peace that, while not universal in applicability, can hasten the end to a war and limit loss of life. Moreover, there is no evidence that private-sector intervention will erode the state. Despite the commercial motives of military companies, their interventions, if anything, have strengthened the ability of governments to control their territory. Yet, military companies are unlikely to resolve conflicts in the long term. Political intervention and postconflict peacebuilding efforts are still necessary.

Although the UN's special rapporteur on the use of mercenaries has acknowledged the difficulties in equating military companies with mercenaries, the debate has not moved beyond that point. Admittedly, the UN is in a sticky position. Although some member states have condemned the use of military companies, others have employed their services or condoned their operations. Meanwhile, the future of private military interests looks bright. "Now entering its eleventh year, MPRI has over 400 employees," declares the company's Web site, noting that in 1997 the volume of business exceeded $48 million. Even with a mercenary label and its associated moral stain, EO and Sandline continue to tout their services to beleaguered governments. Other companies are likely to emerge that offer EO's services, particularly in terms of low-key military training and advising for governments. The most rapid expansion is likely to be linked to the protection of commercial interests, although these can act as a springboard for more aggressive, military actions alongside local companies and power brokers. Mainstream companies, from the United States in particular, are also likely to encroach into low-intensity conflict areas. With backing from a cautious administration not wanting to forgo strategic influence, the temptation to use military companies might prove irresistible.

Regulation of military companies will be problematic, given the diversity of their services and the breadth of their market niche. Yet, in many respects, the private military industry is no different from any other sector in the global economy that is required to conform to codes of practice—except that in the former's case, the risk of political instability and social mayhem is amplified if more unscrupulous actors become involved. There is good reason to glance back in history to a time when private military forces operated more or less freely. Historian Anthony Mockler notes that one hundred years after the first *condottieri* entered Italy: "The lines had become crossed and tangled: mercenaries had become rulers and rulers had become mercenaries."

Want to Know More?

Mercenaries have been around for as long as warfare itself. For detailed accounts of their history, see Anthony Mockler's ***Mercenaries*** (London: MacDonald, 1969) and Janice Thomson's ***Mercenaries, Pirates & Sovereigns: State-Building and Extraterritorial Violence in Early Modern Europe*** (New Jersey: Princeton University Press, 1996).

Several recent articles and studies scrutinize private military companies and their activities worldwide: David Shearer's ***Private Armies and Military Intervention,*** *Adelphi Paper 316* (New York: International Institute for Strategic Studies, February 1998); William Shawcross' ***"In Praise of Sandline"*** (*The Spectator,* August 1, 1998); Al J. Venter's ***"Market Forces: How Hired Guns Succeeded Where the United Nations Failed"*** (*Jane's International Defense Review,* March 1, 1998); Ken Silverstein's ***"Privatizing War"*** (*The Nation,* July 28, 1997); and David Isenberg's ***Soldiers of Fortune Ltd.: A Profile of Today's Private Sector Corporate Mercenary Firms*** (Washington: Center for Defense Information, November 1997).

The legal status of mercenaries is addressed in Francoise Hampson's ***"Mercenaries: Diagnosis Before Prescription"*** (*Netherlands' Yearbook of International Law,* No. 3, 1991) and Edward Kwakwa's ***"The Current Status of Mercenaries in the Law of Armed Conflict"*** (*Hastings International and Comparative Law Review,* vol. 14, 1990).

Martin van Crevald examines the changing dynamics of conflict in ***The Transformation of War*** (New York: The Free Press, 1991). Two studies provide empirical evidence that outright victory, rather than negotiated peace, has ended the greater part of the twentieth century's internal conflicts: Stephen John Stedman's ***Peacemaking in Civil Wars: International Mediation in Zimbabwe 1974–1980*** (Boulder: Lynne Rienner, 1991) and Roy Licklider's ***"The Consequences of Negotiated Settlements in Civil Wars 1954–1993"*** (*American Political Science Review,* September 1995).

On human rights, see a series of reports by the UN's special repporteur on mercenaries that are available online: ***Report on the Question of the Use of Mercenaries as a Means of Violating Human Rights and Impeding the Exercise of the Right of Peoples to Self-Determination.***

For links to this and other relevant Web sites, as well as a comprehensive index of related articles, access **www.foreignpolicy.com.**

David Shearer *is a research associate at the International Institute for Strategic Studies in London. He was a senior adviser to the UN Department of Humanitarian Affairs in Liberia and Rwanda in 1995 and 1996.*

CHILDREN UNDER ARMS: Kalashnikov Kids

Increasingly, children are being used to fight wars, at great cost to themselves and their societies. Discouraging the trend is tricky but not impossible

"We were trapped between acts of heaven and acts of hell," says a young woman in Sierra Leone who spent two unwilling years under arms in her country's civil war. "When the rebels laughed, we laughed." When they were angry, she was punished savagely. Dragged by rebel fighters with 27 other members of her family from their village into the jungle, she found herself a slave to unpredictable violence.

The youngest were forced into Small Boy and Small Girl Units, where they carried stolen goods, ammunition, water and food. They were taught to punish and even kill other children who disobeyed or sought to escape. Each day she and her comrades sang an anthem glorifying their struggle:

> Go and tell the president that Sierra Leone is my home.
> Go and tell my parents they see me no more.
> When fighting in the battlefield I am fighting for ever.
> Every Sierra Leonean is fighting for his land.

After two years, 19 of her family were dead, but she escaped.

Such a story is common in Sierra Leone, where, although the civil war may at last be ending, 6,000 children were recently combatants, according to Radda Barnen, a Swedish charity. It is also common elsewhere.

The United Nations reckons that children, defined as those under 18 years old, are active participants in conflicts stretching from west and central Africa to the Balkans, Latin America, Sri Lanka and Afghanistan. In Uganda, for example, the UN Children's Fund, Unicef, estimates that as many as 8,000 have been abducted by rebels since 1995. Another 15,000 are said by Amnesty International to be in the ranks of Colombia's security forces and many more are in paramilitary groups there. According to the Coalition to Stop the Use of Child Soldiers, a group of religious and peace groups headquartered in Switzerland, 300,000 children in over 60 countries are soldiers.

Are these figures accurate? Do they represent a worrying increase on past practice? It is impossible to say. The phenomenon of child soldiers is far from new. For generations, young men in Africa have taken up weapons alongside their fathers to defend their villages, just as they worked in the fields in peacetime. Drummer boys led armies into battle in America's revolutionary war. In Europe, too, child recruits were common. Admiral Horatio Nelson, like other great seafarers, began his naval career as a ship's boy and saw action in the Indian Ocean. By the end of the second world war, Berlin was defended by 15-year-olds against the might of the Allies. Children have played an active part in wars since at least spartan times.

Then there are problems of definition. What is a child? Is it the same in all cultures? A Tamil might well be married at 14 and expect to fulfil other manly duties, but it is against the law in Britain to take a wife at that age. A 12-year-old gun-toter seems clearly unacceptable; a 17-year-old, less so. And what is a soldier? Not all of them fight, or even risk their lives. Many ordinary children suffer horribly during the kind of vicious civil war that throws up lots of child soldiers. At least the soldiers are likely to get a handful of food for their pains.

Despite these ambiguities, two trends are worth thinking about. Children tend to be used heavily as soldiers during prolonged civil wars; and such civil wars abound at present. And although children were once recruited only when the supply of adult fighters ran short, the youngest are now often recruited first.

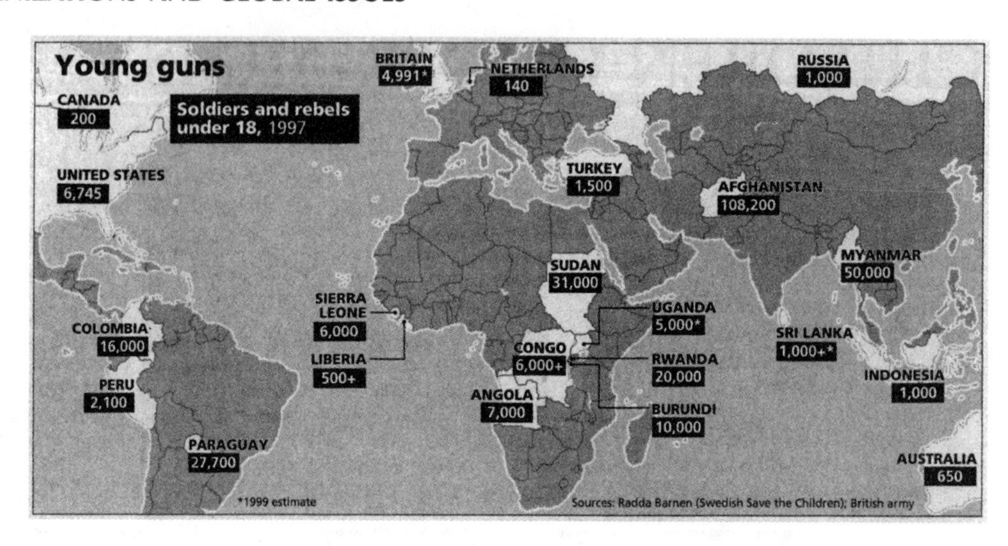

There are logical reasons for this. First there are more children around. Thanks to demography, poverty and persistent fighting, in much of Africa south of the Sahara, for example, half the people are now under 18 years old. Then too children are often easier to attract than adults. Entertainment is in short supply in most villages and what organised recreation there is (watching "Rambo" on mobile video players in rural Liberia and Sierra Leone) may well spur young people to sign up on the spot. Children in most parts of the world can be lured by a gun and a bit of drill into militias or street gangs.

When they cannot be tempted into the ranks, children can be forced more easily than adults. Once secured, they are more readily moulded into unquestioning fighters. Give them only a little alcohol, marijuana or gunpowder to sniff; tell them, as in parts of west Africa, that a magic incantation or membership of a secret society will protect them; give them mirrors and a woollen toy to steer enemy bullets away: then many, more credulous than grown-ups, will run fearless into battle. The youngest will often develop the sort of loyalty that stems from knowing no other way of life.

Despite—sometimes because of—their size, children can do valuable work as scouts, spies, messengers and decoys. Even ten year-olds can learn to carry and use lightweight but lethal weapons, such as M16 semi-automatic rifles or the omnipresent aluminium Kalashnikov AK-47S. They may be more willing than older companions to do the most dangerous jobs, such as laying and clearing mines, serving as suicide bombers or infiltrating villages that are due to be attacked. With no sons or daughters, wives or husbands to think of, they are frequently less terrified of death than most older people.

Finally, children are an economical addition to the force. They need less food than adult soldiers, take up less space and can do without a wage. One Congolese rebel officer explained why *kadogos* (boy fighters) "make very good soldiers": it was because "they obey orders; they are not concerned about getting back to their wife or family; and they don't know fear."

Girls and boys come out to kill

War takes an enormous toll on the young in general. Olara Otunnu, the UN Special Representative for Children and Armed Conflict (and a man with particular knowledge of the subject from his earlier days as spokesman for President Obote of Uganda), says that 2m children have been killed in situations of armed conflict since 1987, and three times that number have been seriously injured or permanently disabled. As civilians' share of casualties in war has rocketed this century (up from 5% in the first world war to 48% in the second and around 90% today), the involvement of children has also grown. They are victims of crossfire and of deliberate attacks, as the evidence of mass graves in Kosovo shows. They are particularly prone to treading on landmines, catching diseases, being poisoned by pollutants. Others are taken hostage or used as human shields. Many simply starve.

But for child soldiers in particular there are more risks. On top of the obvious dangers of injury or death during combat, they tend to live harsh lives. Some are punished, or killed, for making mistakes. Children who have fought for the Lord's Resistance Army in Uganda, for example, report being beaten for dropping a tub of water while under enemy attack. In the same army, if a child fails to raise the alarm when a friend escapes, he is executed by his comrades.

Day-to-day injuries from carrying heavy loads, as well as damage to ears and eyes from gunfire, are well documented. Drug addiction, malnutrition and sexually transmitted diseases are common among bands of child soldiers in different continents.

Then are the emotional effects. Large numbers of children have seen atrocities. In Kosovo, says the UN High Commissioner for Refugees, half of those who fled were under 18 years old. In 1996 Unicef estimated that half of all Rwanda's children had witnessed a massacre. But child soldiers are also made to commit atrocities. Rachel Brett, the author of a book on child soldiers*, argues that "the general brutalisation of child recruits is often a deliberate policy; even in exceptional cases involving ritual cannibalism." Sometimes, in order to humiliate a village under attack and destroy its social order, the youngest boy in the ranks of the attackers is ordered to execute the village chief. Another trick of rebels in Sierra Leone is to use abducted children to attack their own villages and families. Why? So that, feeling cast out from their communities, they will cling to the rebel group.

The impact of all this not only on the child but on society as a whole is dreadful. Children who have had no training or education beyond the use of a gun or a rocket–propelled grenade are harder to demobilise and bring back into routine life than grown-up fighters. Mr. Otunnu argues that groups that recruit child soldiers tend to find themselves with a big problem when peace comes, or even when it does not. "They find a generation of children carrying guns, who know only the gun culture, who hang around on streets everywhere with guns," he says. In Congo, for example, even rebel leaders are keen to see children demobilised, as some child fighters are, it seems, impossible to control.

Where conflicts have dragged on—in Sri Lanka, Afghanistan, Sierra

Leone—many rebel leaders, officers and co-ordinators turn out to have taken part in war first as children. The Taliban leaders in Afghanistan learned to fight as teenagers in the refugee camps of Pakistan. Some of those who abduct children today in Sierra Leone were abducted themselves when the war began in 1991; others started fighting as children in the civil war in neighbouring Liberia. Conflicts involving child soldiers, in other words, may be particularly hard to end.

Under age and under arms

This week about 100 government representatives, UN staff and aid workers gathered in Montevideo, the capital of Uruguay, for the second of four international conferences on child soldiers. They discussed how to stop recruitment of children by armies, paramilitary groups and civil-defence bodies.

That is a difficult (and some would say impossible) task. The differences among the three categories are immense. Some child soldiers are recruited, openly and legally, into national armies where care is taken over their training and welfare. A second lot, such as those with self-defense committees in Mozambique or the "village guards" in Algeria, fight to protect their families and villages. A third type those who are taken away from their communities, often forcibly, by groups that may have started life with a political agenda but frequently end up as common criminals.

The first sort are the easiest to do something about but the least in need of rescue. It is not illegal under international law to recruit a 15-year old as a soldier. The UN Convention on the Rights of the Child, signed in 1989 and ratified by all members except America and Somalia, establishes the age of 18 as the end of childhood. It forbids, for example, the death penalty for children and sets other standards for their protection. An exception has been made for soldiering, allowing recruitment at 15.

The British navy, for example, recruits 16-year-old school-leavers. The British army starts hiring them at 17 and now has 4,991 under-18-year-olds (1,000 more than two years ago) in its employ. Seventeen of them are serving in the Balkans; one of the 381 17-year-old soldiers serving in the Gulf war was killed. The American army, too, recruits and deploys 17-year-olds. Jo Becker of Human Rights Watch, a non-governmental organisation based in America, says that in 1997 the American army had 2,880 17-year-olds on active duty.

The minority of countries that recruit at this age argue that, if they left it any later, the young people would turn to other employment. Some make a different point, that society benefits if lads without job prospects are taken off taken the streets and into useful training before unappealing habits form.

Their opponents say that only the most careful system—for example, that in Australia, where young recruits are monitored by a host of psychologists, chaplains and other folk as well as given training suitable to their age—can protect children from what they see as the unhealthy rigours of military life. It is consistent, they say, for governments that do not allow young people to vote, buy alcohol, drive, marry without their parents' consent or accept certain kinds of civilian employment to send them into mortal danger instead.

Their campaign to realise the minimum age for soldiering from 15 to 18 is gradually gaining momentum, though perhaps not for the reasons put forward. Many western countries want to reduce their armed forces anyway and raising the minimum age is a painless way to cut. Last year Denmark and South Africa increased their recruitment ages to 18. Sierra Leone's government has also said that it will no longer hire soldiers younger than 18. Burundi, Canada and the Netherlands are thinking of raising their recruitment age, and the Netherlands already keeps its youngest soldiers out of combat. So, to some extent, does Britain: soldiers younger than 18 are not sent to patrol the streets in Northern Ireland, though they do go to other trouble spots. The UN, for its part, refuses to employ soldiers younger than 18 in its peacekeeping forces and prefers 21-year-olds for the tougher assignments.

Another step has been taken. On June 17, members of the International Labour Organisation voted unanimously to ban the employment of those younger than 18 in hazardous work, including prostitution, drug-smuggling and soldiering. (Only young conscripts are prohibited; young volunteers will still be allowed—though definitions of "voluntary" among the very poor could prove a touch theoretical.)

Is 18 a reasonable cut-off? It smacks of an attempt by developed countries to force their values on the rest of the world, where children get down to things earlier. But at least, points out Miss Brett, if 18 becomes the legal minimum, then—even allowing for the difficulty of telling a child's age in places where malnutrition may make him look younger than he is or hard labour make him older—13– and 14-year-olds are less likely to end up clutching Kalashnikovs.

If the minimum recruiting age is raised by amending international agreements, (and America and Britain are notable stand-outs against it), it will affect only national armies. A far bigger worry is unofficial armed groups, the civil-defence or rebel-cum-criminal gangs that draws boys and girls during prolonged civil wars. They are not confined to poor countries: a few children fight for the KLA (Kosovo Liberation Army) in Yugoslavia and rather more for the PKK (Kurdistan Worker's Party) in Turkey.

Harder to handle

Civil-defence groups recruit children to fight for their communities along with their friends and fathers. Children with the Kamajors, a secret hunting society turned militia in Sierra Leone, man road blocks, search vehicles, fight and perform rituals in battle. Some children are made to dance naked into battle in order to intimidate the enemy. Algeria's village guards and defence committees in Latin America fall into the same category. They often recruit children at a much earlier age than the government (as young as 12 or 13 in Sierra Leone).

Stopping such groups from using children as soldiers is much harder than stopping governments, as they are unlikely to be much affected by the opinions of either international do-gooders or voters (who might anyway—who knows?—consider enlisting child soldiers preferable to communal destruction). But because these groups usually defend villages, and thus move around less than rebel bands, their activities can be monitored more easily. Some outside carrots and stocks—money to demobilise, the threat of harsh penalties if recruiting child soldiers comes to be classified as a war crime—could have some effect. It is, frankly, a long shot.

Even longer are the odds against winning hearts and minds among the third group. Yet the sort of child soldiers soldier for whom life is worst, and from whom the greatest threat to stability and peace is later likely to come, is an abducted child who becomes a fighter. Wrenched from his community, like the 3,000 or so children in the Lord's Resistance Army in Uganda, such a child risks losing all identity except that which his gun gives him. "Orders have gone out recently from the LRA officers to abduct younger and younger kids. Eleven to 13 is now the preferred age, though they will take up to 17-year-olds," says Keith Wright, Unicef's programme chief in Kampala. "They are slave soldiers, enduring an endless cycle of brutality." In other countries, children as young as three are grabbed, sometimes to secure the loyalty of older siblings, and trained to fight almost as soon as they can walk.

In many civil wars, banditry and competition for resources are as important for the rebels as any political objective. Soldiers do not necessarily fight to win territory but to keep control of wealth. In Uganda a new rebel group, the Allied Democratic Forces, also uses about 500 child soldiers to preserve its sources of revenue. In Colombia factions fight in part for control of the drug trade. In west Africa, Angola and Congo, much of the fighting is for mineral wealth, especially diamonds. Children in such "guerrilla" groups often learn as much about crime as warfare—and perpetuate it.

Authorities that have so far proved unable to halt these groups' obviously criminal activities are unlikely to succeed in stopping their merely immoral ones. But some things could still be done to make it harder to employ children as soldiers. Mr Otunnu is probably optimistic in reckoning that the trade and production of small arms can be limited. But foreign countries and institutions, he argues, should make it clear to any rebel group aspiring to govern that recognition and aid will be harder to win if the group has used child soldiers. This may sound like pie in the sky, but such arguments are making a little progress. The Sudan People's Liberation Army has pledged not to use child soldiers. So have both the Tamil Tigers and the Sri Lankan government.

Until 1998, the UN Security Council had not even discussed the issue of child soldiers. Since then, however, the subject has been raised several times, and expert witnesses have been questioned. The fate of children under arms is now recognised as an important part of peace negotiations in many parts of the world, with implications not only for successful demobilisation but also for policies on health, education and nurturing democracy. As with the campaign to ban landmines, it is the gradual realisation of the problem, rather than any multilateral posturing, that has the best chance of solving it in time.

Note

1. *"Children: The Invisible Soldiers". Radda Barnen, 2nd edition, 1998.

The Dilemma That Confronts the World

Water shortages, global warming and nitrogen pollution threaten the planet's future unless politicians act now, says a UN environment report.

PAUL BROWN reports

IN a devastating assessment on the future for the human race in the early part of the next century Klaus Töpfer, the executive director of the United Nations Environment Programme, said yesterday that the main threats to human survival are posed by water shortages, global warming, and a new danger—worldwide nitrogen pollution.

"A series of looming crises and ultimate catastrophe can only be averted by a massive increase in political will. We have the technology but we are not applying it," he said.

Launching a report called *Global Environment Outlook 2000* in London yesterday, Töpfer said it is possible to reverse the process but conspicuous overconsumption by the world's rich countries has to be cut by 90% to do so. He said it does not mean a lowering of living standards, but an application of existing science, through recycling, for instance.

"The developed world has the technology to bring about the fundamental changes needed to save millions of people from hunger, thirst and ill health. But there is no incentive to apply it because politicians are not forcing manufacturers to do so," he said.

There are signs that targets to cut greenhouse gases from industrialised countries by 5% by 2010 under the Kyoto protocol will not be reached, Töpfer claimed.

He described efforts to curb global warming as inadequate in comparison to the 60% cuts required, and added that the world is already suffering as a result of climate change, which is now unstoppable.

Extreme weather events have left 3-million people dead in the last five years, Töpfer said—the current US hurricane is an example of the destruction that is becoming more common because of climate change.

Töpfer, the former German environment minister, said: "It is possible to get very angry and dismayed about what we are doing to the world, but it does not help. What matters is being constructive and realising that where there is political will, much can be achieved.

"For example, in Europe we have defeated the menace of acid rain by reducing by 75% the amount of sulphur dioxide released from factories since 1980. The worldwide reduction in the manufacture and use of CFCs has put us well on the way to curing the hole in the ozone layer. There are now salmon again in the Thames and the Rhine. We can do it if we try.

"We are improving things further with the urban waste water directive, which will give us cleaner rivers and beaches, but in other parts of the world 15-million children under five die each year from diseases caused by drinking unclean water.

"This could be prevented, but gains made by better management and technology are still being outpaced by degradation.

"Population continues to be a problem. In 1950 the population of Africa was half that of Europe, now it is about equal. In 2050 it will be three times that of Europe. We have to change these trends."

A new problem identified by the report is nitrogen pollution. This is partly caused by untreated sewage from new cities, which pollutes water courses, but mainly by large increases in the use of artificial fertiliser to boost crop growth.

Blooms of algae off the Italian coast and the killing of fisheries in the Black Sea are caused by excessive nutrients.

The report says that in the past it was believed there was time to sort out environment problems but in some cases time has already run out.

Full scale emergencies already exist, says the report: water shortages are hampering developing countries; land degradation has reduced fertility and agricultural potential and destruction of the tropical rainforest has gone too far to be reversed.

Ecological problems across the globe

Africa

Africa is the only continent where poverty is expected to rise in the next century. Twenty-five countries will lack sufficient fresh water by 2025. Some 200-million Africans are undernourished. Deforestation, growing deserts, soil degradation and loss of species are occurring across the continent. Cities are growing faster than governments can develop services for them. Slums are causing serious health problems.

Asia and the Pacific

This area sees 60% of the world's population depending on 30% of the world's land. Rapid economic growth and energy demand is likely to go on causing environmental damage. At least one in three Asians has no safe water to drink. Asia's tendency to develop megacities such as Tokyo, Delhi and Jakarta generates environmental stress. Forest fires are a serious problem—one million hectares of Indonesia's forests were lost in 1997. Marine life has been degraded by overfishing and pollution.

Europe and Central Asia

Road transport is the major source of air pollution and congestion is a serious problem. Europe produces a third of all global warming gases. Each person in Western Europe produces 35% more waste than in 1980. Over-fishing has left North Sea stocks seriously depleted. More than half of the large cities in Europe are using too much of their groundwater supply.

Latin America and the Caribbean

Nearly three-quarters of the population is already urban, many in megacities. In Sao Paulo and Rio de Janeiro air pollution causes an estimated 4000 premature deaths a year. Waste disposal is a big urban problem. Forests are being depleted, particularly in the Amazon. Latin America has 40% of the world's plant and animal types but habitat loss has left many extinct.

North America

Conspicuous over-consumption causes acute problems. Air pollution has been cut but the US generates 25% of the world's greenhouse gases. The average American uses 1600 litres of fuel a year compared with 330 litres in Europe. Marine life has been over-exploited: fish catches off the east coast have collapsed from 2,5-million tons in 1971 to less than 500,000 tons. Exposure to pesticides and toxic compounds is a long-term threat to health.

West Asia (Arabia and Middle East)

Large areas are desert, or classed as dry lands and getting drier. Groundwater sources are critically low as volumes used far exceed natural replenishment. Populations are growing far faster than water resources can be developed. Salt, alkaline deposits and excess nutrients are destroying soil fertility. Pollution is a serious problem. More than 1,2-million gallons of oil a year are spilled into the Gulf.

Polar regions

This area is mainly affected by events elsewhere, but its climate drives the world's weather and ocean currents. Ozone depletion in the atmosphere—which lets in more ultra-violet light—has produced global warming, which sees ice caps and glaciers melting. Pollutants and radioactivity are building up and threatening the food chain. Polar bears are disappearing as ice melts and fish stocks are being overexploited.

Töpfer added: "Many of the planet's species have already been lost or condemned to extinction. One quarter of the world's mammal species are now at significant risk of total extinction."

At sea, fisheries have been grossly overexploited and half the world's coral reefs are threatened with destruction, says the report. Air pollution has reached crisis proportions in many cities and it is too late to prevent global warming. Lack of government control has weakened the ability to solve problems, the report claims.Töpfer said it is essential to force multinational companies to be accountable for their actions and what they produce.

Under a new European directive, car manufacturers are to be made responsible for dealing with their products at the end of their lives.

"Suddenly recycling cars has become easy," said Töpfer. We could do this across a whole range of goods. At a stroke we could re-use materials again and again, making resources go 10 times as far as they do now."

New wars have always threatened the environment of those directly involved, but the effects are being felt ever wider. For example, in the Kosovo crisis, the Danube was closed and those downstream suffered pollution.

The importance of refugees who are forced to destroy the natural environment to survive is another new factor. Invasions of alien species like Great Lakes jellyfish in the Black Sea and water weeds which choke rivers and kill native plants and fish are another growing threat.

"The present course is unsustainable and postponing action is no longer an option. Inspired political leadership and intense co-operation across all regions and sectors will be needed to put both existing and new policy instruments to work," the report concludes.

Index

I

J

K

L

M

N

O

P

R

S

Test Your Knowledge Form

We encourage you to photocopy and use this page as a tool to assess how the articles in ***Annual Editions*** expand on the information in your textbook. By reflecting on the articles you will gain enhanced text information. You can also access this useful form on a product's book support Web site at ***http://www.dushkin.com/online/***.

NAME: DATE:

TITLE AND NUMBER OF ARTICLE:

BRIEFLY STATE THE MAIN IDEA OF THIS ARTICLE:

LIST THREE IMPORTANT FACTS THAT THE AUTHOR USES TO SUPPORT THE MAIN IDEA:

WHAT INFORMATION OR IDEAS DISCUSSED IN THIS ARTICLE ARE ALSO DISCUSSED IN YOUR TEXTBOOK OR OTHER READINGS THAT YOU HAVE DONE? LIST THE TEXTBOOK CHAPTERS AND PAGE NUMBERS:

LIST ANY EXAMPLES OF BIAS OR FAULTY REASONING THAT YOU FOUND IN THE ARTICLE:

LIST ANY NEW TERMS/CONCEPTS THAT WERE DISCUSSED IN THE ARTICLE, AND WRITE A SHORT DEFINITION: